D1414912

# Taking SIDES

Clashing Views on
Controversial
Economic Issues

**Eighth Edition**

**Edited, Selected, and with Introductions by**

## Thomas R. Swartz
*University of Notre Dame*
### and
## Frank J. Bonello
*University of Notre Dame*

Dushkin/McGraw-Hill
A Division of The McGraw-Hill Companies

*This book is dedicated to the thousands of students who have persevered in the "Bonello/Swartz (B.S.)" introductory economics course sequence at the University of Notre Dame. It is also dedicated to our children and grandchildren. In order of their birth dates they are Mary Elizabeth, Karen Ann, Jennifer Lynne, John Anthony, Anne Marie, Rebecca Jourdan, David Joseph, Stephen Thomas, Chelsea Margaret, Kevin Joseph, Meghan Claire, Maureen Keating, and Michael Thomas.*

**Cover Art Acknowledgment**

Charles Vitelli

Manufactured in the United States of America

Eighth Edition

10  9  8  7  6  5  4  3  2

**Library of Congress Cataloging-in-Publication Data**

Main entry under title:
    Taking sides: clashing views on controversial economic issues/edited, selected, and with introductions by Thomas R. Swartz and Frank J. Bonello.—8th ed.
    Includes bibliographical references and index.
    1. United States—Economic policy—1971–1981. 2. United States—Economic policy—1981–1993. 3. United States—Economic policy—1993–. I. Swartz, Thomas R., *comp*. II. Bonello, Frank J., *comp*.

                                             338.9'22
0-697-39105-1                           ISSN: 1094-7612

Printed on Recycled Paper

# PREFACE

*Where there is much desire to learn, there of necessity will be much arguing.*

—John Milton (1608–1674), English poet and essayist

Presented here are 19 debates on important and compelling economic issues, which are designed to stimulate critical thinking skills and initiate lively and informed discussion. These debates take economic theory and show how it is applied to current, real-world public policy decisions, the outcomes of which will have an immediate and personal impact. How these debates are resolved will affect our taxes, jobs, wages, educational system, and so on; in short, they will shape the society in which we live.

It has been our intent throughout each of the eight editions of *Taking Sides: Clashing Views on Controversial Economic Issues* to select issues that reveal something about the nature of economics itself and something about how it relates to current, everyday newspaper headlines and television news stories on public policy issues that deal with economic considerations (and almost all do these days). To assist the reader, we begin each issue with an *issue introduction*, which sets the stage for the debate as it is argued in the YES and NO selections. Each issue concludes with a *postscript* that briefly reviews the arguments and makes some final observations. The introduction and postscript do not preempt what is the reader's own task: to achieve a critical and informed view of the economic issue at stake. Certainly, the reader should not feel confined to adopt one or the other of the positions presented. The views presented should be used as starting points, and the suggestions for further reading that appear in each issue postscript offer additional resources on the topic. At the back of the book is a listing of all the *contributors to this volume*, which provides information on the economists, policymakers, political leaders, and commentators whose views are debated here.

**Changes to this edition**    This new edition of *Taking Sides* represents a considerable revision to this book. Twenty-five of the 38 selections and 11 of the 19 issues are new. Thus, as we rush toward the twenty-first century, this heavily revised book will help us understand the implication of a changing set of economic issues that were not part of our world just a few years ago. The new issues are *Should Cities Subsidize Sports and Sports Venues?* (Issue 3); *Is It Time to Abolish the Minimum Wage?* (Issue 4); *Can Economic Growth Be Increased Just by Using More Inputs and Improving Efficiency?* (Issue 8); *Is Our Social Security Program Securely Anchored?* (Issue 9); *Does the Consumer Price Index Overstate Changes in the Cost of Living?* (Issue 10); *Is There a Need for a Constitutional Amendment to Balance the Budget?* (Issue 11); *Is the Federal Reserve* the Cause of Poor Macroeconomic Performance? (Issue 12); Is the Nonaccelerating Inflation Rate of Unemployment a Useful Guide for Macroeconomic Policy? (Issue 13); Would Adopting Wisconsin's Welfare Reforms End Welfare As We Know It? (Issue 14); Does Free Trade Make the Poor, Poorer? (Issue 16); and Has the North American Free Trade Agreement Been a Success? (Issue 19). For two of the issues, we have retained the topic from the seventh edition but have replaced one or both of the selections in order to bring the debate up to date or to focus more clearly on the controversy: Issue 1 on profits and Issue 6 on managed competition for the health care system.

As with all of the previous editions, the issues in the eighth edition can be used in any sequence. Although the general organization of the book loosely parallels the sequence of topics found in a standard introductory economics textbook, you can pick and choose which issues to read first, since they are designed to stand alone. Note that we have retained the modification to Part 3 introduced in the seventh edition. That part, "The World Around Us," allows us to more fully represent the host of problems our society faces in this ever-changing world we live in.

**A word to the instructor**  An *Instructor's Manual With Test Questions* (multiple-choice and essay) is available through the publisher. A general guidebook, *Using Taking Sides in the Classroom*, which discusses methods and techniques for integrating the pro/con approach into any classroom setting, is also available. An online version of *Using Taking Sides in the Classroom* and a correspondence service for Taking Sides adopters can be found at www.dushkin.com/ usingtakingsides/. For students, we offer a field guide to analyzing argumentative essays, *Analyzing Controversy: An Introductory Guide,* with exercises and techniques to help them to decipher genuine controversies. *Taking Sides: Clashing Views on Controversial Economic Issues* is only one title in the Taking Sides series. If you are interested in seeing the table of contents for any of the other titles, please visit the Taking Sides Web site at http://www.dushkin.com/takingsides/.

**Acknowledgments**  We have received many helpful comments and suggestions from our friends and readers across the United States and Canada. As always, their suggestions were very welcome and have markedly enhanced the quality of this edition of *Taking Sides*. If as you read this book you are reminded of an essay that could be included in a future edition, we hope that you will drop us a note. We very much appreciate your interest and help, and we are always pleased to hear from you.

Our special thanks go to those who responded with suggestions for the eighth edition:

Samuel Bostaph
University of Dallas

Joan G. Buccino
Florida Southern College

Mary Bumgarner
Kennesaw State University

Thomas Curry
Morningside College

John Whitney Evans
College of St. Scholastica

Douglas C. Gordon
Arapahoe Community
   College

James Hornsten
Lake Forest College

Connie Humphreys
Edison Community College

Brian J. McKenna
St. Xavier University

J. R. Morris
Broward Community College
   South

Harold Moses
Daytona Beach Community
   College–Main

Charles J. Mullin
Ohio State
   University–Columbus

Joe Mullin
Columbus State Community
   College

Anatasios Papathanasis
Central Connecticut State
   University

Cy A. Peebles
Towson State University

Kolleen J. Rask
College of the Holy Cross

Aldo Rugai
St. Xavier University

Robert Sobel
Hofstra University

Hubert Spraberry
Howard Payne University

Deborah Thorsen
Palm Beach Community
   College

John Trebnik
Marian College

Carolyn Tuttle
Lake Forest College

Janice Yee
Wartburg College

We also offer our very special thanks to Robert M. Ball, Charles Craypo, and Sylvester J. Schieber, who wrote essays especially for this edition of *Taking Sides*. We deeply appreciate their time and patience, and, most importantly, admire their dedication to increasing the economic understanding of a new generation of students.

We are also indebted to David H. Dean, our editorial adviser, and list manager of the Taking Sides program at Dushkin/McGraw-Hill, for this edition of the book. He provided excellent counsel and gave us much-needed support as we approached our publication deadlines. Those who suffered most in the preparation of this manuscript were those who had to read Swartz's tortured handwriting: our typists Cheryl Reed and Sherry Reichold. Finally we owe much to our graduate assistants here at the University of

Notre Dame: Joseph A. Stevano and Matthew C. Weagle. They were always able to maintain a smile even when our requests to run to the library were outrageous.

To all those mentioned above, we owe a huge debt, many thanks, and none of the blame for any shortcomings that remain in this edition of *Taking Sides*.

Thomas R. Swartz
University of Notre Dame

Frank J. Bonello
University of Notre Dame

# CONTENTS IN BRIEF

# CONTENTS

Orthodox neoclassical economist Thomas Rustici asserts that the minimum wage creates unemployment among least-skilled workers. Labor economist Charles Craypo argues that a high minimum wage is good for the economy.

Journalist William Tucker suggests that there is a substantial correlation between rent controls and homelessness. Sociologist Richard P. Appelbaum and his research associates submit that Tucker's statistical analysis is flawed.

Physician Paul M. Ellwood Jr. and George D. Lundberg, an editor, argue that we cannot return to fee-for-service medicine. Harvard Business School professors John H. McArthur and Francis D. Moore warn that managed care will ensure primarily the profitability of the corporation.

Economist Edwin W. Zedlewski argues that investment in more prisons is
wise social policy. Economist David F. Greenberg contends that the benefits
of more prisons are overestimated.

---

The Clinton administration's Council of Economic Advisers believes in stimulating economic growth by increasing physical capital and improving efficiency. Felix G. Rohatyn, a financial expert, argues that an increase in the
growth rate does not require the redistribution of wealth.

---

Robert M. Ball, former commissioner of Social Security, believes that Social
Security is in good shape financially. Sylvester J. Schieber, a business executive, sees a serious Social Security funding problem.

---

Michael J. Boskin and members of the Advisory Commission to Study the
Consumer Price Index state that changes in the Consumer Price Index over-

state changes in the cost of living. Dean Baker, an economist, argues that it is impossible to determine the direction of the Consumer Price Index.

Martin A. Regalia, an economist, argues in favor of a constitutional amendment to balance the budget. Robert Rubin, secretary of the treasury in the Clinton administration, contends that an amendment would eliminate the government's ability to respond effectively to economic problems.

Lester Thurow, an economics professor at Massachusetts Institute of Technology, states that two major macroeconomic problems are due to Federal Reserve policies. Matthew Miller, senior editor for the *New Republic*, argues that raising aggregate demand will lead to systemic inflation.

Joseph Stiglitz, chairman of the Clinton administration's Council of Economic Advisers, contends that the nonaccelerating inflation rate of unemployment (NAIRU) is a useful guide for macroeconomic policy. James K. Galbraith, professor of economics at the University of Texas, asserts that the NAIRU is a useless guide.

Heritage Foundation senior policy analyst Robert Rector claims that Wisconsin has won more than half the battle against welfare dependence. University of Wisconsin economist Michael Wiseman concludes that the governor of Wisconsin has not found the key to welfare savings.

---

Columnist Robert Kuttner argues that "comparative advantage" is determined by government action, not by free markets. Social critic Michael Kinsley claims that protectionism weakens the economy.

---

Columnist and social critic William Greider warns that blind acceptance of "free-market doctrine" must inevitably lead to inequality. Gary Burtless, a senior fellow at the Brookings Institution, states that although the wages of less-skilled workers have plunged, this shift is not confined to the traded-goods sector.

---

Cynthia Pollock Shea, a senior researcher with the Worldwatch Institute,
argues that immediate action must be taken to halt emissions of chemicals
that deplete the ozone. Professor of economics Lester B. Lave warns that
drastic solutions could be harmful or costly.

---

Alan S. Blinder, a member of the Board of Governors of the Federal Reserve
System, maintains that market energy can solve America's environmental
problems. Social critic David Moberg argues that public policy and direct
government intervention have positive effects on the environment.

---

Paul Krugman, professor of economics at Stanford University, claims that the
North American Free Trade Agreement (NAFTA) has been a success. Sarah
Anderson and John Cavanagh, both from the Institute for Policy Studies,
and David Ranney, professor of urban planning at the University of Illinois,
Chicago, argue that NAFTA is not in the best interests of Canada, Mexico,
and the United States.

# INTRODUCTION

## Economics and Economists: The Basis for Controversy

Thomas R. Swartz
Frank J. Bonello

*I think that Capitalism, wisely managed, can probably be more efficient for attaining economic ends than any alternative system yet in sight, but that in itself it is in many ways extremely objectionable.*

————Lord John Maynard Keynes, *The End of Laissez-Faire* (1926)

Although more than 70 years have passed since Lord Keynes (1883–1946) penned these lines, many economists still struggle with the basic dilemma he outlined. The paradox rests in the fact that a free-market system is extremely efficient. It is purported to produce more at a lower cost than any other economic system. But in producing this wide array of low-cost goods and services, problems arise. These problems—most notably a lack of economic equity and economic stability—concern some economists.

If the problems raised and analyzed in this book were merely the product of intellectual gymnastics undertaken by egg-headed economists, we could sit back and enjoy these confrontations as theoretical exercises. The essays contained in this book, however, touch each and every one of us in tangible ways. Some focus upon macroeconomic topics, such as balancing the budget and the Federal Reserve's monetary policy. Another set of issues deals with microeconomic topics. We refer to these issues as micro problems not because they are small problems, but because they deal with small economic units, such as households, firms, or individual industries. A third set of issues deals with matters that do not fall neatly into the macroeconomic or microeconomic classifications. This set includes three issues relating to the international aspects of economic activity and two involving pollution.

The range of issues and disagreements raises a fundamental question: Why do economists disagree? One explanation is suggested by Lord Keynes's 1926 remark. How various economists will react to the strengths and weaknesses found in an economic system will depend upon how they view the relative importance of efficiency, equity, and stability. These are central terms, and we will define them in detail in the following pages. For now the important point is that some economists may view efficiency as overriding. In other cases, the same economists may be willing to sacrifice the efficiency generated by the market in order to ensure increased economic equity and/or increased economic stability.

Given the extent of conflict, controversy, and diversity, it may appear that economists rarely, if ever, agree on any economic issue. We would be most misleading if we left the reader with this impression. Economists rarely challenge the internal logic of the theoretical models that have been developed and articulated by their colleagues. Rather, they will challenge either the validity of the assumptions used in these models or the value of the ends these models seek to achieve. The challenges typically focus upon such issues as the assumption of functioning, competitive markets, and the desirability of perpetuating the existing distribution of income. In this case, those who support and those who challenge the operation of the market agree on a large number of issues. But they disagree most assuredly on a few issues that have dramatic implications.

This same phenomenon of agreeing more often than disagreeing is also true in the area of economic policy. In this area, where the public is most acutely aware of differences among economists, these differences are not generally over the kinds of changes that will be brought about by a particular policy. The differences more typically concern the timing of the change, the specific characteristics of the policy, and the size of the resulting effect or effects.

## ECONOMISTS: WHAT DO THEY REPRESENT?

Newspaper, magazine, and TV commentators all use handy labels to describe certain members of the economics profession. What do the headlines mean when they refer to the Chicago School, the Keynesians, the institutional economists, or the radical economists? What do these individuals stand for? Since we too use our own labels throughout this book, we feel obliged to identify the principal groups or camps in our profession. Let us warn you that this can be a misleading venture. Some economists—perhaps most of them —defy classification. They drift from one camp to another, selecting a gem of wisdom here and another there. These are practical men and women who believe that no one camp has all the answers to all the economic problems confronting society.

Recognizing this limitation, four major groups of economists can be identified. These groups are differentiated on the basis of two basic criteria: how they view efficiency relative to equity and stability; and what significance they attach to imperfectly competitive market structures. Before describing various views on these criteria, it is essential to understand the meaning of certain terms to be used in this description.

Efficiency, equity, and stability represent goals for an economic system. An economy is efficient when it produces those goods and services that people want without wasting scarce resources. Equity in an economic sense has several dimensions. It means that income and wealth are distributed according to accepted principles of fairness, that those who are unable to care for themselves receive adequate care, and that mainstream economic activity is open to all persons. Stability is viewed as the absence of sharp ups and downs in business activity, in prices, and in employment. In other words, stability is marked by steady increases in output, little inflation, and low unemployment.

When the term market structures is used, it refers to the number of buyers and sellers in the market and the amount of control they exercise over price. At one extreme is a perfectly competitive market where there are so many buyers and sellers that no one has any ability to influence market price. One seller or buyer obviously could have great control over price. This extreme market structure, which we call pure monopoly, and other market structures that result in some control over price are grouped under the broad label of imperfectly competitive markets. With these terms in mind, we can begin to examine the various schools of economic thought.

### Free-Market Economists

One of the most visible groups of economists and perhaps the easiest group to identify and classify is the *free-market economists*. These economists believe that the market, operating freely without interferences from government or labor unions, will generate the greatest amount of well-being for the greatest number of people.

Economic efficiency is one of the priorities for free-market economists. In their well-developed models, *consumer sovereignty*—consumer demand for goods and services—guides the system by directly influencing market prices. The distribution of economic resources caused by these market prices not only results in the production of an array of goods and services that are demanded by consumers, but this production is undertaken in the most cost-effective fashion. The free-market economists claim that, at any point, some individuals must earn incomes that are substantially greater than those of other individuals. They contend that these higher incomes are a reward for greater efficiency or productivity and that this reward-induced efficiency will result in rapid economic growth that will benefit all persons in the society. They might also admit that a system driven by these freely operating markets will be subject to occasional bouts of instability (slow growth, inflation, and unemployment). They maintain, however, that government action to eliminate or reduce this periodic instability will only make matters worse. Consequently, government, according to the free-market economist, should play a minor role in the economic affairs of society.

Although the models of free-market economists are dependent upon functioning, competitive markets, the lack of such markets in the real world does not seriously jeopardize their position. First, they assert that large-size firms are necessary to achieve low per-unit costs; that is, a single large firm may be able to produce a given level of output with fewer scarce resources than a large number of small firms. Second, they suggest that the benefits associated with the free operation of markets are so great compared to government intervention that even a second-best solution of imperfectly competitive markets still yields benefits far in excess of government intervention.

These advocates of the free market have been given various labels over time. The oldest and most persistent label is *classical economists*. This is because the classical economists of the eighteenth century, particularly Adam Smith, were the first to point out the virtues of the market. In *The Wealth of Nations* (1776), Smith captured the essence of the system with the following words:

> Every individual endeavors to employ his capital so that its produce may be of greatest value. He generally neither intends to promote the public interest nor knows how much he is promoting it. He intends only his own security, only his own gain. And he is in this led by an invisible hand to promote an end which was no part of his intention. By pursuing his own interest he frequently promotes that of society more effectively than when he really intends to promote it.

### Liberal Economists

Another significant group of economists in the United States can be classified as *liberal economists*. Liberal here refers to the willingness to intervene in the free operation of the market. These economists share with the free-market economists a great respect for the market. The liberal economist, however, does not believe that the explicit and implicit costs of a freely operating market should or can be ignored. Rather, the liberal maintains that the costs of an uncontrolled marketplace are often borne by those in society who are least capable of bearing them: the poor, the elderly, and the infirm. Additionally, liberal economists maintain that the freely operating market sometimes results in economic instability and the resultant bouts of inflation, unemployment, and slow or negative growth.

Consider for a moment the differences between free-market economists and liberal economists at the microeconomic level. Liberal economists take exception to the free market on two grounds. First, these economists find a basic problem with fairness in the marketplace. Since the market is driven by the forces of consumer spending, there are those who through no fault of their own (they may be aged, young, infirm, or physically or mentally handicapped) may not have the wherewithal to participate in the economic system. Second, the unfettered marketplace does not and cannot handle spillover effects or what are known as externalities. These are the third-party effects that may occur as a result of some action. Will a firm willingly compensate its neighbors for the pollutants it pours into the nearby lake? Will a truck driver willingly drive at the speed limit and in the process reduce the highway accident rate? Liberal economists think not. These economists are therefore willing to have the government intervene in these and other, similar cases.

The liberal economists' role in macroeconomics is more readily apparent. Ever since the failure of free-market economics during the Great Depression of the 1930s, Keynesianism (still another label for liberal economics) has become widely known. In his 1935 book, *The General Theory of Employment, Interest, and Money*, Lord John Maynard Keynes laid the basic groundwork for this school of thought. Keynes argued that the history of freely operating market economies was marked by periods of recurring recessions, sometimes very deep recessions, which we call depressions. He maintained that government intervention through its fiscal policy—government tax and spending power —could eliminate, or at least soften these sharp reductions in economic activity and as a result move the economy along a more stable growth path. Thus for the Keynesians, or liberal economists, one of the extremely objectionable aspects of a free-market economy is its inherent instability.

Liberal economists are also far more concerned about the existence of imperfections in the marketplace than are their free-market counterparts. They reject the notion that imperfect competition is an acceptable substitute for competitive markets. They may agree that the imperfectly competitive firms can achieve some savings because of their large size and efficiency, but they assert that since there is little or no competition the firms are not forced to pass these cost savings on to consumers. Thus liberal economists, who in some circles are labeled antitrusters, are willing to intervene in the market in two ways: They are prepared to allow some monopolies, such as public utilities, to exist, but they contend that these must be regulated by government; or they maintain that there is no justification for monopolies, and they are prepared to invoke the powers of antitrust legislation to break up existing monopolies and/or prevent the formation of new ones.

### Mainstream Critics and Radical Reform Economists

There are two other groups of economists we must identify. One group can be called *mainstream critics*. Included in this group are individuals like Thorstein Veblen (1857–1929), with his critique of conspicuous consumption, and John Kenneth Galbraith (b. 1908), with his views on industrial structure. One reasonably cohesive subgroup of mainstream critics are the post-Keynesians. They are post-Keynesians because they believe that as the principal economic institutions have changed over time, they have remained closer to the spirit of Keynes than have the liberal economists. As some have suggested, the key aspect of Keynes as far as the post-Keynesians are concerned is his assertion that "expectations of the future are not necessarily certain." On a more practical level post-Keynesians assert, among other things, that the productivity of the economic system is not significantly affected by changes in income distribution, that the system can still be efficient without competitive markets, that conventional fiscal policies cannot control inflation, and that "incomes policies" are the means to an effective and equitable answer to the inflationary dilemma. This characterization of post-Keynesianism is drawn from Alfred S. Eichner's introduction in *A Guide to Post-Keynesian Economics* (M. E. Sharpe, 1978).

The fourth and last group can be called the *radical reform economists*. Many in this group trace their ideas back to the nineteenth-century philosopher-economist Karl Marx and his most impressive work, the three volumes of *Das Kapital*. As with the other three groups of economists, there are subgroups of radical reform economists. One subgroup, which may be labeled contemporary Marxists, is best represented by those who have published their research results over the years in the *Review of Radical Political Economics*. These economists examine issues that have been largely ignored by mainstream economists, for example, war, sexism, racism, imperialism, and civil rights. In their analyses of these issues they borrow from and refine the work of Marx. In the process, they emphasize the role of class in shaping society and the role of the economy in determining class structures. Moreover, they see a need to encourage explicitly the development of some form of democratic socialism, for only then will the greatest good for the greatest number be ensured.

In concluding this section, we must warn you to use these labels with extreme care. Our categories are not hard and fast. There is much grayness around the edges and little that is black and white in these classifications. This does not mean, however, that they have no value. It is important to understand the philosophical background of the individual authors. This background does indeed color or shade their work.

## SUMMARY

It is clear that there is no shortage of economic problems that demand solutions. At the same time there is no shortage of proposed solutions. In fact, the problem is often one of oversupply. The nineteen issues included in this volume will acquaint you or, more accurately, reacquaint you with some of these problems. And, of course, there are at least two proposed solutions for each of the problems. Here we hope to provide new insights regarding the alternatives available and the differences and similarities of these alternative remedies.

If this introduction has served its purpose, you will be able to identify common elements in the proposed solutions to the different problems. For example, you will be able to identify the reliance on the forces of the market advocated by free-market economists as the remedy for several economic ills. This introduction should also help you understand why there are at least two proposed solutions for every economic problem; each group of economists tends to interpret a problem from its own philosophical position and to advance a solution that is grounded in that philosophical framework.

Our intention, of course, is not to connect persons to one philosophic position or another. We hope instead to generate discussion and promote understanding. To do this, each of us must see not only a proposed solution, we must also be aware of the foundation that supports that solution. With greater understanding, meaningful progress in addressing economic problems can be achieved.

# *On the Internet . . .*

http://www.dushkin.com

### The Dismal Scientist
Provides free economic data, analysis, and forecasts on a variety of topics.
*http://www.dismal.com/*

### The Economist
The Web edition of the *Economist* is available free to subscribers of the print edition or for an annual fee to those who wish to subscribe online. A selection of articles is available free to those who want to dip into the journal.
*http://www.economist.com/*

### Electronic Policy Network
Timely information and ideas about national policy on economics and politics, welfare and families, education, civic participation, and health policy in the form of a virtual magazine.
*http://epn.org/*

### Resources for Economists on the Internet
This resource of the WWW Virtual Library on Economics is an excellent starting place for any research in economics by academic and practicing economists and anyone interested in economics. Has many Web links.
*http://econwpa.wustl.edu/econFAQ/EconFAQ.html*

### Statistical Resources on the Web/Economics
Here is an excellent source of statistics collated from federal bureaus, economic indicators—both historical and current, the Federal Reserve Board, economic sources, federal statistical tables, a consumer price inflator/deflator, and many links to other sources.
*http://www.lib.umich.edu/libhome/Documents.center/stecon.html*

### WebEc—WWW Resources in Economics
A most complete virtual library of economics facts, figures, and thoughts.
*http://netec.wustl.edu/WebEc.html*

# PART 1

## Microeconomic Issues

*Our lives are profoundly affected by economic decisions made at the microeconomic level. Some important decisions are those regarding profit motives of businesses, city subsidies for sports venues, the minimum wage, the health care industry, rent controls, and more prison space.*

■ Are Profits the Only Business of Business?

■ Should We Encourage the Private Ownership of Guns?

■ Should Cities Subsidize Sports and Sports Venues?

■ Is It Time to Abolish the Minimum Wage?

■ Are Rent Controls the Cause of America's Homelessness?

■ Is Managed Competition the Cure for Our Ailing Health Care Industry?

■ Are More Prisons and Prison Beds the Answer to America's Rising Crime Rate?

# ISSUE 1

## Are Profits the Only Business of Business?

**YES: Milton Friedman,** from "The Social Responsibility of Business Is to Increase Its Profits," *The New York Times Magazine* (September 13, 1970)

**NO: Robert Almeder,** from "Morality in the Marketplace," in Milton Snoeyenbos, Robert Almeder, and James Humber, eds., *Business Ethics*, rev. ed. (Prometheus Press, 1998)

### ISSUE SUMMARY

**YES:** Free-market economist Milton Friedman contends that the sole responsibility of business is to increase its profits.

**NO:** Philosopher Robert Almeder maintains that if capitalism is to survive, it must act in socially responsible ways that go beyond profit making.

Every economic society—whether it is a traditional society in Central Africa, a fossilized planned economy such as Cuba's, or a wealthy capitalist society such as those found in North America, Western Europe, or the Pacific Rim —must address the basic economic problem of resource allocation. These societies must determine *what* goods and services they can and will produce, *how* these goods and services will be produced, and *for whom* these goods and services will be produced.

The *what, how,* and *for whom* questions must be answered because of the problem of scarcity. Even if a given society were indescribably rich, it would still confront the problem of scarcity—in the case of a rich society, "relative scarcity." It might have all the resources it needs to produce all the goods and services it would ever want, but it could not produce all these things simultaneously. Thus, even a very rich society must set priorities and produce first those goods and services with the highest priority and postpone the production of those goods and services with lower priorities. If time is of the essence, this society would determine *how* these goods and services should be produced. And since this wealthy society cannot produce all it wants instantly, it must also determine *for whom* the first bundle of goods and services will be produced.

Few, if any, economic societies are indescribably rich. On the other hand, there are many examples of economic societies that face grinding deprivation daily. In these societies and in all the societies that fall between poverty and great affluence, the *what, how,* and *for whom* questions are immediately apparent. Somehow these questions must be answered.

In some societies, such as the Amish communities of North America, the answers to these questions are found in tradition: Sons and daughters follow in their parents' footsteps. Younger generations produce *what* older generations produced before them. The methods of production—the horsedrawn plow, the hand-held scythe, the use of natural fertilizers—remain unchanged; thus, the *how* question is answered in the same way that the *for whom* question is answered—by following historic patterns. In other societies, such as self-sustaining religious communities, there is a different pattern of responses to these questions. In these communities, the "elder" of the community determines *what* will be produced, *how* it will be produced, and *for whom* it will be produced. If there is a well-defined hierarchical system, it is similar to one of the former stereotypical command economies of Eastern Europe.

Although elements of tradition and command are found in the industrialized societies of Western Europe, North America, and Japan, the basic answers to the three questions of resource allocation in these countries are determined by profit. In these economic societies, *what* will be produced is determined by what will yield the greatest profit. Consumers, in their search for maximum satisfaction, will bid for those goods and services that they want most. This consumer action drives the prices of these goods and services up, which, in turn, increases producers' profits. The higher profits attract new firms into the industry and encourage existing firms to increase their output. Thus, profits are the mechanism that ensures that consumers get what they want. Similarly, the profit-seeking behavior of business firms determines *how* the goods and services that consumers want will be produced. Since firms attempt to maximize their profits, they select those means of production that are economically most efficient. Lastly, the *for whom* question is also linked to profits. Wherever there is a shortage of goods and services, profits will be high. In the producers' attempts to increase their output, they must attract factors of production (land, labor, and capital) away from other economic activities. This bidding increases factor prices or factor incomes and ensures that these factors will be able to buy goods and services in the open marketplace.

Both Milton Friedman and Robert Almeder recognize the merits of a profit-driven economic system. They do not quarrel over the importance of profits. But they do quarrel over whether or not business firms have obligations beyond making profits. Friedman holds that the *only* responsibility of business is to make profits and that anyone who maintains otherwise is "preaching pure and unadulterated socialism." Almeder, who is clearly not a "socialist," contends that business must act in socially responsible ways "if capitalism is to survive."

# YES

Milton Friedman

## THE SOCIAL RESPONSIBILITY OF BUSINESS IS TO INCREASE ITS PROFITS

When I hear businessmen speak eloquently about the "social responsibilities of business in a free-enterprise system," I am reminded of the wonderful line about the Frenchman who discovered at the age of 70 that he had been speaking prose all his life. The businessmen believe that they are defending free enterprise when they declaim that business is not concerned "merely" with profit but also with promoting desirable "social ends; that business has a social conscience" and takes seriously its responsibilities for providing employment, eliminating discrimination, avoiding pollution and whatever else may be the catchwords of the contemporary crop of reformers. In fact they are—or would be if they or anyone else took them seriously—preaching pure and unadulterated socialism. Businessmen who talk this way are unwitting puppets of the intellectual forces that have been undermining the basis of a free society these past decades.

The discussions of the "social responsibilities of business" are notable for their analytical looseness and lack of rigor. What does it mean to say that "business" has responsibilities? Only people can have responsibilities. A corporation is an artificial person and in this sense may have artificial responsibilities, but "business" as a whole cannot be said to have responsibilities, even in this vague sense. The first step toward clarity in examining the doctrine of the social responsibility of business is to ask precisely what it implies for whom.

Presumably, the individuals who are to be responsible are businessmen, which means individual proprietors or corporate executives. Most of the discussion of social responsibility is directed at corporations, so in what follows I shall mostly neglect the individual proprietor and speak of corporate executives.

In a free-enterprise, private-property system, a corporate executive is an employee of the owners of the business. He has direct responsibility to his employers. That responsibility is to conduct the business in accordance with their desires, which generally will be to make as much money as possible while conforming to the basic rules of the society, both those embodied in

From Milton Friedman, "The Social Responsibility of Business Is to Increase Its Profits," *The New York Times Magazine* (September 13, 1970). Copyright © 1970 by The New York Times Co. Reprinted by permission.

law and those embodied in ethical custom. Of course, in some cases his employers may have a different objective. A group of persons might establish a corporation for an eleemosynary purpose —for example, a hospital or a school. The manager of such a corporation will not have money profit as his objective but the rendering of certain services.

In either case, the key point is that, in his capacity as a corporate executive, the manager is the agent of the individuals who own the corporation or establish the eleemosynary institution, and his primary responsibility is to them.

Needless to say, this does not mean that it is easy to judge how well he is performing his task. But at least the criterion of performance is straightforward, and the persons among whom a voluntary contractual arrangement exists are clearly defined.

Of course, the corporate executive is also a person in his own right. As a person, he may have many other responsibilities that he recognizes or assumes voluntarily—to his family, his conscience, his feelings of charity, his church, his clubs, his city, his country. He may feel impelled by these responsibilities to devote part of his income to causes he regards as worthy, to refuse to work for particular corporations, even to leave his job, for example, to join his country's armed forces. If we wish, we may refer to some of these responsibilities as "social responsibilities." But in these respects he is acting as a principal, not an agent; he is spending his own money or time or energy, not the money of his employers or the time or energy he has contracted to devote to their purposes. If these are "social responsibilities," they are the social responsibilities of individuals, not of business.

What does it mean to say that the corporate executive has a "social responsibility" in his capacity as businessman? If this statement is not pure rhetoric, it must mean that he is to act in some way that is not in the interest of his employers. For example, that he is to refrain from increasing the price of the product in order to contribute to the social objective of preventing inflation, even though a price increase would be in the best interests of the corporation. Or that he is to make expenditures on reducing pollution beyond the amount that is in the best interests of the corporation or that is required by law in order to contribute to the social objective of improving the environment. Or that, at the expense of corporate profits, he is to hire "hard-core" unemployed instead of better-qualified available workmen to contribute to the social objective of reducing poverty.

In each of these cases, the corporate executive would be spending someone else's money for a general social interest. Insofar as his actions in accord with his "social responsibility" reduce returns to stockholders, he is spending their money. Insofar as his actions raise the price to customers, he is spending the customers' money. Insofar as his actions lower the wages of some employees, he is spending their money.

The stockholders or the customers or the employees could separately spend their own money on the particular action if they wished to do so. The executive is exercising a distinct "social responsibility," rather than serving as an agent of the stockholders or the customers or the employees, only if he spends the money in a different way than they would have spent it.

But if he does this, he is in effect imposing taxes, on the one hand, and deciding how the tax proceeds shall be spent, on the other.

This process raises political questions on two levels: principle and consequences. On the level of political principle, the imposition of taxes and the expenditure of tax proceeds are governmental functions. We have established elaborate constitutional, parliamentary and judicial provisions to control these functions, to assure that taxes are imposed so far as possible in accordance with the preferences and desires of the public—after all, "taxation without representation" was one of the battle cries of the American Revolution. We have a system of checks and balances to separate the legislative function of imposing taxes and enacting expenditures from the executive function of collecting taxes and administering expenditure programs and from the judicial function of mediating disputes and interpreting the law.

Here the businessman—self-selected or appointed directly or indirectly by stockholders—is to be simultaneously legislator, executive and jurist. He is to decide whom to tax by how much and for what purpose, and he is to spend the proceeds—all this guided only by general exhortations from on high to restrain inflation, improve the environment, fight poverty and so on and on.

The whole justification for permitting the corporate executive to be selected by the stockholders is that the executive is an agent serving the interests of his principal. This justification disappears when the corporate executive imposes taxes and spends the proceeds for "social" purposes. He becomes in effect a public employee, a civil servant, even though he remains in name an employee of a private enterprise. On grounds of political principle, it is intolerable that such civil servants—insofar as their actions in the name of social responsibility are real and not just window-dressing—should be selected as they are now. If they are to be civil servants, then they must be selected through a political process. If they are to impose taxes and make expenditures to foster "social" objectives, then political machinery must be set up to guide the assessment of taxes and to determine through a political process the objectives to be served.

This is the basic reason why the doctrine of "social responsibility" involves the acceptance of the socialist view that political mechanisms, not market mechanisms, are the appropriate way to determine the allocation of scarce resources to alternative uses.

On the grounds of consequences, can the corporate executive in fact discharge his alleged "social responsibilities"? On the one hand, suppose he could get away with spending the stockholders' or customers' or employees' money. How is he to know how to spend it? He is told that he must contribute to fighting inflation. How is he to know what action of his will contribute to that end? He is presumably an expert in running his company—in producing a product or selling it or financing it. But nothing about his selection makes him an expert on inflation. Will his holding down the price of his product reduce inflationary pres- sure? Or, by leaving more spending power in the hands of his customers, simply divert it elsewhere? Or, by forcing him to produce less because of the lower price, will it simply contribute to shortages? Even if he could answer these questions, how much cost is he justified in imposing on his stockholders, customers and employees for this social purpose?

What is the appropriate share and what is the appropriate share of others?

And, whether he wants to or not, can he get away with spending his stockholders', customers' or employees' money? Will not the stockholders fire him? (Either the present ones or those who take over when his actions in the name of social responsibility have reduced the corporation's profits and the price of its stock.) His customers and his employees can desert him for other producers and employers less scrupulous in exercising their social responsibilities.

This facet of "social responsibility" doctrine is brought into sharp relief when the doctrine is used to justify wage restraint by trade unions. The conflict of interest is naked and clear when union officials are asked to subordinate the interest of their members to some more general social purpose. If the union officials try to enforce wage restraint, the consequence is likely to be wildcat strikes, rank-and-file revolts and the emergence of strong competitors for their jobs. We thus have the ironic phenomenon that union leaders—at least in the U.S.—have objected to Government interference with the market far more consistently and courageously than have business leaders.

The difficulty of exercising "social responsibility" illustrates, of course, the great virtue of private competitive enterprise—it forces people to be responsible for their own actions and makes it difficult for them to "exploit" other people for either selfish or unselfish purposes. They can do good—but only at their own expense.

Many a reader who has followed the argument this far may be tempted to remonstrate that it is all well and good to speak of government's having the responsibility to impose taxes and determine expenditures for such "social" purposes as controlling pollution or training the hard-core unemployed, but that the problems are too urgent to wait on the slow course of political processes, that the exercise of social responsibility by businessmen is a quicker and surer way to solve pressing current problems.

Aside from the question of fact—I share Adam Smith's skepticism about the benefits that can be expected from "those who affected to trade for the public good"—this argument must be rejected on grounds of principle. What it amounts to is an assertion that those who favor the taxes and expenditures in question have failed to persuade a majority of their fellow citizens to be of like mind and that they are seeking to attain by undemocratic procedures what they cannot attain by democratic procedures. In a free society, it is hard for "good" people to do "good," but that is a small price to pay for making it hard for "evil" people to do "evil," especially since one man's good is another's evil.

I have, for simplicity, concentrated on the special case of the corporate executive, except only for the brief digression on trade unions. But precisely the same argument applies to the newer phenomenon of calling upon stockholders to require corporations to exercise social responsibility (the recent G.M. crusade, for example). In most of these cases, what is in effect involved is some stockholders trying to get other stockholders (or customers or employees) to contribute against their will to "social" causes favored by the activists. Insofar as they succeed, they are again imposing taxes and spending the proceeds.

The situation of the individual proprietor is somewhat different. If he acts to reduce the returns of his enterprise in order to exercise his "social responsibility," he is spending his own money, not someone else's. If he wishes to spend his money on such purposes, that is his right, and I cannot see that there is any objection to his doing so. In the process, he, too, may impose costs on employees and customers. However, because he is far less likely than a large corporation or union to have monopolistic power, any such side effects will tend to be minor.

Of course, in practice the doctrine of social responsibility is frequently a cloak for actions that are justified on other grounds rather than a reason for those actions.

To illustrate, it may well be in the long-run interest of a corporation that is a major employer in a small community to devote resources to providing amenities to that community or to improving its government. That may make it easier to attract desirable employees, it may reduce the wage bill or lessen losses from pilferage and sabotage or have other worthwhile effects. Or it may be that, given the laws about the deductibility of corporate charitable contributions, the stockholders can contribute more to charities they favor by having the corporation make the gift than by doing it themselves, since they can in that way contribute an amount that would otherwise have been paid as corporate taxes.

In each of these—and many similar —cases, there is a strong temptation to rationalize these actions as an exercise of "social responsibility." In the present climate of opinion, with its widespread aversion to "capitalism," "profits," the "soulless corporation" and so on, this is one way for a corporation to generate goodwill as a by-product of expenditures that are entirely justified in its own self-interest.

It would be inconsistent of me to call on corporate executives to refrain from this hypocritical window-dressing because it harms the foundations of a free society. That would be to call on them to exercise a "social responsibility"! If our institutions, and the attitudes of the public make it in their self-interest to cloak their actions in this way, I cannot summon much indignation to denounce them. At the same time, I can express admiration for those individual proprietors or owners of closely held corporations or stockholders of more broadly held corporations who disdain such tactics as approaching fraud.

Whether blameworthy or not, the use of the cloak of social responsibility, and the nonsense spoken in its name by influential and prestigious businessmen, does clearly harm the foundations of a free society. I have been impressed time and again by the schizophrenic character of many businessmen. They are capable of being extremely far-sighted and clear-headed in matters that are internal to their businesses. They are incredibly short-sighted and muddle-headed in matters that are outside their businesses but affect the possible survival of business in general. This short-sightedness is strikingly exemplified in the calls from many businessmen for wage and price guidelines or controls or incomes policies. There is nothing that could do more in a brief period to destroy a market system and replace it by a centrally controlled system than effective governmental control of prices and wages.

The short-sightedness is also exemplified in speeches by businessmen on social responsibility. This may gain them kudos in the short run. But it helps to strengthen the already too prevalent view that the pursuit of profits is wicked and immoral and must be curbed and controlled by external forces. Once this view is adopted, the external forces that curb the market will not be the social consciences, however highly developed, of the pontificating executives; it will be the iron fist of Government bureaucrats. Here, as with price and wage controls, businessmen seem to me to reveal a suicidal impulse.

The political principle that underlies the market mechanism is unanimity. In an ideal free market resting on private property, no individual can coerce any other, all cooperation is voluntary, all parties to such cooperation benefit or they need not participate. There are no "social" values, no "social" responsibilities in any sense other than the shared values and responsibilities of individuals. Society is a collection of individuals and of the various groups they voluntarily form.

The political principle that underlies the political mechanism is conformity. The individual must serve a more general social interest—whether that be determined by a church or a dictator or a majority. The individual may have a vote and a say in what is to be done, but if he is overruled, he must conform. It is appropriate for some to require others to contribute to a general social purpose whether they wish to or not.

Unfortunately, unanimity is not always feasible. There are some respects in which conformity appears unavoidable, so I do not see how one can avoid the use of the political mechanism altogether.

But the doctrine of "social responsibility" taken seriously would extend the scope of the political mechanism to every human activity. It does not differ in philosophy from the most explicitly collectivist doctrine. It differs only by professing to believe that collectivist ends can be attained without collectivist means. That is why, in my book "Capitalism and Freedom," I have called it a "fundamentally subversive doctrine" in a free society, and have said that in such a society, "there is one and only one social responsibility of business—to use its resources and engage in activities designed to increase its profits so long as it stays within the rules of the game, which is to say, engages in open and free competition without deception or fraud."

# NO

**Robert Almeder**

# MORALITY IN THE MARKETPLACE: REFLECTIONS ON THE FRIEDMAN DOCTRINE

## INTRODUCTION

In seeking to create a climate more favorable for corporate activity, International Telephone and Telegraph allegedly contributed large sums of money to "destabilize" the duly elected government of Chile. Even though advised by the scientific community that the practice is lethal, major chemical companies reportedly continue to dump large amounts of carcinogens and mutagens into the water supply of various areas and, at the same time, lobby strongly to prevent legislation against such practices. General Motors Corporation, other automobile manufacturers, and Firestone Tire and Rubber Corporation have frequently defended themselves against the charge that they knowingly and willingly marketed a product that, owing to defective design, had been reliably predicted to kill a certain percentage of its users and, moreover, refused to recall promptly the product even when government agencies documented the large incidence of death as a result of the defective product. Finally, people often say that numerous advertising companies happily accept, and earnestly solicit, accounts to advertise cigarettes knowing full well that as a direct result of their advertising activities a certain number of people will die considerably prematurely and painfully. Most recently, of course, American Tobacco Companies have been charged with knowingly marketing a very addictive product known to kill untold numbers in slow, painful and costly deaths while the price of the stock of these companies has made fortunes for the shareholders. We need not concern ourselves with whether these and other similar charges are true because our primary concern here is with what might count as a justification for such corporate conduct were it to occur. There can be no question that such corporate behavior sometimes occurs and is frequently legal, or at least not illegal. The question is whether corporate behavior should be constrained by nonlegal or moral considerations. If so, to what extent and how could it be done? As things presently stand, it seems

From Robert Almeder, "Morality in the Marketplace: Reflections on the Friedman Doctrine." Copyright © 1997 by Robert Almeder. Revised and expanded from "Morality in the Marketplace," in Milton Snoeyenbos, Robert Almeder and James Humber, eds., *Business Ethics*, rev. ed. (Prometheus Press, 1992). Reprinted by permission of Robert Almeder.

to be a dogma of contemporary capitalism rapidly emerging throughout the world that the sole responsibility of business is to make as much money as is *legally* possible. But the interesting question is whether this view is rationally defensible.

Sometimes, although not very frequently, corporate executives will admit to the sort of behavior depicted above and then proceed proximately to justify such behavior in the name of their responsibility to the shareholders or owners (if the shareholders are not the owners) to make as much profit as is legally possible. Thereafter, less proximately and more generally, they will proceed to urge the more general utilitarian point that the increase in profit engendered by such corporate behavior begets such an unquestionable overall good for society that the behavior in question is morally acceptable if not quite praiseworthy. More specifically, the justification in question can, and usually does, take two forms.

The first and most common form of justification consists in urging that, as long as one's corporate behavior is not illegal, the behavior will be morally acceptable because the sole purpose of being in business is to make a profit; and the rules of the marketplace are somewhat different from those in other places and must be followed if one is to make a profit. Moreover, proponents of this view hasten to add that, as Adam Smith has claimed, the greatest good for society in the long run is achieved not by corporations seeking to act morally, or with a sense of social responsibility in their pursuit of profit, but rather by each corporation seeking to maximize its own profit, unregulated in that endeavor except by the laws of supply and demand along with whatever other laws are

inherent to the competition process. This, they say, is what has made capitalist societies the envy of the world while ideological socialisms sooner of later fail miserably to meet deep human needs. Smith's view, that there is an invisible hand, as it were, directing an economy governed solely by the profit motive to the greatest good for society in the long run,[1] is still the dominant motivation and justification for those who would want an economy unregulated by any moral concern that would, or could, tend to decrease profits for some *alleged* social or moral good.

Milton Friedman, for example, has frequently asserted that the sole moral responsibility of business is to make as much profit as is legally possible; and by that he means to assert that attempts to regulate or restrain the pursuit of profit in accordance with what some people believe to be socially desirable ends are in fact *subversive* of the common good because the greatest good for the greatest number is achieved by an economy maximally competitive and unregulated by moral rules in its pursuit of profit.[2] So, on Friedman's view, the greatest good for society is achieved by corporations acting legally, but with no further regard for what may be morally desirable; and this view begets the paradox that, *in business,* the greatest good for society can be achieved only by acting without regard for morality, at least in so far as moral rules are not reflected in the legal code. Moreover, adoption of this position constitutes a fairly conscious commitment to the view that while one's personal life may well need moral governance beyond the law, when pursuing profit, it is necessary that one's corporate behavior be unregulated by any moral concern other than that of making as much money as is legally possible; curiously enough, it is only in this way that society achieves the greatest good. So viewed, it is not difficult to see how a corporate executive could sincerely and consistently adopt rigorous standards of morality in his or her personal life and yet feel quite comfortable in abandoning those standards in the pursuit of profit. Albert Carr, for example, likens the conduct of business to that of playing poker.[3] As Carr would have it, moral busybodies who insist on corporations acting morally might do just as well to censure a good bluffer in poker for being deceitful. Society, of course, lacking a perspective such as Friedman's and Carr's is only too willing to view such behavior as strongly hypocritical and fostered by an unwholesome avarice.

The second way of justifying, or defending, corporate practices that may appear morally questionable consists in urging that even if corporations were to take seriously the idea of limiting profits because of a desire to be moral or more responsible to social needs, then corporations would be involved in the unwholesome business of selecting and implementing moral values that may not be shared by a large number of people. Besides, there is the overwhelming question of whether there can be any non-questionable moral values or non-controversial list of social priorities for corporations to adopt. After all, if ethical relativism is true, or if ethical nihilism is true (and philosophers can be counted upon to argue agressively for both positions), then it would be fairly silly of corporations to limit profits for what may be a quite dubious reason, namely, for being moral, when there are no clear grounds for doing it, and when it is not too clear what would count for doing it. In short, business corporations could argue (as Friedman has done)[4] that corporate actions in behalf of society's interests would require of corporations an ability to clearly determine and rank in noncontroversial ways the major needs of society; and it would not appear that this could be done successfully.

Perhaps another, and somewhat easier, way of formulating this second argument consists in urging that because moralists and philosophers generally fail to agree on what are the proper moral rules (if any), as well as on whether we should be moral, it would be imprudent to sacrifice a clear profit for a dubious or controversial moral gain. To authorize such a sacrifice would be to abandon a clear responsibility for one that is unclear or questionable.

If there are any other basic ways of justifying the sort of corporate behavior noted at the outset, I cannot imagine what they might be. So, let us examine these two modes of justification. In doing this, I hope to show that neither argument is sound and, moreover, that corporate behavior of the sort in question is clearly immoral if anything is immoral—and if nothing is immoral, then such corporate behavior is clearly contrary to the long-term interest of a corporation. In the end, we will reflect on ways to prevent such behavior, and on what is philosophically implied by corporate willingness to act in clearly immoral ways.

## II. THE "INVISIBLE HAND"

Essentially, the first argument is that the greatest good for the greatest number will be, and can only be, achieved by corporations acting legally but unregulated by any moral concern in the pursuit of profit.

As we saw earlier, the evidence for this argument rests on a fairly classical and unquestioning acceptance of Adam Smith's view that society achieves a greater good when each person is allowed to pursue her or his own self-interested ends than when each person's pursuit of self-interested ends is regulated in some way or another by moral rules or concern. But I know of no evidence Smith ever offered for this latter claim, although it seems clear that those who adopt it generally do so out of respect for the perceived good that has emerged for various modern societies as a direct result of the free enterprise system and its ability to raise the overall standard of living of all those under it.

However, there is nothing inevitable about the greatest good occurring in an unregulated economy. Indeed, we have good inductive evidence from the age of the Robber Barons that unless the profit motive is regulated in various ways (by statute or otherwise) untold social evil can, and *will*, occur because of the natural tendency of the system to place ever-increasing sums of money in ever-decreasing numbers of hands as a result of the nature of competition unregulated. If all this is so, then so much the worse for all philosophical attempts to justify what would appear to be morally questionable corporate behavior on the grounds that corporate behavior, unregulated by moral concern, is necessarily or even probably productive of the greatest good for the greatest number. Moreover, a rule utilitarian would not be very hard pressed to show the many unsavory implications to society as a whole if society were to take seriously a rule to the effect that, if one acts legally, it is morally permissible to do whatever one wants to do to achieve a profit. We shall discuss some of those implications of this rule below before drawing a conclusion.

The second argument cited above asserts that even if we were to grant, for the sake of argument, that corporations have social responsibilities beyond that of making as much money as is legally possible for the shareholders, there would be no noncontroversial way for corporations to discover just what these responsibilities are in the order of their importance. Owing to the fact that even distinguished moral philosophers predictably disagree on what one's moral responsibilities are, if any, it would seem irresponsible to limit profits to satisfy dubious moral responsibilities.

For one thing, this argument unduly exaggerates our potential for moral disagreement. Admittedly, there might well be important disagreements among corporations (just as there could be among philosophers) as to a priority ranking of major social needs; but that does not mean that most of us could not, or would not, agree that certain things ought not be done in the name of profit even when there is no law prohibiting such acts. Doubtless, there will always be a few who would do most anything for a profit; but that is hardly a good argument in favor of their having the moral right to do so rather than a good argument showing that they refuse to be moral. In sum, it is difficult to see how this second argument favoring corporate moral nihilism is any better than the general argument for ethical nihilism based on the variability of ethical judgments or practices; and apart from the fact that it tacitly presupposes that morality is a matter of what we all in fact would, or should, accept, the argument is maximally counterintuitive (as I shall show) by way of suggesting that we cannot generally agree that corporations have certain clear social responsibilities to avoid certain practices. Accordingly, I would now like to argue that if anything is immoral, a certain kind of corporate behavior is quite immoral although it may not be illegal.

## III. MURDER FOR PROFIT

Without caring to enter into the reasons for the belief, I assume we all believe that it is wrong to kill an innocent human being for no other reason than that doing so would be more financially rewarding for the killer than if he were to earn his livelihood in some other way. Nor, I assume, should our moral feeling on this matter change depending on the amount of money involved. Killing an innocent baby for fifteen million dollars would not seem to be any less objectionable than killing it for twenty cents. It is possible, however, that a self-professing utilitarian might be tempted to argue that the killing of an innocent baby for fifteen million dollars would not be objectionable if the money were to be given to the poor; under these circumstances, greater good would be achieved by the killing of the innocent baby. But, I submit, if anybody were to argue in this fashion, his argument would be quite deficient because he has not established what he needs to establish to make his argument sound. What he needs is a clear, convincing argument that raising the standard of living of an indefinite number of poor persons by the killing of an innocent person is a greater good for all those affected by the act than if the standard of living were not raised by the killing of an innocent person. This is needed because part of what we mean by having a basic right to life is that a person's life cannot be taken from him or her without a good reason. If our utilitarian cannot provide a convincing justification for his claim that a greater good is served by killing an innocent person in order to raise the standard of living for a large number of poor people, then it is hard to see how he can have the good reason that he needs to deprive an innocent person of his or her life. Now, it seems clear that there will be anything but unanimity in the moral community on the question of whether there is a greater good achieved in raising the standard of living by killing an innocent baby than in leaving the standard of living alone and not killing an innocent baby. Moreover, even if everybody were to agree that the greater good is achieved by the killing of the innocent baby, how could that be shown to be true? How does one compare the moral value of a human life with the moral value of raising the standard of living by the taking of that life? Indeed, the more one thinks about it, the more difficult it is to see just what would count as objective evidence for the claim that the greater good is achieved by the killing of the innocent baby. Accordingly, I can see nothing that would justify the utilitarian who might be tempted to argue that if the sum is large enough, and if the sum were to be used for raising the standard of living for an indefinite number of poor people, then it would be morally acceptable to kill an innocent person for money.

These reflections should not be taken to imply, however, that no utilitarian argument could justify the killing of an innocent person for money. After all, if the sum were large enough to save the lives of a large number of people who would surely die if the innocent baby were not killed, then one would as a rule be justified in killing the innocent baby for the sum in question. But this situation is obviously quite different from the situation in which one would attempt to justify the killing of an innocent person in order to raise the standard of living for an indefinite number of poor people. It makes sense to kill one innocent person in order to save, say, twenty innocent persons; but it makes no sense at all to kill one innocent person to raise the standard of living of an indefinite number of people. In the latter case, but not in the former, a comparison is made between things that are incomparable.

Given these considerations, it is remarkable and somewhat perplexing that certain corporations should seek to defend practices that are in fact instances of killing innocent persons for profit. Take, for example, the corporate practice of dumping known carcinogens into rivers. On Milton Friedman's view, we should not regulate or prevent such companies from dumping their effluents into the environment. Rather we should, if we like, tax the company after the effluents are in the water and then have the tax money used to clean up the environment.[5] For Friedman, and others, the fact that so many people will die as a result of this practice seems to be just part of the cost of doing business and making a profit. If there is any moral difference between such corporate practices and murdering innocent human beings for money, it is hard to see what it is. It is even more difficult to see how anyone could justify the practice and see it as no more than a business practice not to be regulated by moral concern. And there are a host of other corporate activities that are morally equivalent to deliberate killing of innocent persons for money. Such practices number among them contributing funds to "destabilize" a foreign government, selling cigarettes while knowing that they are highly addictive killers of innocent people, advertising cigarettes, knowingly marketing children's clothing having a known cancer-causing agent, and refusing to recall (for fear of financial loss) goods known to be sufficiently defective to directly maim or kill a certain percentage of their unsuspecting users because of the defect. On this latter item, we are all familiar, for example, with convincingly documented charges that certain prominent automobile and tire manufacturers will knowingly market equipment sufficiently defective to increase the likelihood of death as a direct result of the defect, and yet refuse to recall the product because the cost of recalling and repairing would have a greater adverse impact on profit than if the product were not recalled and the company paid the projected number of predictably successful suits. Of course, if the projected cost of the predictably successful suits were to outweigh the cost of recall and repair, then the product would be recalled and repaired, but not otherwise.

In cases of this sort, the companies involved may admit to having certain marketing problems or a design problem, and they may even admit to having made a mistake; but, interestingly enough, they do not view themselves as immoral or as murderers for keeping their product in the market place when they know people are dying from it, people who would not die if the defect were corrected.

The important point is not whether in fact these practices have occurred in the past, or occur even now; there can be no doubt that such practices have occurred and continue to occur. Rather the point is that when companies act in such ways as a matter of policy, they must either not know what they do is murder (i.e., unjustifiable killing of an innocent person), or knowing that it is murder, seek to justify it in terms of profit. And I have been arguing that it is difficult to see how any corporate manager could fail to see that these policies amount to murder for money, although there may be no civil statute against such corporate behavior. If so, then where such policies exist, we can only assume that they are designed and implemented by corporate managers who either see nothing wrong with murder for money (which is implausible) or recognize that what they do is wrong but simply refuse to act morally because it is more financially rewarding to act immorally.

Of course, it is possible that corporate executives would not recognize such acts as murder. They may, after all, view murder as a legal concept involving one non-corporate person or persons deliberately killing another non-corporate person or persons and prosecutable only under existing criminal statute. If so, it is somewhat understandable how corporate executives might fail, at least psychologically, to see such corporate policies as murder rather than as, say, calculated risks, tradeoffs, or design errors. Still, for all that, the logic of the situation seems clear enough.

## IV. CONCLUSION

In addition to the fact that the only two plausible arguments favoring the Friedman doctrine are unsatisfactory, a strong case can be made for the claim that corporations *do* have a clear and noncontroversial moral responsibility not to design or implement, for reasons of profit, policies that they know, or have good reason to believe, will kill or otherwise seriously injure innocent persons affected by those policies. Moreover, we have said nothing about wage discrimination, sexism, discrimination in hiring, price fixing, price gouging, questionable but not unlawful competition, or other similar practices that some will think businesses should avoid by virtue of responsibility to society. My main concern has been to show that because we all agree that murder for money is generally wrong, and since there is no discernible difference between that and certain corporate policies that are not in fact illegal, then these corporate practices are clearly immoral (that is, they ought not to be done) and incapable of being morally justified by appeal to the Friedman doctrine since that doctrine does not admit of adequate evidential support. In itself, it seems sad that this argument needs to be made and, if it were not for what appears to be a fairly strong commitment within the business community to the Friedman doctrine in the name of the unquestionable success of the free enterprise system, the argument would not need to be stated.

The fact that such practices do exist —designed and implemented by corporate managers who, for all intents and purposes appear to be upright members of the moral community—only heightens the need for effective social prevention. Presumably, of course, any company willing to put human lives into the profit and loss column is not likely to respond to moral censure. Accordingly, I submit that perhaps the most effective way to deal with the problem of preventing such corporate behavior would consist in structuring legislation such that senior corporate managers who knowingly concur in practices of the sort listed above can effectively be tried, at their own expense, for murder, rather than censured and fined a sum to be paid out of corporate profits. This may seem a somewhat extreme or unrealistic proposal. However, it seems more unrealistic to think that aggressively competitive corporations will respond to what is morally necessary if failure to do so could be very or even minimally profitable. In short, unless we take strong and appropriate steps to prevent such practices, society will be reinforcing a destructive mode of behavior that is maximally disrespectful of human life, just as society will be reinforcing a value system that so emphasizes monetary gain as a standard of human success that murder for profit could be a corporate policy if the penalty for being caught at it were not too dear.

Fortunately, a number of states in America have enacted legislation that makes corporations subject to the criminal code of that state. This practice began to emerge quite strongly after the famous Pinto case in which an Indiana superior court judge refused to dismiss a homicide indictment against the Ford Motor Company. The company was indicted on charges of reckless homicide stemming from a 1978 accident involving a 1973 Pinto in which three girls died when the car burst into flames after being slammed in the rear. This was the first case in which Ford, or any other automobile manufacturer, had been charged with a criminal offense. The indictment went forward because the state of Indiana adopted in 1977 a criminal code provision permitting corporations to be charged with criminal acts. At the time, incidentally, twenty-two other states had similar codes. At any rate, the judge, in refusing to set aside the indictment, agreed with the prosecutor's argument that the charge was based not on the Pinto design fault, but rather on the fact that Ford had permitted the car "to remain on Indiana highways knowing full well its defects." The fact that the Ford Motor company was ultimately found innocent of the charges by the jury is incidental to the point that the increasing number of states that allow corporations to fall under the criminal code is an example of social regulation that could have been avoided had corporations and corporate managers not followed so ardently the Friedman doctrine.

In the long run, of course, corporate and individual willingness to do what is clearly immoral for the sake of monetary gain is a patent commitment of a certain view about the nature of human happiness and success, a view that needs to be placed in the balance with Aristotle's reasoned argument and reflections to the effect that money and all that it brings is a means to an end, and not the sort of end in itself that will justify acting immorally to attain it. What that beautiful end is and why being moral allows us to achieve it, may well be the most rewarding and profitable subject a human being can think about. Properly understood and placed in perspective, Aristotle's view on the nature and attainment of human happiness could go a long way toward alleviating the temptation to kill for money.

In the meantime, any ardent supporter of the capitalistic system will want to see the system thrive and flourish; and this it cannot do if it invites and demands government regulation in the name of the public interest. A *strong* ideological commitment to what I have described above as the Friedman doctrine is counterproductive and not in anyone's long-range interest because it is most likely to beget an ever-increasing regulatory climate. The only way to avoid such encroaching regulation is to find ways to move the business community into the long-term view of what is in its interest, and effect ways of both determining and responding to social needs before society moves to regulate business to that end. To so move the business community is to ask business to regulate its own modes of competition in ways that may seem very difficult to achieve. Indeed, if what I have been suggesting is correct, the only kind of enduring capitalism is humane capitalism, one that is at least as socially responsible as society needs. By the same token, contrary to what is sometimes felt in the business community, the Friedman doctrine, ardently adopted for the dubious reasons generally given, will most likely undermine capitalism and motivate an economic socialism by assuring an erosive regulatory climate in a society that expects the business community to be socially responsible in ways that go beyond just making legal profits.

In sum, being socially responsible in ways that go beyond legal profit making is by no means a dubious luxury for the capitalist in today's world. It is a necessity if capitalism is to survive at all; and, presumably, we shall all profit with the survival of a vibrant capitalism. If anything, then, rigid adherence to the Friedman doctrine is not only philosophically unjustified, and unjustifiable, it is also unprofitable in the long run, and therefore, downright subversive of the long-term common good. Unfortunately, taking the long-run view is difficult for everyone. After all, for each of us, tomorrow may not come. But living for today only does not seem to make much sense either, if that deprives us of any reasonable and happy tomorrow. Living for the future may not be the healthiest thing to do; but do it we must, if we have good reason to think that we will have a future. The trick is to provide for the future without living in it, and that just requires being moral.[6]

*This paper is a revised and expanded version of "Morality in the Marketplace," which appears in* Business Ethics *(revised edition) eds. Milton Snoeyenbos, Robert Almeder and James Humber (Buffalo, N.Y.: Prometheus Press, 1992.) 82–90, and, as such, it is a revised and expanded version of an earlier piece "The Ethics of Profit: Reflections on Corporate Responsibility," which originally appeared in* Business and Society *(Winter 1980, 7–15).*

### NOTES

1. Adam Smith, *The Wealth of Nations,* ed. Edwin Canaan (New York: Modern Library, 1937), p. 423.

2. See Milton Friedman, "The Social Responsibility of Business Is to Increase Its Profits," in *The New York Times Magazine* (September 13, 1970), pp. 33, 122–126 and "Milton Friedman Responds," in *Business and Society Review* no. 1 (Spring 1972), p. 5ff.

3. Albert Z. Carr, "Is Business Bluffing Ethical?" *Harvard Business Review* (January–February 1968).

4. Milton Friedman in "Milton Friedman Responds," in *Business and Society Review* no. 1 (Spring 1972), p. 10.

5. Ibid

6. I would like to thank J. Humber and M. Snoeyenbos for their comments and criticisms of an earlier draft.

# POSTSCRIPT

## Are Profits the Only Business of Business?

Friedman dismisses the pleas of those who argue for socially responsible business action on the grounds that these individuals do not understand the role of the corporate executive in modern society. Friedman points out that the executives are responsible to the corporate owners, and if the corporate executives take a "socially responsible" action that reduces the return on the owners' investment, they have spent the owners' money. This, Friedman maintains, violates the very foundation of the American political-economic system: individual freedom. If the corporate executives wish to take socially responsible actions, they should use their own money; they should not prevent the owners from spending their money on whatever social actions they might wish to support.

Almeder argues that some corporate behavior is immoral and that defense of this immoral behavior imposes great costs on society. He likens corporate acts such as advertising cigarettes, marketing automobiles that cannot sustain moderate rear-end collisions, and contributing funds to destabilize foreign governments to murdering innocent children for profit. He argues that society must not condone this behavior, but instead, through federal and state legislation, it must continue to impose regulations upon businesses until businesses begin to regulate themselves.

Perhaps no single topic is more fundamental to microeconomics than is the issue of profits. Many pages have been written in defense of profits; see, for example, Milton and Rose Friedman's *Free to Choose: A Personal Statement* (Harcourt Brace Jovanovich, 1980). A classic reference is Frank H. Knight's *Risk, Uncertainty, and Profits* (Kelly Press, 1921). Friedrich A. Hayek, the author of many journal articles and books, is a guru for many current free marketers. There are a number of other books and articles, however, that are highly critical of the Friedman-Knight-Hayek position, including Christopher D. Stone's *Where the Law Ends: Social Control of Corporate Behavior* (Harper and Row, 1975). Others who challenge the legitimacy of the notion that markets are morally free zones include Thomas Mulligan, "A Critique of Milton Friedman's Essay 'The Social Responsibility of Business Is to Increase Its Profits,' " *Journal of Business Ethics* (1986); Daniel M. Hausman, "Are Markets Morally Free Zones?" *Philosophy and Public Affairs* (Fall 1989); and Andrew Henley, "Economic Orthodoxy and the Free Market System: A Christian Critique," *International Journal of Social Economics* (vol. 14, no. 10, 1987).

# ISSUE 2

## Should We Encourage the Private Ownership of Guns?

**YES: Daniel D. Polsby,** from "The False Promise of Gun Control," *The Atlantic Monthly* (March 1994)

**NO: Arthur L. Kellermann et al.,** from "Gun Ownership as a Risk Factor for Homicide in the Home," *The New England Journal of Medicine* (October 7, 1993)

### ISSUE SUMMARY

**YES:** Law professor Daniel D. Polsby alleges that guns do not increase crime rates or violence in the streets but that the "proliferation of gun-control laws almost certainly does."

**NO:** The research of emergency room physician Arthur L. Kellermann and his colleagues suggests that gun ownership increases an individual's risk of being murdered rather than providing that person with self-protection.

In 1992 crimes committed with handguns increased by almost 50 percent over the previous five-year annual average. In that year, handguns were used in 931,000 violent crimes. It may be because of statistics such as these that the Brady Bill—federal legislation requiring a five-day waiting period and a background check for individuals wishing to purchase guns—was passed by Congress in November 1993 after numerous attempts to pass gun-control legislation were defeated by the powerful pro-gun lobby during the previous seven years.

The pro-gun interests in the United States are well articulated by the National Rifle Association (NRA) and its members. This organization boasts a membership in excess of 3.3 million, and it claimed liquid assets of more than $90 million in 1990. Throughout its existence, the NRA has effectively blocked nearly every attempt at governmental control over private ownership of guns. Traditionally, the NRA and others have defended their position on the grounds that legislation in this area would violate the "right to bear arms," which they allege is protected by the Second Amendment to the Constitution.

However, in recent years public opinion has increasingly turned against the gun lobby. Also, society has begun to question whether or not the Second Amendment is applicable to private gun ownership. The amendment in full states: "A well regulated Militia, being necessary to the security of a free

State, the right of people to keep and bear Arms, shall not be infringed."
Many argue that the NRA's constitutional argument is rendered invalid by
the reference to a "well regulated Militia." Most legal scholars maintain that
the Supreme Court's 1939 decision in *United States v. Miller* still stands as the
appropriate interpretation of the Second Amendment. Here the Court ruled
that the intent of the amendment was to ensure a collective right having "some
reasonable relationship to the preservation or efficiency of a well-regulated
militia." The Court did not rule that individuals have a right to keep and bear
arms. Indeed, lower courts have turned to the *Miller* decision to *uphold, not
strike down* gun-control legislation.

The most recent Supreme Court ruling in this area came in 1980, when the
Court reaffirmed that attempts to control the use of guns through legislative
action "do not trench upon any constitutionally protected liberties." It is
noteworthy that both Warren E. Burger, the chief justice at that time, and
the current chief justice William H. Rehnquist, both conservatives, joined the
majority of the Court in this interpretation.

If there is no constitutional prohibition against gun control, what are the
costs and benefits of private ownership of handguns? The NRA has long
argued that handguns are necessary for self-protection. The NRA's new advertising slogan, "Refuse to Be a Victim," is directed toward getting that
message across to women, who as a group have traditionally been more
opposed to gun ownership than men. The arguments of those opposed to
gun control go far beyond this, however. This becomes clear in the essay by
Daniel D. Polsby, which follows. Polsby raises fundamental economic questions about the demand for guns, the sources of the supply of guns, and the
elastic characteristics of both supply and demand.

In large measure, the purpose of Polsby's selection is to respond to the
medical community, which has challenged the NRA's contention that guns are
an important means of self-protection. In this regard, Arthur L. Kellermann
and his associates argue that guns are more likely to result in injury to a
member of a gun-owning household than they are to protect the household
from intruders.

# YES
Daniel D. Polsby

# THE FALSE PROMISE OF GUN CONTROL

During the 1960s and 1970s the robbery rate in the United States increased sixfold, and the murder rate doubled; the rate of handgun ownership nearly doubled in that period as well. Handguns and criminal violence grew together apace, and national opinion leaders did not fall to remark on the coincidence.

It has become a bipartisan article of faith that more handguns cause more violence. Such was the unequivocal conclusion of the National Commission on the Causes and Prevention of Violence in 1969, and such is now the editorial opinion of virtually every influential newspaper and magazine, from *The Washington Post* to *The Economist* to the *Chicago Tribune*. Members of the House and Senate who have not dared to confront the gun lobby concede the connection privately. Even if the National Rifle Association [NRA] can produce blizzards of angry calls and letters to the Capitol virtually overnight, House members one by one have been going public, often after some new firearms atrocity at a fast-food restaurant or the like. And last November they passed the Brady bill.

Alas, however well accepted, the conventional wisdom about guns and violence is mistaken. Guns don't increase national rates of crime and violence —but the continued proliferation of gun-control laws almost certainly does. Current rates of crime and violence are a bit below the peaks of the late 1970s, but because of a slight oncoming bulge in the at-risk population of males aged fifteen to thirty-four, the crime rate will soon worsen. The rising generation of criminals will have no more difficulty than their elders did in obtaining the tools of their trade. Growing violence will lead to calls for laws still more severe. Each fresh round of legislation will be followed by renewed frustration.

Gun-control laws don't work. What is worse, they act perversely. While legitimate users of firearms encounter intense regulation, scrutiny, and bureaucratic control, illicit markets easily adapt to whatever difficulties a free society throws in their way. Also, efforts to curtail the supply of firearms inflict collateral damage on freedom and privacy interests that have long been considered central to American public life. Thanks to the seemingly never-ending war on drugs and long experience attempting to suppress prostitution and pornography, we know a great deal about how illicit markets function and how costly to the public attempts to control them can be. It is essential that we make use of this experience in coming to grips with gun control.

The thousands of gun-control laws in the United States are of two general types. The older kind sought to regulate how, where, and by whom firearms could be carried. More recent laws have sought to make it more costly to buy, sell, or use firearms (or certain classes of firearms, such as assault rifles, Saturday-night specials, and so on) by imposing fees, special taxes, or surtaxes on them. The Brady bill is of both types: it has a background-check provision, and its five-day waiting period amounts to a "time tax" on acquiring handguns. All such laws can be called scarcity-inducing, because they seek to raise the cost of buying firearms, as figured in terms of money, time, nuisance, or stigmatization.

Despite the mounting number of scarcity-inducing laws, no one is very satisfied with them. Hobbyists want to get rid of them, and gun-control proponents don't think they go nearly far enough. Everyone seems to agree that gun-control laws have some effect on the distribution of firearms. But it has not been the dramatic and measurable effect their proponents desired.

Opponents of gun control have traditionally wrapped their arguments in the Second Amendment to the Constitution. Indeed, most modern scholarship affirms that so far as the drafters of the Bill of Rights were concerned the right to bear arms was to be enjoyed by everyone, not just a militia, and that one of the principal justifications for an armed populace was to secure the tranquillity and good order of the community. But most people are not dedicated antiquitarians, and would not be impressed by the argument "I admit that my behavior is very dangerous to public safety, but the Second Amendment says I have a right to do it anyway." That would be a case for repealing the Second Amendment, not respecting it.

## FIGHTING THE DEMAND CURVE

Everyone knows that possessing a handgun makes it easier to intimidate, wound, or kill someone. But the implication of this point for social policy has not been so well understood. It is easy to count the bodies of those who have been killed or wounded with guns, but not easy to count the people who have avoided harm because they had access to weapons. Think about uniformed police officers, who carry handguns in plain view not in order to kill people but simply to daunt potential attackers. And it works. Criminals generally do not single out police officers for opportunistic attack. Though officers can expect to draw their guns from time to time, few even in big-city departments will actually fire a shot (except in target practice) in the course of a year. This observation points to an important truth: people who are armed make comparatively unattractive victims. A criminal might not know if any one civilian is armed, but if it becomes known that a large number of civilians do carry weapons, criminals will become warier.

Which weapons laws are the right kinds can be decided only after considering two related questions. First, what is the connection between civilian possession of firearms and social violence? Second, how can we expect gun-control laws to alter people's behavior? Most recent scholarship raises serious questions about the "weapons increase violence" hypothesis. The second question is emphasized here, because it is routinely overlooked and often mocked when noticed; yet it is crucial. Rational gun control requires understanding not only the relationship between weapons and violence but also the relationship between laws and people's behavior. Some things are very hard to accomplish with laws. The purpose of a law and its likely effects are not always the same thing. Many statutes are notorious for the way in which their unintended effects have swamped their intended ones.

In order to predict who will comply with gun-control laws, we should remember that guns are economic goods that are traded in markets. Consumers' interest in them varies. For religious, moral, aesthetic, or practical reasons, some people would refuse to buy firearms at any price. Other people willingly pay very high prices for them.

Handguns, so often the subject of gun-control laws, are desirable for one purpose—to allow a person tactically to dominate a hostile transaction with another person. The value of a weapon to a given person is a function of two factors: how much he or she wants to dominate a confrontation if one occurs, and how likely it is that he or she will actually be in a situation calling for a gun.

Dominating a transaction simply means getting what one wants without being hurt. Where people differ is in how likely it is that they will be involved in a situation in which a gun will be valuable. Someone who *intends* to engage in a transaction involving a gun—a criminal, for example—is obviously in the best possible position to predict that likelihood. Criminals should therefore be will-ing to pay more for a weapon than most other people would. Professors, politicians, and newspaper editors are, as a group, at very low risk of being involved in such transactions, and they thus systematically underrate the value of defensive handguns. (Correlative, perhaps, is their uncritical readiness to accept studies that debunk the utility of firearms for self-defense.) The class of people we wish to deprive of guns, then, is the very class with the most inelastic demand for them —criminals—whereas the people most likely to comply with gun-control laws don't value guns in the first place.

## DO GUNS DRIVE UP CRIME RATES?

Which premise is true—that guns increase crime or that the fear of crime causes people to obtain guns? Most of the country's major newspapers apparently take this problem to have been solved by an article published by Arthur Kellermann and several associates in the October 7, 1993, *New England Journal of Medicine*. Kellermann is an emergency-room physician who has published a number of influential papers that he believes discredit the thesis that private ownership of firearms is a useful means of self-protection. (An indication of his wide influence is that within two months the study received almost 100 mentions in publications and broadcast transcripts indexed in the Nexis data base.) For this study Kellermann and his associates identified fifteen behavioral and fifteen environmental variables that applied to a 388-member set of homicide victims, found a "matching" control group of 388 nonhomicide victims, and then ascertained how the two groups differed in gun ownership. In interviews Kellermann made clear his belief that owning a handgun markedly increases a person's risk of being murdered.

But the study does not prove that point at all. Indeed, as Kellermann explicitly conceded in the text of the article, the causal arrow may very well point in the other direction: the threat of being killed may make people more likely to arm themselves. Many people at risk of being killed, especially people involved in the drug trade or other illegal ventures, might well rationally buy a gun as a precaution, and be willing to pay a price driven up by gun-control laws. Crime, after all, is a dangerous business. Peter Reuter and Mark Kleiman, drug-policy researchers, calculated in 1987 that the average crack dealer's risk of being killed was far greater than his risk of being sent to prison. (Their data cannot, however, support the implication that ownership of a firearm causes or exacerbates the risk of being killed.)

Defending the validity of his work, Kellermann has emphasized that the link between lung cancer and smoking was initially established by studies methodologically no different from his. Gary Kleck, a criminology professor at Florida State University, has pointed out the flaw in this comparison. No one ever thought that lung cancer causes smoking, so when the association between the two was established the direction of the causal arrow was not in doubt. Kleck wrote that it is as though Kellermann, trying to discover how diabetics differ from other people, found that they are much more likely to possess insulin than nondiabetics, and concluded that insulin is a risk factor for diabetes.

*The New York Times*, the *Los Angeles Times*, *The Washington Post*, *The Boston Globe*, and the *Chicago Tribune* all gave prominent coverage to Kellermann's study as soon as it appeared, but none saw fit to discuss the study's limitations. A few, in order to introduce a hint of balance, mentioned that the NRA, or some member of its staff, disagreed with the study. But readers had no way of knowing that Kellermann himself had registered a disclaimer in his text. "It is possible," he conceded. "that reverse causation accounted for some of the association we observed between gun ownership and homicide." Indeed, the point is stronger than that: "reverse causation" may account for *most* of the association between gun ownership and homicide. Kellermann's data simply do not allow one to draw any conclusion.

If firearms increased violence and crime, then rates of spousal homicide would have skyrocketed, because the stock of privately owned handguns has increased rapidly since the mid-1960s. But according to an authoritative study of spousal homicide in the *American Journal of Public Health*, by James Mercy and Linda Saltzman, rates of spousal homicide in the years 1976 to 1985 fell. If firearms increased violence and crime, the crime rate should have increased throughout the 1980s, while the national stock of privately owned handguns increased by more than a million units in every year of the decade. It did not. Nor should the rates of violence and crime in Switzerland, New Zealand, and Israel be as low as they are, since the number of firearms per civilian household is comparable to that in the United States. Conversely, gun-controlled Mexico and South Africa should be islands of peace instead of having murder rates more than twice as high as those [in the United States]. The determinants of crime and law-abidingness are, of course, complex matters, which are not fully understood and certainly not explicable in terms of a country's laws. But gun-control enthusiasts, who have made capital out of the low murder rate in England, which is largely disarmed, simply ignore the counterexamples that don't fit their theory.

If firearms increased violence and crime, Florida's murder rate should not have been falling since the introduction, seven years ago, of a law that makes it easier for ordinary citizens to get permits to carry concealed handguns. Yet the murder rate has remained the same or fallen every year since the law was enacted, and it is now lower than the national murder rate (which has been rising). As of last November 183,561 permits had been issued, and only seventeen of the permits had been revoked because the holder was involved in a firearms offense. It would be precipitate to claim that the new law has "caused" the murder rate to subside. Yet here is a situation that doesn't fit the hypothesis that weapons increase violence.

If firearms increased violence and crime, programs of induced scarcity would suppress violence and crime. But —another anomaly—they don't. Why not? A theorem, which we could call the futility theorem, explains why gun-control laws must either be ineffectual or in the long term actually provoke more violence and crime. Any theorem depends on both observable fact and assumption. An assumption that can be made with confidence is that the higher the number of victims a criminal assumes to be armed, the higher will be the risk—the price—of assaulting them. By definition, gun-control laws should make weapons scarcer and thus more expensive. By our prior reasoning about demand among various types of consumers, after the laws are enacted criminals should be better armed, compared with noncriminals, than they were before. Of course, plenty of noncriminals will remain armed. But even if many noncriminals will pay as high a price as criminals will to obtain firearms, a larger number will not.

Criminals will thus still take the same gamble they already take in assaulting a victim who might or might not be armed. But they may appreciate that the laws have given them a freer field, and that crime still pays—pays even better, in fact, than before. What will happen to the rate of violence? Only a relatively few gun-mediated transactions —currently, five percent of armed robberies committed with firearms—result in someone's actually being shot (the statistics are not broken down into encounters between armed assailants and unarmed victims, and encounters in which both parties are armed). It seems reasonable to fear that if the number of such transactions were to increase because criminals thought they faced fewer deterrents, there would be a corresponding increase in shootings. Conversely, if gun-mediated transactions declined—if criminals initiated fewer of them because they feared encountering an armed victim or an armed good Samaritan—the number of shootings would go down. The magnitude of these effects is, admittedly, uncertain. Yet it is hard to doubt the general tendency of a change in the law that imposes legal burdens on buying guns. The futility theorem suggests that gun-control laws, if effective at all, would unfavorably affect the rate of violent crime.

The futility theorem provides a lens through which to see much of the debate. It is undeniable that gun-control laws work—to an extent. Consider, for example, California's background-check law, which in the past two years has prevented about 12,000 people with a criminal record or a history of mental illness or drug abuse from buying handguns. In the same period Illinois's background-check law prevented the delivery of firearms to more than 2,000 people. Surely some of these people simply turned to an illegal market, but just as surely not all of them did. The laws of large numbers allow us to say that among the foiled thousands, some potential killers were prevented from getting a gun. We do not know whether the number is large or small, but it is implausible to think it is zero. And, as gun-control proponents are inclined to say, "If only one life is saved . . ."

The hypothesis that firearms increase violence does predict that if we can slow down the diffusion of guns, there will be less violence; one life, or more, *will* be saved. But the futility theorem asks that we look not simply at the gross number of bad actors prevented from getting guns but at the effect the law has on *all* the people who want to buy a gun. Suppose we succeed in piling tax burdens on the acquisition of firearms. We can safely assume that a number of people who might use guns to kill will be sufficiently discouraged not to buy them. But we cannot assume this about people who feel that they must have guns in order to survive financially and physically. A few lives might indeed be saved. But the overall rate of violent crime might not go down at all. And if guns are owned predominantly by people who have good reason to think they will use them, the rate might even go up.

Are there empirical studies that can serve to help us choose between the futility theorem and the hypothesis that guns increase violence? Unfortunately, no: the best studies of the effects of gun-control laws are quite inconclusive. Our statistical tools are too weak to allow us to identify an effect clearly enough to persuade an open-minded skeptic. But it is precisely when we are dealing with undetectable statistical effects that we have to be certain we are using the best models available of human behavior. . . .

## ADMINISTERING PROHIBITION

Assume for the sake of argument that to a reasonable degree of criminological certainty, guns are every bit the public-health hazard they are said to be. It follows, and many journalists and a few public officials have already said, that we ought to treat guns the same way we do smallpox viruses or other critical vectors of morbidity and mortality— namely, isolate them from potential hosts and destroy them as speedily as possible. Clearly, firearms have at least one characteristic that distinguishes them from smallpox viruses: nobody wants to keep smallpox viruses in the nightstand drawer. Amazingly enough, gun-control literature seems never to have explored the problem of getting weapons away from people who very much want to keep them in the nightstand drawer.

Our existing gun-control laws are not uniformly permissive, and, indeed, in certain places are tough even by international standards. Advocacy groups seldom stress the considerable differences among American jurisdictions, and media reports regularly assert that firearms are readily available to anybody anywhere in the country. This is not the case. For example, handgun restrictions in Chicago and the District of Columbia are much less flexible than the ones in the United Kingdom. Several hundred thousand British subjects may legally buy and possess sidearms, and anyone who joins a target-shooting club is eligible to do so. But in Chicago and the District of Columbia, excepting peace officers and the like, only grandfathered registrants may legally possess handguns. Of course, tens or hundreds of thousands of people in both those cities—nobody can be sure how many—do in fact possess them illegally.

Although there is, undoubtedly, illegal handgun ownership in the United Kingdom, especially in Northern Ireland (where considerations of personal security and public safety are decidedly unlike those elsewhere in the British Isles), it is probable that Americans and Britons differ in their disposition to obey gun-control laws: there is reputed to be a marked national disparity in compliance behavior. This difference, if it exists, may have something to do with the comparatively marginal value of firearms to British consumers. Even before it had strict firearms regulation, Britain had very low rates of crimes involving guns; British criminals, unlike their American counterparts, prefer burglary (a crime of stealth) to robbery (a crime of intimidation).

Unless people are prepared to surrender their guns voluntarily, how can the U.S. government confiscate an appreciable fraction of our country's nearly 200 million privately owned firearms? We know that it is possible to set up weapons-free zones in certain locations —commercial airports and many courthouses and, lately, some troubled big-city high schools and housing projects. The sacrifices of privacy and convenience, and the costs of paying guards, have been thought worth the (perceived) gain in security. No doubt it would be possible, though it would probably not be easy, to make weapons-free zones of shopping centers, department stores, movie theaters, ball parks. But it is not obvious how one would cordon off the whole of an open society.

Voluntary programs have been ineffectual. From time to time community-action groups or police departments have sponsored "turn in your gun" days, which are nearly always disappointing. Sometimes the government offers to buy guns at some price. This approach has been endorsed by Senator Chafee and the *Los Angeles Times*. Jonathan Alter, of *Newsweek*, has suggested a variation on this theme: youngsters could exchange their guns for a handshake with Michael Jordan or some other sports hero. If the price offered exceeds that at which a gun can be bought on the street, one can expect to see plans of this kind yield some sort of harvest—as indeed they have. But it is implausible that these schemes will actually result in a less-dangerous population. Government programs to buy up surplus cheese cause more cheese to be produced without affecting the availability of cheese to people who want to buy it. So it is with guns....

The solution to the problem of crime lies in improving the chances of young men. Easier said than done, to be sure. No one has yet proposed a convincing program for checking all the dislocating forces that government assistance can set in motion. One relatively straightforward change would be reform of the educational system. Nothing guarantees prudent behavior like a sense of the future, and with average skills in reading, writing, and math, young people can realistically look forward to constructive employment and the straight life that steady work makes possible.

But firearms are nowhere near the root of the problem of violence. As long as people come in unlike sizes, shapes, ages, and temperaments, as long as they diverge in their taste for risk and their willingness and capacity to prey on other people or to defend themselves from predation, and above all as long as some people have little or nothing to lose by spending their lives in crime, dispositions to violence will persist.

This is what makes the case for the right to bear arms, not the Second Amendment. It is foolish to let anything ride on hopes for effective gun control. As long as crime pays as well as it does, we will have plenty of it, and honest folk must choose between being victims and defending themselves.

# NO

# Arthur L. Kellermann et al.

# GUN OWNERSHIP AS A RISK FACTOR FOR HOMICIDE IN THE HOME

Homicide claims the lives of approximately 24,000 Americans each year, making it the 11th leading cause of death among all age groups, the 2nd leading cause of death among all people 15 to 24 years old, and the leading cause of death among male African Americans 15 to 34 years old. Homicide rates declined in the United States during the early 1980s but rebounded thereafter. One category of homicide that is particularly threatening to our sense of safety is homicide in the home.

Unfortunately, the influence of individual and household characteristics on the risk of homicide in the home is poorly understood. Illicit-drug use, alcoholism, and domestic violence are widely believed to increase the risk of homicide, but the relative importance of these factors is unknown. Frequently cited options to improve home security include the installation of electronic security systems, burglar bars, and reinforced security doors. The effectiveness of these protective measures is unclear, however.

Many people also keep firearms (particularly handguns) in the home for personal protection. One recent survey determined that handgun owners are twice as likely as owners of long guns to report "protection from crime" as their single most important reason for keeping a gun in the home. It is possible, however, that the risks of keeping a firearm in the home may outweigh the potential benefits.

To clarify these issues, we conducted a population-based case–control study to determine the strength of the association between a variety of potential risk factors and the incidence of homicide in the home....

## RESULTS

### Study Population
There were 1860 homicides in the three counties [from which samples were taken] during the study period. Four hundred forty-four (23.9 percent) took place in the home of the victim. After we excluded the younger victim in

19 double deaths, 2 homicides that were not reported to project staff, and 3 late changes to a death certificate, 420 cases (94.6 percent) were available for study.

## Reports on the Scene

Most of the homicides occurred inside the victim's home. Eleven percent occurred outside the home but within the immediate property lines. Two hundred sixty-five victims (63.1 percent) were men; 36.9 percent were women. A majority of the homicides (50.9 percent) occurred in the context of a quarrel or a romantic triangle. An additional 4.5 percent of the victims were killed by a family member or an intimate acquaintance as part of a murder–suicide. Thirty-two homicides (7.6 percent) were related to drug dealing, and 92 homicides (21.9 percent) occurred during the commission of another felony, such as a robbery, rape, or burglary. No motive other than homicide could be established in 56 cases (13.3 percent).

The great majority of the victims (76.7 percent) were killed by a relative or someone known to them. Homicides by a stranger accounted for only 15 cases (3.6 percent). The identity of the offender could not be established in 73 cases (17.4 percent). The remaining cases involved other offenders or police acting in the line of duty.

Two hundred nine victims (49.8 percent) died from gunshot wounds. A knife or some other sharp instrument was used to kill 111 victims (26.4 percent). The remaining victims were either bludgeoned (11.7 percent), strangled (6.4 percent), or killed by other means (5.7 percent).

Evidence of forced entry was noted in 59 cases (14.0 percent). Eighteen of these involved an unidentified intruder; six involved strangers. Two involved the police. The rest involved a spouse, family member, or some other person known to the victim.

Attempted resistance was reported in 184 cases (43.8 percent). In 21 of these (5.0 percent) the victim unsuccessfully attempted to use a gun in self-defense. In 56.2 percent of the cases no specific signs of resistance were noted. Fifteen victims (3.6 percent) were killed under legally excusable circumstances. Four were shot by police acting in the line of duty. The rest were killed by another member of the household or a private citizen acting in self-defense.

## Comparability of Case Subjects and Controls

... Interviews with a matching control* were obtained for 99.7 percent of the case interviews, yielding 388 matched pairs. Three hundred fifty-seven pairs were matched for all three variables, 27 for two variables, and 4 for a single variable (sex). The demographic characteristics of the victims and controls were similar, except that the case subjects were more likely to have rented their homes (70.4 percent vs. 47.3 percent) and to have lived alone (26.8 percent vs. 11.9 percent). ...

## Univariate Analysis

Alcohol was more commonly consumed by one or more members of the households of case subjects than by members of the households of controls. Alcohol was also more commonly consumed by the case subjects themselves than by their matched controls. Case subjects were reported to have manifested behavioral correlates of alcoholism (such as trouble at work due to drinking) much more

---

*[Controls were matched with the case subjects according to sex, race, age, and neighborhood of residence.—Eds.]

often than matched controls. Illicit-drug use (by the case subject or another household member) was also reported more commonly by case households than control households.

Previous episodes of violence were reported more frequently by members of case households. When asked if anyone in the household had ever been hit or hurt in a fight in the home, 31.8 percent of the proxies [who were interviewed as representatives of] the case subjects answered affirmatively, as compared with only 5.7 percent of controls. Physical fights in the home while household members were drinking and fighting severe enough to cause injuries were reported much more commonly by case proxies than controls. One or more members of the case households were also more likely to have been arrested or to have been involved in a physical fight outside the home than members of control households.

Similar percentages of case and control households reported using deadbolt locks, window bars, or metal security doors. The case subjects were slightly less likely than the controls to have lived in a home with a burglar alarm, but they were slightly more likely to have controlled security access. Almost identical percentages of case and control households reported owning a dog.

One or more guns were reportedly kept in 45.4 percent of the homes of the case subjects, as compared with 35.8 percent of the homes of the control subjects.... Shotguns and rifles were kept by similar percentages of households, but the case households were significantly more likely to have a handgun.... Case households were also more likely than control households to contain a gun that was kept loaded or unlocked.

## Multivariate Analysis

Six variables were retained in our final conditional logistic-regression model: home rented, case subject or control lived alone, any household member ever hit or hurt in a fight in the home, any household member ever arrested, any household member used illicit drugs, and one or more guns kept in the home. Each of these variables was strongly and independently associated with an increased risk of homicide in the home. No home-security measures retained significance in the final model. After matching for four characteristics and controlling for the effects of five more, we found that the presence of one or more firearms in the home was strongly associated with an increased risk of homicide in the home....

Stratified analyses with our final regression model revealed that the link between guns and homicide in the home was present among women as well as men, blacks as well as whites, and younger as well as older people. Restricting the analysis to pairs with data from case proxies who lived in the home of the victim demonstrated an even stronger association than that noted for the group overall. Gun ownership was most strongly associated with homicide at the hands of a family member or intimate acquaintance.... Guns were not significantly linked to an increased risk of homicide by acquaintances, unidentified intruders, or strangers. We found no evidence of a protective benefit from gun ownership in any subgroup, including one restricted to cases of homicide that followed forced entry into the home and another restricted to cases in which resistance was attempted. Not surprisingly, the link between gun ownership and homicide was due entirely to a strong association between gun ownership and homicide by firearms. Homicide by other means was not significantly linked to the presence or absence of a gun in the home.

Living in a household where someone had previously been hit or hurt in a fight in the home was also strongly and independently associated with homicide, even after we controlled for the effects of gun ownership and the other four variables in our final model.... Previous family violence was linked to an increased risk of homicide among men as well as women, blacks as well as whites, and younger as well as older people. Virtually all of this increased risk was due to a marked association between prior domestic violence and homicide at the hands of a family member or intimate acquaintance....

## DISCUSSION

Although firearms are often kept in homes for personal protection, this study shows that the practice is counterproductive. Our data indicate that keeping a gun in the home is independently associated with an increase in the risk of homicide in the home. The use of illicit drugs and a history of physical fights in the home are also important risk factors. Efforts to increase home security have largely focused on preventing unwanted entry, but the greatest threat to the lives of household members appears to come from within.

We restricted our study to homicides that occurred in the home of the victim, because these events can be most plausibly linked to specific individual and household characteristics. If, for example, the ready availability of a gun increases the risk of homicide, this effect should be most noticeable in the immediate environment where the gun is kept.

Although our case definition excluded the rare instances in which a nonresident intruder was killed by a homeowner, our methodology was capable of demonstrating significant protective effects of gun ownership as readily as any evidence of increased risk....

Four limitations warrant comment. First, our study was restricted to homicides occurring in the home of the victim. The dynamics of homicides occurring in other locations (such as bars, retail establishments, or the street) may be quite different. Second, our research was conducted in three urban counties that lack a substantial percentage of Hispanic citizens. Our results may therefore not be generalizable to more rural communities or to Hispanic households. Third, it is possible that reverse causation accounted for some of the association we observed between gun ownership and homicide—i.e., in a limited numbers of cases, people may have acquired a gun in response to a specific threat. If the source of that threat subsequently caused the homicide, the link between guns in the home and homicide may be due at least in part to the failure of these weapons to provide adequate protection from the assailants. Finally, we cannot exclude the possibility that the association we observed is due to a third, unidentified factor. If, for example, people who keep guns in their homes are more psychologically prone to violence than people who do not, this could explain the link between gun ownership and homicide in the home. Although we examined several behavioral markers of violence and aggression and included two in our final logistic-regression model, "psychological confounding" of this sort is difficult to control for. "Psychological autopsies" have been used to control for psychological differences between adolescent victims of suicide and inpatient controls with psychiatric disorders, but we did not believe this approach was practical for a study of homicide victims and neighborhood controls. At any rate, a link between gun ownership and any psychological tendency toward violence or victimization would have to be extremely strong to account for an adjusted odds ratio of 2.7.

Given the univariate association we observed between alcohol and violence, it may seem odd that no alcohol-related variables were included in our final multivariate model. Although consumption of alcoholic beverages and the behavioral correlates of alcoholism were strongly associated with homicide, they were also related to other variables included in our final model. Forcing the variable "case subject or control drinks" into our model did not substantially alter the adjusted odds ratios for the other variables. Furthermore, the adjusted odds ratio for this variable was not significantly greater than 1.

Large amounts of money are spent each year on home-security systems, locks, and other measures intended to improve home security. Unfortunately, our results suggest that these efforts have little effect on the risk of homicide in the home. This finding should come as no surprise, since most homicides in the home involve disputes between family members, intimate acquaintances, friends, or others who have ready access to the home. It is important to realize, however, that these data offer no insight into the effectiveness of home-security measures against other household crimes such as burglary, robbery, or sexual assault. In a 1983 poll, Seattle homeowners feared "having someone break into your home while you are gone" most and "having someone break into your home while you are at home" 4th on a list of 16 crimes. Although homicide is the most serious of crimes, it occurs far less frequently than other types of household crime. Measures that make a home more difficult to enter are probably more effective against these crimes.

Despite the widely held belief that guns are effective for protection, our results suggest that they actually pose a substantial threat to members of the household. People who keep guns in their homes appear to be at greater risk of homicide in the home than people who do not. Most of this risk is due to a substantially greater risk of homicide at the hands of a family member or intimate acquaintance. We did not find evidence of a protective effect of keeping a gun in the home, even in the small subgroup of cases that involved forced entry.

Saltzman and colleagues recently found that assaults by family members or other intimate acquaintances with a gun are far more likely to end in death than those that involve knives or other weapons. A gun kept in the home is far more likely to be involved in the death of a member of the household than it is to be used to kill in self-defense. Cohort and interrupted time-series studies have demonstrated a strong link between availability of guns and community rates of homicide. Our study confirms this association at the level of individual households.

Previous case–control research has demonstrated a strong association between the ownership of firearms and suicide in the home. Also, unintentional shooting deaths can occur when children play with loaded guns they have found at home. In the light of these observations and our present findings, people should be strongly discouraged from keeping guns in their homes.

The observed association between battering and homicide is also important. In contrast to the money spent on firearms and home security, little has been done to improve society's capacity to respond to the problem of domestic violence. In the absence of effective intervention, battering tends to increase in frequency and severity over time. Our data strongly suggest that the risk of homicide is markedly increased in homes where a person has previously been hit or hurt in a family fight. At the very least, this observation should prompt physicians, social workers, law-enforcement officers, and the courts to work harder to identify and protect victims of battering and other forms of family violence. Early identification and effective intervention may prevent a later homicide.

# POSTSCRIPT

## Should We Encourage the Private Ownership of Guns?

The real issue here is whether or not the firearms industry should go unregulated. Advocates of regulation note that many consumer goods that appear to be far less dangerous than handguns are regulated. If everyday items such as children's toys, over-the-counter drugs, and small kitchen appliances are regulated, why are handguns left unregulated? Surely, more individuals are maimed and killed each year by handguns than by many of the goods that society now regulates.

The NRA would be quick to point out that regulation of the gun industry is not the answer. Indeed, they might argue that the answer is to deregulate all consumer goods. This is the position taken by Jacob Sullivan, the managing editor of *Reason*. In a recent article in *National Review* (February 7, 1994), Sullivan takes great care to show how ineffective regulation such as the Brady Bill will be. Waiting periods and background checks, he argues, will not stop the Colin Fergusons of the world. (Ferguson shot 23 people, fatally wounding 6 of them, on a New York train running from Manhattan to Hicksville on the Long Island Railroad.) Ironically, according to Sullivan, these gun regulations would not have even stopped John Hinckley, who attempted to assassinate President Ronald Reagan and seriously wounded and permanently handicapped Reagan's press secretary James Brady, for whom the Brady Bill is named.

Polsby and other spokespersons for the NRA's position assert that gun control would disarm the law-abiding citizenry and leave the "bad guys" with a monopoly on guns. Kellermann and others within and outside of the medical field, however, find that the cost paid for gun ownership is too high: There are too many accidental shootings; there are too many successful gun-related suicides; and there are too many friends and family members shot in the heat of passion. For Kellermann, guns are too efficient in killing people.

There has been much written about the firearms industry and gun control, particularly after Congress passed the Brady Bill in November 1993. For background, see Jonathan Alter, "How America's Meanest Lobby Ran Out of Ammo," *Newsweek* (May 16, 1994); Frank Lalli, "The Cost of One Bullet: $2 Million," *Money* (February 1994); and Owen Ullmann and Douglas Harbrecht, "Talk About a Loaded Issue," *Business Week* (March 14, 1994). For a good discussion on the limitations of gun control, see David B. Kopel, "Hold Your Fire: Gun Control Won't Stop Rising Violence," *Policy Review* (Winter 1993). And to hear from another member of the medical community, read the editorial by Jerome P. Kassirer entitled "Guns in the Household," which appeared in the October 7, 1993, issue of *The New England Journal of Medicine* along with the Kellermann article.

Finally, we should call your attention to the latest struggle by the NRA: to gain the support of women. In magazines such as *Women and Guns* (published by the Second Amendment Foundation) and in an ad campaign entitled "Refuse to Be a Victim," which has appeared in women's journals such as *Woman's Day* and *Redbook,* the NRA has urged women to "declare your independence from the tragic fear that has become the shameful plague of our times." For a discussion of this campaign, see Sally Chew, "The NRA Goes Courting," *Lear's* (January 1994).

# ISSUE 3

## Should Cities Subsidize Sports and Sports Venues?

**YES: Thomas V. Chema,** from "When Professional Sports Justify the Subsidy: A Reply to Robert Baade," *The Journal of Urban Affairs* (vol. 18, no. 1, 1996)

**NO: Robert A. Baade,** from "Stadium Subsidies Make Little Economic Sense for Cities: A Rejoinder," *The Journal of Urban Affairs* (vol. 18, no. 1, 1996)

### ISSUE SUMMARY

**YES:** Attorney and economic development expert Thomas V. Chema claims that a sports venue has both direct and indirect returns to invested dollars.

**NO:** Economics professor and urban sports facilities consultant Robert A. Baade argues that although one might justify a sports subsidy on the basis of "image" or "enhanced quality of life," one cannot justify spending limited development dollars on the economic returns that come from sports venues.

The cities of Vail, Colorado, Green Bay, Wisconsin, Cooperstown, New York, Indianapolis, Indiana, and Louisville, Kentucky, are all united by a common denominator. Each boasts a well-known sports venue or sporting event. South Bend, Indiana, may be known to most people as the home of the Fighting Irish football team of Notre Dame, but only our family and a few friends know, or for that matter care, that Bonello and Swartz live there too!

Is there an economic value to the city of South Bend that is totally separate and apart from the dollars spent by 90,000 college football fans who will search for the 80,000 tickets that are available six times each fall semester? In broader terms, is there an economic value for the "city fathers and mothers" associated with your ability to correctly connect ski lifts, a football team, a baseball hall of fame, an auto race, and a horse race with their respective cities? This is the essence of the debate found in this issue. Robert A. Baade argues that too few individuals utilize sports facilities to make them worthy candidates for public investment. Thomas V. Chema disagrees, particularly if the venues are strategically placed within the urban community.

We should first examine the impact of a few sports venues. Perhaps no single sports arena has had a longer, more lasting effect on its urban surroundings than the Coliseum in Rome. This marvelous, two-thousand-year-old structure was home to some of the most gruesome "sports" events in Western history. In spite of its crumbling walls and hundreds of years of physical neglect, it still attracts thousands of daily visitors. In fact, this long-abandoned structure still anchors the economic development of the southeast corner of modern Rome.

Alternatively, consider the impact of the America's Cup challenge match to western Australia. The America's Cup is awarded to the winner of a worldwide sailing competition. Until 1986, the competition was always held off the New England coast, since the U.S. team had never lost this international competition. Their first loss came at the hands of the Australians who then had the right to host the challenge match in Fremantle, western Australia. This small, nineteenth-century port city had fallen into serious economic decline prior to the America's Cup challenge match. Although the Australians lost their treasured "Cup" in 1986, they gained much in return. When the sleek racing ships sailed out of the mouth of the Swan River Bay on their return home, they left behind a transformed city awash with cappuccino shops, boutiques, restaurants, microbreweries, and pricey loft condos.

What part of Fremantle's rehabilitation is the direct result of the two or three dozen challenge teams that had to be housed and wined and dined in the two years leading up to the races? What part can be traced to the positive externalities or spillover effects associated with the presence of wealthy sailing teams and the hangers-on who could afford to go halfway around the world to see a sporting event?

Thomas V. Chema attributes large portions of economic development to the presence of sports teams. On the other side, Robert A. Baade contends that it is necessary to carefully measure the dollar costs of sports enterprises to ensure that they do not result in the diversion of leisure dollars to absentee team owners and players.

# YES

## Thomas V. Chema

## WHEN PROFESSIONAL SPORTS JUSTIFY THE SUBSIDY: A REPLY TO ROBERT BAADE

Since virtually the dawn of recorded history the public has been digging into its collective pockets to subsidize the construction of sports venues. Granted, this has not always been a voluntary effort, but then the niceties of democracy were often lost on pharaohs, kings, emperors, and other potentates. The rationale for the public subsidy has varied over time and geography but, with relatively few exceptions, sports have consistently been subsidized.

Robert A. Baade has made a decade long career (or perhaps crusade) arguing against the subsidy. In his most recent paper, "Professional Sports as Catalysts for Metropolitan Economic Development," he purports to demonstrate, using two economic modeling formulae, that subsidy cannot be justified on the basis of economic development and job growth.

For a host of reasons, I disagree with the ultimate conclusion reached by Professor Baade that "cities should be wary of committing substantial portions of their capital budgets to building stadiums." Before cataloging areas of disagreement, let's accept that it is true that professional sports and sport venues are not a panacea for all urban problems. In fact, like Professor Baade, I believe that they are not necessarily even development tools. Their value as catalysts for economic development (job growth and the creation of wealth) depends upon where they are located and how they are integrated into a metropolitan area's growth strategy.

Cities of the future will be important and successful if they can create a critical mass of opportunities for people to socialize within their borders. Several millennia ago, Plato and Aristotle characterized human beings as social creatures. We want to come together, to interact.

For the past 500 years much of that interaction has taken place in cities as people did business and engaged in commerce. Today, with the information superhighway and advanced communications, we tend to be much more isolated in business transactions. Thus, we continually look for other ways to generate human contact and interaction. Cities which understand that

From Thomas V. Chema, "When Professional Sports Justify the Subsidy: A Reply to Robert Baade," *The Journal of Urban Affairs*, vol. 18, no. 1 (1996), pp. 19–22. Copyright © 1996 by JAI Press, Inc. Reprinted by permission of JAI Press, Inc., Greenwich, CT, and London, England.

cultural activities, recreations, sports and plain old socializing not only bring people together, but form a solid base for economic growth, will be the cities which prosper. Cleveland, Baltimore, Indianapolis, and Minneapolis are cities which recognize that sports venues and events can fit into an overall vision for strategic growth. They have integrated the facilities into the urban fabric and they are successful.

The key to sports venues being a catalyst for economic development is locating them in an urban setting and integrating them into the existing city infrastructure. It is the spin-off development generated by two million or more people visiting a specific area of a city during a concentrated time frame which is critical. The return on the public investment in a ballpark or arena, in dollar and cents terms as opposed to the intangible entertainment value comes not from the facility itself, but from the jobs created in new restaurants, taverns, retail, hotels, etc., that spring up on the periphery of the sports venue.

In Cleveland, for example, since the opening of Jacob Field, 20 new restaurants employing nearly 900 people have opened within two blocks of second base. There are two new retail establishments on Prospect Avenue where there had been none since World War II. There are six projects to convert vacant upper stories of office and commercial buildings to market rate apartments and condominiums and the Gateway facility is only two years old.

This development is materializing because 5,000,000 visitors are coming to games and entertainment and they are spending their money outside the walls of the sports venues before and after the events. Moreover, they are discovering

for the first time in 30 years, that downtown has much to offer. They are coming even when there are no sporting events.

Such success dramatizes the flaw in Professor Baade's past and current analyses and conclusions. Baade has researched essentially nonurban facilities which were not intended to be economic development tools. The multiuse stadiums that proliferated in the late 60s and early 70s were specifically designed to be apart from the city. The design characteristics give the impression more of a fort than a marketplace. Moreover, during the period surveyed most new venues were located in suburban or rural locations. The relatively few urban venues might as well have been in suburbs because they were separated from their host city by a moat of surface parking. These facilities became and continue to be isolated attractions. People drive to them, park on surface lots, enjoy the events in the building, and then go home. This is not bad, but it does not generate economic development spin-off. Contrary to Professor Baade's conclusion, however, it is not the sport activity, but the context which is key.

With the exception of Arlington, Texas, the post-1990 ballparks are in urban settings. They connect with the host city and give people an opportunity to spend money in that host city. Given that opportunity, people accept it and the city benefits. Drawing conclusions about the economic development impact from the last generation of sports facility is questionable at best. Certainly, there is no merit in extrapolating from the flying saucers of Pittsburgh, Cincinnati, Philadelphia, etc., and drawing conclusions as to the public return from investment in today's Camden yards and Jacobs Field.

Moreover, the economic model proposed by Dr. Baade intuitively raises several questions. First, emphasis is placed on the assumption that most of the money generated by a stadium is "quickly disbursed beyond the stadium's environs." That may well be, but is that not equally true of a steel mill or auto plant? What is the point here, surely not that a business enterprise to be a growth generator must reinvest the income in the immediate surroundings?

Second, the fact that the current generation of public assembly facilities is a self-contained series of profit centers does not mean that spin-off development will not occur. Given the correct location and avoiding surrounding the venue with a sea of surface parking, entertainment related enterprises will spring up and flourish in the shadow of the stadiums. Witness Cleveland and Denver. Even in the dead times these businesses can survive once the public becomes familiar with them. Indeed in the modern facility there will be less true dead time because the facility will strive to maximize its usefulness, drawing people to its restaurants, team shops, etc., even when there is no event.

Third, the analysis totally ignores the fiscal impact sporting events and revenues have on the host public jurisdiction. Assuming the implausible circumstance where no sports-related revenues stay in the metropolis from a private sector perspective, there still would be the impact of tax revenues left behind. Virtually every host city has a wage or income tax, a sales tax, and/or admissions tax. This reality, multimillions of dollars, seems to be ignored by the models proposed by Professor Baade.

Fourth, it is difficult to accept the rather narrow definition of economic development posited in the study. What is the value in measuring the metropolitan growth vis-à-vis other cities? Moreover, it seems clear that the fully loaded cost of a stadium cannot be recovered from the stadium revenue alone. Indeed, that is why a subsidy is needed. The return on the subsidy investment must be judged not only on the revenue potential of the facility (and players) but on the spin-off as well. Of course, the subsidy is not made only because an economic return on investment is expected, but also because of the entertainment value of the sports activity or venue. This is not an exclusive analysis nor is the sale to the public of the subsidy ever exclusively based on the expected economic development return on investment.

Fifth, what is the rationale for measuring capital investment and sports revenue receipts on a per capita basis? I strongly suspect that any other entertainment-related industry would provide similar results to that which Professor Baade shows in his paper. In fact, if this type of analysis were applied to investments in steel mills, computer factories, supermarkets, or most other industries, the relative results would make stadium investments look pretty good. Contrary to the implication, using Professor Baade's Chicago example, the investment of $150 million in a stadium which equates to approximately $54.00 per capita is returned in less than three years based on $22.00 per capita in sports franchise revenue. A three year payback on investment is generally viewed favorably in the private sector. Such a return on a public sector investment that should last at lest 40 years ought to be viewed very positively.

Sixth, the low wage, seasonal job argument which is typically made by opponents of sports facility investments is, frankly, offensive. Every community, but particularly major urban centers, need to have a diverse mixture of job types in their economy. Not everyone is a rocket scientist. Not everyone could become one even if there were such jobs available, which clearly there are not. Some members or potential members of the labor force need jobs as ushers, ticket takers, vendors, etc. These jobs are neither demeaning to their holders nor do they cause a city to gain "a comparative advantage is unskilled and seasonal labor." This type of reasoning is the product of effete snobbery.

Seventh, how does one measure the opportunity cost involved in public subsidies of sports? I have yet to see or hear of a single instance where the alternative to building a new stadium, for example, was something other than doing nothing. At least since 1989, there have been no proposals of schools v. stadiums or jails v. arenas! The real issue here is collective public investment or individual private expenditures. Economically, this is true of every public investment and sport is no exception.

Eighth, is it really appropriate to measure the economic contribution of an industry based on the growth of the host city rather than on the industry's contribution to the economy of that city? . . .

Finally, it is not clear what jobs are counted as having been created by professional sports in the Baade analysis. Clearly the team and the stadium direct employees, even including all event-related staff, constitute a small number. Most of the jobs created are not going to show up in SIC 794. This model is of very little utility.

It is appropriate for the public to review its investment in a sports venue as an investment in public infrastructure. Like a road, bridge, or water line, the return on the investment comes indirectly as well as directly. A proper analysis includes a review of the entertainment value of the facility and the spin-off value created by the facility. Similarly, a road is justified by transportation utility and the development that it opens on its periphery.

Just as not every road is equal in its economic impact, not every stadium will generate development that justifies a public subsidy. However, when a city establishes a development strategy that includes sports as part of a critical mass of attractions designed to lure people into the urban core, then a sport team or venue can and will provide significant economic value to the city.

# NO

## Robert A. Baade

## STADIUM SUBSIDIES MAKE LITTLE ECONOMIC SENSE FOR CITIES: A REJOINDER

The thoughtful critiques of my research authored by Messrs. Chema and Rosentraub indicate significant agreement among us about the economic impact that professional sports teams and stadiums have on local and regional economies. The areas of alleged disagreement can be broadly characterized as either technical (those monetary benefits and costs that are generally recognized and quantified) or qualitative. Some of the technical issues can be addressed, perhaps resolved, through a clarification of the methods I employed and their outcomes. Other questions can be resolved only with additional data which will enable evaluation of the urban stadiums constructed after 1990. The purpose of this rejoinder is to help advance the stadium debate by commenting on issues raised by Mr. Chema and Dr. Rosentraub.

Before elaborating on specifics relating to these issues, several matters deserve comment. First, I do not have preconceived notions on whether cities, taken individually or collectively, should subsidize the construction of sports facilities. The persistent and ubiquitous use of an economic/investment rationale for public stadium subsidies, however, compels an evaluation of the economic contribution of commercial sport to metropolitan economies. Stadium subsidies represent a classic public finance issue involving both equity and efficiency questions. My research sounds a cautionary note for governments contemplating subsidies on economic grounds. Specifically, cities should reconsider how the stadium is integrated into the urban economy and/or reconsider using the promise of economic gain as a means of selling the subsidy to a skeptical public.

On a personal note, my research about the economic impact of professional sports teams and stadiums has been inspired by my interest in public finance issues and my lifelong experience with sports. In large part my choice to teach

From Robert A. Baade, "Stadium Subsidies Make Little Economic Sense for Cities, A Rejoinder," *The Journal of Urban Affairs*, vol. 18, no. 1 (1996), pp. 33–37. Copyright © 1996 by JAI Press, Inc. Reprinted by permission of JAI Press, Inc., Greenwich, CT, and London, England.

at a liberal arts college was conditioned by my affection for both academics and sport. Lake Forest College gave me an opportunity to coach as well as teach. I raise this point in response to Mr. Chema's reference to my "decade long career (or perhaps crusade) arguing against the subsidy." While he may have mistakenly inferred from my work that I dislike sports, to the contrary, I have valued sports as a participant, coach, educator, and fan.

Given my experience, I may be in a better position than some to evaluate the intangibles so often used in discussing and defending sports. The second point I wish to make is that I have not discussed intangibles in my work except to recognize their potential importance. Because proponents of subsidies rationalize their position first and foremost on economic grounds, it is logical to evaluate first the merits of these arguments. My work focuses exclusively on the economic dimension. If we can resolve the issue as it relates to economics, then it may be necessary to move the stadium subsidy debate to the psychological arena where intangibles are properly the focus.

Third, I have chosen to do retrospective stadium analysis because I recognize that identifying and accurately measuring all the dollar inflows and outflows to an area's economy that are induced by commercial sport is a daunting task. Stadium economic impact studies are prospective in nature and are heavily dependent on the assumptions about the financial inflows and outflows to an area's economy as the consequences of professional sports activities. On a practical level, my approach has been to provide a filter through which the promises of increased economic growth for municipalities through professional

sports can be evaluated. In retrospect it would appear that prospective economic impact studies in general have failed to capture all the significant inflows and outflows that are essential for even a ballpark estimate of the economic contribution of professional sports. On the other hand, retrospective analysis is limited by data availability.

In reacting to specific areas of concern, Mr. Chema notes the importance of stadium context. In referring to stadium location he observed: "Their value as catalysts for economic development... depends upon where they are located and how they are integrated into a metropolitan area's growth strategy." In noting the success of urban sports facilities constructed after 1990, he alleged a flaw in my research. "Such success dramatizes the flaw in Professor Baade's past and current analyses and conclusions." In response to this allegation I would refer him to Baade and Dye (1988, pp. 272–273) where we wrote:

If an urban stadium is being planned, the plan should be expanded to incorporate ancillary development... A stadium is not usually enough of a significant development to anchor an area's economy alone. Rather, in considering the revitalization of an urban neighborhood, a number of potential economic anchors should be developed simultaneously.... Commercial ventures require traffic. The stadium can provide infusions of people, but residential development incorporated with commercial development will ensure a balanced, nonseasonal clientele for business in the stadium neighborhood.

I have emphasized stadium context in public presentations and in my work with stadium planners and architects. Camden Yards and the Gateway Complex in Cleveland represent important experiments relating to stadium context. Research by a number of social scientists, including my own, has identified a stadium and team novelty effect. All else equal, a stadium and team will attract greater interest in the first few years of their existence. So while there is reason to be encouraged by some aspects of the economic performance of Camden Yards and Gateway (not all the financial news from Gateway is good), I am sure that Mr. Chema recognizes that sound statistical analysis of these two projects requires more than a few observations of economic outcomes. As previously noted, retrospective analysis is limited by data availability.

Furthermore, in evaluating the stadium's economic contribution, a model must be constructed that is capable of separating the stadium from other parts of the development. An integrated development complicates the task for the scholar seeking to determine the stadium's economic contribution separate from other elements of the plan.

Mr. Chema's emphasis on context ignores at least one important contextual point. Many of the stadiums that are currently planned or under construction replace stadiums that have been deemed economically obsolete by a team. Boston, Cincinnati, Milwaukee, Minneapolis, New York, and Seattle currently are in the throes of debates about new stadiums for Major League baseball (MLB). Cincinnati, Minneapolis, and Seattle have facilities that are 25 years old or less. The dome in Minneapolis is 13 years old. This shorter stadium shelf life has important economic implications. One concern is how the new generation of facilities born out of economic imperative will affect the neighborhood's economy.

Mr. Chema opines that "the fact that the current generation of public assembly facilities is a self-contained series of profit centers does not mean that spin-off development will not occur." Given the correct developmental context, that may be true, but many stadiums are being designed with the team's bottom line in mind, often to the detriment of the local economy. When a stadium is moved across the street (Chicago's Comiskey Park comes to mind) in the absence of a broader development plan to explicitly include the neighborhood, many of the economic activities are revenues appropriated by local entrepreneurs are appropriated by the stadium operatives seeking to maximize their share of stadium-induced revenues.

In focusing on Cleveland and Camden Yards, Mr. Chema concentrates on the exceptions rather than the rule in stadium planning. The reality is that most stadium deals are signed at the midnight hour by legislators opting to do what is necessary to retain a team rather than formulating a plan that integrates the stadium and team into a broader development package. One could blame legislators alone for myopic stadium legislation, but these outcomes are inspired at least as much by the structure of professional sports leagues which serve their own economic interest by maintaining an excess demand for teams. St. Petersburg, Nashville, and Charlotte do not serve the economic interests of Chicago, Houston, and Milwaukee.

Mr. Chema raised other issues that are more technical in nature. He alleges that my "analysis totally ignores the fiscal impact sporting events and revenues have on the host public jurisdiction." Tax revenues are derived. If the tax base expands, tax revenues increase. Professional sports generate additional tax revenues to the extent that they expand the local economy. If sport is construed as part of the entertainment industry, as no less an authority than Bud Selig, MLB's current commissioner, contends, commercial sport from the perspective of the global economy is arguably a zero-sum game. If all the fans supporting a professional sports team within a city are residents of that city, that team will serve to realign economy activity within the city rather than expanding its tax base. Because taxes are derived, tax revenues do not change in such a situation. Does it matter much to the city whether it derives its revenues from sports entertainment or recreation provided by the local theater?

If we drew an imaginary circle from economic ground zero, the point at which the stadium activity occurs, the larger the circle the smaller the net change in economic activity. This reality should help focus the debate about stadium subsidies for various levels of government. For example, the State of Kentucky on purely economic grounds may not want to use its general funds to build a stadium for Louisville unless it can be demonstrated that either fans will pour across the Indiana, Ohio, West Virginia, and Tennessee borders or that Louisville is in need of urban renewal, a public goods argument that could justify an infusion of state funds. If the stadium replaces leisure and recreational spending in Danville with spending in Louisville, Danville may want to argue against the use of state funds for a stadium in Louisville.

Mr. Chema raised the question "what is the value in measuring the metropolitan growth vis-à-vis other cities?" As Professor Rosentraub has indicated in his critique, commercial sport contributes little in an absolute sense to a metropolitan economy. At present modeling the economies of each city that hosts professional sport is not possible and so an alternative technique must be devised to assess the actual contribution of professional sport relative to the economic promise articulated by boosters. Furthermore, an economist would be remiss if the question of opportunity cost was ignored. Public officials must evaluate the stadium not only on its own merit but relative to alternative uses of those funds. Both issues are considered at length in my paper. An argument can be made that in the municipal auction for professional sports franchises, like the auction for free agent players, the winning bid likely exceeds the team's marginal revenue product. It is likely that the greater the excess demand for professional sports teams, the greater the difference between the team's marginal revenue product and the price the host city pays.

Mr. Chema uses the figures I provided on per capita stadium investments and returns to argue that stadiums provide a good return on investment. The per capita returns were not computed for individual sports, but were calculated for commercial sports in general. For individual cities, I have calculated returns on taxpayer equity on the order of 1–2% for an individual sport and those calculations were based on figures provided from the economic impact studies of subsidy supporters. In football and baseball the trend is decidedly away from multipurpose facilities, a trend that is drive by economic imperatives (individual teams want exclusive control of stadium revenues). By the year 2000, it is not unreasonable to predict that baseball and football will no longer share a single facility in the United States.

With regard to Mr. Chema's claim that "at least since 1989, there have been no proposals of schools v. stadiums", I was puzzled by the use of the word proposals. With all due respect, I would encourage Mr. Chema to listen to the tapes of the 1995 Cincinnati City Council debates on the use of public funds for new stadiums for the NFL Bengals and the MLB Reds.

Mr. Chema understandably found offensive the use of the low wage job creation argument in conjunction with opposition to stadium subsidies. Most of us recognize the need for all types of employment. Rather than construing this argument as the product of "effete snobbery," I would ask him to recognize that some of us are trying to explain why sport might not contribute in absolute dollar terms as much as subsidy proponents suggest. My work should not be construed as a recipe for job creation, but rather as an explanation for why stadium subsidies may not have provided the projected economic boost.

As noted earlier, I argued that a retrospective approach to assessing the economic contribution of a stadium or team is necessary, give the complex manner in which dollar inflows and outflows may be affected. An after-the-fact audit of how a change in the professional sports industry influences a metropolitan economy tacitly includes both direct and indirect effects. Indirect changes include an altered city psyche or vision or a heightened spirit of cooperation. All these indirect changes may, indeed, alter the economic landscape. On page 274 of my 1988 article cited previously, I noted (Baade & Dye, 1988, p. 274):

the most significant contribution of sports is likely to be in the area of intangibles. The image of a city is certainly affected by the presence of professional franchises. Professional sports serve as a focal point for group identification. Sports contests are a part of civic culture. There may well be a willingness of voters to pay taxes to subsidize this kind of activity just like there is for parks and museums.

Professor Rosentraub, in particular, has articulated the less visible ways in which a large public project translates into a more vibrant economy. Without repeating his words, I echo his sentiments.

An after-the-fact audit includes the economic impact of these laudable intangibles and, even then, commercial sport does not emerge as a statistically significant contributor to metropolitan economies. Dr. Rosentraub has emphasized the fact that the professional sports industry is too small to significantly influence a large metropolitan economy. I would only add that it is not only its small size which renders commercial sport relatively unimportant. It is a fact that sports spectating is but one leisure option available to the residents of a large diverse metropolis. Money spent on sports spectating is financed by reduced spending in other recreational venues and that fact contributes to the consistently statistically insignificant results for professional sports my research has yielded using a variety of models.

This fundamental principle is fortified by the fact that the primary beneficiaries of public stadium largesse are owners and players and fans for whom commercial sports produce substantial consumer surplus. For owners and players, particularly those who reside outside the city extending the subsidy, there may be adverse economic effects from diverting leisure dollars from locally owned entertainment centers to absentee owners and players.

In the final analysis I can only repeat what I have said so often. If cities subsidize commercial sports in the quest for an improved image or to enhance the quality of life for its citizens, then taxpayers should be allowed to decide the stadium subsidy issue on these bases. Using economics as a justification for the subsidy is a political expedient, perhaps necessity, but it is inconsonant with the statistical evidence.

## REFERENCES

Baade, R. A., & Dye, R. F. (1988). Sports stadiums and area development: a critical review. *Economic Development Quarterly, 2,* 265–275.

# POSTSCRIPT

## Should Cities Subsidize Sports and Sports Venues?

You probably have been directly or indirectly affected by a sports facility sometime in your life. For many of us this means being part of the crowd that shoulders its way into a baseball park or a basketball arena to watch a favorite team play. For others this means being trapped in a traffic jam as thousands of cars rush home at the end of a football game or the end of a day at the races. Are these modern-day coliseums that dominate the cityscape worth the millions of dollars that taxpayers are asked to pay? Would the community be better advised to spend these dollars attracting industry that supports high-paying jobs or by stabilizing neighborhoods that are in distress?

Chema advocates attracting professional sports teams to a city by offering them substantial subsidies. He argues that Baade has biased his results by focusing his analysis on suburban facilities, which are surrounded by "a moat of surface parking." Chema details benefits such as spin-off development, a whole range of taxes, entertainment value, and relative rates of return in other industries. Baade contends that communities should be wary of the many promises made by prospective professional sports franchises. A city should not be intimidated by the team's threat to leave for another that is willing to build a new, more costly facility. Baade argues that most of the dollars generated by these sports teams are earned by absentee team owners and players and that most of the new employment associated with operating these facilities are at the minimum wage level.

A surprising amount has been written on this topic. In part this can be traced to the fact that a few conservative journals have been persuaded by Baade's position. For example, look for two essays by Raymond J. Keating: "We Wuz Robbed! The Subsidized Stadium Scam," *Policy Review* (March/April 1977) and "Pitching Socialism: Government-Financed Stadiums Invariably Enrich Owners at Public Expense," *National Review* (April 22, 1996). There is plenty written on the other side as well. See Curt Smith, "Comeback: The Triumphant Return of Old-Style Ball Parks Show That Tradition Can Be Popular," *The American Enterprise* (March/April 1997), or, on a related topic, Joanna Cagau and Neil de Mause, "Buy the Bums Out," *In These Times* (December 9, 1996). Finally, there are many articles that examine the economic impact of the Summer Olympics in Atlanta, Georgia. See for example, Matthew Cooper, "Welcome to the Olympic Village," *New Republic* (July 15 and 22, 1996).

# ISSUE 4

## Is It Time to Abolish the Minimum Wage?

**YES: Thomas Rustici,** from "A Public Choice View of the Minimum Wage," *Cato Journal* (Spring/Summer 1985)

**NO: Charles Craypo,** from "In Defense of Minimum Wages," An Original Essay Written for This Volume (1997)

### ISSUE SUMMARY

**YES:** Orthodox neoclassical economist Thomas Rustici asserts that the effects of the minimum wage are clear: it creates unemployment among the least-skilled workers.

**NO:** Labor economist Charles Craypo argues that a high minimum wage is good for workers, employers, and consumers alike, and hence it is good for the economy as a whole.

In the midst of the Great Depression, Congress passed the Fair Labor Standards Act (FLSA) of 1938. In one bold stroke, it established a minimum wage rate of $.25 an hour, placed controls on the use of child labor, designated 44 hours as the normal workweek, and mandated that time and a half be paid to anyone working longer than the normal workweek. Fifty years later the debates concerning child labor, length of the workweek, and overtime pay have long subsided, but the debate over the minimum wage rages on.

The immediate and continued concern over the minimum wage component of the FLSA should surprise few people. Although $.25 an hour is a paltry sum compared to today's wage rates, in 1938 it was a princely reward for work It must be remembered that jobs were hard to come by and unemployment rates at times reached as high as 25 percent of the workforce. When work was found, any wage seemed acceptable to those who roamed the streets with no "safety net" to protect their families. Indeed, consider the fact that $.25 an hour was 40.3 percent of the average manufacturing wage rate for 1938.

Little wonder, then, that the business community in the 1930s was up in arms. Business leaders argued that if wages went up, prices would rise. This would choke off the little demand for goods and services that existed in the marketplace, and the demand for workers would be sure to fall. The end result would be a return to the depths of the Depression where there was little or no hope of employment for the very people who were supposed to benefit from the Fair Labor Standards Act

This dire forecast was demonstrated by simple supply and demand analysis. First, as modern-day introductory textbooks in economics invariably show, unemployment occurs when a minimum wage greater than the equilibrium wage is mandated by law. This simplistic analysis, which assumes competitive conditions in both the product and factor markets, is predicated upon the assumptions that as wages are pushed above the equilibrium level, the quantity of labor demanded will fall and this quantity of labor supplied will increase. The result is that this wage rigidity prevents the market from clearing. The end result is an excess in the quantity of labor supplied relative to the quantity of labor demanded.

The question that should be addressed in this debate is whether or not a simple supply and demand analysis is capable of adequately predicting what happens in real-world labor markets when a minimum wage is introduced or an existing minimum wage is raised. The significance of this is not based on idle curiosity. The minimum wage has been increased numerous times since its introduction in 1938. Most recently, effective September 1, 1997, legislation establishing the current minimum wage of $5.15 was signed into law by President Clinton.

Did this minimum wage increase, and other increases before it, do irreparable harm to those who are least able to defend themselves in the labor market, the marginal worker? That is, if a minimum wage of $5.15 is imposed, what happens to all those marginal workers whose value to the firm is something less than $5.15? Are these workers fired? Do firms simply absorb this cost increase in the form of reduced corporate profits? What happens to productivity?

This is the crux of the debate between Thomas Rustici and Charles Craypo. Rustici argues that the answer is obvious for all to see: there will be an excess in the quantity of labor supplied relative to the quantity demanded. In lay terms, there will be unemployment. Craypo rejects this neoclassical view. He recommends judging the minimum wage on the intent of the original legislation: increased aggregate demand and elimination of predatory labor market practices

.

# YES

Thomas Rustici

# A PUBLIC CHOICE VIEW OF THE MINIMUM WAGE

*Why, when the economist gives advice to his society, is he so often cooly ignored? He never ceases to preach free trade ... and protectionism is growing in the United States. He deplores the perverse effects of minimum wage laws, and the legal minimum is regularly raised each 3 to 5 years. He brands usury laws as a medieval superstition, but no state hurries to repeal its laws.*

—George Stigler

## INTRODUCTION

Much of public policy is allegedly based on the implications of economic theory. However, economic analysis of government policy is often disregarded for political reasons. The minimum wage law is one such example. Every politician openly deplores the spectacle of double-digit teenage unemployment pervading modern society. But, when economists claim that scientific proof, a priori and empirical, dictates that minimum wage laws cause such a regretful outcome, their statements generally fall on deaf congressional ears. Economists too often assume that policymakers are interested in obtaining all the existing economic knowledge before deciding on a specific policy course. This view of the policy-formation process, however, is naive. In framing economic policy politicians will pay some attention to economists' advice, but such advice always will be rejected when it conflicts with the political reality of winning votes..

## ECONOMIC EFFECTS OF THE MINIMUM WAGE

Economic analysis has demonstrated few things as clearly as the effects of the minimum wage law. It is well known that the minimum wage creates unemployment among the least skilled workers by raising wage rates above free market levels. Eight major effects of the minimum wage can be discussed: unemployment effects, employment effects in uncovered sectors of the economy,

From Thomas Rustici, "A Public Choice View of the Minimum Wage," *Cato Journal*, vol. 5, no. 1 (Spring/Summer 1985). Copyright © 1985 by *Cato Journal* Reprinted by permission.

reduction in nonwage benefits, labor substitution effects, capital substitution effects, racial discrimination in hiring practices, human capital development, and distortion of the market process with respect to comparative advantage. Although the minimum wage has other effects, such as a reduction in hours of employment, these eight effects are the most significant ones for this paper.

**Unemployment Effects**
The first federal minimum wage laws were established under the provisions of the National Recovery Administration (NRA). The National Industrial Recovery Act, which became law on 16 June 1933, established industrial minimum wages for 515 classes of labor. Over 90 percent of the minimum wages were set at between 30 and 40 cents per hour.[1] Early empirical evidence attests to the unemployment effects of the minimum wage. Using the estimates of C. F. Roos, who was the director of research at the NRA, Benjamin Anderson states: "Roos estimates that, by reason of the minimum wage provisions of the codes, about 500,000 Negro workers were on relief in 1934. Roos adds that a minimum wage definitely causes the displacement of the young, inexperienced worker and the old worker."[2]

On 27 May 1935 the Supreme Court declared the NRA unconstitutional, burying the minimum wage codes with it. The minimum wage law reappeared at a later date, however, with the support of the Supreme Court. In what became the precedent for the constitutionality of future minimum wage legislation, the Court upheld the Washington State minimum wage law on 29 March 1937 in *West Coast Hotel v. Parrish*.[3] This declaration gave the Roosevelt administra-tion and Labor Secretary Frances Perkins the green light to reestablish the federal minimum wage, which was achieved on 25 June 1938 when President Roosevelt signed into law the Fair Labor Standards Act (FLSA).

The FSLA included legislation affecting work-age requirements, the length of the workweek, pay rates for overtime work, as well as the national minimum wage provision. The law established minimum wage rates of 25 cents per hour the first year, 30 cents per hour for the next six years, and 40 cents per hour after seven years. The penalty for noncompliance was severe: violators faced a $10,000 fine, six months imprisonment, or both. In addition, an aggrieved employee could sue his employer for twice the difference between the statutory wage rate and his actual pay.[4]

With the passage of the FLSA, it became inevitable that major dislocations would result in labor markets, primarily those for low-skilled and low-wage workers. Although the act affected occupations covering only one-fifth of the labor force,[5] leaving a large uncovered sector to minimize the disemployment effects, the minimum wage was still extremely counterproductive. The Labor Department admitted that the new minimum wage had a disemployment effect, and one historian sympathetic to the minimum wage was forced to concede that "[t]he Department of Labor estimated that the 25-cents-an-hour minimum wage caused about 30,000 to 50,000 to lose their job. About 90% of these were in southern industries such as bagging, pecan shelling, and tobacco stemming."[6]

These estimates seriously understate the actual magnitude of the damage. Since only 300,000 workers received an increase as a result of the minimum wage,[7] estimates of 30,000–50,000 lost jobs reveal that 10–13 percent of those covered by the law lost their jobs. But it is highly dubious that only 30,000–50,000 low-wage earners lost their jobs in the entire country; that many unemployed could have been found in the state of Texas alone, where labor authorities saw devastation wrought via the minimum wage on the pecan trade. The *New York Times* reported the following on 24 October 1938:

> Information received today by State labor authorities indicated that more than 40,000 employees of the pecan nut shelling plants in Texas would be thrown out of work tomorrow by the closing down of that industry, due to the new Wages and Hours Law. In San Antonio, sixty plants, employing ten thousand men and women, mostly Mexicans, will close.... Plant owners assert that they cannot remain in business and pay the minimum wage of 25 cents an hour with a maximum working week of forty-four hours. Many garment factories in Texas will also close.[8]

It can reasonably be deduced that even if the Texas estimates had been wildly inaccurate, the national unemployment effect would still have exceeded the Department of Labor's estimates.

The greatest damage, however, did not come in Texas or in any other southern state, but in Puerto Rico. Since a minimum wage law has its greatest unemployment effect on low-wage earners, and since larger proportions of workers in poor regions such as Puerto Rico tend to be at the lower end of the wage scale, Puerto Rico was disproportionately hard-hit. Subject to the same national 25-cents-per-hour rate as workers on the mainland, Puerto Rican workers suffered much more hardship from the minimum wage law. According to Anderson:

> It was thought by many that, in the first year, the provision would not affect many industries outside the South, though the framers of the law apparently forgot about Puerto Rico, and very grave disturbances came in that island.... Immense unemployment resulted there through sheer inability of important industries to pay the 25 cents an hour.[9]

Simon Rottenberg likewise points out the tragic position in which Puerto Rico was placed by the enactment of the minimum wage:

> When the Congress established a minimum wage of 25 cents per hour in 1938, the average hourly wage in the U.S. was 62.7 cents.... It resulted in a mandatory increase for only some 300,000 workers out of a labor force of more than 54 million. In Puerto Rico, in contrast... the new Federal minimum far exceeded the prevailing average hourly wage of the major portion of Puerto Rican workers. If a continuing serious attempt at enforcement... had been made, it would have meant literal economic chaos for the island's economy.[10]...

After two years of economic disruption in Puerto Rico, Congress amended the minimum wage provisions.[11] The minimum wage was reduced to 12.5 cents per hour, but it was too late for many industries and for thousands of low-wage earners employed by them, who suddenly found unemployment the price they had to pay for the minimum wage.

In sum, the tragedy of the minimum wage laws during the NRA and the FLSA was not just textbook-theorizing by academic economists, but real-world disaster for the thousands who became the victims of the law. But these destructive effects have not caused the law to be repealed; to the contrary, it has been expanded in coverage and increased in amount.

... Evidence for the unemployment effects of the minimum wage continues to mount. Many empirical studies since the early 1950s—from early research by Marshall Colberg and Yale Brozen to more recent work by Jacob Mincer and James Ragan—have validated the predictions of economic theory regarding the unemployment effects of the minimum wage law. In virtually every case it was found that the net employment effects and labor-force participation rates were negatively related to changes in the minimum wage. In the face of 50 years of evidence, the question is no longer if the minimum wage law creates unemployment, but *how much* current or future increases in the minimum wage will adversely affect the labor market.

## Employment in Uncovered Sectors

The labor market can be divided into two sectors: that covered by the minimum wage law, and that not covered. In a partially covered market, the effects of the minimum wage are somewhat disguised. Increasing it disemploys workers in the covered sector, prompting them to search for work in the uncovered sector if they are trainable and mobile. This then drives down the wage rate in the uncovered sector, making it lower than it otherwise would have been. Since perfect knowledge and flexibility is not observed in real-world labor markets, substantial unemployment can occur during the transition period.

Employees in the covered sector who do not lose their jobs get a wage-rate increase through the higher minimum wage. But this comes only at the expense of (1) the disemployed workers who lose their jobs and suffer unemployment during the transition to employment in the uncovered sector, and (2) everyone in the uncovered sector, as their wage rate falls due to the influx of unemployed workers from the covered sector. While increasing the incomes of some low-wage earners, increasing the minimum wage tends to make the lowest wage earners in the uncovered sector even poorer than they otherwise would have been.

Yale Brozen has found that the uncovered household sector served to absorb the minimum wage-induced disemployed in the past.[12] But the "safety valve" of the uncovered portion of the economy is rapidly vanishing with the continual elimination of various exemptions.[13] Because of this trend we can expect to see the level of structural unemployment increase with escalation of the minimum wage.[14]

## Nonwage Benefits

Wage rates are not the only costs associated with the employment of workers by firms. The effective labor cost a firm incurs is usually a package of pecuniary and nonpecuniary benefits. As such, contends Richard McKenzie,

employers can be expected to respond to a minimum wage law by cutting back or eliminating altogether those fringe benefits and conditions of work, like the company parties, that increase the supply of labor but which do not affect the productivity of labor. By reducing such non-money benefits of employment, the employer reduces his labor costs from what they otherwise would have been and loses nothing in the way of reduced labor productivity."[15]

If one takes the view that employees desire both pecuniary and nonpecu-

*Table 1*

## Value of the Minimum Wage, 1955–1995

| Year | Value of the Minimum Wage, Nominal Dollars | Value of the Minimum Wage, 1995 Dollars† | Minimum Wage as a Percent of the Average Private Nonsupervisory Wage |
|---|---|---|---|
| 1955 | $0.75 | $3.94 | 43.9% |
| 1956 | 1.00 | 5.16 | 55.6 |
| 1957 | 1.00 | 5.01 | 52.9 |
| 1958 | 1.00 | 4.87 | 51.3 |
| 1959 | 1.00 | 4.84 | 49.5 |
| 1960 | 1.00 | 4.75 | 47.8 |
| 1961 | 1.15 | 5.41 | 53.7 |
| 1962 | 1.15 | 5.36 | 51.8 |
| 1963 | 1.25 | 5.74 | 54.8 |
| 1964 | 1.25 | 5.67 | 53.0 |
| 1965 | 1.25 | 5.59 | 50.8 |
| 1966 | 1.25 | 5.43 | 48.8 |
| 1967 | 1.40 | 5.90 | 52.2 |
| 1968 | 1.60 | 6.49 | 56.1 |
| 1969 | 1.60 | 6.21 | 52.6 |
| 1970 | 1.60 | 5.92 | 49.5 |
| 1971 | 1.60 | 5.67 | 46.4 |
| 1972 | 1.60 | 5.51 | 43.2 |
| 1973 | 1.60 | 5.18 | 40.6 |
| 1974 | 2.00 | 5.89 | 47.2 |
| 1975 | 2.10 | 5.71 | 46.4 |
| 1976 | 2.30 | 5.92 | 47.3 |
| 1977 | 2.30 | 5.56 | 43.8 |
| 1978 | 2.65 | 6.00 | 46.6 |
| 1979 | 2.90 | 5.99 | 47.1 |
| 1980 | 3.10 | 5.76 | 46.5 |
| 1981 | 3.35 | 5.68 | 46.2 |
| 1982 | 3.35 | 5.36 | 43.6 |
| 1983 | 3.35 | 5.14 | 41.8 |
| 1984 | 3.35 | 4.93 | 40.3 |
| 1985 | 3.35 | 4.76 | 39.1 |
| 1986 | 3.35 | 4.67 | 38.2 |
| 1987 | 3.35 | 4.51 | 37.3 |
| 1988 | 3.35 | 4.33 | 36.1 |
| 1989 | 3.35 | 4.13 | 34.7 |
| 1990 | 3.80 | 4.44 | 37.9 |
| 1991 | 4.25 | 4.77 | 41.1 |
| 1992 | 4.25 | 4.63 | 40.2 |
| 1993 | 4.25 | 4.50 | 39.2 |
| 1994 | 4.25 | 4.38 | n/a |
| 1995 | 4.25 | 4.25 | n/a |

†Adjusted for inflation using the CPI-U-X1.

Source: Center on Budget and Policy Priorities.

niary income, then anything forcing them to accept another mix of benefits would clearly make them worse off. For example, suppose worker A desires his income in the form of $3.00 per hour in wages, an air-conditioned workplace, carpeted floors, safety precautions, and stereo music. If he is *forced* by the minimum wage law to accept $3.25 per hour and fewer nonpecuniary benefits, he is worse off than at the preminimum wage and the *higher* level of nonpecuniary income. A priori, the enactment of minimum wage laws must place the worker and employer in a less-than-optimal state. Thus it may not be the case that only unemployed workers suffer from the minimum wage; even workers who receive a higher wage and retain employment may be net losers if their nonpecuniary benefits are reduced.

## Labor Substitution Effects

The economic world is characterized by a plethora of substitutes. In the labor market low-skill, low-wage earners are substitutes for high-skill, high-wage earners. As Walter Williams points out:

> Suppose a fence can be produced by using either one high skilled worker or by using three low skilled workers. If the wage of high skilled workers is $38 per day, and that of a low skilled worker is $13 per day, the firm employs the high skilled worker because costs would be less and profits higher ($38 versus $39). The high skilled worker would soon recognize that one of the ways to increase his wealth would be to advocate a minimum wage of, say, $20 per day in the fencing industry.... After enactment of the minimum wage laws, the high skilled worker can now demand any wage up to $60 per day... and retain employment. Prior to the enactment of the minimum wage of $20 per day, a

demand of $60 per day would have cost the high skilled worker his job. Thus the effect of the minimum wage is to price the high skilled worker's competition out of the market.[16]

Labor competes against labor, not against management. Since low-skill labor competes with high-skill labor, the minimum wage works against the lower-skill, lower-paid worker in favor of higher-paid workers. Hence, the consequences of the law are exactly opposite its alleged purpose.

## Capital Substitution Effects

To produce a given quantity of goods, some bundle of inputs is required. The ratio of inputs used to produce the desired output is not fixed by natural law but by the relative prices of inputs, which change continuously with new demand and supply conditions. Based on relative input prices, producers attempt to minimize costs for a given output. Since many inputs are substitutes for one another in the production process, a given output can be achieved by increasing the use of one and diminishing the use of another. The optimal mix will depend on the relative supply and demand for competing substitute inputs.

As a production input, low-skill labor is often in direct competition with highly technical machinery. A Whirlpool dishwasher can be substituted for low-skill manual dishwashers in the dishwashing process, and an automatic elevator can take the place of a nonautomatic elevator and a manual operator. This [is] not to imply that automation "destroys jobs," a common Luddite myth. As Frederic Bastiat explained over a century ago, jobs are obstacles to be overcome.[17] Automation shifts the *kinds* of jobs to be done in society but does not reduce their total number. Low-skill jobs are done away with, but higher-skill jobs are created simultaneously. When the minimum wage raises the cost of employing low-skill workers, it makes the substitute of automated machinery an attractive option.

### Racial Discrimination in Hiring Practices

At first glance the connection between the level of racial discrimination in hiring practices and the minimum wage may not seem evident. On closer examination, however, it is apparent that the minimum wage law gives employers strong incentives to exercise their existing racial preferences.[18] The minimum wage burdens minority groups in general and minority teenagers most specifically. Although outright racism has often been blamed as the sole cause of heavy minority teenage unemployment, it is clearly not the only factor. William Keyes informs us that

> In the late 1940's and early 1950's, young blacks had a lower unemployment rate than did whites of the same age group. But after the minimum wage increased significantly, especially in 1961, the black youth unemployment rate has increased to the extent that it is now a multiple of the white youth unemployment rate.[19]

To make the case that racism itself is the cause of the employment and unemployment disparity among blacks and whites, one would have to claim that America was more racially harmonious in the past than it is now. In fact, during the racially hostile times of the early 1900s 71 percent of blacks over nine years of age were employed, as compared with 51 percent for whites.[20] The minimum wage means that employers are not free to decide among low-wage workers on the basis of price differentials; hence, they face fewer disincentives to deciding according to some other (possibly racial) criteria.

To see the racial implications of minimum wage legislation, it is helpful to look at proponents of the law in a country where racial hostility is very strong, South Africa. Since minimum wage laws share characteristics in common with equal pay laws, white racist unions in South Africa continually support both minimum wage and equal-pay-for-equal-work laws for blacks. According to Williams:

> Right-wing white unions in the building trades have complained to the South African government that laws reserving skilled jobs for whites have been broken and should be abandoned in favor of equal pay for equal work laws.... The conservative building trades made it clear that they are not motivated by concern for black workers but had come to feel that legal job reservation had been so eroded by government exemptions that it no longer protected the white worker.[21]

The reason white trade unions are restless in South Africa is a $1.52-per-hour wage differential between black and white construction workers.[22] Although the owners of the construction firms are white, they cannot afford to restrict employment to whites when blacks are willing to work for $1.52 per hour less. As minimum wages eliminate the wage differential, the cost to employers of hiring workers with the skin color they prefer is reduced. As the cost of discrimination falls, and with all else remaining the same, the law of demand would dictate that more discrimination in employment practices will occur.

Markets frequently respond where they can, even to the obstacles the minimum wage presents minority groups. In fact, during the NRA blacks would frequently be advanced to the higher rank of "executives" in order to receive exemptions from the minimum wage.[23] The free market demands that firms remain color-blind in the conduct of business: profit, not racial preference, is the primary concern of the profit-maximizing firm. Those firms who fail the profit test get driven out of business by those who put prejudice aside to maximize profits. When markets are restricted by such laws as the minimum wage, the prospects for eliminating racial discrimination in hiring practices and the shocking 40–50 percent rate of black teenage unemployment in our cities are bleak.

## Human Capital Development

Minimum wage laws restrict the employment of low-skill workers when the wage rate exceeds the workers' marginal productivity. By doing so, the law prevents workers with the least skills from acquiring the marketable skills necessary for increasing their future productivity, that is, it keeps them from receiving on-the-job training.

It is an observable fact, true across ethnic groups, that income rises with age.[24] As human capital accumulates over time, it makes teenagers more valuable to employers than workers with no labor-market experience. But when teenagers are priced out of the labor market by the minimum wage, they lose their first and most crucial opportunity to accumulate the human capital that would make them more valuable to future employers. This stunting reduces their lifetime potential earnings. As Martin Feldstein has commented:

[F]or the disadvantaged young worker, with few skills and below average education, producing enough to earn the minimum wage is incompatible with the opportunity for adequate on-the-job learning. For this group, the minimum wage implies high short-run unemployment and the chronic poverty of a life of low wage jobs.[25]

Feldstein also finds a significant irony in the minimum wage: "It is unfortunate and ironic that we encourage and subsidize expenditure on formal education while blocking the opportunity for individuals to 'buy' on-the-job training."[26] This is especially hard on teenagers from the poorest minority groups, such as blacks and hispanics—a truly sad state of affairs, since the law is instituted in the name of the poor.

## Distortion of the Market Process

Relative prices provide the transmission mechanism by which information is delivered to participants in the market about the underlying relative scarcities of competing factor inputs. They serve as signals for people to substitute relatively less scarce resources for relatively more scarce resources, in many cases without their even being aware of it.[27]

Whenever relative price differentials exist for input substitutes in the production process, entrepreneurs will switch from higher-priced inputs to lower-priced inputs. In a dynamically changing economy, this switching occurs continually. But when prices are not allowed to transmit market information accurately, as in the case of prices artificially controlled by government, then distorted information skews the market and guides it to something clearly less than optimal.[28]

Minimum wages, being such a distortion of the price system, lead to the wrong

*Table 2*
## Dates and Amounts of Minimum Wage Changes

| Date | Amount | As a Percent of the Average Wage in Manufacturing (Old Minimum/New Minimum) |
| --- | --- | --- |
| February 1967 | $1.40 | 44.8% / 50.2% |
| February 1968 | $1.60 | 47.6% / 54.4% |
| May 1974 | $2.00 | 37.8% / 47.3% |
| January 1975 | $2.10 | 42.7% / 44.9% |
| January 1976 | $2.30 | 41.7% / 45.6% |
| January 1978 | $2.65 | 38.5% / 44.4% |
| January 1979 | $2.90 | 40.8% / 44.6% |
| January 1980 | $3.20 | 41.7% / 44.5% |
| January 1981 | $3.35 | 40.1% / 43.3% |
| April 1990 | $3.80 | 31.4% / 35.6% |
| April 1991 | $4.25 | 33.6% / 37.6% |

factor input mix between labor and all other inputs. As a result, industry migrates to locations of greater labor supply more slowly, and labor-intensive industries tend to remain fixed in non-optimal areas, areas with greater labor scarcity. Large labor pools of labor-abundant geographical areas are not tapped because the controlled price of labor conveys the wrong information to all the parties involved. Thus, the existence of price differentials, as knowledge to be transmitted through relative prices, is hidden.[29] The slowdown of industrial migration keeps labor-abundant regions poorer than they otherwise would be because economic growth there is stifled. As Simon Rottenberg explains for the case of Puerto Rico:

> The aggregate effect of all these distortions was that Puerto Rico could be expected to produce fewer goods and services than would have otherwise been produced and that the rate at which insular per capita income rose toward mainland United States income standards could be expected to be dampened. In sum, the minimum wage law could be expected to reduce the rate of improve-

ment in the standard of life of the Puerto Rican people and to intensify poverty in the island.[30]

In summary, the evidence is in on the minimum wage. All eight major effects of the minimum wage examined here make the poor, disadvantaged, or young in society worse off—the alleged beneficiaries turn out to be the law's major victims. . . .

## CONCLUSION

George Stigler may have startled some economists in 1946 when he claimed that minimum wage laws create unemployment and make people who had been receiving less than the minimum poorer.[31] Fifty years of experience with the law has proven Stigler correct, leaving very few defenders in the economics profession.[32]

But economists have had little success in criticizing this very destructive law. Simon Rottenberg demonstrated the government's disregard for what most economists have to say about this issue in his investigation of the Minimum Wage

Study Commission created by Congress in 1977. He noted the numerous studies presented to the commission that without exception found that the law had a negative impact on employment and intensified the poverty of low-income earners. The commission spent over $17 million to conduct the investigation and on the basis of the evidence should have eliminated the law. What was the outcome? The commission voted to *increase the minimum wage by indexing and expanding coverage*. As dissenting commissioner S. Warne Robinson commented about the investigation:

> The evidence is now in, and the findings of dozens of major economic studies show that the damage done by the minimum wage has been far more severe than even the critics of forty years ago predicted. Indeed, the evidence against the minimum wage is so overwhelming that the only way the Commission's majority was able to recommend it be retained was to ask us not to base any decisions on the facts.[33]

It cannot be that our elected representatives in Congress are just misinformed with respect to the minimum wage law. To the contrary, the *Congressional Record* demonstrates that they fully understand the law's effects and how the utilization of those effects can ensure reelection. Economists would do well to realize that governments have little interest in the truth when its implementation would contradict self-serving government policies. Rather than attempting to bring government the "facts," economists should educate the public. This is the only solution to the malaise created when people uncritically accept such governmental edicts as the minimum wage.

## NOTES

1. Leverett Lyon et al. *The National Recovery Administration: An Analysis and Appraisal* (New York: Da Capo Press, 1972), pp. 318–19.
2. Benjamin M. Anderson, *Economics and the Public Welfare: A Financial and Economic History of the United States, 1914–1946* (Indianapolis: Liberty Press, 1979), p. 336.
3. Jonathan Grossman, "Fair Labor Standards Act of 1938: Maximum Struggle for a Minimum Wage," *Monthly Labor Review* 101 (June 1978): 23.
4. "Wage and Hours Law," *New York Times*, 24 October 1938, p. 2.
5. Grossman, "Fair Labor Standards Act," p. 29.
6. Ibid., p. 28.
7. Ibid., p. 29.
8. "Report 40,000 Jobs Lost," *New York Times*, 24 October 1938, p. 2.
9. Anderson, *Economics and the Public Welfare*, p. 458.
10. Simon Rottenberg, "Minimum Wages in Puerto Rico," in *Economics of Legal Minimum Wages*, edited by Simon Rottenberg (Washington, D.C.: American Enterprise Institute, 1981), p. 330.
11. Rottenberg, "Minimum Wages in Puerto Rico," p. 333.
12. Yale Brozen, "Minimum Wage Rates and Household Workers," *Journal of Law and Economics* 5 (October 1962): 103–10.
13. Finis Welch, "Minimum Wage Legislation in the United States," *Economic Inquiry* 12 (September 1974): 286.
14. Brozen, "Minimum Wage Rates and Household Workers," pp. 107–08.
15. Richard McKenzie, "The Labor Market Effects of Minimum Wage Laws: A New Perspective," *Journal of Labor Research* 1 (Fall 1980): 258–59.
16. Walter Williams, *The State Against Blacks* (New York: McGraw-Hill, 1982), pp. 44–45.
17. Frederic Bastiat, *Economic Sophisms* (Irvington-on-Hudson, N.Y.: Foundation for Economic Education, 1946), pp. 16–19.
18. Walter Williams, "Government Sanctioned Restraints That Reduce the Economic Opportunities for Minorities," *Policy Review* 22 (Fall 1977): 15.
19. William Keyes,"The Minimum Wage and the Davis Bacon Act: Employment Effects on Minorities and Youth," *Journal of Labor Research* 3 (Fall 1982): 402.
20. Williams, *State Against Blacks*, p. 41.
21. Ibid., p. 43.
22. Ibid., pp. 43–44.
23. Lyon, *National Recovery Administration*, p. 339.
24. U.S. Department of Commerce, Bureau of the Census, *Statistical Abstract of the United States 1982–83*, p. 431.

25. Martin Feldstein, "The Economics of the New Unemployment," *The Public Interest*, no. 33 (Fall 1973): 14–15.

26. Ibid., p. 15.

27. Thomas Sowell, *Knowledge and Decisions* (New York: Basic Books, 1980), p. 79.

28. Ibid.

29. Ibid., pp. 167–68.

30. Rottenberg, "Minimum Wages in Puerto Rico," p. 329.

31. George Stigler, "The Economies of Minimum Wage Legislation," *American Economic Review* 36 (June 1946): 358–65.

32. Although there are a few supporters left such as John K. Galbraith, many "liberal" economists such as Paul Samuelson and James Tobin have recently come out against the minimum wage. See Emerson Schmidt, *Union Power and the Public Interest* (Los Angeles: Nash, 1973).

33. Simon Rottenberg, "National Commissions: Preaching in the Garb of Analysis," *Policy Review* no. 23 (Winter 1983): 139.

# NO

Charles Craypo

# IN DEFENSE OF MINIMUM WAGES

This article refutes the dominant view held by orthodox neoclassical economists such as Thomas Rustici. These economists assert that minimum wage
laws should be abolished because they misallocate resources and cause production inefficiencies. I reject Rustici's conclusion and instead take the position that in most instances high minimum wages are good for workers,
employers and consumers alike and hence are good for the economy as a
whole.

Three things are wrong with Rustici's neoclassical view of things. It depends on an idealized world that by assumption favors more rather than less
market competition as the solution to economic problems. Second, it ignores
the reasons why governments enact minimum wage laws in the first place
and instead interprets and judges them on inappropriate grounds. Third, the
neoclassical argument against minimum wages is supported by contradictory
empirical evidence that casts doubt on its theoretical validity and practical
significance.

Critics of the orthodox neoclassical interpretation of minimum wages include both neoclassical and institutional applied labor economists. In fact,
most of the contradictory empirical studies in recent years have produced by
neoclassical economists whose findings prompt them to question the dominant view. In addition to the research of mainstream economists, research critical of the orthodox position has come from the various institutional schools
of thought which emphasize evolutionary change and systemic rather than
deductive reasoning from an idealized model.

Most of the debate surrounds the federal minimum wage law contained
in the Fair Labor Standards Act (FLSA) of 1938, which represented an essential part of President Roosevelt's agenda to get the nation out of the Great
Depression. Labor law reformers had long advocated federal wage and hour
laws in response to an historic pattern of low earnings among working families and intense wage competition among employers. The courts, however,
struck down early attempts to establish federal standards on grounds the

separate states had constitutional primacy in such matters. Individual states were reluctant to pass regulatory laws, however, because they feared industry would avoid locating there. The enormities of the depression nevertheless drove working people to strike employers and protest politically. Soon the Supreme Court changed directions and ruled that the constitution does in fact allow Congress to regulate interstate commerce; Congress responded with numerous regulatory laws including the FLSA.

*The inherent bias in neoclassical analysis.* When polled, a large majority of American economists support Rustici in his opposition to minimum wage increases. This reflects their prior training in the neoclassical wage model, which generally rejects labor standards legislation on grounds that market outcomes are superior to anything government can achieve through regulation. Employers and others lobbying to abolish or weaken minimum wage laws therefore can count on the support of orthodox economists, despite widespread public approval of these laws. Indeed, in 1993, three-fourths of economists polled said that an increase in the minimum wage would increase unemployment, while a similar poll in 1996 found that 84% of the public favored an increase.

This vastly different view of the world underscores the first problem with Rustici's neoclassical analysis. The competitive market model it uses simply does not depict real labor markets accurately. It imagines all sorts of things that do not exist and ignores a great many other things that do. When this analysis is applied to particular labor market problems, such as declining real wages, it is likely to misdiagnose the ailment and to prescribe inappropriate public policy.

The problem is that in explaining how the interaction between worker skill and output determines wages the neoclassical model uses circular reasoning. It presumes that if we know the wage we also know the worth of the worker because market competition ensures that each worker is paid the value of his or her worth, as measured by the value of what each produces. It further presumes that the worker's productive value is determined by his or her level of skill and education, that is, by their accumulated "human capital." Therefore, if one worker is paid more than another worker, then the first worker must be worth more (that is, must have more skill and education) than the second; because the wage is, by definition, equal to output value, which in turn is determined by skill and education. Consequently, every worker must be worth what he or she is being paid, no more and no less. Workers who think they are not being paid enough must be wrong, because if they possessed more human capital they would be worth more therefore paid more.

This is tautological reasoning. It explains everything and nothing because it uses the thing it is trying to explain as the evidence with which to explain it. It does, however, allow neoclassical economists to reject any attempt to regulate wages on the grounds that the worker currently is being paid what he or she is worth. In the world of the neoclassical economist, forcing employers to pay a higher wage will simply place the individual employer at a competitive disadvantage and at the same time discriminate against workers who did not benefit from the regulated wage increase. As a result, neoclassical investigations of minimum wage effects usually ask a single question. How many workers will become unemployable following an increase in the minimum wage. The question derives from the competitive wage model, not from observed experiences or policy objectives.

With this mind-set, it is understandable that Rustici and other orthodox neoclassical economists see the solution to labor market problems, such as low earnings and unemployment, as more rather than less market determination and the elimination of existing regulations. If labor markets deliver less than ideal results it is because they are not free enough. Public policy must be to remove the imperfections. Unions and minimum wages are logical targets in this regard.

The problem with such deductive reasoning is that employers and employees seldom meet as equals in the labor market, although the model assumes that they do. In blue-collar settings, for example, the employment relationship favors employers, who typically offer jobs on a take-it-or-leave-it basis. Individual workers find there are far more workers than there are good jobs and they take what they can get on the terms that are offered. Employers simply have more options in the hiring process than do workers—except perhaps when unemployment is low and workers scarce in the lowest paying, least desirable occupations and industries, at which point employers turn to immigrant labor to fill job vacancies at the going wage levels. Additionally, employers know far more than hourly workers do about supply and demand conditions in local labor markets and are more mobile in terms of where and when to hire. They also can hold out much longer financially than can workers in the event of differences over wages and working conditions. Finally, and importantly, because they own the plant and equipment upon which the worker's livelihood depends, they can threaten to relocate the workplace or to replace the workers with machines or other workers.

In the absence of institutional protections such as union contracts and minimum wages, workers are in constant danger of having to compete with one another to see which of them will work for less pay and under the worst conditions. If one or a few employers are able to reduce labor standards by taking advantage of labor's inherent bargaining weakness, and in the process they expand markets and increase their profits, then the race is on among all employers to take down labor standards. The labor market degenerates into what institutional labor economists call destructive competition. As two institutional labor economists observed decades ago, "When an employer can hire workers for practically his own price, he can be slack and inefficient in his methods, and yet, by reducing wages, reduce his cost of production to the level of his more able competitor" (Commons and Andrews, 1936:48).

*The irrelevancy of the neoclassical analysis.* This demonstrates the second thing wrong with Rustici's neoclassical interpretation. It examines and evaluates minimum wage laws only on the basis of what would result in a competitive market model. In doing so, it ignores the reasons why such laws are enacted in the first place and whether or not they solve the problems they were intended to solve. The problem with this approach is that it focuses on only one of the three forms of economic efficiency that are essential for a nation to sustain high-levels of production and consumption: a nation's need to provide high standards of living for its citizens.

Robert Kuttner (1997) argues that neoclassical preoccupation with allocative efficiency prevents an examination of macroefficiency and technical efficiency. Macroefficiency concerns a nation's ability to sustain or enhance total production, employment, and family living standards; whereas technical efficiency refers to the ability to generate new products and production methods through industrial invention and innovation. Allocative efficiency, on the other hand, is limited to looking after the immediate interests of the consumer by minimizing production costs and product prices. If only allocative efficiency is taken into account, the long-term interests of both producers and consumers is ignored as the nation neglects its overall economic growth, job and earnings performance, and progress in research/development.

It must be remembered that neither macro- nor technical efficiency necessarily results in optimal allocation efficiency in the short run, that is, in the lowest possible costs of production and consumer prices. Nor does optimal allocative efficiency necessarily help to maximize either macro- or technical efficiency. The postwar success of certain West European and Asian economies, led by Germany and Japan, testifies to the need to distinguish between alternative forms of economic efficiency and between short- and long-run goals and performance. Japanese industrial strategists made these distinctions for example when they targeted the global auto market in the late 1950s. They gave up short-run cost efficiency in return for long-term product and workforce quality on their way to world supremacy in autos by the 1980s (Halberstam 1986).

Because neoclassical economists largely ignore macro- and technical efficiency in their analysis of competitive labor markets, their competitive model cannot estimate the macroeffects of incremental changes in prices and quantities in particular markets. The 1930s, for example, were characterized by the kind of intense wage and price competition that neoclassical economists associate with allocative efficiency. Consequently, the economy should have been performing at its best. But we still refer to what happened instead as the Great Depression.

Remember that the question deriving from the neoclassical market model is "How many workers are made unemployable because the new wage prices them out of competitive labor markets?" That is not, however, the question that advocates of the FLSA were concerned with in 1938, nor what people are concerned with today in view of the long-term decline in median real wages and the increase in unstable jobs. The problem then and now is not the ability to produce enough goods and services, but rather it is creating jobs at wages high enough to buy back what is produced and in the process sustain high living standards for everyone.

This was the task of the 1938 federal minimum wage. It was designed to do two things: (i) increase employment and purchasing power in order to stimulate the slumping economy; and (ii) drive out of the market employers who competed on the basis of cheap labor instead of through better products and state-of-the-art production methods. The country had been in economic crisis for the better part of a decade. It had become increasingly clear that much of the problem was due to low pay, long workweeks, and growing use of child rather than adult labor.

Advocates of minimum wages were not the least dissuaded by neoclassical forecasts that some jobs would be lost and some employers driven out of business. That is precisely what they wanted to do, on grounds that a job that does not pay enough to support a family should not exist and an employer who cannot pay a living wage, even though other employers in that industry can and do pay the mandated living wage, should be driven from the marketplace.

In brief, if a job pays less than enough to sustain workers and their dependents at the customary standard of living, then that job is not paying its way in a productive economy because it is being subsidized by some household, charitable organization, or government transfer payment. The beneficiary of this subsidy is either the employer paying the low wage and making a profit by doing so, or the customer paying a low price for the good or service. Fast-food restaurant fare, for example, is cheap in part because fast-food workers earn poverty level wages. Home owners in wealthy suburbs can get their houses cleaned cheaply because the women who clean them live in low-income areas, need the money, and have few job options. A subsidy is a subsidy, whether the worker is part of a poor household or an affluent household and whether the employer is a large or a small business.

If you work for a fast-food restaurant why should your family subsidize the owners of that restaurant? In a like manner, why should taxpayers subsidize manufacturers that employ fathers and mothers who cannot support their families without receiving food stamps or a tax rebate from the government? Why should the large employer have to compete with a smaller rival that is being sub-sidized by low-income households and taxpayers.

This subsidization does not have to occur. In Australia, for example, restaurant workers, "bag boys" in grocery stores, bartenders in taverns, and other workers who are generally low paid in the United States are paid in excess of $12 an hour. Nevertheless, McDonalds hamburgers and Pizza Hut pizzas still abound in Australia. In the United States unionized waitresses in Las Vegas also earn $12 an hour, before tips, and Las Vegas is one of the fastest growing economic regions in America. Waitresses in other parts of the country commonly receive about half the level of the minimum wage, before tips, which forces them to show a certain amount of servitude in order to earn enough tips to make the job worthwhile (a subsidy to the employer from the customer) and leaves the worker unsure of her or his earnings from day-to-day and week-to-week. Such market outcomes reflect the low-status, devalued nature of these workers and occupations more than it does their value to both customers and employers.

*Contradictory evidence for the neoclassical view.* Rustici's neoclassical approach necessarily ignores the economic and social problems associated with low-wage jobs because it concentrates on workers rather than jobs. Such focus also shifts responsibility for low-wage incomes from jobs to workers by focusing on worker behavior rather than industrial strategies and government policies. Recall that the theory assumes the individual worker's wage is determined by his or her worth on the job; it further presumes that this worth is determined in large part by the amount of human capital the worker possesses in terms of formal education (college degrees) and occupational training (vocational and on-the-job training). Thus the job and its requirements are excluded from the analysis and low-wages are linked to the worker's efforts to acquire skill and education. When neoclassical researchers like Thomas Rustici want to verify their theory they study the earnings and employment experiences of groups of workers having low educational and vocational skills on grounds such workers are most likely to lose jobs as a result of minimum wage raises. Most neoclassical studies do indeed find greater unemployment among such groups following minimum wage increases.

But the findings of empirical studies themselves pose the third problem with Rustici's analysis. The results of far too many empirical studies—those conducted by neoclassical as well as institutional labor economists—have contradicted the neoclassical model for it to remain very convincing. During the Progressive Era prior to World War I, for example, government economists surveyed jobs before and after passage of state minimum wage laws covering women workers (Obenauer and von der Nienburg 1915). This and a later study conducted by Commons and Andrews (1936), found that mandated wages alleviated the degenerative effects of low wages and actually enhanced productivity by increasing worker desire and ability to produce. Only "parasitic" employers were threatened by minimum wages and relatively small numbers of jobs were eliminated.

Some years later, Princeton labor economist Richard Lester surveyed southern manufacturing employers after World War II and found they had not laid-off marginal workers in response to minimum wage increases, but instead had maintained their workforces and tried to offset the higher labor cost by increasing output and sales. This allowed them to take advantage of the economies of scale (lower per-unit costs of production) that accompany higher levels of plant and equipment utilization. Lester went on to note that workers doing the same jobs in different plants received different wages over long periods of time—another finding at odds with neoclassical reasoning - therefore, it was not possible to predict the employment effects of a minimum wage raise. His and other studies thus refuted the neoclassical notion of a single competitive wage. Workers with comparable skills often make quite different wages over long periods of time and those with different skills often earn the same wages. "Such matters are elementary and commonplace to a student of labor, but they seem to be largely overlooked by theorists of the [neoclassical] marginalist faith," he concluded (1947:148).

In the 1990s, another group of neoclassical revisionists using much the same investigative methods as Lester, but with more sophisticated equipment and techniques at their disposal, produced similar findings and came to much the same conclusion. Princeton economists David Card and Alan Krueger demonstrated that modest increases in minimum wage rates have little if any negative impact on the most exposed workers—teenagers. Instead of analyzing what happens to workers following minimum wage increases, they, like Lester before them, asked what happened to the jobs themselves. And like Lester, they discovered that employers did not respond as anticipated. Jobs in fast-food restaurants and other low-wage establishments did not decline, and in fact they even increased slightly in New Jersey when that state increased its minimum wage above the federal level. More surprising perhaps, in adjacent Pennsylvania, where no increase in the state minimum wage had occurred, fast-food employment actually fell slightly! Card and Krueger substantiated these findings in similar studies involving fast-food restaurant jobs in Texas and teenage workers in all industries in California (Card and Krueger 1995: Chapters 2 and 3).

These results, clearly at odds with the neoclassical literature, prompted one somewhat shaken but faithful neoclassical reviewer of Card and Krueger's work to conclude in 1995, just as the debate was getting underway on a proposal to raise the federal minimum wage to $5.15, that "we just don't know how many jobs would be lost if the minimum wage were increased to $5.15" (Kennan 1995:1964). Orthodox certainty was beginning to be eroded by the contradictory findings, but the basic model was not questioned. Many neoclassical economists hold doggedly to the view that jobs *must be* lost if minimum wages are increased. Consider, for example, a standard neoclassical labor economics text now in its sixth edition. The authors dismiss the Card-Krueger findings and insist instead that: "While the impact of the minimum wage on employment, especially that of young workers will undoubtedly continue to receive a great deal of research and public policy discussion, the best evidence remains that the overall impact of the law is to lower employment of unskilled workers while increasing the earnings of those who are able to get jobs" (Filer, Hamermesh, and Rees 1996:175).

In sum, neoclassical economists like Rustici find fault with the minimum wage because they contrast it with a theoretical system that is said to provide optimal results; but it is a system that ultimately is nonfalsifiable because of its tautological nature. They purport to refute the minimum wage on grounds it destroys low-wage jobs despite the fact that this is precisely what it is supposed to do. Finally, by limiting the inquiry to the dictates of a model that is inherently hostile to government regulation, they preclude serious debate on regulation as a policy tool.

*Alternative analyses of minimum wage laws.* The shortcomings of traditional neoclassical analysis become apparent when considered in terms of macro- and technical efficiency. Wage-based competition during the 1930s reduced already depressed earnings and worker purchasing power, which in turn decreased product demand and caused additional workers to be unemployed. The effect was to cut output, incomes, and profits. With no recovery in sight, large firms could not be expected to make more cars, radios, and appliances than they could sell, nor could they be expected to design and manufacture new products when consumers could afford neither old nor new models.

Economic recovery did not occur until total war production during 1940–45, when all the neoclassical rules of allocative efficiency were repealed: industry was cartelized, wages and prices were controlled, and productive decision making was centralized. Yet, despite the total violation of market rules, the defense plants were running day and night, workers were acquiring formal and informal education and training, incomes and profits were high. Then, from the late 1940s until the mid-1970s, industrial oligopolies and labor unions replaced government in administering the productive system, again in violation of allocative efficiency. But we look back fondly on those decades as the golden age of increased living standards and job security.

Since then, however, the economy has been deregulated in keeping with neoclassical doctrine and both product and labor markets made more competitive by domestic and global changes in industrial structure and behavior. Labor productivity has been increasing, albeit modestly, and labor resources probably have been allocated more efficiently than in the postwar decades, but real earnings are falling, job security declining, and living standards stagnating (Mishel, et al. 1996).

As a society we have three broad policy responses. One, we can remove a certain portion of the population from the productive system by offering social insurance and welfare benefits to able-bodied individuals including laid-off or displaced males and single mothers. This should raise wages by reducing the supply of workers. Two, we can force some idle workers into productive roles by abolishing their financial support and subsidy systems, giving them no practical choice but to work under the terms offered. This should lower wages by putting the new low-wage workers in competition with existing ones. Finally, we can legislate high minimum wages and other protective labor measures to ensure the lowest paid workers a conventional standard of living. This would raise wages directly.

The first alternative has been the favorite of conservative economists and moral reformers since the early 1880s when industrial poverty appeared in Britain (Persky 1997). Free market advocates urged the abolition of welfare support and wage supplements on grounds that its elimination would increase the number of laborers and their productivity while also lowering taxes and birth rates. As a secondary benefit, they went on to claim, this would also enhance family stability and values by making parents responsible for their children and both children and mothers/wives dependent on and therefore respectful of and obedient to wage-earning fathers/husbands. Conservatives still argue generally along these lines.

The second alternative is preferred by liberal economists and policy makers. It seeks to assure low-wage workers a living income by supplementing their inadequate earnings through the Earned Income Tax Credit, a tax rebate of up to several thousand dollars a year to the employee based on his or her payments into the Social Security fund. Advocates favor this approach because it effectively increases the employee's real wage rate and at the same time it offsets undesirable market outcomes of low wages without distorting wage and employment structures and obstructing allocative efficiency. They also believe that the long-run solution is worker training and education to enhance human capital. Conservative and liberal economists and policy makers tend to agree on that. They differ, however, on whether it should be publicly financed and broadly available.

In view of the bipartisan support for more education, a word of caution is in order. More education is always laudable, but by itself cannot solve the problem of low wages. This is because employers use formal educational credentials, especially college degrees, to screen applicants for good jobs. Therefore, as the overall educational level of the workforce rises, the amount of education needed to get a given job also increases. This jeopardizes the effectiveness of education as the justification for high pay. For if a college degree were to be conferred magically upon the entire working population tomorrow, who would bus and wait tables the day after? Employers would find and apply other screening criteria, perhaps a graduate or professional degree, in order to determine which college grads would manage restaurants and which would bus and wait tables.

Moreover, the supply of educated workers does not automatically create the demand for them. American engineering students, for instance, may wonder exactly what it is they are going to engineer when they read about U.S. companies hiring pools of low wage but college trained information technologists in developing countries to work on computer software projects using high-speed satellite information links, or when they hear about domestic aerospace companies transferring technology overseas in exchange for sales contracts, or of NASA purchasing rocketry equipment from other industrialized countries in order to get the lowest possible price (Barlett and Steele 1996: 49–52, 93–9).

The third alternative favors policies that increase earnings and incomes directly, that is, before taxes and transfer payments. High minimum wages are a logical policy choice in this analysis because they contribute directly to sustained economic growth (macroefficiency) and industrial capitalization and innovation (technical efficiency). It is based on the premise that with rare exceptions people want the dignity and independence that comes with gainful employment, and therefore they should work because it is good for them as individuals and good for the society in which they are stakeholder producers and consumers. But this is true only if the jobs available to them pay wages that afford a decent living.

In addition, the high wage economy is most consistent over time with the three economic efficiencies. It is true that minimum wages are inconsistent with the neoclassical definition of allocative efficiency in the short run; but it is the long term that should concern us as a nation. High-paid workers stay with their employers, which encourages the latter to invest in worker skill and education, which in turn encourages employers to adopt state-of-the-art production methods and sophisticated product design and performance. High-paid workers also have the purchasing power to buy the goods and services that they and other high-paid workers produce.

A high wage policy is the best hope for a bright future for the American economy. It ensures a proficient labor force in a stable macroeconomy and encourages steady technological advancement. The larger society is only as prosperous as its individual parts. Thus when labor standards are high the larger society prospers.

## REFERENCES

Barlett, Donald L., and James B. Steele. 1996. *America: who Stole the Dream?* Kansas City: Andrews & McMeel.

Card, David Edward, and Alan B. Krueger. 1995. *Myth and Measurement: The New Economics of the Minimum Wage.* Princeton, NJ: Princeton University Press.

Commons, John R., and John B. Andrews. 1936. *Principles of Labor Legislation* (fourth edition). New York: Augustus M. Kelley (1967 Reprint).

Filer, Randall K., Daniel S. Hamermesh, and Albert Rees. 1996. *The Economics of Work and Pay*, sixth edition. New York: Harper Collins.

Halberstam, David. 1986. *The Reckoning.* New York: Morrow.

Kuttner, Robert. 1997. *Everything For Sale: The Virtues and Limits of Markets*. New York: Alfred A. Knopf.

Lester, Richard A. 1947. "Marginalism, Minimum Wages, and Labor Markets." *American Economic Review* 37 (March) pp. 135–48.

Mishel, Lawrence, Jared Bernstein, and John Schmitt. 1977. *The State of Working America, 1996–97*. Armonk, NY: M. E. Sharpe.

Obenauer, Marie L., and Bertha von der Nienburg. 1915. *Effect of Minimum Wage Determinations in Oregon*. Bureau of Labor Statistics, Bulletin No. 176. Washington: GPO.

Persky, Joseph. 1997. "Classical Family Values: Ending the Poor Laws as They Knew Them." *Journal of Economic Perspectives* 11 (Winter) pp. 179–89.

# POSTSCRIPT

## Is It Time to Abolish the Minimum Wage?

The impact of the minimum wage can be expressed in many ways. Two particularly rewarding ways of looking at such legislative initiatives are to examine minimum wages over time in real dollars and as a percent of manufacturing wages.

A clear pattern should emerge from an examination of this data. The 1965–1970 period saw the highest level of the minimum wage in real terms. In constant 1982–84 dollars, the minimum wage for these years was approximately $4 an hour and reached nearly 50 percent of the prevailing manufacturing wage. For the next 20 years, however, the value of the minimum wage in real terms and as a percentage of the manufacturing wage fell. It is only in recent years that it has begun to recover.

The renewed interest in the minimum wage can be traced in part to the research findings of David Card and Alan Krueger. These economists, as Craypo points out, have shaken the economics profession with their empirical research findings that moderate increases in the minimum wage have few negative consequences on employment patterns and in some cases are associated with the increases in employment. Their work has been published widely in professional journals: *Industrial and Labor Relations Review* (October 1992 and April 1994) and in the *American Economic Review* (1994 and 1995). They have also detailed their findings in a book entitled *Myth and Measurement: The New Economics of the Minimum Wage* (Princeton University Press, 1995).

Two vocal critics of the Card/Krueger research are David Newmark and William Wascher. Their empirical studies are supportive of the traditional neoclassical findings that the minimum wage causes unemployment, particularly among teenagers and young adults. See their work published in *Industrial and Labor Relations Review* (September 1992 and April 1994); *NBER Working Paper No. 4617* (1994); *Journal of Business and Economic Statistics* (1995); and *American Economic Review Papers and Proceedings* (May 1995). Still often considered the best antiminimum wage statement, however, is George J. Stigler's 1946 essay entitled "The Economics of Minimum Wage Legislation," *American Economic Review*.

# ISSUE 5

## Are Rent Controls the Cause of America's Homelessness?

**YES: William Tucker,** from "How Housing Regulations Cause Homelessness," *The Public Interest* (Winter 1991)

**NO: Richard P. Appelbaum et al.,** from "Scapegoating Rent Control: Masking the Causes of Homelessness," *Journal of the American Planning Association* (Spring 1991)

### ISSUE SUMMARY

**YES:** Journalist William Tucker analyzes the problem of homelessness across the United States and suggests that rent controls and homelessness are correlated.

**NO:** Sociologist Richard P. Appelbaum and his research associates submit that Tucker's statistical analysis is flawed and that he ignores the real causes of homelessness: poverty, the lack of affordable housing, and inadequate support services for those who suffer from mental illness and alcoholism.

Most principles of economics textbooks spend some time discussing rent controls and how they distort the operation of the market system. Most use rent controls as an example of a price ceiling, which is a legal maximum on the price that may be charged for a commodity. The objective of rent control is, of course, to protect the consumer from high rents. However, supply and demand analysis suggests that, as a result of rent controls, an excess in the quantity demanded for rental housing occurs. This in turn forces landlords to ration the limited supply of rental units on some nonprice basis (personal habits, family size, and length of residence in the community, for example). With the imposition of rent controls, the market is not allowed to reach its equilibrium level, and a "net loss" to society is assumed to result as consumers are forced to pay a high price for the relatively small quantity that suppliers of housing units make available to the market.

Some textbooks go beyond discussing the efficiency implications of these market interferences and examine the historical experiences of New York City, Boston, Los Angeles, San Francisco, Washington, D.C., and other U.S. cities that have experimented with rent controls. These textbooks generally assume that purely competitive market conditions, which are necessary to utilize a supply and demand analysis, are or would be present in these housing markets if there were no rent controls. They conclude that these well-meaning governmental interventions in housing markets have left those in search of affordable housing worse off than if the market were allowed to operate on its own. They allege that renters hold on to apartments because rents are low, while at the same time these low rents discourage landlords from maintaining, upgrading, and/or investing in new units. Thus there are simply fewer housing units on the market.

It is only in recent years, however, that homelessness has been linked to the imposition of rent controls. This connection can be directly traced to the research findings of William Tucker.

In the early 1980s, under pressure from groups charged with the responsibility to provide social services to the homeless, the Reagan administration began to count the number of homeless persons. In 1984, the U.S. Department of Housing and Urban Development issued a study entitled "Report to the Secretary on the Homeless and Emergency Shelters," which estimated that the national homeless population was somewhere between 250,000 and 350,000 persons. (This study forms the statistical foundation for the Tucker selection in this debate.) This estimate and the Reagan administration's hands-off policy to deal with this problem came under intense attack. Groups such as the Coalition for the Homeless in New York and the Committee for Creative Non-Violence in Washington, D.C., estimated that this population was in reality between 2 and 3 million persons in 1984.

Who are these people who find themselves homeless? (*Homeless* refers to an individual who regularly has no place to sleep and must seek refuge in a shelter or remain on the streets after nightfall.) Besides the mentally ill who have not found adequate community care following deinstitutionalization and the drug and alcohol addicts, there are low-income families who have been evicted for nonpayment of rent; the unemployed; those who have lost their benefits from federal or state welfare or unemployment programs; battered women; and individuals and families who have been displaced by condominium conversions, gentrification, and urban renewal.

It seems reasonable to ask, Why has the market not responded by providing "affordable housing" for these people? If we are to believe Tucker, it is because of rent controls. Prospective landlords do not believe that they can earn a financial return sufficient to compensate them for the risk that they must bear. Richard P. Appelbaum and his research team reject Tucker's analysis and his conclusion, largely on the basis of a systematic statistical critique of the Tucker study.

# YES
William Tucker

# HOW HOUSING REGULATIONS CAUSE HOMELESSNESS

The problem of homelessness in the 1980s has puzzled liberals and conservatives alike. Both have tended to fit the problem into their preconceived views, without looking at what is new and different about the phenomenon.

For liberals, the issue has been fairly straightforward. Homelessness, they say, stems from a lack of government effort and compassion. Reacting almost reflexively, liberals have blamed homelessness on federal spending cuts and the heartlessness of the Reagan administration. The most commonly cited figure is that budget authorizations for the Department of Housing and Urban Development (HUD) were cut 75 percent in the Reagan years, from $32 billion in 1981 to $8 billion in 1988. Everything else is presumably self-explanatory. This compelling logic has even been repeated in the *Wall Street Journal*.

Conservatives, on the other hand, have taken two approaches. Either they deny the problem's existence or they assert that homelessness is almost always the result of personal pathologies. On the first count, it has often been argued (as in Martin Morse Wooster's June 1987 *Reason* article, "The Homeless: An Adman's Dream") that homelessness is really no worse than it ever was, but that the problem has been exaggerated to justify increases in government spending. On the other, conservatives have also argued that most of the homeless are insane, alcoholics, or drug addicts, and that their personal failings make it impossible for them to find housing, even when it is available.

## UNPERSUASIVE EXPLANATIONS

But these arguments, whether liberal or conservative, do not really hold up under close scrutiny.

The most obviously flawed explanation lies in the figures that seem to indicate a massive federal cutback in housing assistance. There has been no such cutback. Federal low-income housing assistance actually *increased* from $5.7 billion in 1980 to $13.8 billion in 1988. The number of households receiving low-income housing assistance also rose, going from 3.1 million to 4.2 million during the same period.

The commonly cited "cutback" from $32 billion to $8 billion is the figure for HUD's future authorizations. This figure has nothing to do with actual housing assistance, however, since it only indicates the amount of money that Congress authorized HUD to spend in the future. These authorizations often run forty years in advance—and much of the money is never spent anyway.

The reason for this cutback has been the changeover from a program centered around public-housing construction to one centered around housing vouchers. When Congress authorizes a unit of new public housing, it must include all future mortgage payments, running decades ahead. In authorizing a housing voucher, Congress pledges money for only five years—the lifetime of the voucher.

In addition, vouchers provide the same housing at only half the price. A unit of public housing costs the federal government $8,000 a year, while a voucher costs only $4,000. Thus, twice as many people can be reached with the same amount of money. This is why HUD has been able to extend housing aid to more low-income people without an equivalent increase in spending.

But if the liberal argument about "spending cuts" is based largely on a misunderstanding of the budgetary process, the conservative argument that homelessness has not really increased at all seems equally ill-founded.

There were indeed homeless people long before 1980, and their numbers have always been difficult to count. But it is hard to ignore the almost unanimous reports from shelter providers (many of them old-line conservative church groups) that the problem has been getting steadily worse since 1980. The anecdotal evidence is also abundant. Anyone who has walked the streets of New York or Washington over the last decade knows that there are more beggars sitting on the sidewalks and sleeping on park benches than there were ten years ago.

Although many of the homeless are obviously alcoholics, drug addicts, and people who are clinically insane, large numbers appear only to be down on their luck. The most widely accepted statistical breakdown was first proposed in a 1988 Urban Institute paper: "Feeding the Homeless: Does the Prepared Meals Provision Help?" According to authors Martha Burt and Barbara Cohen, one-third of the homeless can be categorized as released mental patients, one-third as alcoholics and drug abusers, and one-third as people who are homeless for purely economic reasons.

Thus the component of homeless people who are not affected by personal pathologies is large. It should also be noted that being a chronic alcoholic or drug addict does not condemn a person to living in the streets. Even "winos" or "stumblebums" were able to find minimal housing in the past.

And so paradoxes remain. How can we have such a large homeless population at a time when rental vacancy rates are near postwar highs? How can there be plenty of housing but not enough "affordable housing"? In short, how can there be scarcity in the housing market when so much housing is still available?

## VARIATIONS AMONG HOUSING MARKETS

These paradoxes can be resolved when we recognize that the housing market is not a national market but is instead the sum of many regional and local markets. Rental vacancy rates probably serve as the best measure of the availability of affordable housing, since most poor people rent. These rates vary widely from city to city. During the 1980s, rental vacancy rates in Dallas and Houston were rarely below 12 percent—a figure that is about twice what is considered a normal vacancy rate. At the same time, housing has been absurdly scarce in other cities. New York has not had vacancy rates over 3 percent since 1972. San Francisco had normal vacancy rates during the 1970s, but they plunged to 2 percent during the 1980s, where they remain today.

Since the poor tend to be limited in their mobility, vacancy rates significantly affect their ability to find housing. Although southern and southwestern cities claim to receive a regular seasonal migration of homeless people during the winter months, there is little evidence that people are moving from city to city to find housing. Other factors, like work opportunities, proximity to family members, and sheer inertia, seem to dominate people's choice of locale.

What should be far more mobile is the capital that builds housing and has created such a superabundance in specific cities. If it is difficult to find tenants for new apartments in Dallas and Phoenix, why don't builders shift to Boston or San Francisco, where housing is desperately needed?

Once we start asking this question, the impediments in the housing market suddenly become visible. It is obviously not equally easy to build housing in all cities. In particular, the local regulatory climate has a tremendous impact on the housing supply. Dallas and Houston are free-wheeling, market-oriented cities with little or no zoning regulation and negligible antigrowth sentiment. They have been able to keep abreast of hous-

ing demand even as their populations grew rapidly. Boston and San Francisco, on the other hand, have highly regulated housing markets. Both are surrounded by tight rings of exclusionary suburbs, where zoning and growth-control sentiment make new construction extremely difficult. In addition, both have adopted rent control as a way of "solving" local housing shortages. As a result, both have extremely high housing prices and extremely tight rental markets. The median home price in each approaches $200,000, while in Dallas and Phoenix the median price is below the national median of $88,000.

Thus it makes little sense to talk about a national housing market's effect on homelessness. Local markets vary widely, and municipal regulation seems to be the deciding factor.

This is what has misled both liberals and conservatives. Conservatives look at the national superabundance of housing and conclude that local problems do not exist. Liberals look at local shortages and conclude that there is a national housing problem. In fact, housing shortages are a local problem created by local regulation, which is the work of local municipal governments.

It is not surprising, then, to find that homelessness varies widely from city to city, with local housing policies once again the decisive factor. These conclusions are supported by research that I conducted in 1988: I calculated comparative rates of per-capita homelessness for various cities, using the homelessness figures for the largest thirty-five cities investigated in the 1984 *Report to the Secretary of Housing and Urban Development on the Homeless and Emergency Shelters.* I also added fifteen other large cities that were not included in the initial HUD survey.

I then subjected the comparative rates of homelessness to regression analysis, in order to look for possible associations with other factors.

Among the independent variables that I considered were the local unemployment rate, the poverty rate, city size, the availability of public housing, the median rent, annual mean temperature, annual rainfall, the size of the minority population, population growth over the past fifteen years, the rental vacancy rate, the presence or absence of rent control, and the median home price in the metropolitan area surrounding each city.

Of all these variables, only four showed a significant correlation: the median home price, the rental vacancy rate, the presence of rent control, and the size of the minority population. The first three formed an overlapping cluster, with the median home price being the strongest predictor (accounting for around 42 percent of the variation, with a chance of error of less than .001 percent). The size of the minority population added about another 10 percent. The total predictive value for both factors was 51 percent, with a margin of error below .00001 percent.

When combined on a single graph (see Figure 1), the figures for the forty cities for which all of the relevant data are available show a strong trendline for median home prices; the cities with rent control are predominantly clustered in the top right-hand quadrant. Of the four major cities with minority populations of more than 60 percent, the two with rent control (Newark and Washington) are right on the trendline, while the two without it (Miami and Detroit) are the sole "outliers"—cities whose rates of homelessness do not seem to correspond with their positions in correlation with median home prices.

Altogether, these data suggest that housing variables are a better indicator of homelessness than are the traditional measures of unemployment, poverty, and the relative size of a city's public housing stock. High median home prices are usually found in cities with strict zoning ordinances and a strong no-growth effort. Cities with a tight ring of exclusionary suburbs (such as Boston, New York, Washington, San Francisco, and Los Angeles) have high home prices. Strangely enough, most have also adopted rent control.

At the same time, rent control is closely correlated with low rental vacancy rates. Every city in the country with rent control (except Los Angeles) has a vacancy rate below 4 percent, while the average for cities without rent control is over 8 percent.

When viewed historically, these low vacancy rates are obviously the result of rent control rather than its cause. When most of these cities adopted rent control in the 1970s, all had vacancy rates around the norm of 6 percent. Rather than being spurred by low vacancies, the rent-control ordinances that swept the East and West Coasts during the 1970s were advertised as a response to inflation. The housing shortages came later. (New York, on the other hand, has had rent control since 1943, when it was imposed as part of World War II price controls. Vacancy rates stood at 10 percent in 1940, but have never been above 5 percent since the war ended; they have been below 3 percent since the late 1960s.)

Given these facts, the most plausible explanation of the relation of homelessness to high median home prices, low rental vacancies, and the presence

*Figure 1*

**Homelessness in Forty American Cities, Correlated with Rent Control, Size of Minority Population, and Median Home Price**

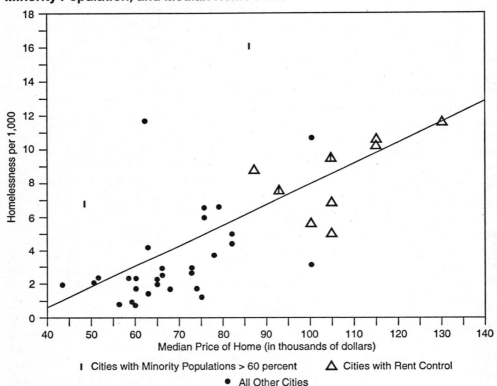

I Cities with Minority Populations > 60 percent  △ Cities with Rent Control
● All Other Cities

$(R = .649; P < .0001)$

of rent control seems to be what might be called "intense housing regulation." Many cities, such as San Francisco, Berkeley, and Santa Monica, have adopted rent control as part of municipal efforts to slow growth and stop development. These efforts are often aimed against new housing construction, particularly of apartments and rentals.

Since most communities that adopt no-growth ordinances usually like to think of themselves as liberal-minded, they do not like to admit to limiting housing opportunities for low-income people. So they try to compensate by imposing rent control, which they claim "protects" tenants from rising rents.

But of course rent control makes things only worse, by causing vacancy rates to decline and apartments to become much harder to find. The words of Assa Lindbeck, the Swedish socialist (and now chairman of the Nobel Prize Committee for Economics) can hardly be improved upon:

The effects of rent control have in fact been exactly what can be predicted from the simplest type of supply-and-demand analysis—"housing shortage" (excess demand for housing), black markets, privileges for those who happen to have a contract for a rent-controlled apartment, nepotism in the distribution of the available apartments, difficulties in getting apartments for families with children, and, in many places, deterioration of the housing stock. In fact, next to bombing, rent control seems in many cases to be the most efficient technique so far known for destroying cities.

## ATTACKS ON GROWTH AND SRO'S

Perhaps the best place to see this syndrome at work is in the San Francisco area, which has some of the country's most intense and innovative housing regulation and is also generally considered to be the center of some of the nation's worst homelessness.

It may be hard to believe, but housing prices in California in 1970 were no higher than the national average—even though the state experienced astonishing population growth during the 1950s and 1960s. It was not until the wave of environmental regulation and no-growth sentiment emerged in the 1970s that housing prices began to climb. Throughout California, the increase in home prices has consistently outpaced the national average over the last two decades. By 1988, the median price for a home stood at $158,000 there, in contrast to the nationwide figure of $88,000. In the highly regulated San Francisco Bay area, the median was $178,000, more than twice the national median.

California also experienced a wave of rent-control ordinances in the 1970s. Berkeley adopted rent control in 1971, shortly after imposing a "neighborhood preservation ordinance" that all but prohibited new development. The ordinance was eventually overturned in the California courts in 1975. Then in 1978, Howard Jarvis made an ill-fated promise that Proposition 13 would lower rents by reducing property taxes. When rent reductions failed to materialize, angry tenants in more than a dozen cities retaliated by adopting rent control.

As a result, housing in highly regulated metropolitan regions around San Francisco, San Jose, and Los Angeles has become very scarce. At the same time, homelessness has become a pronounced problem. Santa Monica, which imposed rent control in 1979 as part of an intense antidevelopment campaign, has become the homelessness capital of the West Coast.

Once growth control, tight zoning, and rent control are in place, even middle-class people may have trouble finding housing. A municipality in effect becomes a closed community, open only to its current residents (who either experience remarkable run-ups in the value of their homes or live at rents far below market) and people with strong inside connections. Mark Kann's 1986 book *Middle Class Radicalism in Santa Monica*, which generally praised the city's housing policies, speaks of a "woman who tried to get a Santa Monica apartment for more than a year without success[;] . . . she broke into the city, finally, by marrying someone who already had an apartment there."

No-growth ordinances and rent control have not, of course, been embraced everywhere; but city administrations have often produced comparable results through intense housing-code enforcement, designed to drive "undesirable" housing (and the people who live in it) out of their jurisdictions.

In *New Homeless and Old: Community and the Skid Row Hotel*, Charles Hoch and Robert Slayton have traced the disappearance of the single-room occupancy (SRO) and "cubicle" hotels that once provided cheap housing to thousands of marginal tenants in downtown Chicago. Over 8,000 of these hotel rooms—still available to Chicago's low-income transients in 1963—have disappeared, leaving barely 2,000 today. These lost accommodations were all supplied by the private market. Although remarkably inexpensive (often costing only $2 a night), these rooms offered residents exactly what they wanted—security and privacy. Most of the hotels had elaborate security systems, with desk clerks screening visitors and protecting residents from unwanted ones. In addition, the cheap hotels were usually convenient to stores and public transportation, allowing low-income residents with few family connections to lead frugal but relatively dignified lives.

What happened to these old SRO hotels? Almost without exception, they became the target of urban-renewal efforts and municipal campaigns to "clean up downtown." Intense building-code enforcement and outright condemnation drove most of them out of business. Strict zoning ordinances have since made it virtually impossible to build replacements. Hoch and Slayton conclude:

> We do not believe that the demise of Skid Row and the SRO hotels was the inevitable result of market forces, or that Skid Row residents embodied peculiar social and psychological characteristics that produced deviant and pathological social behavior.... [Instead,] this loss was the result of decades of antagonism from civic and business leaders, legitimated from the 1950s on by so-

cial scientists, and incorporated into dramatic change-oriented programs like urban renewal.

Nor have these policies abated today. Despite the hue and cry over the loss of SRO hotels, their replacement is still generally forbidden by zoning ordinances. In Los Angeles, there is a movement afoot to close down SRO hotels—even those subsidized by the city government—because they are not built to withstand earthquakes. Peter Smith, president of the New York City Partnership for the Homeless, comments: "It's essentially illegal for private developers to build SRO hotels in New York anymore."

## RESTRICTING DEVELOPMENT

What is causing homelessness, then, is the familiar phenomenon of government regulation. This regulation tends to escape the attention of the public and the enthusiasts of deregulation, because it is done at the local rather than the state or national level.

The truth is that cities and towns do not always welcome new development. At bottom, even the most enthusiastic advocates of progress would often prefer to see their own neighborhoods remain just as they are. People will usually settle for higher-priced housing, because it raises the value of their own homes; but few want tenements, rentals, or other forms of "low-income" housing.

Through regulation, most cities and towns hold a tight rein on their housing markets. Suburbs are particularly exclusionary, zoning out everything but high-priced single-family homes (which require large lot sizes), and prohibiting the rental of rooms or apartments. Cities themselves, although sometimes offering rhetorical welcomes, often play the same exclusionary games.

An example can be seen in Takoma Park, Maryland, a nineteenth-century "streetcar suburb" of Washington, D.C., which until recently had a long history of tolerant housing policies. Takoma Park is a hodgepodge of two-, three-, and four-family homes within easy commuting distance of Washington. During World War II, homeowners rented attics and spare bedrooms to wartime officials who could not find housing in Washington. This tradition continued after the war, when many returning GI's sought housing while attending nearby Columbia Union College. Many homeowners permanently converted their homes to two- and three-family units.

During the 1970s, however, a group of homeowners living in a recently constructed, more suburban part of the city asked Montgomery County to enforce a sixty-year-old zoning ordinance that prohibited rentals in single-family zones. (Zoning is controlled by county governments in Maryland.) After a long dispute, the city council adopted a compromise in 1978, which permitted anyone who was renting before 1954 to continue to do so for another ten years. In 1988 the reprieve expired, however, and evictions began. More than six hundred tenants were forced to leave their homes.

## THE APPEAL OF UTOPIANISM

It is important to realize that housing regulations are to blame for a lot of homelessness. But at the same time, we must acknowledge the impulses that make people want to intervene in the housing marketplace.

About a year ago, I spent a few days in San Francisco's Market Street dis-trict, a notorious skid row. Although not particularly dangerous, the surroundings were decidedly unpleasant. Weather-beaten young men, each of whom seemed to have his entire worldly belongings wrapped in a sleeping bag, lounged along the sidewalks. Ragged holdovers from the sixties perched on public monuments, performing drunken imitations of rock singers. Veterans of motorcycle gangs weaved past timid pedestrians, carrying on garrulous arguments with their equally disheveled girlfriends. Along the side streets, tattoo parlors jostled with cheap cafeterias, pornography shops, and the inevitable flophouse hotels.

It is easy enough to imagine some ambitious politician surveying the scene and deciding that it was time to "clean up Market Street." Such campaigns have occurred all over the country and have inevitably produced the disjuncture that we now find between the supply of housing and the price that poor people can afford to pay for it.

Yet distasteful as it may seem, skid rows play a crucial role in providing the poor and near-poor with cheap housing. Not everyone can live in suburban sub-divisions or high-rise condominiums. To provide for everyone, we also need rooms for rent, fleabag hotels, tenements, trailer parks—and the "slumlords" who often run them. Although usually imagined to be rich and powerful, these bottom-rung entrepreneurs almost always turn out to be only slightly more affluent than the people for whom they are providing housing.

In the utopian dreams of regulators and "housing activists," such landlords are always eliminated. They are inevitably replaced by the federal government and the "non-profits," orchestrated by the city planners and visionary architects who would "tear down the slums" and replace them with "model tenements" and the "garden cities of tomorrow."

It is not wrong to have such visions. But let us do things in stages. Let us build the new housing *first*—and only then tear down the old "substandard" housing that is no longer needed. If we let the best become the enemy of the good—or even the barely adequate—the homeless will have nothing more substantial to live in than the dreams of the housing visionaries themselves.

# NO

# Richard P. Appelbaum et al.

## SCAPEGOATING RENT CONTROL: MASKING THE CAUSES OF HOMELESSNESS

The U.S. Congress has recently considered legislation that would withhold federal housing funds from the numerous locales that have adopted rent control. Such legislation is supported by HUD [Department of Housing and Urban Development] Secretary Jack Kemp, who strongly believes that rent control is partly responsible for discouraging badly needed investment in rental housing. Sixteen states currently have laws that restrict the ability of localities to enact rent control, while another 29 have been targeted for such laws by the National Apartment Owners' Association and the National Multi-Housing Council. While the belief that rent control has adverse consequences for housing markets has long been advanced by housing economists, a new claim has recently emerged in support of anti-rent control legislation: the assertion that rent control should be dismantled because it is the chief underlying cause of homelessness. The evidence for this claim can be traced to a single study by journalist William Tucker (1987a, 1987b, 1989a, 1989b). Since homelessness is such a visible national issue, local rent regulations —affecting millions of tenants nationwide—are more vulnerable to federal anti–rent-control legislation than at any time in the recent past....

Despite the widespread attention it has received, Tucker's research is seriously flawed. The link between rent control and homelessness it purports to demonstrate does not withstand serious scrutiny. Given the political context in which the research appears, the following critique of Tucker's thesis is doubly important. Unchallenged, Tucker's work represents a serious threat to local rent control by linking it with a national problem of high concern. Pointing the finger at rent control can only divert attention from a serious effort to uncover and address the actual causes of homelessness.

The growth of homelessness during the 1980s is not linked with the efforts by a handful of local governments to regulate skyrocketing rents. Homelessness is directly related to the overall level of poverty, to the availability of affordable housing, and to the accessibility of support services for people

From Richard P. Appelbaum, Michael Dolny, Peter Dreier, and John I. Gilderbloom, "Scapegoating Rent Control: Masking the Causes of Homelessness," *Journal of the American Planning Association*, vol. 57, no. 2 (Spring 1991). Copyright © 1991 by The American Planning Association. Reprinted by permission. Notes and references omitted.

suffering from mental illness or alcoholism. It is no accident that the number of homeless Americans increased dramatically during the 1980s. The past decade has witnessed growing poverty, especially among the "working poor"; a decline in low-rent housing, including sharp cuts in federal low-income housing assistance; and a failure to adequately serve the deinstitutionalized mentally ill. As a result, since the early 1980s the homeless population has increased between 20 and 25 percent a year, according to the U.S. Conference of Mayors annual surveys (1989, 2). Moreover, the profile of the homeless population includes a growing number of families with young children, as well as individuals with jobs (U.S. Conference of Mayors 1989).

This assessment of the underlying causes of America's homeless problem would seem to suggest fairly straightforward remedies directed at increasing the wages of America's working poor, expanding the supply of affordable housing, and providing residential and social support programs for the nation's mentally ill. A comprehensive examination of the evidence gives no support to the claim that rent control is the root cause of homelessness in the United States....

## THE EFFECT OF RENT CONTROL ON INVESTMENT IN RENTAL HOUSING

Two hundred cities and counties currently have some form of rent regulation. This group includes over 100 communities in New Jersey, as well as cities and counties in Massachusetts, New York, Virginia, Maryland, Alaska, Connecticut, and California. Most of these ordinances were first enacted in the early 1970s. Approximately 10 percent of the nation's rental housing stock is estimated to be covered by some form of rent control (Baar 1983). Current rent control measures can be categorized as *moderate*, in comparison with the more *restrictive* rent control that was in effect in New York City during the immediate postwar period.

Moderate rent controls permit rent increases sufficient for the landlord to maintain an adequate return on investment, while protecting tenants against rent gouging. All ordinances currently in effect are moderate in nature. Such controls typically peg annual rent increases to increases in the landlords' costs, and exempt newly constructed rental units from controls altogether. They also often require adequate maintenance as a condition for annual rent adjustments: tenants in buildings that are inadequately maintained can appeal their rent increases. Some rent control laws permit vacated units to be temporarily decontrolled so that rents can be raised to market levels for incoming tenants, after which they are recontrolled. Moderate rent controls thus contain a number of provisions explicitly designed to encourage both construction of new rental housing and maintenance of existing units.

In a few highly inflationary California housing markets, some controls are coupled with an additional provision: they exclude increased mortgage costs from the formulas relating landlords' costs and allowable rent increases. This provision is designed to discourage speculation in rental housing. Under such an exclusion, a landlord who has incurred increased capital costs (either through recent purchase or through refinancing to obtain equity capital) cannot pass the higher financing costs through to tenants in the form of rent increases.

In sum, current rent controls contain provisions that are intended to guarantee the landlord a fair and reasonable rate of return on investment, while protecting the interests of tenants by preserving affordable housing. Maintenance is strongly encouraged; newly built units are not controlled at all.

Nonetheless, critics continue to argue that rent control discourages investment in rental housing. According to Tucker (1987a, 1987b, 1989a), for example, localities that enact rent control rob landlords of their rightful returns. So deprived, landlords cut costs. Maintenance suffers; buildings are abandoned. Badly needed new units are never constructed. Although rents may be lowered in the short run, the argument goes, housing scarcity eventually results. Scarcity, in turn, causes homelessness. In posh areas like Santa Monica, Cambridge, or the Upper West Side of Manhattan, yuppies squeeze out low income tenants in the fight for scarce apartments. In blighted areas like the South Bronx, buildings are abandoned, and eventually razed by arsonists or government bulldozers. Either way, says Tucker, the poor are relegated to the streets and shelters.

This analysis is not original to Tucker; on the contrary, it is shared by a number of housing economists as well as many people in the real estate community. For example, ten years ago a national survey of economists found virtually unanimous agreement that "a ceiling on rents reduces the quantity and quality of housing available" (Kearl et al. 1979). These conclusions are not based on empirical studies, but on theoretical assumptions about how housing markets are supposed to operate. The real estate lobby has been highly effective in communicating this analysis to its members and the media. Major news organizations, including the *Wall Street Journal* and *Forbes* magazine, have editorialized against rent controls (Gilderbloom 1983).

Numerous empirical studies have been conducted on the effects of moderate rent control on rental housing investment; none support the views just described. A comprehensive review ... finds that such controls have not caused a decline in construction, capital improvements, maintenance, abandonment, or demolition of controlled units relative to noncontrolled ones. This is because of the nonrestrictive nature of moderate controls, which, as we have seen, guarantee landlords a fair and reasonable rate of return. Rent controls eliminate extreme rent increases, particularly in highly inflationary markets, but they do not eliminate the profits necessary to encourage investment in private rental housing (Gilderbloom 1984, 1986; Heffley and Santerre 1985; Mollenkopf and Pynoos 1973; Daugherbaugh 1975; Vitaliano 1983). In particular, the vacancy decontrol-recontrol provision in some localities results in significantly higher average rents than those that would occur in the absence of such a provision (Gilderbloom and Keating 1982; Hartman 1984; Clark and Heskin 1982; Rydell 1981; Los Angeles Rent Stabilization Division 1985). While moderate rent control is successful in eliminating exorbitant rent increases, its impact on redistributing income from landlords to tenants clearly depends on the degree to which market conditions would otherwise have led to rent increases that greatly exceed the allowable rent levels.

## RENT CONTROL AND HOMELESSNESS: TUCKER'S ANALYSIS

Tucker's study is the first to look at the impact of rent control on homelessness. In order to support his argument that rent control produces homelessness by discouraging investment and thereby creating housing scarcity, Tucker sought to show that cities with rent control had lower vacancy rates and greater homelessness than cities without rent control.

For his primary data set, Tucker relied on the single comparative study of homelessness that had been done at the time of his study—the HUD survey of homelessness in 60 metropolitan areas (1984). HUD had conducted a random sample of 20 cities in each of three size strata (50,000– 250,000; 250,000–1,000,000; and over, 1,000,000). For each city, HUD telephoned people they labeled "knowledgeable informants" and asked for their estimates of the homeless street population in their areas. (Shelter estimates were more accurately obtained from information provided by shelter operators.) The various estimates for each locale were then combined into an average figure that was weighted to reflect the presumed reliability of the different sources. Tucker took the HUD estimates for the 40 metropolitan areas in the two largest strata. He then computed a homeless rate for each city by dividing HUD's estimate of the total number of homeless by the population of the core city for each metropolitan area.

Tucker did not rely exclusively on HUD's random sample of places; rather, he modified the HUD sample in several ways. First, he dropped six cities from among HUD's 40 metropolitan areas over 250,000 in population: Dayton, Davenport, Colorado Springs, Scranton, Raleigh, and Baton Rouge. These six places were reportedly eliminated because of "the great difficulty in determining local vacancy rates" (Tucker 1989a, 5, n. 4). For unexplained reasons, Tucker then added to his list one of HUD's smallest (under 250,000) metropolitan areas— Lincoln, Nebraska. He also mistakenly classified Hartford as a city with rent control. Finally, he added 15 additional cities "to include some notable HUD omissions" (1987a, 1); he does not explain how these cities were selected out of thousands of possible places across the United States. Since these cities were not a part of HUD's original study, Tucker developed his own homeless estimates by making telephone calls to unspecified informants in each city. This misguided sampling methodology yielded a final list of 50 places for his analysis.

Once he had obtained his list of places, Tucker identified factors that might be important determinants of homelessness. He originally chose rates of poverty, unemployment, public housing availability, and rental housing vacancy; total population; mean annual temperature; and the presence (or absence) of rent control. Two additional variables— population growth rate and mean annual rainfall—are employed in a recent study (1989a) but apparently not in the original studies (1987a, 1987b); nonetheless, the appendix in the recent study reports only the seven original variables. High rates of poverty and unemployment are indicative of an economically marginal population, and therefore should be associated with greater homelessness. Public housing availability, on the other hand, provides one form of protection against homelessness, and so should be associated with lower rates. Low vacancy rates indicate scarcity in the private rental housing market, and —according to Tucker—should be associated with both rent control and homelessness. Larger, faster-growing places may well attract the unemployed with the lure of jobs, thereby contributing to homelessness in such cities. Finally, locales with warm temperatures and low rainfalls have an obvious appeal to the homeless.

Having selected these key variables, Tucker employed them in two- and three-variable regression equations predicting homelessness. While his results vary somewhat among his various reports, he generally found that the only variables that made any substantial difference in the rate of homelessness were the local vacancy rate and rent control—and that the latter statistically accounts for much of the impact of the former. In fact, Tucker found that rent control by itself explains fully 27 percent of the difference in homelessness among cities; when combined with mean temperature, it accounts for 31 percent. According to these findings, homeless people are attracted to cities with hospitable climates; when such places have rent control, increased housing scarcity is assumed to result, and —with it—greater homelessness.

In evaluating Tucker's findings, it is important to bear in mind that he classified only 9 of the 50 cities as having any form of rent control at all. Since all of the cities had homeless problems to varying degrees, it is obvious that rent control cannot be the principal cause of homelessness, as Tucker contends. Miami, with the highest rate of homelessness in the cities under study, does not currently have rent control. Nor does St. Louis, which ranks second. Nor does Worcester, which ranks fourth. The fact that three out of four places with the most severe homeless problems lack rent control would seem to provide a prima facie case for rejecting Tucker's claim out of hand.

The first major difficulty in Tucker's study lies with his use of HUD's measure of homelessness (1984) as his key variable. According to two congressional hearings that examined HUD's methods in detail, that measure was highly unreliable. HUD relied on what it called "knowledgeable informants"—police departments, social service agencies, shelter staffs—who simply *guessed* at the numbers of homeless people in the 60 areas HUD reviewed. There was no actual count of the number of homeless in the streets, park benches, abandoned cars, and elsewhere—and certainly no estimate of the "invisible" homeless temporarily living in overcrowded apartments with friends or relatives. Although the guesses were mainly for downtown neighborhoods, HUD acted as if they applied to much larger metropolitan areas—Rand McNally marketing areas (RMAs), areas with four or five times as many people. This method, not surprisingly, produced very low rates of homelessness for the metropolitan areas HUD studied, since they guaranteed that homeless people outside the downtown areas would be excluded from the study. Tucker's principal variable, therefore, substantially undercounts the homeless.

The second major problem results from the questionable procedures by which Tucker arrived at his 50 cities, which —as will be demonstrated in the next section of this article—skew his results towards his foregone conclusions. As noted above, he began with HUD's random sample of 40 medium and large metropolitan areas, added one smaller HUD metropolitan area, selectively eliminated six places, and then added 15 others of his own choosing. Since only five of HUD's cities were among the more than 200 places with rent control, Tucker made certain that three rent-controlled cities were included among those he added. But sampling problems are compounded by the fact that the three rent-controlled cities he added are already presumably included in HUD's homeless estimates: Newark and Yonkers are part of the New York City metropolitan area, while Santa Monica is part of Los Angeles.

Tucker's third major error is his failure to consider the possibility that high rents might themselves be a chief cause of homelessness, while at the same time causing tenants to demand rent control. In other words, his reported correlation between rent control and homelessness might be an artifact of the association of both with high rents. He nowhere looks at the possible causal effect of rent on homelessness....

## WHY DO WE HAVE A HOMELESSNESS PROBLEM?

The United States now faces the worst housing crisis since the Great Depression. The underlying problem is a widening gap between what Americans can afford to pay and what it costs to build and operate housing. In this situation, the poor are the most vulnerable to joining the ranks of those without a home.

The number of poor Americans, now about 33 million people, is growing, and the poor are getting poorer (Center on Budget and Policy Priorities 1988, 1; Children's Defense Fund 1989, 16–26, 100–106, 115; U.S. Joint Economic Committee of Congress 1988, ch. VII). The largest increase is among the "working poor"—people who earn their poverty on the job because of low wages. Among the "welfare poor"—primarily single mothers and their children—Aid to Families with Dependent Children (AFDC) and other benefits have declined far below the poverty level. These are people who are only one rent increase, hospital stay, or layoff from becoming homeless. In fact, a recent report by the U.S. Conference of Mayors (1989, 2) found that almost one-quarter of the homeless *work*, but simply have wages too low to afford permanent housing.

The plight of the poor is worsened by the steadily rising housing costs that have plagued the economy throughout the past decade (see U.S. Comptroller General 1979 for an early announcement of the housing crisis). On one hand, rising homeownership costs have forced many would-be first-time buyers into the status of reluctant long-term renters, greatly increasing pressures on the rental housing market. Homeownership rates have been declining steadily since 1980, particularly among first-time homebuyers. Among households where the head was under 25, for example, ownership has declined from 23.4 percent to 15.1 percent of all households, a drop of 36 percent; for those headed by someone aged 25 to 34, the decline has been from 51.4 percent to 45.1 percent, or 12 percent (Apgar 1988, 24). In 1973, it took 23 percent of the median income of a young family with children to carry a new mortgage on an average-priced house. Today, it takes over half of a young family's income (Children's Defense Fund 1988, 57).

On the other hand, renters confront chronic production shortages and rising rents. Between 1970 and 1983 rents tripled, while renters' income only doubled. As a result the average rent-income ratio grew from roughly one-quarter to one-third; the proportion of tenants paying 25 percent or more income into rent increased from one-third to one-half. By 1985, close to one out of every four renters paid over half of their income for housing costs. Eleven million families now pay over one-third of income on rent; 5 million pay over half.

The problem is especially acute for the poor, who are now competing with the middle class for scarce apartments. It is estimated that by 1985 there was a national shortage of some 3.3 million affordable units for households earning under $5,000—an increase of more than 80 percent since 1978 (Leonard et al. 1989, 9). Among the nation's nearly 7 million poor renter households, 45 percent spent more than 70 percent of their income on housing in 1985; 65 percent paid more than half; while 85 percent—some 5.8 million households—paid more than the 30 percent officially regarded as "affordable" under current federal standards. The median tenant household paid almost two-thirds of its income on rent (Leonard et al. 1989, 1–2). The typical young single parent pays 81 percent of her meager income just to keep a roof over her children's heads (Children's Defense Fund 1988, 59).

Despite the severity of these problems, less than one-third of poor households receive any kind of housing subsidy (Leonard et al. 1989, 27; U.S. Congressional Budget Office 1988, 3). This housing subsidy level is the lowest of any industrial nation in the world. Some 6 to 7 million low-income renter families receive no housing assistance whatsoever, and are therefore completely at the mercy of housing markets that place them immediately at risk of being homeless. And, while the number of poor families has risen during the 1980s, the number of low-rent private apartments has plummeted as a result of rising rents, urban redevelopment activities, condo conversions, and arson. Between 1974 and 1985, the number of privately owned, unsubsidized apartments renting for less than $300 (measured in 1988 dollars) fell by one-third, a loss of nearly 3 million units (Apgar et al. 1989, 4). The swelling waiting lists of even the most deteriorated subsidized housing projects are telling evidence of the desperation of the poor looking for affordable homes.

The already existing shortages of affordable private housing were worsened considerably by the short-sighted actions of the Reagan administration. The 1986 Tax Reform Act, for example, removed many of the tax benefits that previously made it profitable for the private sector to rent housing to poorer families. It is estimated that the loss of tax shelters for housing will eventually reduce the value of income property by 20 percent, forcing compensating rent increases of 25 percent by the early 1990s. The National Association of Home Builders predicted that rental housing construction would decline by half as a direct result (Furlong 1986, 16); an MIT market simulation predicted an eventual loss of 1.4 million units (Apgar et al. 1985, 1).

The Reagan administration's budget cutbacks virtually eviscerated publicly owned and subsidized housing, all but eliminating the already small federal commitment to providing housing for the poor. Not only were safety net programs cut in general, but housing was selected to bear the brunt of budgetary retrenchment. Between 1981 and 1989 federal expenditures for subsidized housing declined by four-fifths, from $32 billion to $6 billion. Total federal housing starts declined from 183,000 in 1980 to 20,000 in 1989 (Low Income Housing Information Service 1989). The administration even proposed to sell off 100,000 units of public housing, an effort that was stymied largely because public housing tenants were too poor to afford their units. A number of specific programs, including several directed at the needs of the homeless, were "zeroed out" in the 1989 budget. It should be pointed out that, as severe as these measures may appear, President Reagan's proposed cuts were still deeper: philosophically committed to ending federal involvement in housing altogether, he was prevented from doing so only by the lobbying efforts of low-income housing advocates before a Democrat-controlled Congress. A single statistic tells the story in unambiguous terms. When President Reagan came to office in 1981, the federal government spent seven dollars on defense for every dollar on housing. When he left office in 1989, the ratio of dollars spent was 46 to one.

In sum, declining incomes at the bottom have converged with rising housing costs to produce a potentially explosive situation, which unwise short-term federal policies have served to worsen. Rent control plays no role in this unfolding tragedy. According to one estimate (Clay 1987, i), by 2003 "the gap between the total low-rent housing supply (subsidized and unsubsidized) and households needing such housing is expected to grow to 7.8 million units," representing an affordable housing loss for nearly 19 million people. This figure represents the probable constituency of the homeless, as the United States moves into the twenty-first century.

On its own, rent control can't solve the housing crisis. It is merely one tool available to local governments for confronting skyrocketing rents and a shortage of affordable housing. Tucker's study does not demonstrate what it sets out to do, and so cannot be used to justify a scapegoating of rent control for the mounting tragedy of homelessness.

## AUTHOR'S NOTE

We would like to thank Jon Lorence and William Bielby for giving us special assistance in the analysis of this data. Carrie Donald, Gary Dworkin, Neal King, and Bob Nideffer also provided important technical assistance. Special thanks go to Kevin Quinn and the staff of the Economic Policy Institute, who published an earlier version as a briefing paper. Authors are listed in alphabetical order.

# POSTSCRIPT

## Are Rent Controls the Cause of America's Homelessness?

This is a debate where the protagonists defend their positions with reasoned arguments and statistical evidence. But note, the provision of statistical evidence can itself be subject to challenge. Your task here is to bring critical questions to bear on the statistics used as you untangle the conflicting claims made in these two essays. Which essay provides the most reasonable set of assumptions? Which analysis employs data that are least subject to question? Which set of conclusions is justifiable?

These are not easy questions to answer. Yet if we do not attempt to systematically examine the assumptions, data, economic theories, and conclusions of empirical studies such as those of Tucker and Appelbaum et al., we would simply allow our uninformed preconceptions to determine which argument we would accept as the foundation for the public policy we endorse. If we lean toward the conservative, free-market camp, we might be inclined to accept unquestioningly Tucker's analysis, since it suggests that government interferences in the market rent controls cause the social problem of homelessness. If, on the other hand, we find ourselves sympathetic toward the liberal, institutional, or even the radical view of economics, we would tend to accept without question the Appelbaum et al. work, since they suggest that the interference-free market fails to provide affordable housing to the large majority of individuals and families who find themselves homeless. By now we hope we have convinced you that a knee-jerk reaction is never correct. That means that, on occasion, we must reject the arguments of some researchers, even if we want to believe them.

To help you make this determination, we suggest that you look at other published work in this area. In the anti–rent control camp you will find noted housing authority Anthony Downs, *Residential Rent Controls: An Evaluation* (Urban Land Institute, 1988). You will also find other works published by Tucker, since his work provides the empirical foundation for the anti–rent control camp. See, for example, *The Excluded Americans: Homelessness and Housing Policies* (Regnery Gateway, 1990) and *The Source of America's Housing Problem: Look in Your Own Back Yard*, Policy Analysis Series, no. 127 (Cato Institute, February 6, 1990). On the other side we suggest that you read some of the other work published by Appelbaum and Gilderbloom. Among other contributions to this literature, Appelbaum has published *Rent Controls: Facts, Not Fiction* (California State Senate Rules Committee, 1990). Gilderbloom has also written widely in this area, including "Towards A Sociology of Rent," *Social Problems* (vol. 34, no. 3, 1987).

# ISSUE 6

## Is Managed Competition the Cure for Our Ailing Health Care System?

**YES: Paul M. Ellwood Jr. and George D. Lundberg,** from "Managed Care: A Work in Progress," *Journal of the American Medical Association* (October 2, 1996)

**NO: John H. McArthur and Francis D. Moore,** from "The Two Cultures and the Health Care Revolution: Commerce and Professionalism in Medical Care," *Journal of the American Medical Association* (March 26, 1997)

### ISSUE SUMMARY

**YES:** Physician and long-time advocate of managed health care Paul M. Ellwood Jr. and George D. Lundberg, an editor of *JAMA (The Journal of the American Medical Association)*, argue that it is unrealistic to expect a return to unmanaged, autonomous, fee-for-service medicine.

**NO:** Harvard Business School professor John H. McArthur and Harvard Medical School professor Francis D. Moore warn that, if unchecked, professional commitment to patient care will be subordinated to new rules of practice that ensure the profitability of the corporation.

A quiet revolution has taken place in our health care industry. Overnight we have gone from a fee-for-service system, where health care users (consumers) had maximum choice and doctors and hospitals (producers) had maximum autonomy, to a system of health maintenance organizations (HMOs) and preferred provider organizations (PPOs), where both consumers and producers of health care are subject to the discipline excercised by those who pay for the large majority of privately provided health care: the insurance industry.

The results have been remarkable. In the 30 years from 1965 to 1995, the consumer price index (CPI) for all items increased almost fivefold. The cost of health care, on the other hand, increased nearly tenfold. Yet, if we compare the all-item CPI and the medical care sector of the economy since 1993, the rate of inflation in the latter sector has fallen each year so that by 1996 it is actually less than the overall rate of inflation in the economy.

Those who would like to blame the government for all the problems in our economy are quick to point out that the public sector is no stranger to the health care industry. For more than 30 years the U.S. government has actively shaped both the supply and the demand for services in this industry. Although governmental involvement can be traced back to the passage of the personal income tax in 1913, which explicitly excluded the cost of employer-provided, health insurance fringe benefits from taxation—a policy which reduced the relative price of health care—most agree that the real impact of government was not felt until the mid-1960s.

In an attempt to provide access to the U.S. health care system for the aged and often poverty-stricken retired population, Congress amended the Social Security Act in 1965 and created what is known as Medicare. A short time later, it extended these benefits to the non-aged poor by passing Medicaid. These two pillars of President Lyndon B. Johnson's War on Poverty brought about fundamental changes in the health care industry. Few can deny that some of these changes were good. Indeed, large numbers of American citizens were provided with much-needed health care, which they could not otherwise have purchased. But few can also deny that this government intrusion into the marketplace set in motion a tidal wave of price increases in the industry that are easily discernible four decades later.

These increases in price and relatively small (but very significant) increases in consumption of medical services have had major consequences. Consider how much of the U.S. income is devoted to health care. In 1965 it was 5.9 percent. By 1992 it had skyrocketed to 14 percent. Some estimated that without intervention it might have reached 19 percent of the nation's total gross domestic product (GDP) by the year 2000. In the face of these rapidly rising health care costs, President Bill Clinton proposed a new federal initiative: managed health care. This ambitious program, designed to provide universal coverage, was a market-based system that attempted to preserve consumer choice and build upon the employer-based private insurance system that was already in place. When the president's proposals were defeated by Congress, employers took matters into their own hands. They turned to the insurance industry, demanded lower costs, and threatened to take their business elsewhere if their demands were not met.

Seemingly overnight, doctors who were in a solo practice or who practiced in small groups found that if they did not join an HMO or a PPO, the large insurance carriers that represented the major employers in their community would not cover their medical charges. Indeed, when they did join these groups out of necessity, they found that they had to agree to a fixed, often low, price for their services and abide by a set of medical policies established by the HMO or PPO.

# YES

Paul M. Ellwood Jr.
and George D. Lundberg

# MANAGED CARE: A WORK IN PROGRESS

The modern *JAMA* [*Journal of the American Medical Association*] has been working toward comprehensive American health system reform since 1987, emphasizing cost control, access for all, and promotion of quality.[1] One of us (P.M.E.) has been developing market-based health system thinking for more than 25 years.[2] The concept of managed care is hardly new. The Kaiser plans began in the American West in the 1930s.[3] The massive reform that has occurred in the 1990s has been phenomenal and largely unpredicted, although much of it has been called for by many authors.[4-6] Many patients, providers, and purchasers alike consider the system to be in turmoil, some even in chaos. But movement is profound and irreversible, at least in the short run.

As we go forward, we believe that physicians should be more involved and influential in determining where the American health system is going. It is unrealistic to expect to return to unmanaged, autonomous, fee-for-service medicine where those who paid the bill often exerted little influence over medical practice. We should expect a more integrated, selective, epidemiologic data-dependent, and consumer-driven health system. We physicians no longer have a health system that was built by us and sometimes for us.

The new American health system works. It has contained costs, it provides easily accessible comprehensive health care to its insured members, and, on the whole, it has not yet jeopardized quality. But patients, physicians, the uninsured, and the country deserve better. The American health system is a work in progress; it can and, we believe, will get better.

## ORIGINS OF THE NEW AMERICAN HEALTH SYSTEM

Only 5 years after the establishment of Medicare, the Nixon administration became alarmed by the program's unanticipated run-up costs. Searching for remedies, the leadership of the Department of Health, Education, and Welfare in 1970 found—and the president accepted—a unique American approach to health reform combining social insurance with market forces.

The idea, labeled the "health maintenance strategy,"[7] was to allow Medicare beneficiaries to make a choice between health maintenance organizations (HMOs) and traditional fee-for-service systems that were competing on price and quality. It was anticipated that the government's actions would catalyze similar restructuring in the private, largely employer-financed segment of the health economy that also was having difficulty coping with medical inflation.

The HMOs were designed to take 2 forms: nongroup independent practice associations (IPAs) favored and pioneered by medical societies in the far West, and prepaid group practices (Kaiser Permanente Health Plan was the prototype). Both organizational arrangements were to combine in a variety of ways the health insurance risk-bearing function with the responsibility to deliver health care to voluntary enrollees for 1 year or more. In keeping with the free market philosophy of the Republican administration, rapid expansion of HMOs was encouraged by placing few limitations on the ownership or tax status of the fledgling HMO firms. The suggestion of the architects of the health maintenance strategy, that an independent commission be formed to establish measures to make HMOs publicly accountable for the impact on their enrollees' health, was not incorporated into the Nixon administration proposal.

The health maintenance strategy assumed that IPAs, which resembled more closely the existing arrangement of health care, would initially be more appealing to consumers and most practicing physicians. Later, as competition over prices and the novel approach to quality accountability took hold, the group practices were expected to be better posi-tioned to manage a carefully selected professional workforce and its attendant information systems and capital resources to produce more consistent health value for patients and purchasers. The health delivery function was so much more central, and difficult to manage, than the marketing and insurance activities that physician leadership in managing the health enterprise seemed assured—but it was not guaranteed by law or precedent.

Beyond the structural arrangements and the distribution of power and revenue so important to the supply side of health care, the demand side of the health maintenance strategy represented much more of an experiment. Would consumers be motivated to choose the best value based on a mysterious balance of untested financial incentives and as yet unavailable objective comparisons of health care results? It may seem obvious now, but early advocates of market forces could not prove that demand based on prices of HMO care would be elastic.

## THE TRANSITION

After rapid, unheralded passage by the House of Representatives, the more conservative Senate Finance Committee rejected the Nixon administration's proposals for HMO market-based "voucherized" Medicare. Although many years later Medicare risk contracting by HMOs was approved by Congress and the White House, no Health Care Financing Administration (HCFA) administrator has chosen to aggressively sell off to the private sector the opportunity HCFA has to run a huge public conventional health insurance organization. Furthermore, most of the new "health plans" were not quite ready for the high-risk, inevitably sick Medicare population. State-managed Medicaid also lagged despite a contrarian but successful switch to capitation in Arizona in 1982. Far from being the catalyst for public sector and private sector reforms, the government's program preferred the status quo except for complex encounter-based payment tinkering like diagnosis related groups for hospitals and relative value scales for physicians. Unfortunately, these approaches to price controls failed to contain Medicare costs.

The large private-employee-benefits purchasers of health insurance lagged by a decade in taking advantage of the concepts held within the ill-fated employee-oriented 1973 HMO Act. Then, in the mid-1980s, faced with the prospect of intensifying global competition for sale of products and uncontrollable health care costs, employer purchasers began seriously encouraging their employees to join health plans. But the employers, too, defied the health maintenance strategists by offering a very limited number of health plan choices (usually 1 or 2 health plans and an indemnity plan) in each community. The resulting health plans, consisting of rapidly assembled broad provider networks with rich benefit packages and low prices, appealed to employers and employees. Quality was dealt with the old-fashioned way, by word of mouth, and by satisfaction with patient-physician relationships. This approach to purchasing by large corporations more than anything else shaped the new health care marketplace. Large, overlapping provider networks required less financial commitment by health plans and less professional commitment by physicians. Most provider-controlled group practice and hospital-based entities couldn't cover the urgent territorial demands of the typical employer. Their unstandardized, unadjusted, and unaudited claims of qualitative superiority didn't sell to consumers.

The potential unprecedented growth in earnings in the burgeoning, formerly nonprofit, health industry attracted entrepreneurs and venture capital to the hot new health plans. Naturally, for-profit health plans, responding to Wall Street's short-term earnings growth mentality, avoided major capital investments except for acquisitions, and sought to circumvent the uncertainty that objectively competing overtly on quality might bring.

Individual consumers, especially those who had long-standing relationships with physicians, were cautious and slow to switch from the company's traditional indemnity plans. Ultimately they succumbed to the lower out-of-pocket costs, lack of hassle, and aggressive marketing of the new health plans. After all, the physician and hospital panels of the loosely integrated health plans were almost like the familiar Blues. Then, with the advent of point-of-service health plans, the door was open for consumers to go out of their own plan to any provider if it was worth the extra out-of-pocket payments. But they continued to rely on the informal advice of others about the quality of the health plan, supplemented often with information supplied by the health plan about the availability of primary physicians.

In the past 3 years, the Clinton plan of "managed competition" and the Republican "Health Contract for America" foundered on more than politics. Congressional Budget Office (CBO) uncertainty over whether savings would accrue from price competition induced delays and revisions. The arithmetic of the CBO—rather than just political ineptitude and organized backlash—killed major government health reforms.

Following all of this recent political posturing over a market-based approach to medical care was federal government inaction and a demand-side private sector revolution. But the character of the resulting 1996 managed care system (not health maintenance) has been a surprise.

Extraordinarily effective price competition has developed between various health plans. Prices were very elastic and the old system was even more poorly managed and inefficient than anticipated. There remains a moribund indemnity fee-for-service system (mainly Medicare) that may stay alive for a year or 2 on political life support. Consumers, especially healthy families, have been remarkably price sensitive, exhibiting surprisingly little loyalty to physicians or health plans....

## THE CURRENT ENVIRONMENT

Thomas Pyle has called health care's revolutionary changes "the unbungling" of health care; others regard it as the rebungling (personal communication, August 10, 1996, Jackson Hole, Wyo). The largest and fastest-growing health plans are national or regional for-profit entities over which providers exert little control. The health plan's power is exercised through legal contracts with purchasers, consumers, and providers. Genuine collaboration between most health plans' management and providers is tenuous, but the understanding of what the health insurance money is buying and its compatibility with sound medical practice have vastly improved. Physicians typically work for several health plans, making it virtually impossible to differentiate between them on the basis of population-based outcome data. The more highly integrated group practice plans (most of them nonprofits and provider controlled) have grown more slowly and locally but think they've found a way to reassert themselves.

Why does the new house of medicine look so different from what the HMO architects designed? The customers weren't ready for a spartan, efficient, high-tech, computerized, Saarinen-like house of scientific medicine. Instead, their tastes were traditional and tended to favor a new home that looked and felt like their old home—cluttered, warm, and secure, close to school, to work, to shopping, and to freeways. The demand side of health care preferred a much more traditional health system than the planners expected —one that was paid for in a new way but felt like the old system.

During the years since Medicare was enacted, American medicine has become, by some calculations, the world's largest business. The pace of restructuring in the American health system has been continuous, responding to innovations in health delivery, advances in medical technology rising public expectations, and the demands of other sectors of the economy. Now the new health system is faced with a congruence of discontinuities that could produce clinical advances along with economic ones more like the health maintenance strategists envisioned.

There will be no letup in cost-containment pressures. If anything resembling the Republican Medicare plan passes, it will be difficult to rely on the old underfunded Medicare as an income source. Medicare enrollees are already joining risk-based health plans at a record pace, and more plans are becoming risk contractors. Medicare consists of individual purchasers who do not require the broad dispersed networks originally sought by employers. Many have chronic illnesses and are particularly concerned about quality. The rush by states to Medicaid managed care plans opens up yet another individual-choice market that is not attached to any existing insurer except the state.

The public media have chosen to feature some health plans' highly paid executives, gag rules, and physicians' being paid to "undertreat." Anecdotes about skimping on care are hyped enough to make the cover of *Time. Barron's, Newsweek,* and *Consumer Reports* all have attempted to rate differences in plan quality based on inadequate information; yet despite anecdotes (some lurid) we have no objective evidence of any overall decline in the quality of care in the new system. Consumers are confused. State legislators—alerted by the headlines encouraged by offbeat and conventional providers—see votes in designing laws to inhibit health plans. More than 100 health care bills have been introduced in the California legislature alone.

Employers continue to demand low price increases in the 1% and 3% range but now want proof of quality. Employers are joining purchasing coalitions on a regional basis (like the Pacific Business Group on Health) and national scale (Washington Business Group on Health) to coordinate contracting and to assess quality. Some (like GTE) are paying higher portions of the premiums for those employees who join what the company believes to be the highest-quality health plans....

The easy ways to cut costs—like shorter hospital stays—are reaching their limits. Now it is time to evaluate the content of care, but few health plans have information systems or organizational structures to fundamentally challenge traditional approaches to medical care. The IPAs, group practices, and physician management corporations detect an opening. Many believe they can manage quality better than the large, more entrepreneurial health plans. Does quality competition, more choices, and the loyal chronically ill Medicare constituency provide an opportunity for physicians to bypass the managing health plan and contract directly with the purchasers? But even the best of the provider-controlled group practice plans have a long way to go in successfully practicing population-based medicine. At present, their largely uncomputerized clinical record systems and weak epidemiologic perspective leaves them unprepared for population-based medical care. However, advances in medical computing projects, like the Medical Group Management Association's conduct of outcomes management trials, and the accumulation of large open databases, like that of the American College of Surgeons on cancer, give a glimpse of the opportunity.

## WHAT'S NEXT

Health plans have become enormous and important actors in the new American health system. They have the capital and character to influence how care is delivered and how resources are used. If pointed in the right direction, even the most entrepreneurial Wall Street–oriented health plan has the opportunity to compete on quality. Such plans can establish extensive premier medical networks (PriMe) within their larger organization, assemble their own selective provider networks, integrate financial management (and rewards) more closely with clinical practice, and build a culture of excellence. Furthermore, they have the capital to buy advanced information technology to support the delivery of more scientifically based and more efficient medical care.

But we have no assurances that the competition of such plans in the current market will reward those who deliver higher-quality care. First, we lack strong national standards that hold these plans accountable for the results they achieve —either in terms of clinical quality, improving the health of their enrolled population, or even satisfying the expectations of their enrollees. Second, we have no evidence that the economic success of these plans is being affected by their clinical performance—purchasers and consumers have not, so far, rewarded or punished plans based on quality. Third, a sound market is always a work in progress. The large for-profit plans that appear to be dominant today may not be as important tomorrow. If purchasers and consumers had tools that allowed them to buy on quality, and if they could actually begin to use that power to shape the market, the thinking that lay behind the original HMO movement may still play out: provider-managed organizations might demonstrate that they are better able to meet patient expectations and get good results and operate more efficiently than their less integrated and disciplined competitors....

Two alternatives exist: strong public policy or effective public interest collaboration. Congress may ultimately be the proper body to articulate standards for health care quality, but it is unlikely to take this on soon or in the short-term. The recently established not-for-profit Foundation for Accountability (FACCT)

is an attempt to meet this need through a voluntary collaboration. Led by purchaser and patient groups, FACCT has just published its first recommended set of patient-oriented outcomes measures. These measures are the product of measurement science that focuses on patients' perceptions of their own function and well-being. Their initial measures cover diabetes, cancer of the breast, major depression, health risk behaviors, and patient satisfaction with care. The foundation will not be in the auditing business but is urging various accrediting and auditing organizations to apply their measures.

At this stage of our health system reconstruction, there is good reason to be hopeful. Compared with 25 years ago, we have achieved a great deal: creation of new organizations that can allocate money and talent in a rational way, reliable and pervasive tools for measuring health outcomes, growing consensus on the importance of preventive services, uniform screening and other "best practices" incorporated into guidelines, initial systems for reporting to the public on the quality of care they are receiving and the impact of the health system on the public's overall health, and information systems that support, monitor, and provide feedback on the effects of health services.

The signs are good for American health care. Consumers are being offered more choices that are more easily understood. Medicare is evolving from a traditional and unorganized array of providers to a more appropriate set of offerings that allow individuals to choose arrangements that best meet their own needs. And we are recognizing that the easiest, crude approaches to cost containment have reached their limits. Purchasers and consumers know that it is possible to compare plans and providers based on quality and are becoming more sophisticated in demanding this information.

Ultimately, this trend may lead to a sound, efficient, and truly effective health system. If we document the benefits achieved by our health care systems, we can respond properly to public concerns about expenditures, entitlements, and reform. At the same time, we will be ensuring that consumers are themselves responsible for their choices and that they are capable of making those choices in an informed manner to the greatest extent possible.

The health care system is coming out of the closet. Professional black boxes and undocumented claims of superior individual credentials and results are no longer enough! Organizational transparency and readily available objective evidence of health improvement is in!

Getting there will require the application of the following principles.

## PRINCIPLES OF ACCOUNTABILITY TO THE PUBLIC FOR HEALTH QUALITY

*The quality measures must be powerful enough to provide direction to the new American health system.* Plans and providers will seek to achieve the results on which they are measured and for which they are accountable. If the measures are sound and the public understands and values them, they will become the central tool of health care reform and redesign.

*The measures must anticipate the behavioral changes they induce.* If one plan or system proves to be exceptional at treating AIDS or diabetes, it will attract the sickest people in the community—and that's good! We should want the most competent and committed organizations to care

for those most in need. But we should pay them for the additional responsibility and costs they incur. Quality measures and payment systems must be risk adjusted in order to shape the kind of health system we want. Despite its importance, there is no well-funded coordinated effort to devise risk adjustors and to reward health plans that serve the sickest patients well.

*Patient opinions should come first.* Our patients pay us, receive our services, and have faith in our skill. In the market environment, they increasingly judge us. In the last 20 years, the science of measuring health outcomes and patient satisfaction has made enormous progress.[6,8] Although not without limits, many self-report measures are more reliable and rigorous than traditional clinical measures. The new measures of quality should emphasize consumers' perceptions of their own health function and well-being. At the same time, they should provide the level of feedback to providers that allows them to continuously improve medical practice.

*It's time for outcomes accountability.* Managed care organizations are structured to facilitate accountability. We finally have the measures and the structures in place to assess whether different practices or systems perform better. And we have an audience in purchasers and patients that is craving that information. As organizations become responsible for outcomes, we will see a growing link between the maturing disciplines of health services research and the clinical practices embraced by health systems.[9] Already many large health plans have created sophisticated research centers to help infuse their practices with evidence-based strategies, and they are building large observational series to continuously refine the care they provide.

*The influence of health plans on the measures chosen should be minimized.* Health plans are one important device for organizing and financing medical services, but there are others—some not invented yet. The standards for assessing performance must be based on the patient's experience of health and illness, independent of the particular structure or philosophy of the care providers. With billions of competitive dollars at stake, no plan can be objective about how it should be judged. The measures used to assess quality should not be constrained by the self-interest of the provider or financing organizations. We should not ignore the practical experience of health plans that have learned a great deal about measuring and managing quality, and we should remain sensitive to unnecessary burden or cost. But our health system is accountable to the public, and the public must decide what level of reporting or burden is appropriate.

The first phase of the health maintenance strategy was a bold and successful experiment that focused on and produced lower-cost health care. Now we are ready for the next phase that will measure and produce better-quality health care. And, surely, from the enormous savings that have been made through this revolution, we also will be able to find an incremental way to provide access to basic health care for all of our people.[10]

## NOTES

1. Lundberg GD, Bodine L. Fifty hours for the poor. *JAMA.* 1987;258:3157.

2. Ellwood PM, Enthoven AC. 'Responsible choices': the Jackson Hole Group plan for health reform. *Health Aff (Millwood).* 1995;14(2):24–39.

3. Smillie JG. *Can Physicians Manage the Quality and Costs of Health Care? The Story of the Permanente Medical Group.* New York, NY: McGraw-Hill Book Co; 1991.

4. Williams AP. Memorandum to the president-elect: parameters for health system reform. *JAMA.* 1992;268:2699–2700.

5. Lundberg GD. United States health care system reform: an era of shared sacrifice and responsibility begins. *JAMA.* 1994;271:1530–1533.

6. Ellwood PM. The Shattuck Lecture: outcomes management: a technology of patient experience. *N Engl J Med.* 1988;318:1549–1556.

7. Ellwood PM Jr, Anderson NN, Billings JE, Carlson RJ, Hoagberg EJ, McClure W. Health maintenance strategy. *Med Care.* 1971;9:291–298.

8. Ware JE Jr, Bayliss MS, Rogers WH, Kosinski M, Tarlov AR. Differences in 4-year health outcomes for elderly and poor, chronically ill patients treated in HMO and fee-for-service systems: results from the Medical Outcomes Study. *JAMA.* 1996;276:1039–1047.

9. Yelin, EH, Criswell LA, Feigenbaum PG. Health care utilization and outcomes among persons with rheumatoid arthritis in fee-for-service and prepaid group practice settings. *JAMA.* 1996;276:1048–1053.

10. Davis K. Incremental coverage of the uninsured. *JAMA.* 1996;276:831–832.

# NO

John H. McArthur
and Francis D. Moore

# THE TWO CULTURES AND THE HEALTH CARE REVOLUTION

There are two contrasting streams, two distinct cultural traditions, for providing services in the United States: the commercial and the professional. While these two traditions stand in sharp contrast to each other, they have shared a central role in the evolution of our society and its institutions. It is our purpose here to explore threats to the quality and scope of medical care that arise when the tradition of medical professionalism is overtaken by the commercial ethic and by corporations seeking profit for investors from the clinical care of the sick. We also explore the extent to which commercial behavior has invaded the nonprofit sector through the merger of the insurance function with the clinical provider in prepaid health plans. Widespread pressures to reduce the out-of-control costs of health care in this country, as well as the cost to individual patients, families, and employers, have accentuated some of these threats to clinical quality.

Effective communication between the commercial and the professional communities has been wanting with respect to their traditions, technology, and motivation in the medical arena. To the interested public, it appears that people are not listening to each other. It is our hope here to open communication between these two contrasting cultures, an idea expressed by C. P. Snow in his Rede Lecture at Cambridge, in which he contrasted the traditions of science and humanism.[1] ...

## THE TWO CULTURES: PROFESSIONAL AND COMMERCIAL

The fundamental act of professional medical care is the assumption of responsibility for the patient's welfare—an unwritten contract assured by a few words, a handshake, eye contact denoting mutual understanding, or acknowledgment by the physician that "We will take care of you." The essential image of the professional is that of a practitioner who values the patient's welfare above his or her own and provides service even at a fiscal loss and

Excerpted from John H. McArthur and Francis D. Moore, "The Two Cultures and the Health Care Revolution: Commerce and Professionalism in Medical Care," *Journal of the American Medical Association*, vol. 277, no. 12 (March 26, 1997), pp. 985–989. Copyright © 1997 by The American Medical Association. Reprinted by permission.

despite physical discomfort or inconvenience. There is no outside invested capital seeking returns from the physician's work.

The fundamental objective of commerce in providing medical care is achieving an excess of revenue over costs while caring for the sick, ensuring profit for corporate providers, investors, or insurers. A central feature in enhancing net of income over expense in a competitive market is a reduction in volume or quality of services so as to reduce costs, while maintaining prices to the purchaser. While cost reductions often diminish the quality of services, such economies are not always passed along to the public as lowered prices. Many families who seek insurance coverage but are excluded by unaffordable prices are forced to seek public providers outside prepaid plans and the commercial insurance system.

In this setting, the operation of market forces is hampered because patients and families can rarely acquire the information necessary to discriminate as to suitability and quality among alternative clinical services or providers. Without consumer input, market forces often fail completely, or behave perversely, acting strongly on price without regard to quality or breadth.

In purchasing commercial services, the public has learned to beware both of low quality and excessive pricing, as expressed in the Latin phrase *caveat emptor*—"let the buyer beware." The American public is gradually becoming aware that *caveat emptor* may soon become *caveat morbidus*—"let the patient beware."

## THE TWO CULTURES IN CONFLICT

When a corporation employing physicians seeks profit by selling their services, the physician-employees cease to act as free agents. Professional commitment to patient care is subordinated to new rules of practice that assure the profitability of the corporation.

Surprisingly, much the same enigma is becoming evident in the voluntary nonprofit private sector, particularly in prepaid health plans and teaching hospitals. Physicians working in such plans, as well as those in fee-for-service plans—both of them in the private, nonprofit sector—are finding themselves increasingly burdened by clinical constraints intended to ensure survival of the hospital, the plan, or the insurance carrier in a fiercely competitive market. While there is no legally defined profit for tax purposes in a nonprofit institution, the same results are threatened by the accumulation of large operating reserves, excessive construction programs, large executive cohorts at high salaries with business support structures, acquisition of other hospitals, or uncontrolled growth of research and teaching programs funded from patient-derived income. A teaching-research hospital that seeks excessive profit from patient care to support its nonprofit activities (teaching, research, community outreach, and education of nurses and paramedical personnel) behaves like a for-profit facility. Both in the commercial and the nonprofit sectors, an appropriate balance must be sought between patient-derived income, reinvestment, scientific and educational obligations.

Prepaid health plans inevitably involve a conflict between the commercial and professional cultures. As Gradison[2] has pointed out, prepaid health plans "merge the insurance function with the delivery function." This mixture is dangerous because when markets are saturated and/or premiums fixed, with costs still rising, financial ruin can be avoided only by reducing quality and breadth of services, endangering the health of individuals, families, or whole communities.

Sensing this inherent conflict, Enthoven and Kronick[3,4] introduced the term "managed competition," which signified protection for the public from exploitation under the pressure of commercial competition, giving further currency to the term "managed care."[3,4]

At the same time, while acting within the framework of professional commitment, some physicians and administrators have taken earnings out of the system that were beyond reasonable and customary rewards for such services.

## COMMERCIAL MEDICINE: POTENTIAL HAZARDS

### 1. Diversion of Funds

Funds for the care of the sick—whether from private sources, employers, or taxation—are intended to support disease prevention, public health, and the care of disease: public health and the health of the public. When a portion of this highly targeted national fund is diverted for corporate objectives (such as dividends, advertising, executive salaries), the resources available for health care are thereby reduced.

The same diversion from health care objectives results from excessive earnings by physicians or administrators in the nonprofit sector and the fee-for-service establishment.

### 2. Pricing

In the familiar commercial market for everyday goods and services, a less affluent population is assumed to exist that is unable to afford certain products or services and must "get along without." In medical care there is no such population: need is universal. The charity threshold is defined as the income level below which family costs for medical care must be borne by church, charity, or government. Unless regulated, this threshold will inevitably rise as health plans and other insured providers increase prices and/or decrease services to ensure profitability.

### 3. Risk Avoidance

Exclusion of individuals and families from coverage because of prior disease, genetic constitution, predisposition, or high cost is already noticeable in our health insurance system. Such risk avoidance denies care to those most in need and is not a characteristic of national health insurance plans in other industrialized countries.

### 4. Increased Load on Public Providers

Exclusion of individuals or families because of high risk or unaffordable prices will shift the burden of their care to other providers, including tax-supported public clinics and hospitals (federal, state, county, or municipal) and charity or church hospitals. Any economic overview of recent trends in the total cost of health care in the nation must quantify the increased burden borne by these public institutions.

### 5. Downgrading of Personnel

Expertise is expensive. Among physicians, nurses, and paramedical personnel, those who are most highly qualified require the highest compensation. These highly qualified but expensive personnel will be threatened by discharge in favor of others with less experience and fewer credentials but lower income expectations.

### 6. Loss of Free Speech

Another cause for dismissal is adverse comment or criticism about the quality of care being given. This amounts to a gag rule and is an example of the loss of free speech, not by order of public law but by the dictates of health care corporations that have confused commercial success (and a favorable public image) with professional obligation.

### 7. Distortions of Clinical Care and Ethical Dilemmas

It is in these areas that most complaints have surfaced, as frequently reported in the media. Problems include delayed admission, premature discharge, sloppy or unskilled services delivered in a shoddy and ill-kempt or unfriendly environment, avoidance of surgery or radiologic scanning, and the overuse of multiple profitable blood tests rather than definitive expert consultation or operation. Limitations in ambulatory care include denying prescriptions written by the physician in favor of similar drugs marketed by favored vendors and strict constraints on the amount of time a physician can spend with each patient. Time limitations on patient-physician contacts are particularly destructive to patient confidence and comfort. Rehabilitation and long-term care including psychiatry and terminal cancer care, care of the frail elderly, and care for those with advanced heart disease or stroke are nonremunerative. In a commercial environment seeking to maximize revenue from each clinical encounter, both volume and quality of such clinical services are inevitably threatened. These economies attract the attention of the media when they occur in a health plan providing extravagant expenditures for executive salaries, public relations, and advertising.

Such compromises and distortions of clinical care place physicians in a severe ethical dilemma: shall they follow the dictates of conscience and known good practice in giving every consideration to the aid and comfort of the patient, or shall they save money for their employers? Such dilemmas are among the most severe ethical challenges in the practice of physicians and surgeons today.

### 8. Managed Care—Cui Bono?

The term "managed care" came into common currency in the late 1980s to denote clinical practices in prepaid plans. It implied that an element of beneficial professional management, based on concern for patient welfare, would be essential to ensure both equity and quality in the highly competitive environment of corporate medicine. While it was never clearly specified by whom complex management choices would be made, or in whose interest clinical care would be managed, there was a tacit assumption that the provider would supply management in the best interest primarily of the patient, as well as the insurer or parent corporation. Now, only 7 years later, to many the term "managed care" implies the need for concern about the welfare of the patient because they suspect that care is being managed to minimize expense and perhaps even maximize income for the employer, provider, and/or insurer, while masquerading as a benefit for the patient. The term is increasingly interpreted as meaning "managed costs" rather than "managed care."

### 9. Commercial Insurance in the Nonprofit Sector

As mentioned above, many of the pressures of commercial medicine are already becoming evident even in the nonprofit sector, especially in prepaid health plans, because of their structural combination of the insurance function and the delivery obligation. In addition, indemnity insurance carriers apply continuous pressure on hospitals and physicians to lower costs of diagnosis and treatment, limit hospital stay, and curtail therapy.

### 10. Physicians as Entrepreneurs in Care and Research

The entry of physicians and biomedical scientists into the world of for-profit commerce is becoming an increasingly prominent feature of this landscape. Many physicians have become owners and managers of commercial hospital chains and treatment centers. Biomedical scientists long accustomed to receiving charitably deductible support from commerce are now becoming the owners, stockholders, and operators of corporations seeking profit from the marketing of their own scientific discoveries.

Sale of securities as well as the sale of products has sometimes led to large earnings for physicians. In some cases, the very scientists whose research was originally supported by public funds are owners of corporations that are often risky and financially unstable but sometimes very profitable. Every taxpayer has made an investment in these biotechnical corporations. It seems inevitable that some sort or repayment to a special government research fund will be mandated for some fraction of the profit accruing to scientific corporations when their product development has been based on research supported by public funds.

### 11. Neglect of Community Responsibility and Teaching and Research

Many community hospitals were established to include care for the poor, usually at a fiscal loss, accommodated by income from endowment or by shifting funds from other revenue sources within the hospital. As financial insecurity threatens their continuing support, community hospitals are faced with takeover by commercial for-profit corporations. The purchase of such hospitals by for-profit chains (often based in another city or state) generates transition funds that can be used to cover immediate welfare needs. Continuing support is often lacking.

Teaching hospitals have assumed responsibility for a share of the university functions of teaching and research as well as responsibility to the broader community they serve. This support is threatened by commercial takeover.

### 12. Monopoly: Loss of Free Choice

Free enterprise commerce fosters compensation and encourages consumer choice among alternatives, but these choices cannot operate in rural areas, smaller communities, or inner-city ghettos where the population and financial resources are insufficient to attract more than a single prepaid health plan or HMO. Freedom of choice, long considered an ideal by-product of free competition, is compromised.

### STANDARDS

Whether by voluntary self-regulation or by the passage of regional or national legislation, minimum standards will inevitably be required to abate some of the hazards to society and abuses of patient care arising from commercial pressures on professional behavior. These standards address the potential hazards we mentioned in the foregoing.

Acceptable profit levels will require definition, as well as allowable diversion of money to dividends, executive bonuses, promotional expenses, advertising, etc. By the same token, earnings of administrators, business consultants, and physicians in the nonprofit or private sectors will need to be subject to guidelines in the interest of equity and economy. Pricing will necessarily be viewed in light of prevalent income and affordability. Assumption of risk will inevitably be required of all carriers and providers to share the risk for particularly high-cost cohorts such as congenital anomalies, familial disorders, human immunodeficiency virus infection, and chronic vascular disease.

Criteria for effectiveness, quality, and patient satisfaction will need definition. Patient satisfaction, while clearly important, must be viewed with suspicion because approximately 80% of a covered population will, in any one year, be free of any disorder requiring medical care. Their "satisfaction" is easily assured. Only evaluation of the opinion of those patients and families afflicted with serious illness can patient satisfaction be a meaningful criteria. Morbidity and mortality should never become the principal criteria of effectiveness since they are both subject to manipulation by avoidance of risk.

Staff organization is best served by the unit system common in most teaching hospitals whereby distinct medical and surgical disciplines are under the clinical direction of highly qualified expert physicians rather than administrative executives.

Decoupling the individual physician from the insurance function frees physicians to manage their own clinical care procedures while maintaining the identity of the prepaid plan for business purposes. In decoupling, the physicians, as a group, contract or make other group arrangements with their front office (ie, the insurance function) to deliver patient care or community preventive medicine at a group price to the insurer, thus reestablishing the primacy of professional judgment and supervision of clinical care for individual patients.

Regular input of complaints and suggestions from both patients and physicians must be facilitated. Community responsibility should be accepted by all carriers and prepaid plans to avoid skimming—the enrollment of the low-risk, prosperous segment of a community—leaving newborns, the elderly, and those with prior illness to be cared for at public expense. For teaching hospitals this responsibility to their broader community includes a continuing commitment to share in the support of postgraduate teaching and research....

## POTENTIAL BENEFITS OF CORPORATE-COMMERCIAL MEDICINE

Cost control (ie, a decline in the national budget for health care) has been anticipated in the cost-cutting competitive atmosphere of a commercial marketplace. This may become increasingly difficult either to secure or to demonstrate because all patient costs must be embraced in such an accounting, including the increased burden on church, charity, tax-supported institutions, or the patient's own pocketbook. Physician earnings have already shown a decline; total remuneration of executives and administrators appears to have risen over the last decade.

If, as a result of the entry of commerce into American medical care, national standards become a reality—with appropriate agencies for surveillance, reporting, and local assessment of the adequacy of health practices—this will be a major benefit from the commercialization of American medical care.

While access to capital investment will be a benefit from the entry of commerce into medical care, some caution and some years of experience will be necessary before realizing this benefit. Capital investment in medical care that assumes responsibility only for the welfare of stockholders, investors, or executives will arouse public opposition and invite political attack. If private capital disregards community needs, communities will be less well off and the attractiveness of such ventures for investment will decline.

## REFERENCES

Snow CP. *The Two Cultures and the Scientific Revolution: The Rede Lectures.* New York, NY: Cambridge University Press; 1959.

Gradison W. Issues in employment and insurance. *Bull N Y Acad Med.* 1995;72:586–594.

Enthoven A, Kronick R. A consumer-choice health plan for the 1990's: universal health insurance in a system designed to promote quality and economy (in two parts). *N Engl J Med.* 1989;320:29–37.

Enthoven A, Kronick R. A consumer-choice health plan for the 1990's: universal health insurance in a system designed to promote quality and economy (in two parts). *N Engl J Med.* 1989;320:94–101.

# POSTSCRIPT

## Is Managed Competition the Cure for Our Ailing Health Care System?

Often considered the two most vocal advocates of managed care are Paul Ellwood and Alain Enthoven. Enthoven served as the principal architect of President Clinton's failed health care reform. Three books by Enthoven that discuss his viewpoint are *Health Plan: The Only Practical Solution to the Soaring Cost of Medical Care* (Addison-Wesley, 1980); *New Directions in Public Health Care: A Prescription for the 1980s* (Institute for Contemporary Studies, 1980); and *Theory and Practice of Managed Competition in Health Care Finance* (Elsevier Science, 1988). Ellwood and Enthoven are coauthors of an essay entitled "Responsible Choices: The Jackson Hole Group Plan for Health Reform," *Health Affairs* (1995).

Finally, there are several books by Henry J. Aaron, the director of the Brookings Economic Studies Program, which provide a more middle-of-the-road analysis. In general he believes that there are still major changes in the future of the health care industry that probably include a regulatory role for government. See *The Problem That Won't Go Away: Reforming U.S. Health Care Financing* (The Brookings Institution, 1996) and *Rationing Health Care: The Choice Before Us* (The Brookings Institution, 1990).

# ISSUE 7

## Are More Prisons and Prison Beds the Answer to America's Rising Crime Rate?

**YES: Edwin W. Zedlewski,** from "When Have We Punished Enough?" *Public Administration Review* (November 1985)

**NO: David F. Greenberg,** from "The Cost-Benefit Analysis of Imprisonment," *Social Justice* (Winter 1990)

### ISSUE SUMMARY

**YES:** Edwin W. Zedlewski, an economist with the National Institute of Justice, argues that investment in more prison capacity is wise social policy because the associated costs are more than compensated for by the value of the benefits society would enjoy.

**NO:** Economist David F. Greenberg alleges that many of the costs of imprisonment are excluded from Zedlewski's calculations and that he has significantly overestimated the benefits.

Few people feel totally safe walking the streets of urban America or even pitching a tent in a wilderness area. It is well known that the country is plagued by a terrifying crime rate. Crime reports in newspapers, on radio, and on television are daily reminders that nearly 6 million people in the United States annually suffer the effects of violent crimes—murder, rape, robbery, and aggravated assault. Another 29 million Americans suffer the effects of property crime—arson, burglary, and larceny/theft. Stated differently, the 1992 "crime clock" indicates that there is an automobile stolen every 20 seconds, a burglary committed every 11 seconds, a theft perpetrated every 4 seconds, a murder committed every 22 minutes, a rape reported every 5 minutes, and at least 1 robbery and 2 assaults occurring every minute of every day!

These figures suggest that the American criminal justice system is under siege, and there is no letup in sight. In fact, the 1990s may prove to be the most violent period in the nation's history. In the 10-year period 1983–1992, the numbers of persons arrested each year for committing a violent crime increased from 391,000 to 590,000, which translates to a 50.8 percent increase. Rather than winning the war against crime, America seems to be losing it on a grand scale.

Perhaps even more frustrating is the fact that the country's incarceration rate has increased at an even faster rate than the criminal activity it is intended to contain. More than three-quarters of a million individuals are behind bars; that is a population equal to the whole of Baltimore, Maryland, or Milwaukee, Wisconsin, and substantially greater than the population of Atlanta, Georgia, or Boston, Massachusetts. If we add together the prison population with those on probation and parole, our "city of criminals" would be equal to more than 4 million persons—the second largest city in the United States.

In spite of this burgeoning prison population, Edwin W. Zedlewski argues that the U.S. prison system is woefully inadequate. For him an efficient determination of how many criminals should be sent to prison is predicated on equating the marginal social costs with the marginal social benefits. This cost-benefit analysis would compare the costs associated with incarceration with the economic value of the benefits society would enjoy if these individuals were no longer free. In a cost-benefit analysis, as long as the value of the benefits of one more prison bed is equal to or greater than the costs society must pay for this bed, society should increase its prison capacity.

The two readings that follow take up the challenge of determining the associated benefits and costs of increased incarceration. This is not a simple summation of easily identifiable expenditures and costs. We caution you to read with great care the assumptions made by Zedlewski and by David F. Greenberg.

# YES
## Edwin W. Zedlewski

# WHEN HAVE WE PUNISHED ENOUGH?

Today's criminal justice system is in a state of crisis over prison crowding. Even though national prison capacity has expanded, it has not kept pace with demands.... National attention has focused on prison crowding. But the common cry among corrections professionals is not a need for more prisons but a need for alternatives to incarceration.

The search for alternatives to prison is curious inasmuch as public sentiment calls for more punishment. Recent legislative changes to penal codes in the form of mandatory prison terms for drunk drivers and for gun crimes, plus calls for the abolition of parole boards, argue for more prison space. Yet many professionals resist, arguing that prison construction is too expensive and does little for the reduction of crime.[1]

Do we need more prisons or more alternatives to prison construction? Before such questions can be answered, we need more information on both the costs and benefits of punishment. Since so many elements of the sentencing decision, such as victim harm, justice, and public fear, defy quantification, any picture will be necessarily incomplete. Nonetheless, the data assembled here quantify many of the missing benefits of prison capacity and thereby contribute to debate over prison crowding and alternative sentencing.

Significantly, even discarding the emotional and psychological costs mentioned, the data strongly support the need for more prison capacity. Subsequent sections of this paper apply the social cost-benefit framework to alternate uses of scarce prison space and the choice of alternatives to incarceration. These sections are less prescriptive because research findings are less definitive. They are sufficient, however, to offer at least some recommendations for policy makers.

### THE SOCIAL COST OF CRIME

Gary Becker first sketched an analytic framework for deciding upon optimal expenditure for crime control.[2] By advancing the notion that the criminal justice system ought to minimize the "net social harm" of crime, Becker recognized that while expenditures to reduce crime drained resources, crime imposed other costs upon a community. There is nothing mystical about these so-called social costs. Home and business security systems, victim losses, and prematurely abandoned buildings are as much expenditures on crime as prisons and police salaries.

Three kinds of costs are involved: harm to victims, combating or preventing crime, and punishing offenders. Their sum represents the social cost of crime. These elements are interdependent in that an increase in punishment can simultaneously increase punishment costs and decrease victim and prevention expenditures. The trick is to find the balance among the elements that minimizes the total crime bill.

Available data cannot determine with precise accuracy what criminal justice expenditures ought to be to minimize net social costs. However, the logic of spending no more on a problem than one can realize in return is useful in examining sentencing decisions. There is now, moreover, sufficient data available to enable us to assess the direction—more or less prison—toward which sentencing should move.

Estimates of the social costs relevant to imprisonment decisions are generated using the notion of balancing the harm from crime against the costs of incarceration. Admittedly, this exercise is artificial in that defendants are imprisoned for a variety of reasons—retribution, rehabilitation, just deserts among them. Minimizing social harm may not even be among the reasons articulated by policy makers. Yet, judges and policy makers do in some sense weigh the safety of the community against the costs of punishment in their decisions and in that sense they are performing a social cost-benefit balancing.

Through their balancing, judges and corrections officials decide whether society will be better off if certain defendants are set free. They are concerned with the future: whether defendants will produce useful social products through jobs; whether the correctional system should expend several thousands of dollars to confine them; and whether society will be spared damage from future criminal acts. Two "costs," at least implicitly, are compared, the costs of imprisonment and the costs to society of setting a defendant free.

## What Is a Year in Prison Worth?

What is the social cost of a year in prison? That figure can be obtained with reasonable accuracy. Custodial costs for a year in prison are about $15,000 according to the American Correctional Association. Construction and financing costs, if viewed improperly, can make building seem overwhelmingly expensive.[3] But construction financing costs are in fact like mortgage costs facing homebuyers who quickly find the relevant comparisons. To assess annual capital costs, one simply discounts future repayments into current dollars (to obtain the discounted present value of the investment) and then prorates total costs over the projected life of the facility. More simply, one can multiply the current interest rate times the value of the construction. Construction costs for new prisons average about $50,000 per bed space according to a recent General Accounting Office report.[4] Using a 10 percent interest rate on state bonds as the rental cost of capital, a prison space, with its share of the rest of the prison structure, costs about $5,000 per year.

Lost social output from the defendant is somewhat more difficult to value.

If a prisoner had been unique in his gainful employment, there would indeed be a loss. But, if imprisonment means that some unemployed person replaces him in the work force, then there might actually be a social gain. Added into these social dynamics are the net transfers of dependents, if there are any, into and out of other welfare support programs. A net social loss of $5,000 per year should generously account for lost social output.[5] Decisions to imprison, therefore, imply system costs of roughly $20,000 and total social costs of about $25,000. Subsequent development of this analysis shows that results are not sensitive to substantial errors in any one cost figure.

## Letting Them Go Free, Is Not

The social cost of an imprisonment decision, about $25,000 per year, must be weighed against the social cost incurred by the release decision. That cost can be approximated, albeit crudely, by estimating the number of crimes per year an offender is likely to commit if left free and multiplying that number by an estimate of the average social cost of a crime. We develop estimates of these two figures here, realizing in advance the substantial imprecision of the results. It is virtually meaningless to say that "the average criminal in the United States commits $q$ crimes per year" or that "the average American crime costs $X$ dollars." The numbers help focus attention on important issues, however. The number of crimes averted by imprisonment and the social costs attendant with crime are critical determinants of how much prison space we should have. The results here suggest the direction that sentencing policy should take, even if they do not suggest the magnitude of change.

Given that prison space is limited, judges try to reserve it for the most active criminals.[6] For expository purposes, we can envision omniscient judges trying to gauge a defendant's criminality in terms of past and future offenses per year. If he were to focus on crime control, the judge would send to prison those with the greatest annual offense rates, $q$. Since prison space is limited, he would eventually set free all those with offense rates greater than some $q$. The question is whether the $q$ crimes saved is greater than the expenditure to save them.

Judges are neither omniscient nor do they sentence offenders to prison solely on the basis of criminality. The average criminality of currently imprisoned offenders is, therefore, less than it would be under a pure and omniscient crime control sentencing policy. Still, knowing something about the criminality of current inmates at least helps us assess the benefits attained from current prison capacity.

In order to approximate the numbers of crimes likely to be committed by freed offenders, we used information about annual crime rates obtained from inmate interviews. Inmate characteristics should resemble those of marginal releasees—defendants that judges decided were almost but not quite deserving of a prison term. It is this group of borderline cases that would have been imprisoned if additional space were available and their crimes that would have been averted. Because of the severe limitations in predicting which defendants are most criminal, there is good reason to believe that inmate offense rates approximate those of borderline releasees.[7]

The estimates of annual offense rates here are taken from a survey by the Rand Corporation of 2,190 inmates who were housed in jails and prisons in California, Michigan, and Texas.[8] The average number of crimes per inmate serves well to assess the crime savings attained under current abilities to predict criminality.

... Rates varied from 1 to 1,000 offenses per year, and individual offenders specialized to varying degrees (a burglar for instance, may have been involved in few other kinds of theft).... Inmates averaged somewhere between 187 and 278 property crimes of various kinds per year, excluding drug deals. Those who said they had committed no property offenses —some 18 percent of the sample—have been excluded in order to sidestep difficulties in valuing violent crimes.

### The Victim's Bill
A final estimate is the value of a crime to society. It is the most troubling element in the exercise, partly because of the statistical errors, and partly because of the conceptual difficulties in defining social value. Rather than exhaust the reader with a long digression on the relationship between social value and market costs or between average expenditure on crime versus expected savings, we shall simply state our procedure. We counted every published expenditure on crime we could find and updated them to reach $99.8 billion (1983). We counted every victimization we could estimate for 1983 and obtained 43.4 million crimes. We divided dollars by crimes to get expenditures of $2,300 per crime....

Admitting the inaccuracies involved in the estimation, does $2,300 per crime seem plausible, nonetheless? Expenditures have some merit as measures of value because people do not spend more for services than the value they derive from them. Because the figure is a gross average, it probably overvalues petty larcenies and undervalues rapes or vicious beatings. Some overestimation occurs because not all criminal justice expenditures are crime-related. On the other hand, many household and urban expenditures are uncounted. At any rate, even fairly large errors will not alter the conclusions reached.

The estimates indicate that if judges were to sentence 1,000 more offenders (similar to current inmates) to prison, they would obligate the correctional system to roughly $25 million per year. About 187,000 felonies would be averted through incapacitation of these offenders. These crimes would represent about $430 million in social costs. The conclusion is insensitive to rather large errors in estimates. If we were to double the annual cost of confinement, halve the average crimes per offender, and halve the average cost per crime, we would still conclude that $50 million in confinement investments would account for $107 million in social costs.

Since estimates of social costs were based on money spent, not costs avoided, what actual savings would be realized is open to speculation. One can, however, envision several kinds of savings from declining crime rates. If householders and businessmen are objective in their expenditures, they would divert some money from protection of goods to the purchase of more goods. Fewer buildings would be abandoned because of crime risks. Inner city businesses would enjoy lower operating expenses due to reduced incidences of thefts. Mass transportation would be safer and more popular. The potential savings seem large.[9]

## The Fat Half of the Wishbone

Our cost comparisons were based on an implicit assumption that incapacitation of offenders was the only source of crime savings. An extensive literature[10] argues that in fact the majority of crime savings are attributable to deterrence. General deterrence is the crime savings accrued because potential offenders take into account the risks of punishment (as measured by the fraction of crimes that result in punishment) in their crime commission decisions. As the risk of punishment increases, the number of people willing to commit crimes decreases.

Estimates of the savings attributable to punishment risk vary with the data used and the crimes and sanctions studied. Ehrlich,[11] using state-aggregated data from 1960, estimated that a 1 percent increase in imprisonment risk (prisoners per crime) would produce a 1 percent decrease in crimes per capita. Wolpin,[12] using a national-aggregate time series of England and Wales, estimated that a 1 percent increase in imprisonment produced a four-fifths (0.839) percent decrease in crime rates. Wolpin also separated the deterrence savings from incapacitation or imprisonment savings and estimated that slightly more than half the savings were due to deterrence for both property and violent crimes.

Other studies suggest that the deterrent component is even larger. Cohen's[13] review of incapacitation research uncovered a range of 2 to 25 percent estimated for incapacitation's share. Nagin and Blumstein[14] estimated that if sentencing policies in effect in 1970 had been changed from a 25 percent chance of prison upon conviction of a serious crime to 100 percent and if prison terms had been reduced from 2.6 years on average to 1, crime rates would have been reduced by 25 percent while prison populations would have risen by 25,000 inmates. Focusing on the appealing concept of preventing crime through imprisonment misses most of the benefits of the punishment.

Deterrence estimates of crime savings help corroborate our findings. A 1 percent increase in 1983 state prison populations would amount to 4,390 more prisoners, or about $110 million in expenditures. Using Wolpin's estimate of a 0.839 percent reduction in crime rates means that 364,000 crimes would have been averted at an assumed value of about $837 million.

Not surprisingly, the cost-benefit ratio has fallen from about 17:1 to 7:1 as we moved from using inmate-based estimates of crimes averted to general population estimates; inmates are likely to contain a disproportionate number of high-rate offenders. So long as incoming prisoners resemble current inmates, the higher benefit ratio is pertinent. If incarcerations increased to the point that additional inmates more nearly represented the general population's propensities for crime, cost-benefit ratios would move toward the lower figure. Society is likely to receive a substantial rate of return on prison investments in either case.[15]

## SELECTIVE INCAPACITATION

Some opponents of prison expansion have argued that improved identification of high-rate offenders coupled with a policy of "selective incapacitation" might obviate the need for additional capacity. Selective incapacitation emphasizes future criminality as a cornerstone of sentencing decisions. It argues that long terms for high-rate offenders and short terms or non-prison sanctions for lesser criminals can increase crime savings without construction. It is in contrast to what many perceive current policies to be; namely, a balance between the offense committed and the offender committing.

The potential for selective incapacitation can be seen... from the Rand survey data.[16] Nearly half the sample admitted to fewer than 10 crimes per year. At the other extreme, some 20 percent admitted to more than 200 crimes per year. Imprisoning more high-rate offenders for longer periods would increase the incapacitation benefits of prisons.

Enhanced prediction of criminality would be desirable even if current policies were maintained. Unfortunately, the near-term prospects for improvements are severely clouded.

Greenwood and Abrahamse[17] scored prison inmates on a scale of 0 to 7 on bases such as prior record, drug use, and employment history and then predicted which among a sample from the 781 robbers and burglars from the Chaiken and Chaiken survey were likely to be high-, medium-, and low-rate offenders. They compared their predictions to inmate reports and concluded that they had predicted with fair accuracy. Unfortunately, this conclusion is sensitive to how their predictions are aggregated.

... The hypothetical policy under consideration gives long prison terms to high rate offenders and very short terms or probation to lesser offenders. This is consistent with a policy of targeting prison space for high-rate offenders. Using the study's classification scheme, judges would err by nearly 50 percent in both directions: every high-rate offender sentenced to a long term (15 percent) would be accompanied by a misclassified lesser offender (14 percent), and large numbers of high-rate offenders (13 out of 28 percent) would receive minor sentences.[18] One would expect classification errors to be even greater in any operational setting because a new set of offenders would differ from the study sample in terms of prediction characteristics.

Subsequent research in a decision-making environment reinforced pessimism over near-term prospects for identifying habitual offenders. Petersilia et al.[19] found that even comprehensive sentence investigations, which documented employment history, family structure, and criminal records, were poor predictors of the recidivists among a convicted population. Felons recommended for probation and felons recommended for prison but not incarcerated were back into the court system in nearly equal proportions. Only 3 percent of their sample of incoming prison inmates were predicted to be good probation risks.

Other problems requiring attention are the ethical questions raised for the nation's judiciary. Among them are the proportionality of punishment to the offense and the need to provide some sense of justice to victims. How should a judge decide between a first-time murderer and a career thief? Between imprisoning one habitual offender for 10 years and five lesser offenders for 2 years each? Such questions, largely resolved under current policies, must be reconsidered for selective incapacitation.

A final consideration is whether public sentiment would support long-term incarceration of juveniles. Youths under 18 accounted for over 30 percent of arrests for serious crimes in 1983; youths under 21 accounted for over 47 percent.[20] Thus, youths must figure into any crime savings calculated. Either current juvenile punishment policy, which minimizes the use of confinement, would have to be discarded or the hypothetical crime savings estimated from selective incapacitation would have to be revised.

The implications of this section are that selective incapacitation has many obstacles to overcome before it can be advanced as a viable policy. Besides the ethical issues of punishment structure and the social concerns over treatment of juvenile offenders, there is the distinct possibility that predicted crime savings are mythical. Increasing sentence lengths for some offenders means that bed spaces are taken away from other offenders. Reductions in punishment certainty are reductions in the deterrence power of sanctioning. Crimes saved through increased incapacitation may be fewer than those lost through reduced deterrence. Also, our current abilities to identify high-rate offenders from official statistics seem so limited that half the offenders sentenced to lengthy terms would likely be lesser criminals.

## IF NOT PRISON, WHAT?

The same statistics that earlier argued for additional prison capacity support the notion that some offenders are not worth imprisoning. Indeed, most convicted offenders serve no prison time. Few who do serve prison time serve their full term. In 1983 American correctional systems were supervising 2.4 million persons. Some 73 percent of these persons were in the community, 252,000 as parolees from their prison terms and 1,502,000 probationers who had not been sent to prison. Jails, which house both convicted and some pretrial persons, held 224,000 and prisons held 439,000 inmates.[21] Persons who received only fines or suspended sentences are not counted in these figures because they receive no supervision. Incarceration is the extreme, not the standard, punishment for a crime.

The criminal justice system operates under a punitive philosophy nonetheless, and 20th century penologists have designed many alternatives to incarceration. Fines, restitution, forfeitures, community service, supervised and unsupervised probation, and suspended sentences are among the current alternatives. But despite the flexibility implied by the range of possibilities, alternatives to prison use either of two mechanisms: expropriation of assets (or work equivalent of assets) or monitoring of subsequent behavior in the community.

### The World of Fines

Becker argued that fines were socially efficient because they punished offenders without draining significant amounts of resources for their administration. While correct in theory, the argument is eroded somewhat by two related considerations: a convict's ability to pay and the state's ability to enforce its fine policies. In *Tate v. Short*,[22] the Supreme Court ruled that fines could not be set beyond a defendant's ability to pay and then converted to imprisonment. This decision was buttressed by *Bearden v. Georgia*[23] in 1983 where the court ruled that unpaid fines could not be converted to imprisonment unless the state determined that the defendant had not made a *bona fide* effort to pay.

These decisions do not reflect disfavor of fines by the Supreme Court. In *Bearden*, the court explicitly recognized the enforcement of fines by imprisonment. What the court called attention to was the need for a rational and equitable fine structure. Amounts levied must be subjected to some sort of means test and enforcement must be tempered by subsequent considerations of ability to pay.

These restrictions do not appear to have severely restricted the use of fines. Hillsman *et al.*[24] found that fines were the predominant sanction for non-traffic violations in courts of limited jurisdiction (misdemeanors and lesser felonies) which handled 90 percent of all criminal cases brought and were also used in general jurisdiction felony courts. Only 2 of the 24 felony courts surveyed said they never imposed fines. The fraction of fine amounts actually collected, as much as 90 percent of the amounts levied, depended on the interest and persistence of the courts in collecting them.

Credible enforcement of fines requires the establishment and monitoring of payment schedules if the amounts set are anything but nominal. Setting fair but punitive fines requires information on the legitimate incomes of convicts. The equity problem has been solved in part in Sweden and West Germany by implementation of "day fines." Fines in these countries are levied in units of work days of the defendant. Defendant income is used to estimate the value of his work day and transform the days fined into a payable fine amount. Swedish and German courts enjoy easy access to a defendant's salary information, but it is not clear that easy access is an important ingredient of success. Simply asking the defendant his salary may be sufficient, particularly if the alternative to a fine is a jail term.

A popular American variation of the fine is restitution. Although the defendant is in essence fined, the fine amount is determined by the harm done to his victim and is paid to the victim, either in cash or labor. By combining punishment and compensation, restitution offers a strong sense of redress. But, only victims lucky enough to have a convicted assailant can receive compensation through restitution sentences. The large majority will have to look to other mechanisms. Victim compensation funds financed through fines and forfeitures, as established by the Victims of Crime Act of 1984, can offer more efficient and equitable restoration of damages.

## Probation and Public Safety

While fines are popular in misdemeanor cases, the courts sentence the majority of felons and serious misdemeanants to probation.... [T]he relative use of probation and imprisonment has remained fairly stable despite perceptions of a large-scale shift toward imprisonment. What has changed is the absolute use of both sanctions and their use relative to the number of serious crimes.

As practiced in the early 1970s, probation was a cornerstone of rehabilitation. Probation officers operated in part as social workers. They either gave referrals for job and family counseling, drug and alcohol treatment, and vocational training, or provided these services personally. As disappointment over the prospects for rehabilitation grew in the late 1970s, probation officers gradually took on more of a watchman's role even though many social services were still provided.

Whatever the underlying rationale, probation has been perceived to be a minor sanction. Polling college students, Sebba[25] found that they ranked one year's probation just below a 12-month suspended sentence and above a $250 fine in terms of severity. Surveying prosecutors, Jacoby and Ratledge[26] found that one year's unsupervised probation ranked between fines of $10 and $100; a year's supervised probation ranked on a par with a 30-day suspension of a driver's license.

Concern over the severity of punishment implied by probation and the threat to community safety has caused several states, among them Delaware, New Jersey, Georgia, and Washington, to implement special probation programs that have increased oversight and restricted freedom in varying degrees.[27] Perhaps typical, Georgia's Intensive Probation Supervision (IPS) is designed for prison-bound cases. IPS probationers must either hold a full-time job or be a full-time student, perform community service, and pay part of their supervisory costs. They average 16 contacts per month with their supervisors.

State officials regard the program as successful. Although IPS probationers have been more expensive to monitor than regular probationers ($1,595 versus $275 per year), they are still less expensive than confinement at $10,814 per year. Earnings and taxes paid by IPS probationers are offsets to program costs and their higher revocation rates—25.5 percent versus 16.7 percent for a matched group given regular probation—suggests that the increased supervision increases community safety.[28]

Many costs are not captured in this assessment, however. Among the missing are victim losses, repeated criminal justice costs for apprehensions and court procedures, and confinement costs for some of those revoked. Thus the efficacy of the program is unclear in a more complete cost environment.

Haynes and Larsen[29] made similar comparisons among correctional treatments under fuller accounting of costs.

They estimated the social costs incurred from a cohort of Arizona burglars in three supervisory settings: confinement in prison or jail; community supervision under probation, parole, and halfway houses; and, unsupervised release, possibly after one of the aforementioned treatments. They captured a substantial number of the relevant cost components: corrections supervision, welfare and other social support, crime prevention, victim losses, and subsequent apprehensions. Costs were estimated for a variety of crimes and were applied to information on crimes committed obtained from interviews with the burglars. No attempt was made to estimate deterrence savings.

They found that incarceration was considerably less expensive than community supervision when identified crimes and costs were accounted for—$11,640 versus $26,868 per year. As previous studies found, small numbers of offenders (10 percent) committed most of the crimes (90 percent).[30] Haynes and Larsen also found that recurring system costs were substantial: $2,640 for arrest and prosecution of a burglary and $701 or a simple shoplifting, exclusive of general crime prevention and victim losses.

### Twisting Punishment to Fit Crimes

Given that large numbers of convicted offenders are going to be released, how should one choose among alternatives to incarceration? Should a minor offense by a habitual offender receive the same sentence as a more serious offense by a first offender? Should equal offenses be treated the same if the defendants differ in criminal record?

If the answer to the last question is no, then there must be combinations of offender characteristics and crime seriousness that deserve equal amounts of punishment. This does not mean that identical punishments should be handed down to dissimilar convicts. We suggest that differences in propensities to commit future crimes, perhaps as evidenced by prior record, argue for different forms of punishment. Extending the cost-benefit reasoning presented at the outset, it is suggested that defendants with low propensities to commit future crimes should be punished as inexpensively as possible. As perceived future danger increases, the punishment should provide an opportunity to curtail future social costs. This logic suggests fines for first offenders and appropriately supervised probation for repeat offenders....

Absent evidence of habitual involvement in crime, the system should try to punish efficiently; that is, exact the penalty consuming the least resources. Properly set, fines can be made painful. If properly administered, nearly full payment can be extracted at low cost. Thus, fines produce economical deterrence. Evidence of future criminality, on the other hand, suggests that society may suffer additional crimes. The data presented here indicate that these costs are likely to exceed any reasonable costs of monitoring several times over. Supervised probation has a potential for detecting and limiting crimes.

Sanctions need not be administered separately. Judges can combined probation with a fine or with other forms of punishment. The important principle is that the punishment selected should minimize social costs while maintaining punishment equity.

## CONCLUSION

The objective of this paper was to present research findings pertinent to the questions of how much offenders should be punished. Rather than rely on traditional but difficult to quantify *desiderata* [desired needs] of punishment such as retribution and justice, a cost-benefit perspective was used to investigate whether society spends more money punishing than it gains from punishment. Existing data are adequate only for a crude answer to that question. Yet, the results overwhelmingly support the case for more prison capacity. The case for current use of probation and fines is less clear because there is less data on the application of these sanctions. It appears, nonetheless, that social costs would be reduced if more probationers were given either prison terms or fines. Incapacitating borderline offenders now crowded out by today's space constraints would likely cost communities less in crime expenditure than they now pay in social damages and prevention. Punitive fines for first offenders would deter others and reduce system expenditures on supervision while producing revenues and perhaps compensating victims.

## NOTES

1. See, for example, *Prison Crowding—A Crisis in Corrections*, a Report of the Task Force on Criminal Justice issues of the Policy Committee of the Center for Metropolitan Planning and Research (Baltimore: Johns Hopkins University Press, December 1984), p. 6.

2. Gary S. Becker, "Crime and Punishment: An Economic Approach," *Journal of Political Economy*, vol. 76 (March 1968), pp. 169–217.

3. See, for example, Gail S. Funke, *Who's Buried in Grant's Tomb?* (Alexandria, Va.: Institute for Economic and Policy Studies, Inc., 1982).

4. *Federal, District of Columbia, and State Future Prison and Correctional Institution Populations and*

*Capacities*, GAO/GOD-84-56 (Washington, D.C.: U.S. General Accounting Office, February 27, 1984), p. 30.

5. Clark R. Larsen estimated tax losses per prisoner at $408 per year and average welfare payments at $84 per year in *Costs of Incarceration and Alternatives* (Phoenix: Arizona State University Center for the Study of Justice, May 1983). The reason for such low average costs was that few of the inmates were employed in legitimate occupations or married at the time of imprisonment.

6. Some weight is undoubtedly given to a need for punishment of major criminal events rather than personalities. Justice demands that spouse killers be punished, for instance, even though repetition of the crime is unlikely.

7. Prior convictions alone have been found to be a weak predictor of underlying criminal activity. See Barbara Boland, *Age, Crime, and Punishment* (Washington, D.C.: The Urban Institute, 1978).

8. Jan Chaiken and Marcia Chaiken, *Varieties of Criminal Behavior*, R-2814-NIJ (Santa Monica, Calif.: Rand Corporation, 1982).

9. See William W. Greer, "What Is the Cost of Rising Crime?" *New York Affairs* (January 1984), pp. 6–16 or a comprehensive enumeration of social costs due to crime.

10. See A. Blumstein, J. Cohen, and D. Nagin (eds.), *Deterrence and Incapacitation: Estimating the Effects of Criminal Sanctions and Crime Rates* (Washington, D.C.: National Academy of Sciences, 1978) for an extensive review and assessment of the deterrence literature and evidence.

11. Isaac Ehrlich, "Participation in Illegitimate Activities: A Theoretical and Empirical Investigation," *Journal of Political Economy*, vol. 81 (May/June 1973), pp. 531–567.

12. Kenneth L. Wolpin, "An Economic Analysis of Crime and Punishment in England and Wales, 1894–1967," *Journal of Political Economy*, vol. 86 (October 1978), pp, 815–839.

13. Jacqueline Cohen, "The Incapacitative Effect of Imprisonment: A Critical Review of the Literature," in Blumstein, Cohen, and Nagin (eds.), *op. cit.*, pp. 187–243.

14. Daniel Nagin and Alfred Blumstein, "On the Optimum Use of Incarceration for Crime Control," *Operations Research*, vol. 26 (May 1978), pp. 381–405.

15. One cannot safely extrapolate too far from observed values of the data. A 50 percent increase in prison populations may generate more or fewer crime savings depending on how much deterrence is created by sizable increases in prison risks.

16. Table A.15 in Chaiken and Chaiken, *op. cit.*

17. Peter Greenwood and Allan Abrahamse, *Selective Incapacitation*, R2815-NIJ (Santa Monica, Calif.: Rand Corporation, 1982).

18. From Table 4.8, *ibid.*, all robbers and burglars in the study. Definition of low, medium, and high rates of criminal activity differed with each state and crime in the sample.

19. J. Petersilia, S. Turner, J. Kahan, and J. Peterson, *Granting Felons Probation*, R-3186-NIJ (Santa Monica, Calif.: Rand Corporation, 1985).

20. Federal Bureau of Investigation, *Crime in the United States: Uniform Crime Reports* (Washington, D.C.: U.S. Government Printing Office, 1984).

21. Bureau of Justice Statistics, *Probation and Parole 1983*, September 1984; *The 1983 Jail Census*, November 1984; and *Prisoners in 1983*, April 1984.

22. *Tate v. Short*, 401 U.S. 395 (1971).

23. *Bearden v. Georgia*, 461 U.S. 660 (1983).

24. S. Hillsman, J. Sichel, and B. Mahoney, *Fines in Sentencing: A Study of the Use of the Fine as a Criminal Sanction* (Washington, D.C.: National Institute of Justice, 1984).

25. Leslie Sebba, "Some Explorations in the Scaling of Penalties," *Journal of Research in Crime and Delinquency*, vol. 15 (July 1978), pp. 247–265.

26. Joan Jacoby and Edward Ratledge, *Measuring the Severity of Criminal Penalties: Provisional Results* (Washington, D.C.: Jefferson Institute of Justice Studies, 1982).

27. The Delaware program is part of a comprehensive revision of its criminal sanctions. See former Governor Pierre S. duPont's *Expanding Sentencing Options: A Governor's Perspective, Research in Brief* (Washington, D.C.: National Institute of Justice, 1985).

28. Billie S. Erwin, *Evaluation of Intensive Probation Supervision in Georgia* (Atlanta: Georgia Department of Offender Rehabilitation, 1984).

29. P. Haynes and C. Larsen, "Financial Consequences of Incarceration and Alternatives," *Crime and Delinquency*, vol. 30 (October 1984), pp. 529–550.

30. See for comparison J. Petersilia, P. Greenwood, and M. Lavin, *Criminal Careers of Habitual Felons*, R-2144-DOJ (Santa Monica, Calif.: Rand Corporation, 1977).

# NO

David F. Greenberg

# THE COST-BENEFIT ANALYSIS OF IMPRISONMENT

## INTRODUCTION

For more than a decade, U.S. prison populations have grown at an historically unprecedented rate. In 1974 there were 218,466 sentenced prisoners in state and federal institutions; by the end of June 1989, there were 673,565. The annual growth rate in this period was approximately 8%, much larger than the 2.8% overall growth rate for the six decades between 1925 and 1985. Jail populations have also grown—from 141,588 in 1972, to more than 300,000 at the end of 1989. So far there have been no signs of leveling off.

Critics of this expansion have long argued that the expansion of the incarcerated population is a terribly inefficient way of reducing crime rates. Pointing to the high cost of building and operating new facilities, these critics have called for shorter sentences and/or greater use of alternatives to incarceration for many persons who are now sent to prison (President's Commission, 1967: 38; AFSC Working Party, 1971; Keller and Alper, 1970; Citizen's Study Committee, 1972: 1; Board of Directors, 1973; Mitford, 1973; National Advisory Commission, 1973; Killinger and Cromwell, 1974; Hahn, 1975; Perlstein and Phelps, 1975; Fox, 1977; Dodge, 1979; Irwin and Austin, 1987). Greater use of these alternatives would reduce the prison population, or at least prevent further increases. The anti-expansionist critics have recently been challenged by Edwin Zedlewski, a staff economist at the National Institute of Justice. In a journal article, and in a summary of his research issued by the National Institute of Justice, Zedlewski (1985, 1987) concludes that prisons are a highly cost-effective method of reducing crime, one whose use should be greatly expanded. During the summer of 1988, newspapers gave his findings and recommendations wide publicity.

Zedlewski's recommendations come in the wake of public campaigns in which politicians and mass media editorialists have both attacked judges for being too lenient and advocated putting more people in prison. President George Bush has proposed adding one billion dollars to the federal budget

From David F. Greenberg, "The Cost-Benefit Analysis of Imprisonment," *Social Justice*, vol. 17, no. 4 (Winter 1990). Copyright © 1990 by *Social Justice*. Reprinted by permission. Notes and references omitted.

to pay for the addition of 24,000 beds to the federal prison system—a 77% increase in capacity—and the recent director of federal drug policy, William J. Bennett, called for even larger increases (Berke, 1989).

Zedlewski's cost-benefit analysis provides a seemingly scientific rationale for these proposals. Under this circumstance, his analysis must be subjected to especially close scrutiny. When this is done, it quickly becomes apparent that his computations are badly flawed. Once these flaws are corrected, Zedlewski's conclusions no longer follow.

In the pages below, I review Zedlewski's procedures and then show that they are invalid. I conclude with a broader discussion of the use of cost-benefit analyses in criminal justice policy-formation.

## ZEDLEWSKI'S COST-BENEFIT ANALYSIS

The fundamental premise of a cost-benefit analysis of crime is that the resources a society deploys in preventing or coping with crime could, in the absence of crime, be used in other ways. It follows that a policy designed to minimize the costs of crime must consider not merely injuries to persons and the destruction of property, but also the "opportunity costs" of preventing crime—the costs of paying for police, courts, prisons, watchdogs, locks, private security forces, taxi fares, etc. (Votey and Phillips, 1973; Cook, 1983).

It is assumed that increases in prevention costs will reduce crime, but if total costs are to be minimized, prevention costs should be increased only to the point where an extra dollar spent on prevention yields a dollar's worth of pre-

vented crime. Thus Hellman (1980: 59–60) remarks:

> The optimum amount of crime prevention for society to produce can now be defined; society should produce units of crime prevention up to the point at which the marginal benefit of the last unit of crime prevention equals the marginal costs of producing it. The marginal benefit of preventing one more crime is the harm avoided. The marginal cost is the additional cost of producing one more unit of prevention.

Eventually a point of diminishing returns will be reached, beyond which further spending on prevention will not produce commensurate benefits in lower crime rates. It is an empirical question to determine just what that point is.

To determine whether the benefits gained by putting people in prison to prevent crime are commensurate with the costs of incarceration, Zedlewski estimates both the costs and the benefits of doing so.

### The Costs of Imprisonment

To compute the costs of putting more people in prison, Zedlewski quotes from a 1984 report of the General Accounting Office the figure of $50,000 construction costs per bed, which, assuming a 10% interest rate for borrowed money, leads to an annualized construction cost of $5,000 per prisoner. This figure will obviously rise and fall with the interest rate. To this he adds an annual maintenance cost of $15,000 for a medium-security prison, and $5,000 per prisoner/year in social costs (loss of economic production, taxes, and welfare payments to families of inmates), for a total of about $25,000 a year.

## The Benefits of Imprisonment

Zedlewski restricts his consideration of the benefits of imprisonment to crime prevention. He estimates the number of crimes prevented by locking people up, taking into account both the incapacitative (restraining) function of imprisonment and its deterrent effect.

To estimate the incapacitative effect of imprisonment, Zedlewski draws on a survey sponsored by the National Institute of Justice and conducted by the Rand Corporation of 2,190 inmates of prisons and jails in California, Michigan, and Texas. The inmates told interviewers that they had, on the average, committed between 187 and 287 property crimes per year, not counting drug dealing. To be on the safe side, Zedlewski uses the smaller of these figures in his computations.

Because Zedlewski wants to examine the implications of expanding the prison population by sending to prison "borderline offenders—those . . . who would have gone to prison had space been available" (1987: 3)—(rather than by extending the sentences of those who are now incarcerated), he proceeds on the assumption that this figure can be applied to persons who are now not imprisoned, but are instead placed on probation or fined. If that assumption is correct, he reasons, then the imprisonment of a convicted defendant—who under present sentencing policies is not imprisoned—would prevent at least 187 felonies a year.

Further crime reduction, above and beyond what is achieved through incapacitation, can be achieved by deterring potential offenders. Zedlewski cites several studies on the magnitude of this effect, which found crime rates to be fairly sensitive to the size of the prison population. Interpreted causally, these findings suggest that the crime rate could be lowered by increasing the chances that a person who commits a crime will be imprisoned for it.

Translating an estimate for the number of crimes a given policy prevents into dollars is always a problem in cost-benefit analyses. The standard procedure is to value stolen property at its cost, to set the cost of injuries at medical costs and lost income, and loss of life on the basis of lost earnings for a person the victim's age, or at an arbitrary large figure such as $1 million.

This procedure is highly problematic. Victims are probably less likely to report a crime to the police when their loss is small; consequently, police records of losses are likely to be biased upward. Victims may also inflate their losses for insurance purposes. The psychic costs of crime, which often greatly exceed financial losses, are difficult to quantify meaningfully, but for many victims, they undoubtedly exceed the monetary value of lost property or the cost of medical care.

Zedlewski's highly original approach to the quantification of victims' costs is to abandon any attempt to establish an "objective" value for the cost of a crime. His alternate approach is based on the assumption that criminal justice policy can be regarded as if it were formulated by a rational actor. In the restricted sense that the term is conventionally used in economics, a rational person will try to minimize the total cost of crime and crime prevention by spending money to prevent crime only so long as the marginal cost of preventing a crime is smaller than the marginal cost of the crime prevented. Counting every conceivable cost of the criminal justice system, as well as private expenditures to prevent crime (and victim losses),

Zedlewski arrives at a figure of $99.8 billion per year as the total cost of crime in 1983. Victimization surveys suggest that there were 43.4 million crimes against victims committed in 1983. Dividing one figure by the other yields a cost per crime of $2,300.

Zedlewski reasons that imprisoning a thousand additional offenders comparable to those in the survey would cost an extra $25 million each year, and leading to 187,000 fewer crimes, worth an aggregate of $430,000,000. With benefits exceeding costs by a factor of 17, the conclusion that benefits substantially exceed costs remains valid even if there are some errors in the computation:

> Doubling the annual cost of confinement, halving the average cost per offender, and halving the average cost per crime would indicate that $50 million in confinement investments would avert $107 million in social costs (Zedlewski, 1987: 4).

### How Large an Expansion?
Zedlewski does not say by how much prison populations should be expanded. The critical question is the size of the population of offenders that is committing crimes at very high rates without being imprisoned. Presumably Zedlewski believes this population to be substantial; otherwise there would be little point to his advocacy. But how large is it?

Some research suggests that the proportion of offenders who are not in prison at any given moment is high. Greene and Stollmack (1981) used arrest records to estimate the number of criminals actively committing index crimes in the District of Columbia. Their estimate for the years 1974–1975 was about 30,000. In those years, the average total jail and prison population for the District was 2,187, about 7.3% of the total. The ratio of prison population to the number of reported index crimes is roughly twice as high in the District of Columbia as in the rest of the United States. Consequently, the percentage of the U.S. criminal population that was incarcerated in those years was probably somewhat lower than 7.3% (U.S. Department of Justice, 1977: 16–21).

In a model of the Canadian criminal justice system devised and estimated by Blumstein, Cohen, and Nagin (1976), the ratio of prisoners to active criminals was found to be about 0.05 in equilibrium. Of course, the Canadian prison population is far smaller than that of the U.S. But so is its population, and the magnitude of its crime problem. Cross-national comparisons of crime rates are always a bit fuzzy, but if one takes index crimes as a rough measure of the volume of crime, then the ratio of prison population to crime volume is only slightly higher in the United States than in Canada. This does not suggest that a much higher proportion of criminals is behind bars in the U.S.

If the estimate that only one criminal in 20 is incarcerated at any given time, then there are approximately 19 million offenders at large who are potential candidates for incarceration. This could imply a call for prison construction that would truly gladden the hearts of construction contractors. For reasons that will be discussed below, however, the figure of 19 million is quite misleading.

## A CRITIQUE OF ZEDLEWSKI'S COMPUTATIONS

### The Cost Computations
The procedure Zedlewski uses to estimate the costs of more imprisonment is,

as far as it goes, unexceptional. He simply adds up government expenditures and loss of revenue to arrive at $25,000 per year for each additional prisoner. These figures will undoubtedly vary from state to state because of regional differences in the costs of construction, standards of living considered appropriate for prisoners, etc.

However, as an overall figure, Zedlewski's number is unobjectionable. Yet, there are some costs of imprisonment not included in Zedlewski's estimation.

... [A] problem posed by Zedlewski's analysis is his assumption that the judicial processing of offenders will be unaffected by a tougher sentencing policy. There is every indication that this assumption is mistaken. Because most defendants want to avoid being put in prison, a sentencing policy that would incarcerate large numbers of persons who are not now incarcerated would entail additional court processing costs. Many defendants who now plead guilty on the promise of being sentenced to probation or to "time served" in jail awaiting trial would surely contest their charges if threatened with a substantial prison sentence. The proportion of cases that go to trial would undoubtedly increase. Defendants would be paying more for private attorneys, and governments would have to pay more for prosecutors, judges, subsidized defense lawyers, court reporters, and miscellaneous support staff.

Another consequence has been higher acquittal rates. In Massachusetts, a 1974 law required a one-year prison sentence without parole for illegal possession of a gun. Faced with this mandatory sentence, more defendants declined to plead guilty, went to trial, and were *acquitted.* Indeed, the acquittal rate rose from about 50% to about 80%. The net effect was to reduce the number of people going to prison on gun charges (Carlson, 1982; Currie, 1985: 63–64).

We can obtain a rough estimate of the magnitude of these costs by noting that in 1985, the total cost to federal, state, and local governments of judicial and legal services was $10.07 billion (Jamieson and Flanagan, 1987: 2). In 1984 there were 180,418 new court commitments to state and federal institutions. If judicial costs were allocated entirely to those cases that result in a commitment, the court costs per commitment come to $55,800.

Of course, a substantial fraction of these costs must be allocated to the prosecution of cases that do not result in such commitments. Judges and attorneys must still be paid for cases that are dismissed, or where sentences involving fines, probations, or short jail sentences are imposed. Numerically, those cases considerably exceed those that result in a prison sentence. On the other hand, the cases where prison sentences are imposed tend to be the more serious ones. They take more of the court's time, and they involve greater prosecutorial and defense efforts. It would be arbitrary to assign any given fraction of $55,800 to the prosecution of these cases, but the fraction may be large enough to add appreciably to Zedlewski's estimate of the cost of expanded imprisonment.

A further cost of imprisoning people is imposed on those who now benefit from the crimes prevented. Most of these crimes involve theft. Most of these thefts materially benefit someone, either the offenders themselves, or customers who purchase stolen goods at a discounted price. The savings to low-income consumers who live on the margins of subsistence may have substantially larger marginal utility to them than the marginal costs to middle- and upper-income victims of the loss of their property. The aggregate benefit to low-income communities of cheaper goods is probably quite large. Some of these benefits are documented in such ethnographic studies as Ianni (1974) and Walsh (1977). In the absence of such benefits, social welfare costs, which are ultimately borne by taxpayers, might rise appreciably.

These benefits of theft can be ignored only if one decides *a priori* that, as a matter of policy, benefits arising from illegal acts should not be counted. Such a procedure, however, skews an analysis in favor of the legal and economic *status quo*. Insofar as a cost-benefit analysis seeks to assess the implications of different policies or procedures, such an *a prior* decision should not be made without explicit justification.

**The Benefit Computations**

Zedlewski's use of the Rand survey to determine the benefits of expanded incarceration is, for a number of reasons, extremely problematic. First, the figure of 187 crimes per person per year pertains only to that fraction of the subject population that reported committing the particular felonies under consideration. Yet, 53.3% of the prison inmates said that they had not committed *any* of those crimes (these inmates had committed crimes that were not among those listed, e.g., drug offenses or kidnapping) (Chaiken and Chaiken, 1979: 6, 210). For this reason, the appropriate mean offense rate for the prison sample is not 187 offenses per year but $(187)(.467) = 87.3$ property offenses per year. This error alone leads Zedlewski to overestimate the benefits of imprisonment by a factor of two.

Second, the survey was conducted in three states—Texas, California, and Michigan—whose crime rates are all higher than the national average. These higher rates could stem from a higher proportion of the population engaging in crime, with the average offense rate per criminal being the same as in other parts of the country; or the proportion of the population that engages in crime could be about the same as elsewhere, but with active criminals violating the law more often. If the latter case holds, Zedlewski's procedure overestimates the national benefits of incarceration, because the incapacitation of offenders in other states will not yield as great a reduction in crime as in Texas, California, and Michigan. To take this possibility into account, Zedlewski's estimate of the crimes that might be prevented nationally should be reduced by about 20%.

In addition, the population that is now sentenced to prison is likely to be unrepresentative of the population that is now convicted but not incarcerated. There are several reasons why this is so. First, among those who violate the law, the frequency of violation is highly skewed. Recall Zedlewski's estimate that 43.4 million crimes are committed each year. Dividing that figure by the roughly 19 million offenders we estimated to be active every year, we find the average number of crimes committed by each offender to be only 2.28, far smaller than the 187 crimes per offender posited by Zedlewski.

The discrepancy is easily resolved: the offender population at large is extremely heterogeneous. What research has shown to be true of prison inmates is no doubt true of offenders outside prison as well—a small proportion commits many crimes, while a much larger proportion commits few. Surely this is true of probationers as well. Some may be committing crime at rates comparable to the high-frequency offenders in the Rand study. How many of them are doing so is unknown, as the shape of the distribution of offenses across offenders is not yet well known.

Selection from this heterogeneous population of offenders is unlikely to be totally random. Other things being equal, the more often people violate the law, the greater the likelihood that they will be arrested for at least one of the violations. Thus, the apprehended population is likely in the aggregate to commit crimes at higher frequencies than the offender population at large.

After conviction, further selection occurs. A study of federal sentencing in San Francisco found that probationers differed from those sent to prison in many ways—educational attainment, marital status, stability of residence and employment, dishonorable discharge from military status, pre-arrest income, participation in church activities, and length of prior criminal record—that are expected to be associated with lower rates of criminality (Robison et al., 1969). Indeed, many studies of the determinants of sentencing have found that length of prior record is a major influence on a judge's decision to imprison or release a convicted defendant (Vera Institute of Justice, 1977; Greenwood, 1980; Hagan and Bumiller, 1983; Panel on Sentencing Research, 1983). Within the Rand inmate sample, there is a positive relationship between self-reported offending rates and having a previous official record (Chaiken and Chaiken, 1979: 85–124).

These expectations are confirmed by studies comparing the recidivism of probationers and ex-prisoners. In the San Francisco study, 19.4% of the probationers recidivated, as did 35.4% of those sentenced to prison and then released. Wisconsin felony offenders placed on probation recidivated less often than parolees (29.4% vs. 39.4%), though the difference was largely confined to those without a prior record (Babst and Mannering, 1965). Adults placed on probation by the Superior Court in California's largest counties avoided rearrest more often than those who had been jailed (65.8% versus 48.6% after one year) (Beattie and Bridges, 1970). In a recent study of offenders from urban Los Angeles and Alameda counties, 63% of probationers and 72% of parolees were rearrested on new charges within two years (Petersilia and Turner, 1986). And in two other studies, the rate of recidivism was 22% lower for probationers than for released prisoners (Vito, 1987a; 1987b). Naturally enough, the magnitude of the differences varies with the jurisdiction, as do the absolute levels of recidivism; but the direction of the differences is consistent.

These findings have extremely important implications. The use of self-reports from existing prison inmates to determine how much crime would be prevented by incarcerating persons now placed on probation depends critically on the assumption that the distribution of offense rates in the target population is similar to the distribution of offense rates in the study sample. For the reasons just rehearsed, that assumption is most unlikely to be true. The target population is likely to be less criminally active than the study sample, and less seriously criminal.

Had we a reliable method for identifying the high-frequency offenders, it might matter little for a policy designed to achieve marginal effects that many offenders violate the law at low frequencies. Yet, the accuracy of prediction methods is notoriously poor. While one can select high-frequency offenders with a precision that exceeds random guessing, the improvement is usually modest. This means that any selection scheme is likely to miss some high-frequency offenders, and incarcerate many low-frequency offenders, a process that reduces the volume of crime prevented (AFSC Working Party, 1971; Von Hirsch, 1972, 1985: 105–114; Greenberg, 1975; Monahan, 1981; Blackmore and Welsh, 1983). Moreover, some predictors that could be used for predictive purposes are presumably already available to judges and play a role in the decision to grant or deny probation now. This makes it seem unlikely that there is a substantial body of identifiable high-crime probationers who are not being imprisoned already. . . .

It is also possible that incarcerating convicted criminals leads them to commit more crimes. Incarceration can do this by stigmatizing convicts, weakening their ties to others who are not engaged in crime (family members, fellow workers, and community members), placing them in a milieu that facilitates affiliation with other criminals, generating feelings of bitterness toward "the law" or "respectable" people, attenuating their work skills, etc. These processes could lengthen crime careers or increase rates of return to crime by released prisoners.

It is not altogether easy to determine whether this happens, and if so, to what extent. A naive comparison of recidivism rates of probationers and ex-prisoners falters because the selection procedures that determine who is sent to prison serve as a filter that tends to keep those with low rates of involvement in crime out of prison. So the two populations are not entirely comparable; that is, they may differ in ways that account for differences in recidivism,

independently of the criminal justice disposition they receive. However, one recent study that attempted to take account of such differences statistically found that imprisonment tended to *enhance* rates of return to crime (Petersilia and Turner, 1986).

If criminal careers are on the average long, even modest enhancements of this sort could negate much of the crime reduction that incapacitation achieves. Moreover, they will increase imprisonment costs, because recidivist criminals will return to the courts more often, and be imprisoned in the future for parole violations and new convictions.

A check of Zedlewski's high estimates for the amount of crime more imprisonment would prevent can be obtained by noting that changes over time in prison populations create "natural experiments" whose consequences for the crime rate can be readily assessed. If it is true that large increases in prison populations produce large reductions in crime rates, then the large increases in prison populations seen in recent years should already have produced large reductions in crime. A few simple "back of the envelope" calculations provide telling evidence that this has not occurred.

Between 1980 and 1985, for example, U.S. prison populations grew by 165,642, while index crimes reported to the police fell by 978,300. This comes to 5.91 index crimes per prisoner. This figure, unlike Zedlewski's, is comparable in magnitude to empirical estimates others have obtained (Greenberg, 1975; Cohen, 1978, 1983; Moore et al., 1984). Assuming a causal relationship, it follows that an increase in the prison population of 100,000 (an increase of 31.6%) would have reduced the number of index crimes committed by 591,000—a reduction of approximately 4%. This very modest reduction, corresponding to an elasticity of about −.123, suggests that imprisonment is a relatively inefficient way to reduce crime.

Our conclusion that rates of crime are relatively insensitive to the size of the prison population is confirmed by a study of imprisonment and crime rates in Illinois, where a program designed to relieve prison overcrowding reduced the size of the prison population by about 10% from the level to which it would otherwise have grown. Austin (1986) estimates that this reduction increased the crime rate by less than 1% (corresponding to an elasticity of approximately −.10).

Had Zedlewski's estimate of 187 felonies been valid, the number of index crimes (assuming for the sake of simplicity that all those felonies were index crimes) committed in the United States would have fallen by 30,975,054. Since there were 13,408,300 index crimes reported to the police in 1980, the index crime rate would have fallen to zero by 1985 (even if we take crimes not reported to the police into account) had Zedlewski's estimate been valid.

Alternately, we can look at victimization surveys. Between 1980 and 1985, victimizations (as estimated by household surveys) declined from 40,252,000 to 34,864,000. If this reduction is attributed entirely to the growth in prison population, the imprisonment of a single offender prevents 32.65 victimizations per year. Had the Zedlewski estimate of 187 victimizations been valid, victimizations would have fallen to 9,276,946, less than one-third their actual level. Further growth in prison populations after 1985 would have brought the victimization rate down to zero. Nothing of the kind has happened.

It must be stressed that these estimates are not to be taken too literally. My choice of years was arbitrary. Had I chosen a different set of years my estimates would have been somewhat different. For example, a comparison of index crime rates in 1981 and 1985 leads to the conclusion that the average prisoner commits 8.13 crimes while at large. With 1982 as a base year, the figure would have been 5.60. Comparing 1985 with 1979, one would conclude that the growth in the prison population did not prevent any crimes at all (the crime rate was higher in 1985 than in 1979 even though the prison population had grown).

It could be objected that other factors, which tend to increase the crime rate, may have been at work in these years. In the absence of the rapid expansion of prison populations that occurred, perhaps the crime rate would have risen more dramatically. There is, no doubt, some validity to this argument. The population was growing, and cultural and life-style changes contributing to the growth in crime may also have been taking place. Yet the upheavals of the 1960s were over. Though social change was continuing, it was not of such a large magnitude that it could conceivably have nullified the crime-prevention effects of such a large increase in the prison population, if Zedlewski's figures bear any resemblance to reality. The more plausible conclusion is that they do not.

This conclusion is strengthened when demographic changes occurring during this period are taken into account. Between 1980 and 1985, the age composition of the U.S. population shifted. In 1985 there were fewer people in the youthful high-crime-rate age brackets than there were in 1980. This demographic shift undoubtedly contributed to the observed decline in crime rates (Blumstein, 1985; Cohen, 1985; Blumstein, Cohen, and Rosenfeld, 1986; Steffensmeier and Harer, 1987). Taking this demographic shift into account would *reduce* one's estimates of the crime reduction that might be accomplished through an expansion of the prison population.

Before proceeding to the final step in Zedlewski's analysis—attaching a monetary value to each crime prevented, we may pause to point out the implications for the comparison of costs and benefits to the scaling down of the average rate of crimes per marginal candidate for incarceration. Taking without question Zedlewski's estimate of the dollar value of preventing a crime to be $2,300, the value of the crimes prevented by locking up a marginal offender who commits 10 crimes a year is $23,000 per year, slightly *less* than the cost of a year's incarceration.

But can the figure of $2,300 be trusted? There are several reasons it cannot. First, a substantial fraction of the amount of money spent on crime prevention and control goes for traffic offenses, and crimes that are not victimizing at all, such as narcotics violations and prostitution. Taxpayers do not pick and choose the kinds of crimes the criminal justice system prosecutes; given that choice, some of us might opt for a very different allocation of resources than the present one. As Zimring and Hawkins (1988) note, the figure of $2,300 is an average over all kinds of offenses, some of which would no doubt be costed at much more than $2,300, others at less. Under these circumstances, an average figure may not mean much.

Second, budgeting procedures for public goods can create a "fiscal illusion" that makes it difficult for taxpayers to know the full costs of providing those services

publicly. This difficulty biases the provision of public goods toward overspending (Buchanan, 1967: Chapter 10).

Third, Zedlewski forgets that if public spending were increased exogenously, individuals might simply reduce their own private spending on crime prevention (Clotfelder, 1977). Depending on whether private or public expenditures are more efficient in preventing crime, a change in the mix of private and public expenditures might raise or lower crime rates.

Fourth, the procedure by which Zedlewski derives his figure for the amount individuals are willing to pay to prevent crime is entirely mistaken. Recall that Zedlewski derived this figure by adding victim losses of $35.4 billion to miscellaneous private and public expenditures for the prevention and punishment of crime ($61.4 billion). Though this may be the total cost of crime, it is not the appropriate figure to use for the amount that the public is willing to spend to reduce crime.

Within the cost-benefit framework, $61.4 billion is the amount being spent to reduce crime to its present level from the higher levels of crime that would presumably prevail in the absence of any spending for crime prevention and control. It is anyone's guess just what that level would be. It could conceivably be extremely large, far higher than present levels.

If one were to include only material losses in the cost-benefit calculus, it would be irrational to spend more money to prevent victim losses than the $35.4 billion those losses cost. If, as seems likely, it would cost more than that to prevent all those crimes, it would be cheaper to compensate victims.

Of course, people may be willing to pay to avoid the psychological costs associated with victimization as well. Yet Zedlewski's computation is still not the correct way of taking that willingness into account. The subjective value of a *marginal* reduction in crime below its present level depends on how much *additional* spending *beyond current expenditures* individuals would be willing to accept to achieve that reduction. This, too, is unknown. However, a recent survey of 400 Alabama residents suggests that it might not be high. Although 69% of the sample said that Alabama needed more prisons, only 19% favored paying for them with more taxes. Cutting back on state spending in other areas, such as education or health care, to pay for more prisons, was even less popular—only 3% supported that option (Doble and Klein, 1989: 22, 27).

In the abstract, then, the public may favor greater use of imprisonment, but it does not appear to be willing to pay for it. In any event, because Zedlewski uses an irrelevant figure for the number of crimes (those not prevented, rather than those prevented by present policy) and an incorrect dollar figure (total costs of crime rather than costs of crime prevention), his procedure cannot be taken as offering even a rough estimate of the marginal value of preventing a crime.

In sum, even when his caveats and qualifications are taken into account, Zedlewski grossly overestimates the potential benefits of expanded prison construction, and greatly underestimates the costs. Unfortunately, it is not easy to offer superior estimates of some factors that figure in his analysis because the empirical base for improved estimation is lacking.

To say that Zedlewsi's conclusions cannot be supported by the line of reasoning he advances is not to say that they cannot be supported in other ways. The question of how many people should be in prison is a difficult one that the present essay does not even attempt to address. The question of alternate sentences is equally outside the scope of the present discussion.

## COST-BENEFIT ANALYSIS RECONSIDERED

Apart from the details of his computations, the terms in which Zedlewski develops his argument can themselves be criticized on a number of counts. First, by restricting the policy analysis to whether more prisons should be constructed, he fails to consider whether other alternatives might not be more cost effective than prisons. Even if all his calculations had been valid, it would still not follow that prison construction would be rational; after all, other alternate strategies might be even more efficient. Note that this is not an argument against cost-benefit analyses, only an insistence that the range of policy options needs to be broadened before such analyses are used to decide in favor of a given policy.

Second, governments have only a limited amount of funds to spend. Crime control is only one of many claims competing for the public purse. Even if further funding for crime control would in itself be desirable, it may not be desirable to take funds away from education, pollution abatement, or public health. Of course, by raising taxes or borrowing, funding or crime control can be increased without taking funds away from other public programs. However, there is a limit beyond which governments cannot tax or borrow. The reluctance of today's politicians to propose higher taxes to reduce the federal deficit suggests some of the political problems raising taxes can entail....

In a culture where utilitarian considerations are a widely accepted basis for legitimating policy decisions, it is inevitable that cost-benefit analyses will continue to be produced and disseminated to justify penal policy innovations. In itself, this is not a bad thing; at times, such analyses can illuminate policy choices. In other circumstances, such as the present one, cost-benefit analyses will be inconclusive because they will not be able to produce reasonable estimates of costs and benefits, or will not be able to cope with interpersonal comparisons of costs and benefits. On such occasions, social scientists, who may be called upon by policymakers to formulate and justify administrative initiatives, have a special responsibility not to suspend their critical sensibilities. When a policy cannot be justified, we should say so.

# POSTSCRIPT

## Are More Prisons and Prison Beds the Answer to America's Rising Crime Rate?

The most recent articulation of the call for a massive increase in the number of prison cells is voiced by Princeton professor of politics and public affairs John J. DiLulio Jr. DiLulio, along with Joan R. Petersilia, heads the Brookings Institution project "The New Consensus on Crime Policy." See, for example, the following two articles that have appeared in the *Brookings Review:* "Does Prison Pay?" (Fall 1991) and "Does Prison Pay?: Revisited" (Winter 1993). Anne Morrison Piehl was coauthor of both these essays. In numerous essays, which appear in a wide variety of publications from professional journals to *Readers Digest*, DiLulio warns that the next generation of teenagers is a "wolf pack" of depraved "superpredators." His comment is, "If incarceration is not the answer, then what, precisely is, is the question."

DiLulio is not without his critics. See, for example, Bruce Shapiro, "How the War on Crime Imprisons America," *The Nation* (April 22, 1996). Shapiro argues that DiLulio is not an objective observer. His immigrant grandmother was mugged and severely beaten a few blocks from her home by black teens, and his uncle was stabbed to death by a murderer, who was a drug addict out of prison on parole. Shapiro reminds us that DiLulio himself has said that these experiences "sure as hell concentrate your mind."

Another variation on this theme is captured in an exchange of views that appeared in the June 1996 issue of *Social Science Quarterly.* Here J. R. Clark and Dwight R. Lee argue that a short-run policy to reduce prison sentences, and of course fiscal pressures, will in the long run increase criminal activity and the demand for prison cells. They liken this to a Laffer Curve: At zero sentencing length, there is a zero demand for prison space and correspondingly high crime rates; as sentencing rates increase so does the demand for prison space. But after a point, an increase in sentencing length decreases the required prison capacity because you have locked up most of the bad guys and deterred most of the other want-to-be bad guys. As you would expect, this hypothesis is challenged in other essays in the June 1996 issue of *Social Science Quarterly.* See in particular the essays by M. Dwayne Smith, "The Folly of a 'Lock Em Up' Laffer Curve," and Dale O. Cloninger's "Sentence, Length, Severity, and the Demand for Prison Space."

# On the Internet . . .

### Consolidated Financial Statements of the U.S. Government, 1995 (Prototype)
The Consolidated Financial Statements (CFS) of the U.S. government provide information about government financial operations on an accrual basis. Links to the statements, notes about them, and supplemental tables can be found at this site.
*http://www.fms.treas.gov/cfs/cfs95.html*

### Joint Economic Committee
Start here to explore the work and opinions of the members of the Joint Economic Committee on many topics—tax reform and government spending, Clintonomics, and the growth debate, to name just a few.,
*http://www.senate.gov/~jec/jechmpgt.html*

### The Public Debt
Here you will find links to The Public Debt of the United States to the Penny, Historical Debt, Interest Expense and the Public Debt, and Frequently Asked Questions.
*http://www.publicdebt.treas.gov/opd/opd.htm*

### U.S. Macroeconomic and Regional Data
Hosted by the Department of Economics at the State University of New York, Oswego, this site contains the full text of recent economic reports to the president and links to various global and regional economic indicators.
*http://www.oswego.edu/~economic/mac-data.htm*

### U. S. Treasury
Select Browse at this site to open up the U.S. Treasury, which is divided into accessible areas: Banking and Finance, Money, Taxes, Treasury Services, to name just a few.
*http://www.ustreas.gov/*

# PART 2

## Macroeconomic Issues

*Government policy and economics are tightly intertwined. Fiscal policy and monetary policy have dramatic input on the economy as a whole, and the state of the economy can often determine policy actions. Decisions regarding balancing the budget or welfare reform must be made in the context of broad macroeconomic goals, and the debates on these issues are more than theoretical discussions. Each has a significant impact on our economic lives.*

■ Can Economic Growth Be Increased Just by Using More Inputs and Improving Efficiency?

■ Is Our Current Social Security Program Securely Anchored?

■ Does the Consumer Price Index Overstate Changes in the Cost of Living?

■ Is There a Need for a Consitutional Amendment to Balance the Budget?

■ Is the Federal Reserve the Cause of Poor Macroeconomic Performance?

■ Is the Nonaccelerating Inflation Rate of Unemployment a Useful Guide for Macroeconomic Policy?

■ Would Adopting Wisconsin's Welfare Reforms End Welfare As We Know It?

# ISSUE 8

## Can Economic Growth Be Increased Just by Using More Inputs and Improving Efficiency?

**YES: Council of Economic Advisers,** from *Economic Report of the President 1997* (Government Printing Office, 1997)

**NO: Felix G. Rohatyn,** from "Recipe for Growth," *Wall Street Journal* (April 11, 1996)

### ISSUE SUMMARY

**YES:** The Clinton administration's Council of Economic Advisers believes that the way to stimulate economic growth is to increase the availability of physical capital and to improve efficiency.

**NO:** Felix G. Rohatyn, U.S. ambassador to France and former partner of an investment firm, argues that an increase in the growth rate does not require the redistribution of wealth and that the government must play an active role in education, in infrastructure investment, and in the maintenance of a corporate safety net.

Economic growth is generally defined as an increase in an economy's production of goods and services. Because productive activity generates real income, output and income are simply two sides of the same coin; that is, economic growth is also referred to as an increase in real income. Societies desire economic growth because an increase in the availability of goods and services means that persons in that society are better off, at least in a material sense.

Economic growth has always been a central concern of economists. Consider the beginnings of modern economics, Adam Smith's *Wealth of Nations*. Published in 1776, its title conjures up images of material well-being and the forces that cause variations in material well-being between countries and over time. The Full Employment and Balanced Growth Act captures the importance of economic growth from an economic policy perspective. This legislation, passed in 1978, states that "it is the continuing policy and responsibility of the Federal government ... to foster and promote ... increased real income."

In measuring economic growth, economists typically use the concept of real gross domestic product (GDP). Simply defined, real GDP is the value of an economy's production of goods and services measured in constant prices. The percentage change in real GDP is typically referred to as the economic growth rate.

In explaining economic growth, economists typically use the growth accounting framework. This framework views production as the process of converting inputs into output. An increase in the quantity of output occurs with either an increase in the quantity of inputs employed or an increase in the ability of the inputs to produce output. Accordingly, three sources of economic growth are identified: increases in labor inputs, increases in capital inputs, and increases in total factor productivity or efficiency.

Although the growth accounting framework is conceptually simple, its estimation is not. There are direct and independent measurements available for real GDP, labor inputs, and capital inputs, but no direct and independent measurement of total factor productivity. Therefore, total factor productivity is measured indirectly as a residual. This means that whatever changes in real GDP are left unexplained by changes in labor and capital inputs are attributed to changes in total factor productivity. As a consequence, total factor productivity, when it is estimated, not only includes the true contribution of productivity to economic growth but also any errors in the measurement of economic growth and changes in labor and capital inputs. For this reason the empirical estimate of the contribution of total factor productivity to economic growth has been called "a measure of our ignorance."

Policy concern with economic growth develops when growth performance is less than desired. This is the current situation for the United States. During the 1960s economic growth, measured as the simple arithmetic average of yearly percentage changes in real GDP, was 4.4 percent, 3.2 percent during the 1970s, 2.8 percent during the 1980s, and 1.8 percent during the first six years of the 1990s. In short, during the 1990s, the growth rate for the U.S. economy has been quite low by historical standards. The question then is, What should be done to increase the growth rate?

The solution offered by Clinton's Council of Economic Advisers follows almost directly from the growth accounting framework. Advisers say we need to increase physical capital or capital inputs. They believe this will happen if the government reduces its budget deficits. They also say we need to increase total factor productivity. They believe this will happen if the government takes actions to improve human capital, to stimulate research and development, to increase competition, to expand trade, and to improve public sector efficiency. Felix G. Rohatyn, on the other hand, takes a more fundamental political view. He believes that improving economic growth requires, among other things, the acceptance of a new definition of fairness by the Democrats and a new definition of the proper role of government by the Republicans. These new definitions will allow the American economy to break out of the "financial iron triangle," which restricts economic growth and generates serious social tensions.

# YES

## Council of Economic Advisers

# THE ECONOMIC AGENDA

The United States still faces major economic challenges. American technology, the economy, and society are all changing rapidly. Instead of ignoring or lamenting these changes, the Nation must embrace them, transforming problems into opportunities. We can do this only if we set a coherent economic agenda. This [Clinton] Administration has already accomplished much with the policies of the last 4 years. In the next 4 years the Administration will continue to build on those policies, holding fast to its new vision of the government's role in the economy as the basis for an agenda to promote growth, opportunity, and responsibility.

### GROWTH

Productivity growth has been slow since the early 1970s. Since 1973, annual rises in productivity in nonfarm businesses have averaged 1.1 percent, a drastic decline from the 2.8 percent annual average that the Nation enjoyed between 1960 and 1973 (Figure 1). Biases in the methods used to calculate these numbers may exaggerate the slowdown, but something has undoubtedly happened to slow the pace at which output per hour increases. Slower productivity growth has the direct consequence of retarding increases in the Nation's standard of living. It also places obstacles in the way of solving some of the Nation's other challenges. Americans may be less supportive of freer trade when trade liberalization has been associated, however spuriously, with slower growth. It will be harder to balance the budget over the long term, especially while supporting a growing aged population, when productivity growth is slow. And workers are more reluctant to share their resources with those who are worse off when they feel that their own wages are stagnant.

The sources of economic growth can be grouped under three headings: increases in physical capital, improvements in human capital, and increases in the overall efficiency of the economy—the amount of output per unit of

From Executive Office of the President, Council of Economic Advisers, *Economic Report of the President 1997* (Government Printing Office, 1997).

input. The Administration's economic agenda is based on strengthening each of these three pillars of economic growth.

### Increasing Physical Capital

The first pillar of economic growth is increases in physical capital, which enable workers to produce more goods and services. Because it reduces the government's borrowing, deficit reduction will remain the key to how much of national saving is available for private investment in physical capital. The Nation has made great progress in bringing down the deficit in the last 4 years, but this ground will be lost unless we address the strains that some of the major entitlement programs will place on the budget over the long term. As the population ages, expenditures on Social Security are expected to grow from an estimated 4.7 percent of GDP [Gross Domestic Product] in 1996 to around 6.4 percent in 2030, then stabilize. A much more serious challenge is posed by Medicare and Medicaid. If nothing is done to reform these programs, their outlays are projected to grow from an estimated 3.9 percent of GDP in 1996 to 13.0 percent in 2050. Their projected growth is due not just to the aging of the population, as in the case of Social Security, but also to the expectation that the volume and intensity of medical services consumed will continue their rapid rise. . . .

Assuming Federal tax revenues remain at their historically constant level of around 18 percent of GDP, the projected increase in entitlements, especially Medicare and Medicaid, will have one of two effects: either it will balloon the budget deficit, or it will all but crowd out other vital government expenditures, including those necessary to sustain long-term economic growth, such as education and research and development. The deficit reduction of the last 4 years, however, has put the Nation in a position to address these long-term issues in a manner that preserves the important achievements of Medicare, Medicaid, and Social Security.

When the government runs a smaller deficit, it absorbs less private saving and frees up resources for private sector investment. But *public* investments in infrastructure, such as roads, schools, and airports, are also important. It is false economy to release funds for investment in one area by cutting back in another where the need and the return are just as great. Entrepreneurs will be reluctant to build new factories, homes, and offices if the highways and bridges that link them are inadequate for the new traffic they generate.

To be sure, government must take pains to see that every dollar it invests, like every other government dollar, is well spent. We have to think hard about how to put into place incentives that make such outcomes more likely. And we have to think carefully about which public investments should be the responsibility of the Federal Government and which the responsibility of States and localities. But fear of misdirected investment should not lead to underinvestment, because too little investment is costly to future growth. In short, we should not create an infrastructure deficit while attempting to improve the budget deficit.

### Improving Human Capital

The second pillar of economic growth is improvements in what economists call human capital: the knowledge, experience, and skills of the workforce. As the economy has changed, the demands imposed on the brainpower of the American workforce have increased enormously.

*Figure 1*

**Actual and Trend Labor Productivity**

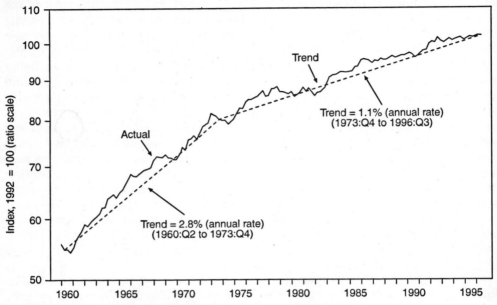

Labor productivity has grown at a 1.1 percent average annual rate since 1973.

Note: Data are for the nonfarm business sector.

Source: Department of Labor

[T]he returns to education, as measured by the difference in incomes between college and high school graduates, have risen sharply in the last 20 years. Much of this difference probably reflects the increasing importance of computer skills in the workplace.

Many American schools do a superb job of human capital formation, but some are failing at the task. Standardized test scores reflect only part of the learning that goes on in schools, yet the fact that American children perform less well on standard science and mathematics tests than many of their foreign counterparts is a continuing source of concern. There is no easy answer.

Recognizing the challenge that these changes pose, the President has set ambitious goals for the Nation's education system: every 8-year-old should be able to read, every 12-year-old should be able to log onto the Internet, every 18-year-old should be able to go to college, and every classroom and library in America should be linked to the Internet.

An array of policies, current and proposed, are directed toward achieving these goals. The America Reads initiative, working through the National Service program, will call on thousands of people to mobilize an army of a million volunteer tutors, dedicated to ensuring that every child in America can read by the age of 8. A good education in the early years of a child's life is necessary, but hardly sufficient to endow that child with the skills that our technological society demands. Therefore, in addition to early-education programs, we need to promote technology in the classroom and encourage young people to take more years of college.

Although the returns to additional years of education are substantial—between 5 percent and 15 percent—without government involvement many students would find it difficult to borrow for college. Not only do they lack a credit history, but they cannot borrow against expected future earnings—human capital cannot be pledged as collateral. The result is a classic market failure: markets by themselves do not provide all the education for which the benefits exceed the costs, even when the benefits are measured only in narrow economic terms. Since the G.I. Bill was passed in the 1940s, the Federal Government has had an acknowledged role in making higher education more affordable. Policies already implemented by this Administration are bringing us much closer to the day when every American who wants to will be able to attend at least 2 years of college. Under the new direct student loan program, for example, individuals can borrow money for college directly from the Federal Government and tailor their repayments to suit their own financial circumstances. Seeking to build on the success of this program, the President has also proposed tuition tax credits, to support those seeking higher education, and penalty-free withdrawals from individual retirement accounts, to encourage them to save for it themselves.

Meanwhile the Technology and Literacy Challenge initiative is bringing advanced computer technology into every classroom in the Nation. It is making significant progress toward ensuring that all American students are computer literate, equipped with the skills they will need in the 21st century. Under this initiative, 20 percent of all the schools in California have already been wired to the Internet —a good example of government and the private sector complementing each other. The Federal Government served as entrepreneur for this initiative, but much of the work was done by 50,000 volunteers, with many of the Nation's leading high-technology firms donating equipment. The initiative also stresses the development of educational software and the training of teachers to harness the potential of these new technologies.

Other steps are important in preparing the Nation's educational system for the 21st century. Recent reports have documented the extent to which America's public schools have become dilapidated. Schools with leaky and collapsing roofs have had to be closed. Because students need a more conducive environment in which to learn, the President has proposed $5 billion in Federal funding to support a program, administered by the States, that would spend $20 billion for school construction and renovation. Additional efforts are focused on enhancing resources for those communities facing the hardest problems (e.g., those with disproportionate numbers of disadvantaged children), improving standards through the Goals 2000 program, and promoting new approaches through the charter school movement.

Education does not end with college. That is why this Administration has consistently emphasized lifelong learning and employability security, to boost economic growth and reduce the adjustment costs associated with a vibrant economy.

Unfortunately, the legacy of past efforts in this sphere has left workers facing a complicated maze of dozens of government-assisted training programs, each with its own rules, regulations, and restrictions. The President has proposed replacing this complex system with a single choice-based system for adults. This system should use a market-oriented approach, relying on training vouchers or grants to empower people directly to seek the training that will help them the most.

## Research and Development

The third pillar of growth is greater economic efficiency—learning to produce more output with fewer inputs. Additions to the Nation's technological arsenal through research and development are an important contributor to efficiency: private industry invests over $100 billion in research and development each year. This is a huge sum, but it may not be enough: history and economic theory suggest that, left to their own devices, private firms will not invest sufficiently in improving technology, because they themselves do not realize the full benefit therefrom. Even though the patent system encourages invention by guaranteeing that inventors retain property rights to their innovations, many very useful ideas developed in more basic scientific research cannot (and should not) be patented.

The Federal Government has long played a critical role in promoting research and development. It has financed growth in telecommunications, for instance, from that industry's inception, with the first Baltimore-to-Washington telegraph line, to its latest major development, the Internet. In agriculture, government-funded research provided the basis for enormous improvements in productivity that today allow less than 3 percent of the workforce to feed the entire Nation, and have made the United States one of the world's leading agricultural exporters.

Detractors of government support for research have often distorted the issue. Some have posed a false dichotomy between basic research, for which public support is almost universal, and technology, which they say should remain the province of the private sector. Yet many areas of technology have huge spillover benefits and therefore would be under provided without government support. Critics have also accused government of trying to "pick winners"—of seeking to supplant the market at one of the things it does best. But government support of technology is not aimed at outguessing the market. Rather, it is focused on setting up partnerships and other structures to identify, together with the private sector, those areas in which large benefits to society are not likely to be produced by the market alone.

In the spirit of the Administration's new vision for the economy, the Federal Government has placed public-private partnerships at the center of its research and development policy. The Advanced Technology Program (ATP), expanded substantially under this Administration, is a good example. ATP awards matching funds to industry, on a competitive basis, to conduct research on cutting-edge technologies and processes that, despite their great economic potential, might otherwise not have been pursued. The firms themselves set much of the research agenda, but this pairing has been an effective way to leverage government funding into larger increases in research and development. The record shows that the success rate of this and similar programs is indeed formidable.

### Increasing Competition

Improving the efficiency of the economy is not just a matter of improving technology. How the economy is organized plays just as important a role in creating incentives for firms to use their capital and labor as efficiently as possible. If the market economy is to deliver on its promise of growth and prosperity, markets have to be competitive, because it is competition that drives firms to be efficient and innovative. Firms, however, often find it easier to increase profits by reducing competition than by improving efficiency in response to competition. Monopolies and oligopolies not only can charge inefficiently high prices and restrict output, but may also have a diminished drive to innovate.

The traditional way to increase competition is to prevent the growth of monopoly power in the first place. This Administration has restored vigor to the enforcement of the antitrust laws, blocking anticompetitive mergers and, where warranted, prosecuting alleged violators. But competition is not viable in some industries, namely, those called natural monopolies. Antitrust enforcement may be of little help in these areas; instead government regulation can help to ensure that monopoly power is not abused.

The extent and the form of competition are constantly changing. Joseph Schumpeter, one of the 20th century's great economists, described capitalism as a process of creative destruction. New industries constantly come into existence as old industries are destroyed. The late 19th and early 20th centuries saw the transformation of the economy from a mostly agricultural to a mostly industrial one. Today services and information are assuming the lead position, while at the same time demand for U.S. goods is increasingly coming from abroad. Sometimes analysts focus on manufacturing as if it still represented the core of the economy. Manufacturing is important—it is the Nation's largest investor in research and development and its leading exporter—but manufacturing employment today represents only 15 percent of total employment, and service industries also produce many of our important exports, for example in telecommunications, financial services, and other intellectual property.

Today, new technologies have expanded the scope for competition in many sectors that have historically been highly regulated, such as telecommunications and electric power. Traditional regulatory structures, however, with their rigid categories of regulation versus deregulation, and competition versus monopoly, have become increasingly unhelpful in guiding policy in these areas. These new technologies do not call for wholesale deregulation because not all parts of these industries are adequately competitive. Instead they call for appropriate changes in regulatory structure to meet the new challenges. Such changes must recognize the existence of hybrid areas of the economy, some parts of which are more suited to competition, while others are more vulnerable to domination by a few. Market power in one part of a regulated industry cannot be allowed to maneuver itself into a stranglehold over other parts, or else economic efficiency may be severely compromised. The Administration's regulatory reforms in the telecommunications and electric power industries have attempted to achieve competitive balance.

Even as these changes have intensified competition in some parts of the economy, it remains limited in others. In particular, where goods and services are locally provided, and where transportation costs are high, consumers in some areas may have too little choice, even if providers in the country as a whole are numerous. In parts of the country, for example, a single hospital may be the only one serving a large rural area. In the health care sector, new guidelines for antitrust enforcement were recently issued in response to concerns such as these, and the Administration has resisted attempts to scale back antitrust enforcement in this area. The benefits of competition can be seen in our university system, where competition remains keen—and perhaps partly accounts for the dominant position American universities hold in the world of higher education.

### Expanding Trade

The third source of increasing efficiency in the economy is more-open markets abroad. Like the freeing up of domestic markets, opening of foreign markets shifts resources into relatively more productive areas. The Administration will continue to pursue its outward-oriented, protrade agenda through multilateral, regional, and bilateral means, expanding on and bringing to fruition initiatives like the Asia-Pacific Economic Cooperation group and the proposed Free Trade Area of the Americas.

The global economy, like the domestic economy, is evolving, and its change brings with it new challenges. A clean environment, a safe workplace, and competitive markets are important to us internationally just as they are at home. Trade liberalization can complement these goals in many ways. Anti-competitive practices abroad, for example, frequently cohabit with restrictions on trade and may forestall entry of American firms into foreign markets. Liberalizing trade in agriculture can lead to a more environmentally sound international allocation of farming activity. The side agreements to NAFTA [North American Free Trade Agreement], on which the Administration conditioned its approval of the agreement, demonstrate that safeguarding a shared environment, promoting better working conditions, and liberalizing trade are not mutually exclusive goods to be traded off against each other. Pursuing these goals in the multilateral framework of the WTO [World Trade Organization] will be increasingly important. At the same time, it is important that countries not allow domestic regulation to become a pretext for nontariff trade barriers whose real purpose is to restrict competition.

Some of the fastest-growing economies are the emerging markets of the developing world, many of them in East and Southeast Asia. To grasp fully the opportunities that these new markets offer, the United States needs to strengthen economic relations with these countries.

### Improving Public Sector Efficiency

The fourth and final way to increase the overall efficiency of the economy is by improving the efficiency with which the government itself does its job. By freeing up resources for potentially more productive uses in other sectors, and by reducing the cost of regulation, government reform can raise economy-wide productivity. The Vice President's reinventing government initiative has been doing just that. Thousands of pages of Federal regulations have been eliminated, and thousands more are being streamlined or improved in other ways. Hundreds of obsolete Federal programs have been eliminated, and red tape has been reduced dramatically. The Federal civilian workforce has been cut by more than 250,000, and as a percentage of the Nation's total employment it is now smaller than at any time since the early 1930s.

# NO

Felix G. Rohatyn

## RECIPE FOR GROWTH

The American economy is now constrained by a financial iron triangle, in part created by the Republican majority together with the Clinton administration, from which it is difficult to break out and which is beginning to generate serious social tensions.

* The first leg of this triangle is the commitment to balance the budget in seven years. Even though there has never been a rational explanation for this time frame, it has now become part of the political theology. It would be as dangerous for either party to depart from it, say by suggesting that eight or nine years would be equally logical, as it was for George Bush to abandon his "No new taxes" pledge.

* The second leg is an extension of the first and is more restrictive in its effect: It is the acceptance, by both parties and blessed by the Congressional Budget Office, that our economic growth rate will be 2.2% for the seven-year period. Even though projections are notoriously inaccurate even over much shorter periods, this particular projection is becoming both a prediction and a self-limitation. It implies that this rate of growth is the limit of what our economy is capable of without inflation. Since this view has the support of the Federal Reserve, the Treasure and the financial markets, it has become a de facto limit on economic growth. The markets and the Fed react to any appearance of acceleration with higher interest rates and the economy then falls back to 2.2% or below.

* The third leg of this triangle is the impact of technology and global competition on incomes and employment. The lethal political combination of corporate downsizing together with ever-increasing differentials in wealth and income among Americans of differing levels of education and skills, and the huge rewards to capital as the result of the boom in the securities markets, are creating serious social tensions and political pressures.

Unless we can somehow break out of this iron triangle, we could face serious difficulties, and the best hope for a breakout is to make a determined effort for a higher rate of economic growth. Only higher growth, as a result of higher investment and greater productivity, can make these processes socially tolerable. In order to deal constructively with the realities of technology and the global economy, Democrats and Republicans may have to abandon cherished traditional positions and turn their thinking upside down: Democrats may have to redefine their concept of fairness, while Republicans may have to rethink the role of Government.

## ECONOMIC INSECURITY

The American economy is growing very slowly despite occasional upward blips. Growth and inflation are both around 2%. Our main trading partners, Europe and Japan, are undergoing serious economic strains of their own, with German unemployment nearing 10% and French unemployment near 12%. Fiscal contraction is taking place on both sides of the ocean as the Maastricht criteria are maintained in Europe and deficit reduction continues as a priority here, feeding a general sense of economic insecurity. The winds of deflation could be stronger than the winds of inflation.

At the same time, the Dow Jones Industrial Average is near its all-time high of 5700, mergers and restructurings are still taking place at a record pace, and layoffs and downsizing are continuing as the inevitable result of global competition and technological change. And Pat Buchanan has created a political groundswell, on the left as well as on the right, by identifying real problems but proposing solutions based on fear, xenophobia, isolationism and protectionism. It is frightening to think of the political impact of a Buchanan if unemployment were now 7.5% instead of 5.5%. All that it requires is the next recession.

The social and economic problems we face today are varied. They include job insecurity, enormous income differentials, significant pressures on average incomes,

urban quality-of-life and many others. Even though all of these require different approaches, the single most important requirement to deal with all of them is the wealth and revenues generated by a higher rate of economic growth. John Kennedy was right: A rising tide lifts all boats. Although it may not lift all of them at the same time and at the same rate, without more growth we are simply redistributing the same pie. That is a zero sum game and it is simply not good enough.

The fact that our 2%–2.5% present growth rate is inadequate is proven by the very problems we face. The question of when, and especially how, to balance the federal budget deserves a great deal more intelligent discussion than the political sloganeering we have heard so far. The budget is a document that reflects neither economic reality nor valid accounting practices. If the budget is to be balanced in order to satisfy the financial markets, only real justification of this goal, then it must be done with growth rather than with retrenchment. That higher growth, together with controlling costs of entitlement like Medicare, Medicaid and Social Security, will generate the capital needed to provide both private and pubic investment adequate to the country's needs.

Bringing the rate of growth from its present 2%–2.5% to a level of 3%–3.5% would generate as much as an additional $1 trillion over the next decade. It could provide both for significant tax cuts for the private sector as well as for the higher level of public investment in infrastructure and education required as we move into the 21st Century. It would obviously generate millions of new jobs. The present bipartisan commitment to balance the budget in seven years, based on the present anemic growth, is economically unrealistic and probably socially unsustainable. In all likelihood, higher growth is in fact the only way to achieve budget balance. The question is how to achieve it.

The conventional wisdom among most academic economists as well as the Treasury, the Federal Reserve Board and Wall Street is that our economy cannot generate higher growth without running the risk of triggering inflation. Not everyone shares that view. In particular, the leaders of many of this country's leading industrial corporations believe that we could sustain significantly higher growth rates based on the very significant productivity improvements they are generating in their own businesses, year-after-year.

Economics is not an exact science as we have painfully learned over and over again. It is the product of the psychology of millions of consumers, of business leaders making long-term investment decisions, of capital flows instantaneously triggered by events and ideas. We must do away with the false notion that we must choose between growth or inflation. Our experience, even in the more recent past, shows that technology and competition can produce growth without serious inflationary pressures. In the face of today's totally new environment of almost daily revolutions in technology combined with globalization, we should be willing to be bolder, both in fiscal and monetary policy.

As a traditional Democrat, I have always believed that freedom, fairness and wealth, basic to a modern democracy, required an essentially redistributionist philosophy of wealth, that a fairly steeply graduated income tax was required as a matter of fairness and that lower deficits would guarantee adequate growth and a fair distribution of wealth. The experience of the last two decades, with the advent of the global economy, has very much shaken that view.

Fairness does not require the redistribution of wealth; it requires the creation of wealth; it requires the creation of wealth, geared to an economy that can provide employment for everyone willing and able to work, and the opportunity for a consistently higher standard-of-living for those employed. Only strong private sector growth, driven by higher levels of investment and superior public services, can hope to provide the job opportunities required to deal with technological change and globalization. Only higher growth will allow that process to take place within the framework of a market economy and a functioning democracy.

We should have no illusions about the likelihood of reducing the level of present income and wealth differentials; they are likely to increase in the near future as the requirements for skills and education increase. The world is not fair; we must, however, make it better for those in the middle as well as at the lower end of the economic scale. The key is enough growth that, even if initially the lower end does not gain as rapidly as the upper, it can improve its absolute standard of living, and being a process of closing the gap.

Higher growth requires a tax system that promotes growth as its main objective. It must encourage higher investment and savings. That is not the case today. Today's tax system aims at a concept of fairness dictated by distribution tables. That may not be the best test. A tax system with growth as its main objective may be a variation of the flat tax; or it may be a national sales tax; or it may be another system aimed at taxing consumption instead of investment such as proposed by Sens. Sam Nunn and Pete Domenici.

The power and dominance of global capital markets in today's world would seem to aid in the latter direction. Lowering taxes on capital would at first blush seem to help the already wealthy, current holders of capital. But whatever its effect on the distribution tables, it could unleash powerful capital flows, both domestic and foreign, that would lower interest rates significantly and make investment in the U.S. even more competitive than it is today. At the same time, they would maintain the strength of the dollar and maintain lower rates of inflation.

Achieving the objective of higher growth could also include the gradual privatization of Social Security in order to create a massive investment pool with higher returns for the beneficiaries and greater investment capabilities for the private and the pubic sector. The key to economic success in the 21st Century will be cheap and ample capital, high levels of private investment to increase productivity, high levels of education and advanced technology. It also includes higher levels of public investment in building a national infrastructure supportive of the 21st century economy.

If the Democrats can redefine their concept of fairness, Republicans, on the other hand, may have to abandon their view of passive government. If growth and opportunity are to be the prime objectives of our society, the government must play an active role in some areas. The first is education; the second is higher levels of infrastructure investment; the third is the maintenance of a corporate safety net.

Public school reform, driven by higher standards, is an absolute priority. Even though that is a state responsibility, it is a national problem. These standards, regardless of today's political conventional wisdom, will ultimately be national in scope. Access to higher education should be made available to any graduating high school senior meeting stringent national test levels and demonstrably in need of financial assistance. The equivalent of the GI Bill, providing national college scholarships to needy students, should be created and federally funded. It should be the primary affirmative action program funded by the federal government.

As part of a higher economic growth rate, state and local governments should provide higher levels of infrastructure investment. In addition to the creation of private employment, this could also provide public sector jobs to meet the work requirements of welfare reform, as well as to provide the support to a high capacity modern economy. Financial assistance from the federal government would encourage the states in that endeavor. Higher growth would enable federal as well as state and local budgets to take on this responsibility.

A corporate safety net should be provided in order to deal with the inevitable dislocations which corporate downsizings and restructurings will continue to create. Business, labor and government should cooperate to create a system of portable pensions and portable health care to cushion the transition from one job to another. Incentives should be provided for business to make use of stock grants for employees laid off as a result of mergers and restructuring. If losing one's job creates wealth for the shareholders, the person losing his or her job should share in some of that wealth creation. Corporate pension funds, to the extent they are overfunded as a result of the stock market boom, could be part of a process to provide larger severance and retraining payments for laid-off employees.

Other than in areas such as pensions and health care, it is counterproductive to try to legislate the social side of "corporate responsibility"; it is almost impossible to define. To begin with, most large U.S. corporations are majority-owned by financial institutions including the pension funds of the very employees who are in danger of displacements. These institutions, driven by their own competitive requirements, were the source of the pressures on management which resulted in the dramatic restructuring of American industry over the last decade. Those restructurings have made American industry highly competitive in world markets; they must continue and we must continue the opening of world trade.

Board of directors are not blind to the risks of political backlash. The issue of executive compensation, made starkly visible by its tie-in with the rise in stock market values, will be dealt with responsibly or boards will find themselves under great shareholder pressure. The use of profit-sharing, stock options and stock grants to practically all levels of the corporation will be significantly expanded and should create greater common interests between executives, shareholders and employees. However, the main role of the corporation must remain to be competitive, to grow, to invest, to hire and to generate profits for its shareholders; a significant portion of employee compensation should be related to the growing productivity of its employees.

The benefits to business in such an approach are obvious, but labor also has a large stake in such a re-examination.

Some of the proposals put forth at present would have very negative results for working Americans. It is too late to return to a protected American economy; the only result would be to trigger a financial crisis that would harm America and our trading partners. It is impossible to stop the effect of global information, technology, capital and labor. What is important for working people, union or non-union, is the creation of more well-paying jobs as a result of high levels of investment and high levels of education; to share in the profits of their employers through profit-sharing and stock ownership; to share in the benefit potential of pension funds vastly increased by the boom in the financial markets; to have access to permanent health care security and to high levels of education and training to deal with the 21st century requirements.

Business and labor, together, should hammer out such an agenda. If we are serious about balancing the budget in a responsible manner, the president and the congressional leadership could set a national objective that the economy's rate of growth reach a minimum sustainable level of 3% annually by the year 2000. They could ask the best minds in the country, from government, from business, from labor and from academia to provide a set of options which could lead to such a result. Many of these options would be politically difficult, both for Democrats and for Republicans, and some would probably be impossible. But the only way to abandon long-held notions that may no longer apply to today's world is to discuss them within the framework of a very simple and definite objective: higher growth.

## A DIFFERENT PERSPECTIVE

Setting the U.S. on a path to higher growth will require coordination with our partners in the G–7 [Group of Seven]. The Europeans should welcome such an initiative since they are in greater need for growth than we are. Nevertheless, the process will be slow and it must be put into motion.

The president's setting an objective of higher growth would have an important psychological impact; the economy is, after all, heavily influenced by psychological factors. If the president were to set an ambitious growth objective, then all elements affecting the economy would be subject to review from a different perspective. They would include fiscal and monetary policy; investments and savings; education and training; international trade. Most importantly, these activities should take place within a framework in which the Democratic Party redefines its concept of fairness and the Republican Party redefines its concept of the role of government. At present, neither is appropriate for the revolution that technology, globalization and the inclusion of an additional one billion people to the global workforce will bring about tomorrow.

Ultimately, a rising tide will float all ships, and both political parties can help bring this about. If they fail to do so, at a minimum the present malaise will turn uglier, and it is even conceivable that another tide will sweep away existing parties. If that were to happen, arguments about growth or fairness will be totally irrelevant.

# POSTSCRIPT

## Can Economic Growth Be Increased Just by Using More Inputs and Improving Efficiency?

The Clinton administration's Council of Economic Advisers begins its discussion of economic growth by focusing on the behavior of productivity. It documents the current slowdown in productivity growth by comparing the period 1960–73 to the period since 1973. Annual increases in productivity in nonfarm business averaged 2.8 percent during the first period and 1.1 percent during the second period. The advisers state that the administration's growth strategy is to increase physical capital, improve human capital, and improve the overall efficiency of the economy. To increase physical capital, they want to balance the budget: with less government borrowing more funds will be available for business firms to borrow for investment purposes. To improve human capital, they propose several initiatives: establish goals for education, make higher education more affordable, and reform training programs. To improve the overall efficiency of the economy, they recommend expansion of the Advance Technology Program to encourage research and development, a combination of more vigorous antitrust enforcement in some industries and greater government regulation in others, expansion of trade, and greater governmental efficiency.

Rohatyn argues on a more fundamental level. He begins by stating that the economy's growth is currently constrained by a financial iron triangle. This iron triangle consists of the commitment to balance the federal government's budget in seven years, the acceptance of a 2.2 percent growth rate for the seven-year period, and the impact of technology and increasing global competition. In order to break out of this iron triangle, Rohatyn believes that both Democrats and Republicans need to abandon long-held positions. He states that the Democrats need to redefine their concept of fairness. Instead of viewing fairness in terms of the redistribution of income and wealth, Democrats need to define fairness in terms of a consistently higher standard of living. If the Democrats accept this new definition, they could lend support to a restructuring of the tax system so that it promotes growth. Rohatyn claims that the Republicans need to redefine their view of the proper economic role of government. Instead of a passive role for government, Republicans need to accept an active role for government in education, in the attainment of higher levels of infrastructure investment, and in the maintenance of a corporate safety net.

Additional readings on the issue of economic growth include "Saving, Economic Growth, and the Arrow of Causality," by Robert Eisner, *Challenge* (May/June 1995); "True Tax Reform: Encouraging Saving and Investment," by Murray Weidenbaum, *Business Horizons* (May/June 1995); "Technology and Growth: An Overview," by Jeffrey C. Fuhrer and Jane Sneddon Little, *New England Economic Review* (November/December 1996); "The Productivity Growth Slowdown: Diverging Trends in the Manufacturing and Service Sectors," by Sharon Kozicki, *Economic Review, Federal Reserve Bank of Kansas City* (First Quarter 1997); "Is the U.S. Economy Really Growing Too Slowly? Maybe We're Measuring Growth Wrong," by Leonard Nakamura, *Business Review, Federal Reserve Bank of Philadelphia* (March/April 1997); and "Breaking Down the Barriers to Technological Progress," by Preston J. Miller and James A. Schmitz Jr., *Federal Reserve Bank of Minneapolis 1996 Annual Report.*

# ISSUE 9

## Is Our Current Social Security Program Securely Anchored?

**YES: Robert M. Ball,** from "Keeping the Social Security Promise," An Original Essay Written for This Volume (1997)

**NO: Sylvester J. Schieber,** from "Social Security: Avoiding the Downstream Catastrophe," An Original Essay Written for This Volume (1997)

### ISSUE SUMMARY

**YES:** Robert M. Ball, former commissioner of Social Security, believes that Social Security is in good shape financially, and that the projected imbalances can be addressed through a series of minor adjustments.

**NO:** Sylvester J. Schieber, a business executive, sees a serious Social Security funding problem, and calls for fundamental change: movement from a completely defined benefits program to a partially defined benefits program.

It is not surprising, in retrospect, that an event as catastrophic as the Great Depression of the 1930s would produce fundamental changes in the American economy. The reality of the human suffering generated by the collapse of one-third of the nation's banks, an unemployment rate of 25 percent, and 30 percent declines in the production of goods, services, and household net worth led to a rush of legislation, which, in general terms, was intended to achieve two objectives: to restore confidence in the economy and to provide greater economic security. The institutions and programs created by this legislative avalanche are today familiar to almost all Americans: the Federal Deposit Insurance Corporation (FDIC), the Securities and Exchange Commission (SEC), and Social Security.

Social Security, more formally Old Age, Survivors, and Disability Insurance (OASDI), was signed into law on August 14, 1935, by President Franklin D. Roosevelt. As originally designed, OASDI provided three types of benefits: retirement benefits to the elderly who were no longer working, survivor benefits to the spouses and children of persons who have died, and disability benefits to persons who experience nonwork-related illness or injury. The Medicare portion of Social Security, which provides benefits for hospital, doctor, and medical expenses, was not created until 1965.

There are many terms used to describe OASDI. It is an entitlement program, that is, everyone who satisfies the eligibility requirements receives benefits. Eligibility is established by employment and contributions to the system (in the form of payroll taxes) for a minimum period of time. It is also a defined benefits program; that is, the level of benefits is determined by legislation. The opposite of a defined benefits program is a defined contributions program where benefits are determined by contributions and whatever investment income is generated by those contributions. OASDI is also described as a pay-as-you-go system; this means that payments received by recipients are financed primarily by the contributions of current workers. Still another description of OASDI is that it is an income security program. This refers to a whole set of government programs designed to provide minimum levels of income to various persons. Other income security programs include workmen's compensation, unemployment compensation, supplemental security income (SSI), and general assistance. Finally, OASDI is described as a social insurance program to distinguish it from private insurance programs. The insurance feature rests on the fact that OASDI protects against certain unforeseen events like disability or early death. The social feature arises from the fact that contributions and the level of benefits are determined by legislation as well as the fact that the contributions are mandatory (payroll taxes that must be paid).

With respect to the administration of OASDI, there are several components to consider. One component is the Social Security and Medicare Trustees. This six-member panel annually prepares estimates of the inflows and outflows of funds and examines the long-term actuarial soundness of the system. A second component is the Advisory Council, which is constituted every four years and reviews the projections of the trustees. In the process the council may offer suggestions for changes in the program. The third component involves both the Congress and the president because any changes to the system, in terms of contributions and benefits, require the passage of legislation.

All this serves as background for understanding the current issue. For the last several years the trustee projections have indicated that OASDI trust funds would fall below the "safe level" by the year 2030. These predictions were widely reported by the media as the "Social Security Crisis." The Advisory Council that was formed in 1994 met periodically during 1994 and 1995 to explore alternative solutions to the crisis and in early 1996 issued its own report. But the 13-member council could not agree on a single overall strategy to resolve the crisis; instead, it offered three different strategies.

In this issue two members of the Advisory Council present their views on the magnitude of the Social Security underfunding and then detail and defend their strategies for dealing with it. Robert M. Ball, along with five other members of the council, supports what has been called the Maintenance of Benefits Option that retains the basic structure of OASDI as a completely defined benefits program. Sylvester J. Schieber, along with four other members of the Advisory Council, supports a fundamental restructuring of OASDI, involving partial privatization with the creation of personal security accounts. This is an important issue, for it affects all of us. What we do with OASDI affects the amount of taxes we pay while we are working and our economic well-being during retirement.

# YES

Robert M. Ball

## SOCIAL SECURITY: KEEPING
## THE PROMISE

For 60 years, the United States has had a deliberate policy of promoting income security in retirement through a four-tier system: (1) a nearly universal, wage-related, contributory, defined-benefit Social Security plan; (2) supplementary employer-sponsored private pensions (now covering about one-half of the workforce); (3) individual savings; and (4) underlying the whole, a means-tested safety-net program, now called Supplemental Security Income (SSI). Social Security and SSI are federally-operated and financed, and private pensions and savings are explicitly promoted by federal tax policy.

Over 30 years ago, the Medicare program was added to this four-tier system because it was recognized that while a cash income could meet regular and recurring expenses, only a health insurance system could meet the unpredictable and sometimes very heavy cost of health care in retirement and during disability. So we now have a five-tier federally-promoted system for retirement security, each tier with a distinct mission and complementing the others.

Unlike Medicare, Social Security is in quite good shape financially, and can rather easily be brought into long-range balance. It is important that this be done promptly because what is now easy will become difficult if unattended to. The recently released 1997 report of the Trustees is the third in a row to report that *without any changes of any kind in the program*, the system will be able to pay full benefits on time until about 2030, and that after that date the continuing income from the payments of employers and employees (augmented by income from the taxes on benefits) would meet three-fourths of the cost. Even with the cost of benefits rising, after 75 years these sources of income alone would still meet about two-thirds of the cost.

Social Security is not "going broke." The long-range financing challenge is how to cope with a shortfall. In designing a financing plan we aren't starting from scratch after 2030 but rather with 75 percent of benefit costs already being financed by the tax rates in current law.

Another point about Social Security financing that is greatly misunderstood concerns the ratio of workers (those paying in) to the number of beneficiaries (those taking out). This ratio is dropping, and the change accounts for the increasing cost of Social Security in future years as the baby-boom generation retires. However, this ratio has always been recognized as the most important factor in the program's long-range costs and has been addressed in all the long-range estimates and provisions for financing. There are no surprises here. Yet commentators routinely treat the changing ratio as though we had suddenly discovered a situation that will make it overwhelmingly difficult to meet rising costs as the baby-boomers retire.

This is not the case. The current anticipated deficit has to do entirely with other factors. Half the new deficit is the result of a change in actuarial methods and in new sources of data, and half in changes in assumptions about the future growth of real wages, disability incidence, and other cost-controlling factors. (And it is entirely possible, of course, that similar adjustments resulting in either higher or lower cost estimates will need to be incorporated in future forecasts made over a 75-year period.)

## STRATEGIES TO STRENGTHEN SOCIAL SECURITY

A deficit of 2.23 percent of payroll could be eliminated by simply raising contribution rates 1.12 percentage points for workers and employers alike. It is doubtful, however, that such a big increase in taxes would be generally accepted as the best way of meeting the shortfall, and it is not necessary. There are other ways. Yet it is to be noted that the two groups of Advisory Council members advocating partial privatization of Social Security call for very large tax increases—deductions of an additional 1.6 percent from earnings

in one case and an increase of 1.52 percent in the combined payroll tax in the other case. As a matter of fact, if tax increases of this size were adopted, there would be no need for benefit cuts and certainly no financial reason for basic changes in Social Security, such as partial privatization. These tax increases alone would bring Social Security very close to the long-range balance; the remaining gap would be 0.6 percent of payroll in one plan and only slightly more in the other. If coupled with a correction of about −0.2 percent in the Consumer Price Index, which governs Social Security's cost-of-living adjustments—a correction very likely to be made as the result of the current reevaluation of the CPI by the Bureau of Labor Statistics—these tax increases would bring Social Security well within the definition of close actuarial balance as traditionally defined, i.e., with estimated benefit expenditures falling within 5 percent of estimated income. No other changes in benefits or taxes would be needed.

But instead of relying on big tax increases, there are several more attractive alternatives. The most important change would be to shift from pay-as-you-go financing to partial reserve financing so that part of the increasing costs in the future can be met from earnings on a fund build-up. The recent Advisory Council was unanimous on the desirability of this shift. And once partial reserve financing is adopted, the rate of return in the funds' investments becomes important.

In Social Security, the government is the administrator and fund manager of an enormous pension and group insurance plan. It collects dedicated taxes which are the equivalent of the premiums in a private insurance plan and the payments into the defined benefits plan of a private corporation or state retirement system. And it administers benefits which, like the dedicated tax contributions, are spelled out in detail in the law. There are, of course, important differences between Social Security's defined-benefit plan and the defined-benefit plans managed by the private sector and the states, but the broad characteristics are similar.

The administration of Social Security is very efficiently handled, costing less than one percent of income. But the government is not doing as well as it might in its role as fund manager. This is not because of any failure on the part of those managing the system but because Social Security by law is allowed to invest only in the most conservative of all investments: long-term, low-yield government bonds. Trustees of private pension systems and managers of state pension systems who have the authority to invest much more broadly would surely be replaced if they were to pursue such an ultraconservative investment policy.

To deny Social Security managers the same investment opportunities available to private fund managers means that Social Security will pay smaller benefits than private pensions can pay for each dollar of contribution (except to the extent that Social Security's low administrative costs offset the smaller investment gain). This differential, caused by prohibiting investments in private securities, accounts for much of the pressure to switch to a system of private savings plans as a partial substitute for Social Security. It leads to the cry, "Give me the money—I can do better on my own."

Yet increasing the investment return on Social Security contributions cannot be the whole answer to balancing Social Security nor is it a necessary part of the answer. The attached table shows a series of changes which together with an increase in the investment return would bring the program into long-range balance. The items in the chart alone eliminate about two-thirds of the long-range deficit and postpone the date of Trust Fund exhaustion from 2030 to 2050. Investing 40 percent of the fund build-up in stocks would do the rest.

If for whatever reason it were decided to keep all Trust Fund investments in government bonds, balance over the 75-year estimating period could still be maintained by implementing additional moderate tax increases or benefit cuts now or providing for gradual benefit cuts in the future by scheduling increases in the normal retirement age beyond the age 67 provided in present law.

Proposals to substitute a compulsory savings plan for part of Social Security seem undesirable for a variety of reasons and certainly unnecessary. But before looking more closely at the issues raised by privatization, it is important to put the debate in context by examining the nature of the Social Security system—both in law and by tradition.

## SOCIAL SECURITY AS AN ENTITLEMENT

Social Security is an "entitlement" program. In spite of the fact that entitlements on the whole have recently been given a bad name, the concept is of great importance to the future economic security of those covered by Social Security. The term deserves to be rehabilitated. In the case of Social Security, "entitlement" means that all people without distinction of sex, race, income, or behavior receive benefits in an amount specified by law once they have met the objective criteria of having worked in employment cov-

---

### STRENGTHENING SOCIAL SECURITY: RECOMMENDED STEPS FOR CONSIDERATION[1]

- **Starting point:** Over the long run (75 years), Social Security revenues are expected to fall short of outlays by . . . 2.23% of payroll.[2]
- **Goals:** Preserve long-term balance without making major changes in the program, and improve the benefit-contribution ration for younger workers.
- **Initial Steps:**

| Proposed Change | Rationale for Change | Impact on Deficit |
|---|---|---|
| 1. Increase taxation of benefits | Benefits should be taxed to the extent they exceed what the worker paid in, as is done with other contributory defined-benefit pension plans. | − 0.31 |
| 2. Change Cost of Living Adjustment (COLA) to reflect corrections to Consumer Price Index (CPI) | COLA is determined by CPI, which is widely believed to overstate inflation; anticipated corrections should result in downward adjustment of at least 0.2%. | − 0.20 |
| 3. Extend Social Security coverage to all newly hired state and local employees | Most state and local employees are already covered; the 3.7 million who are not are the last major group in labor force not covered. | − 0.22 |
| 4. Change wage-averaging period for benefits-computation purposes from 35 to 38 years. | Reduces benefits for future retirees an average of 3%. | − 0.28 |
| 5. Increase contribution rate 0.50% (0.25% for workers and employers alike) | Future workers as well as current and future beneficiaries should share modestly in correction of imbalance. | − 0.50 |

*(Box continued on next page)*

---

ered by the program for a specified period of time and have met other objective qualifications—by reaching age 62 for reduced retirement benefits, or by reaching age 65 for full benefits, or by having a total disability estimated to last for a long and indefinite period, or by having a relationship with a covered worker that gives them entitlement to benefits as a widow or widower, or by being the child of an insured worker.

In the case of Social Security and Medicare, as distinct from certain other entitlement programs such as food stamps, there is not only a *legal* entitlement, but since the benefits grow out of past earnings and contributions, they are looked on as an *earned* entitlement. Thus, although benefits and conditions for payment can be changed by law if the changes affect a broad category of participants in ways that are reasonable and

- **Long-term deficit remaining** after implementation of above changes . . . 0.75% of payroll.[3]
- **Conventional options** to eliminate this remaining deficit include: additional moderate tax increases or benefit cuts now or providing for gradual benefit cuts in the future by scheduling increases in the normal retirement age beyond the age 67 provided in present law. But all of these changes have the disadvantage of making Social Security less attractive to younger workers (by lowering the ratio of benefits to contributions), which strengthens the case for—
- **Investing some of Social Security's accumulating funds in equities:** Under present law, funds may be invested only in low-yield government bonds. Passively investing 40% of these funds in stocks indexed to the broad market would yield higher returns, closing the deficit and improving the benefit/contribution ratio for younger workers.[4]

[1]By Robert M. Ball, commissioner of Social Security 1962–73 and member of the Social Security Advisory Council 1994–96. [2]1997 estimate by the Social Security trustees, expressed as a percent of total covered payrolls: in other words, if Social Security payroll-tax rates had been increased by 2.23 percentage points in 1997, the long-term deficit would be eliminated. [3]Adjusted for interaction of proposed changes. [4]To help maintain the program in balance even beyond the traditional 75-year estimating period, a contribution-rate increase of 1.6% should be scheduled to go into effect in 2045, with the understanding that at that time, depending on actual experience, the increase may not be needed.

nondiscriminatory, there is a considerable reluctance on the part of Congress or the President to reduce protection or make radical changes. There is good reason for this. Social Security commitments are very long-term. People are contributing now to pay for benefits that may not be due for more than 40 years in the future, and a high degree of stability in both contribution rates and benefit levels is a valued part of the Social Security tradition—so much so that discussions of possible benefit reductions or other major changes make participants very uneasy.

The opposite of an entitlement is a discretionary payment, which if applied to

Social Security could mean—as it does in some programs—that benefit levels would be determined not by long-term considerations but by short-term budget cycles, in which various programs compete against each other for funding. It could even mean—as once was the case in welfare programs and may soon be again in some states (now that basic welfare policy has been turned back to the states) —that payments could vary according to the policies of individual administrators seeking to encourage or discourage certain behavior. Social insurance is designed to get away from all that, and the fundamental principle that determines the character of the program is that it is an *earned entitlement*. There would be little security in a Social Security system if benefits were to be altered every few years to adjust to short-term budget considerations. To make Social Security work, it has to be backed by long-term commitments —an entitlement, but an entitlement in return for work and contribution, not an entitlement granted simply by legislative fiat.

It is important also to the concept of Social Security that it have its own financing through earmarked contributions by participants. Thus, over the years, the test of adequate financing for Social Security has not been short-run, as with other programs, but rather whether the best estimates, projected across a very long period—75 years—show an approximate balance between earmarked income and benefits as specified in law.

## WHAT PARTIAL PRIVATIZATION MEANS

Proponents of partial privatization on the 1994–1996 Advisory Council on Social Security would significantly reduce the guarantee of an entitlement by, in one case, limiting benefits to what could be supported by present tax rates and, in the other proposal, by substituting a low, flat benefit. The first approach would require, over time, an average cut of 30 percent in the guaranteed benefit, and the second would cut the guaranteed benefit even more on average. Both plans call for substituting, for a part of the entitlement, a compulsory savings plan that would guarantee only that the worker be given an amount taken from his or her wages to invest, as with a 401(k) plan, for future income in retirement. So there would be two major changes: the Social Security en-

titlement would be cut back and, instead of being entitled to a full defined *benefit,* contributors would make defined *contributions* to various investment vehicles, with future income dependent in part on the success or failure of individual investment strategies. Under one plan, individual investments would be limited to a number of government-operated plans; under the other, investors could channel their deductions from wages to virtually any generally available investment account or broker.

The argument over privatization divides into two parts. First, why not invest part of the Social Security fund directly in private stocks? This increases the return on contributions and thus substantially improves the benefit/contribution ratio for younger workers as well as helping with the long-range balance. The main fear expressed by some is that if Social Security invests in stocks, Congress would force Social Security to make politically motivated investments. The fear is that instead of following a neutral policy of passive investment in indexed funds, Congress would steer investments toward or away from particular stocks according to some political agenda and would interfere in other ways with the best interest of the participants and with the operations of individual companies or industries.

Based on experience to date, this fear is entirely unwarranted. Managers of the Thrift Savings Plan (TSP), a major retirement plan for federal employees, and of the defined benefit plans of the Federal Reserve System and the Tennessee Valley Authority, all of which have been investing in private securities for many years, have remained entirely independent in their fund management. However, to provide additional safeguards, it would be possible to create an organization, modeled on the Board of Governors of the Federal Reserve System, to have broad responsibility for Social Security Trust Fund investments. The board would consist of experts confirmed by Congress and appointed for lengthy, staggered terms. By law the board would be required to pursue a policy of investment neutrality, a policy buttressed by being required to invest in broadly indexed funds and to select private portfolio managers experienced in handling large indexed accounts. While under our political system there can obviously be no absolutely iron-clad guarantees against attempts at political manipulation, the record of the Board of Governors of the Federal Reserve makes clear that this approach can insulate decision-makers and protect the principle of independence in policy-making.

Second, what, if anything, is wrong with shifting part of Social Security protection over to personal savings-and-investment accounts? There are several problems.

### Individual Accounts

First let us consider the plan of one group within the Advisory Council called "Individual Accounts" (IA). This plan, it should be noted, would modify the present program less than just about any of the other proposals for privatization that have been discussed both within and outside of the Advisory Council, but it still seems entirely unsatisfactory.

In discussing the IA plan, it is important to bear in mind that, as previously noted, the plan requires an additional deduction from workers' earnings of 1.6 percent. I am inclined to think that this alone might well be enough to make the proposal unacceptable to the public,

since no corresponding increase in Social Security protection is proposed. The whole objective of the IA plan is to reduce the benefits covered by the government guarantee to a level where over the long run they can be financed by present Social Security contribution rates, while hoping that the new Individual Accounts will, on average, make up for the cuts in the guaranteed Social Security plan. Since the objective is only to make up for the cuts *on average*, it may be assumed that for many people, in spite of the increase in deductions from their earnings, the combined benefits of the residual government plan and the savings benefits will actually be substantially lower than those of the government plan under present law. This does not seem to be a very attractive proposition: higher deductions from workers' earnings than under present law, but a considerable risk that one might be in the group that will get less in benefits than the present government guarantee.

To be fair, in making comparisons with today's guarantees it needs to be recognized that the present level of benefits is not adequately funded for the long run. So people will need to choose—to decide whether a menu of modest proposals to bring the present program into balance is as onerous as having earnings reduced an additional 1.6 percent coupled with lower benefits for those who get a less-than-average return from their individual account and in all cases lose guaranteed defined benefit protection.

Under the IA plan, individual savers would have a limited choice of investment vehicles, perhaps five to ten indexed funds, managed and invested by the federal government as in the case of the Thrift Savings Plan. At retirement age, the retiree would be required to take out a lifetime annuity underwritten by the government with a guaranteed period of payment and with protection against inflation by price indexing. The annuitant also would be required to take out a joint and survivors annuity to protect the annuitant's spouse—unless, as is the case under the Employee Retirement Income Security Act (ERISA) requirement for private pension plans, the spouse agrees in writing to waive this right. It should be noted that with the government directly handling the investment of the funds in the savings accounts, this plan does not do much for the financial industry. The Advisory Council assumed that the cost of financial management would be low—only 10 basis points.

Perhaps the worst thing about this plan is that it increases the risk that retirement income will be inadequate. The IA plan shifts Social Security away from a defined-*benefit* plan toward a defined-*contribution* plan. This is a bad idea. By definition, defined-contribution plans contain no guarantees regarding the amount of the benefit. With more and more private-sector employers offering only defined-contribution 401(k) pension plans, it is all the more important that the nation's *basic* plan be maintained as a defined-benefit plan with amounts available in retirement determined by law rather than by the risks and uncertainties of individual investment.

The increased risk arises, of course, not solely from the general risk of picking investments that perform badly but also from the fact that individuals are inevitably exposed to the risk of being forced to begin or end an investment period at a bad time. Workers are required to start making the investments when they go to work and end them when they re-

tire and convert the accumulation to an annuity. But they have no control over conditions in the stock market at these times.

Moreover, although the intent of the IA plan is to create a nationwide system of individual retirement accounts, with both the principal and the income available only in retirement, it is very doubtful that this objective could be preserved in practice. As with today's IRAs and 401(k) plans, people will want to use individual savings accounts for medical, educational, housing, or other needs. With funds going into *individually-named* accounts, as provided for under the IA plan, account holders will assuredly find it unreasonable to be denied access to their "personal" funds in an emergency situation—or indeed for any purpose that seems worthwhile—and Congress and the Executive Branch can be expected to go along, as is already happening with IRAs and 401(k)s. As a result, the amounts that would actually be available at retirement under the IA plan would almost certainly be much lower than predicted by the plan's proponents.

Looking at the two parts of the plan together—the part guaranteed by the government plus the individual savings part—the IA plan would achieve a better return on total investment than the current Social Security system, assuming pay-as-you-go increases in the contribution rates to make up for the shortfall under present law. However, the residual Social Security part of the IA plan, looked at separately, would not do at all well on this test—a fact that could lead to the unraveling of the whole plan.

As the plan developed over time, with beneficiaries doing less and less well under the reduced Social Security plan compared to individual accounts (at least in the case of the more successful investors), there would be every reason for many above-average earners to press for further reductions in contributions to Social Security in order to be able to shift more of their Social Security contributions to their individual accounts. Thus the IA plan is inherently unstable, and would probably lead to further cutbacks in government-guaranteed benefit levels.

This approach to retirement security raises another troubling issue. How far should we go in compelling people to save for retirement? It is not doing average and below-average earners any favors to make them save more for the sole purpose of trying to increase their income in retirement. Millions of workers are living from paycheck to paycheck, spending whatever they have on food, clothing, shelter, schooling and other immediate needs—and still falling short of an adequate standard of living. And for many workers, protecting against the unforeseeable cost of health care may be a higher priority than setting aside more income for retirement. Yet the IA plan's sponsors take no note of these needs.

Partial-privatization proponents simply accept, as a given, that more should be deducted from workers' wages now to improve their cash income in retirement. But many workers, if asked, might prefer to earmark any deductions from earnings beyond those needed to support the present level of Social Security either for current health insurance or for Medicare in their retirement. After all, Medicare is just as important as cash benefits to the financial security of retirees and the disabled, and the Medicare Hospital Insurance (HI) fund faces problems in the near term. To ignore Medicare's immediate needs in order to finance a long-term re-

design of Social Security strikes me as a serious inversion of priorities.

If Congress is willing to support a payroll tax increase of 1.6 percent (which is doubtful), directing it to Medicare would be sufficient to postpone the HI's fund exhaustion by about 15 years, thus providing a substantial planning period in which to design and implement needed structural changes. When combined with these changes, a tax rate increase of a small fraction of 1.6 percent is enough to support the present level of Social Security benefits. The IA plan puts the whole burden of maintaining the present benefit level on deductions from worker wages.

### Personal Security Accounts

The other plan proposed by some members of the Advisory Council to privatize a part of Social Security—the "Personal Security Accounts" (PSA) plan—would, over time, completely abolish the present Social Security system and substitute a flat benefit payment varying only by the length of time under the system—with full coverage, one would have a guaranteed benefit of $410 a month, increased over time to keep up with rising wages—augmented by 5 percent of earnings invested by the individual in any generally available investment vehicle.

The combined payroll tax on employers and employees would be increased 1.52 percent, with the increase maintained over the next 70 years or so to meet the cost of paying benefits to current retirees and others with a stake in the present system while at the same time funding a new compulsory savings plan for those under age 55. This 1.52 percent of payroll is the so-called "transition" cost of switching from a pay-as-you-go system (Social Security today) to a funded savings plan. It is a very long and very costly "transition." For many years —across the span of two generations— workers must pay twice: once for their own protection and once for the protection of those already retired and older workers with an investment under the old system.

In addition, to make the financing of the plan work, it is necessary to borrow very large amounts from the federal government—as much as $2 trillion in 1997 dollars at the peak, $15 trillion in nominal dollars. Borrowing on this scale is required because, although the payroll tax increase of 1.52 percent meets the *average* transition cost over some 70 years, the cost is above average at first—for about 30 years, in fact. Then, with the cost gradually declining after 30 years, it becomes possible to gradually repay the loan out of the tax increase.

This larger privatization scheme has all the disadvantages of the IA plan —plus many more. In the first place, it is doubtful whether such a plan could be administered. The government would need to see that 5 percent of workers' earnings were deducted each payday and sent to any of thousands of financial institutions or brokers and kept invested until retirement, while at the same time allowing workers to shift from one investment arrangement to another and adding new funds each payday to the same or a different account. It is difficult to see how this would work with smaller employers and an unlimited number of investment opportunities. And administration also entails trying to make clear to people what their individual benefits would be: how benefits are computed under the old plan, how the transitional benefits work, and how this new hybrid system's

benefits all fit together. Each part of the plan is complicated within itself and when combined with the others creates a situation that defies explanation. The total job of administration would be chaotic, expensive, and quite likely unmanageable at any price. (It should be noted, however, that no allowance has been made for administration in the estimated cost of this plan except for an allowance of 100 basis points for the cost of investing.)

There are other problems. The PSA plan does not provide for inflation protection or annuitization. (Individuals desiring annuities would have to buy them in the private market, which necessarily has to charge an extra premium to protect against the fact that those who buy annuities ordinarily have longer than average life expectancies.) Moreover, the plan does not require protection for a spouse. And, although survivors and disability protection are continued as part of the government guaranteed plan, over time the disability benefits would be cut about 30 percent below present law.

Finally, a government system supported by a wage tax but with a benefit unrelated to wages will clearly be a bad deal for above-average earners, who are therefore likely to give the government part of the PSA plan little support. Thus this whole plan could easily end up as simply a compulsory individual savings plan—without the present program's ability to redistribute income from the higher-paid to the lower-paid— supplemented by a government safety-net program testing individual need (as in the case of SSI). This would represent a major loss of security for many workers, particularly those with lower-than-average lifetime earnings. For society as a whole, that loss of security would mean greater reliance on welfare programs, with all their flaws, difficulty of administration, and lack of political support.

## BUILDING ON WHAT WORKS

Whatever their attractions, partial-privatization schemes have seemingly insurmountable disadvantages. They are a high-cost, high-risk approach to retirement security. In essence, they require workers to contribute more of their wages than at present in order to fund two distinct systems: one offering reduced benefits and the other promising uncertain returns. One can imagine workers and beneficiaries choosing this approach only if they believe the present system is going broke and needs to be replaced, and only if they are unaware of the philosophy that has made Social Security so successful for so long.

Social Security is a blend of reward for individual effort and, at the same time, a strong affirmation of community solidarity. Social Security is based on the premise that we're all in this together, with everyone sharing responsibility not only for contributing to their own and their family's security but also to the security of everyone else, present and future.

There is nothing sentimental about this approach; it is neither liberal nor conservative. It simply makes sense. Lacking a crystal ball—unable to know in advance who will succeed and who will struggle unsuccessfully, who will suffer early death or disability and who will live long into retirement, in good health or ill—we pool our resources and are thus able to guard against the average risk at manageable cost to each of us. Social Security's redistributive benefit formula, feasible only in a system in which nearly everyone participates, not only helps to protect us all against impoverishment but, because it is part of a universal system, does so at much lower administrative cost than private insurance and without the stigma of a welfare program.

The unique strengths of this approach argue for retaining our traditional multi-tier retirement system with Social Security as the foundation. Basic protection that one can count on is particularly important in a dynamic, risk-taking economy such as ours, in which long-established businesses, sometimes whole industries, may fade even as new ones are springing up. More than most, our economy rewards rapid adaptation to changing conditions; that is one reason why it functions well at the aggregate level. But the more dynamic the economy, the greater the need for individuals to be protected against economic circumstances beyond their control. In short, we need the basic security that Social Security uniquely supplies regardless of downsizing, mergers, bankruptcies, the volatility of the job market, and the uncertainty of individual investments.

Social Security as presently constituted clearly meets the test of what Lincoln described as the legitimate objective of government: "to do for a community of people whatever they need to have done but cannot do at all or cannot do so well for themselves in their separate and individual capacities." Compulsory individual savings plans do not meet this test—and we would be well advised to keep Lincoln's wise words in mind as we consider various proposals to "individualize" our Social Security system.

# NO

**Sylvester J. Schieber**

# SOCIAL SECURITY: AVOIDING THE DOWNSTREAM CATASTROPHE

## INTRODUCTION

For more than 20 years now, the movie *To Fly* has been shown several times each day at the Air and Space Museum of the Smithsonian Institution in Washington, DC. The beginning of the movie is set in 1876 and in an early scene a balloonist is seen floating over a very peaceful river as he notices a trapper paddling below in a canoe. After a bit, from his high perch the balloonist sees some dangerous white water and waterfalls down river. The balloonist, seeing that the trapper has no clue of the pending danger, screams down to the trapper that there is white water down river and he must get to shore for his own safety. In the movie, the trapper paddles safely toward shore. This scene is a good analogy for the nature and scope of the financing problem now facing Social Security.

## THE NATURE AND SCOPE OF THE SOCIAL SECURITY FINANCING PROBLEM

This year Social Security will collect approximately $60 billion more in revenues than it will incur in expenses through the Old Age and Survivors Insurance and the Disability Insurance (OASDI) programs. Trust fund balances in the combined programs currently exceed $500 billion. Social Security's current funding flows and trust fund balances might encourage us to be tranquil about the downstream prospects of its operations. But its actuaries and trustees have been telling us for some time that the program is significantly underfunded for future generations of retirees. The most recent Trustees Report suggests that the payroll tax would have to be about 2.23 percentage points higher than it is today to provide promised benefits over the next 75 years.[1]

Some students of the program trivialize its underfunding by saying that 2.23 percent of covered payroll over the next 75 years is no big deal; that current law tax rates would meet two-thirds of promised benefits even after the trust funds are depleted; and that there are some very simple marginal adjustments that can rebalance the system. These arguments are misleading.

If the current actuarial imbalance is to be made up through a tax increase, it would represent an 18 percent increase in the program's cost over the next 75 years. Such an increase in the tax that has become the largest federal tax for many workers is no trivial matter. If it were imposed this year, it would amount to $72 billion and it would grow at the compound rate of average wage growth in the future. In addition, the 2.23 percent figure assumes that we could have raised the payroll tax rate 2.23 percentage points early in 1997 and "banked" the added accumulation, or cut benefits by a comparable amount. This assumption is problematic for several reasons: it does not consider the deteriorating funding status of the program at the end of the 75-year projection period; there are questions about the government's ability to convert added payroll tax collections into national savings; and by the time action is finally taken, the funding gap will be much larger than it is currently.

Social Security today is no more in "crisis" than the man in the canoe described earlier. But the man in the canoe, with the benefit of the downstream perspective of the balloonist, realized that he would be in danger if he did not change his course. Our situation with Social Security is similar to that of the man in the canoe. The program's actuaries have warned us several times that there is a significant problem downstream. Not only have they warned us repeatedly of Social Security's actuarial imbalance, their estimates of the magnitude of the imbalance

have consistently worsened over the last 15 years as reflected in Table 1.

The table shows that since 1983 the projected accumulation in the trust funds has diminished significantly in virtually every subsequent valuation of the ongoing operations of the program. The actuarial underfunding of the program, stated as a percentage of covered payroll over the 75-year projection period, has also worsened in almost every projection year since 1983. The year that we expect the trust fund to be depleted has also worsened significantly over the the projection period. Finally, the projected underfunding of the program has grown by more than $3 trillion since 1983. We have been told repeatedly that this program is significantly underfunded downstream, and each subsequent valuation tells us that the underfunding is worse than that revealed in the last valuation. One Canadian actuary characterizes the unfolding picture as a "predictable surprise." The essence of his characterization is that the problems we face are highly predictable, but it is likely that we will still be surprised when we finally experience them because we have refused to deal with them.

## BALANCING SOCIAL SECURITY WITHIN THE CONTEXT OF GOVERNMENT'S TOTAL OPERATIONS

In 1997, total expenditures under the OASDI programs will be an estimated 4.66 percent of our gross domestic product (GDP). By 2030, the OASDI claim on the economy is expected to rise to 6.57 percent of GDP and by 2035 to 6.64 percent. In other words, over the next 30 to 35 years, we expect Social Security's claim on the economy

*Table 1*

**Projected Maximum OASDI Trust Fund Accumulations in Current Dollars, Projected 75-Year Actuarial Balance as a Percentage of Covered Payroll, and Estimated Year Trust Funds Will Be Depleted by Year of Actuarial Estimate and Present Values of 75-Year Surpluses of OASDI Funds Relative to Obligations**

| Year of Estimate | Projected Maximum Trust Fund Balance ($ billions) | Actuarial Balance as Percent of Payroll | Year Trust Fund Projected to Be Depleted | Present Value of Tax Income **plus** Current Fund **minus** Obligations ($ billions) |
|---|---|---|---|---|
| 1983 | $20,750 | 0.02 | 2063 | $148.3 |
| 1984 | 18,393 | −0.06 | 2059 | 37.4 |
| 1985 | 11,955 | −0.41 | 2049 | −268.8 |
| 1986 | 12,739 | −0.44 | 2051 | −342.6 |
| 1987 | 12,411 | −0.62 | 2051 | −377.6 |
| 1988 | 11,838 | −0.58 | 2048 | −664.0 |
| 1989 | 11,930 | −0.70 | 2046 | −849.5 |
| 1990 | 9,233 | −0.91 | 2045 | −1,242.7 |
| 1991 | 8,020 | −1.08 | 2041 | −1,185.1 |
| 1992 | 5,535 | −1.46 | 2036 | −1,772.6 |
| 1993 | 4,923 | −1.46 | 2036 | −1,863.7 |
| 1994 | 2,976 | −2.13 | 2029 | −2,841.9 |
| 1995 | 3,275 | −2.17 | 2030 | −2,832.7 |
| 1996 | 2,829 | −2.19 | 2029 | −3,094.2 |
| 1997 | 2,834 | −2.23 | 2029 | |

Sources: 1983 to 1997 Annual Reports of the Board of Trustees of the Federal Old-Age and Survivors Insurance and Disability Insurance Trust Funds (Washington, DC: Social Security Administration) and the Office of the Actuary, Social Security Administration.

to grow by about 2 percentage points. Some analysts would have us believe that such a shift in national resources to this vital retirement program can be achieved without significant difficulty. One of the problems that we face in rebalancing Social Security is that it is only one of several governmental programs that will be affected by the aging of our society. The combination of these programs, including Social Security, Medicare, Medicaid, and other federal retirement programs, will place a tremendous strain on the government's fiscal operations.

Figure 1 shows three-year averages of the total receipts of the federal government as a percentage of gross domestic product (GDP) starting with Fiscal Year 1951 through Fiscal Year 1996. Three-year averages are used here rather than the actual annual data to smooth the effects of economic cycles on tax revenues. Over the 45-year period from the end of the Korean War, total federal tax receipts have varied from a low of 17.1 percent of GDP to a high of 19.3 percent, only about a 2 percentage point variation in the claim that the federal government has made on

Figure 1

**Three-Year Averages of Total Federal Receipts as a Percentage of GDP**

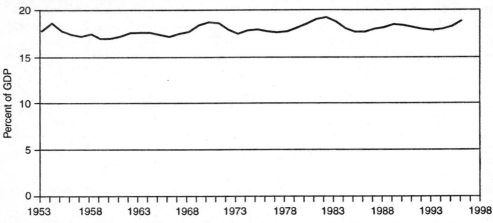

Source: *Historical Tables: Budget of the United States Government, Fiscal Year 1998*, pp. 21–22.

taxpayers. Even looking at actual year-to-year numbers, the maximum claim in any year was 19.7 percent of GDP.

While there is no natural limit to government's claim on the economy, there are clearly political forces that have narrowly limited the amount U.S. taxpayers have rendered to it over virtually all of the last half century. If total government revenue claims on the economy are narrowly limited and Social Security is scheduled to make a bigger claim than currently, then some other government expenditures must shrink. It is here that projected expansions in Social Security's economic claims would seem to be particularly constrained.

Figure 2 shows the projected increases in the claims on the economy by various federal entitlement programs between 1996 and 2030. The graphic shows the projected increasing claim of Social Security as discussed earlier. The projected relative growth in Medicare claims is expected to far outstrip that of OASDI. Some analysts conclude from

this picture that we should really focus our energies for managing entitlement growth on federal medical programs in general and Medicare in particular. They claim that if we can restrain the rapid growth in the health care programs, we can sustain projected growth in the cash retirement programs.[2]

While constraining federal health programs for the elderly may be desirable, it will be more difficult to do so than constraining the cash programs for retirees for four reasons. First, old people simply use more health care services than younger ones. Second, the percentage of our population over age 65 is expected to grow by as much between 2010 and 2030 as it had in the prior 80 years. The third factor that will make it difficult to reduce Medicare expenditures is the excessive price inflation that persists in the health sector of our economy. The fourth factor that will drive up future health costs is the continued technological development in the health sector and increasingly intensive treatment of patients.[3]

These four factors are all compounding factors that will drive up the cost of Medicare claims even in the face of program reforms. Current projections suggest that under present law Medicare's claim on the economy will grow from 2.5 percent of GDP today to 7.5 percent by 2030. The underlying assumptions in that projection, however, assume that the added price inflationary pressures and the increased costs of treatment due to cost expanding technologies will largely be eliminated by the end of the first decade of the next century, just as the first of the baby boomers begin to turn age 65. In other words, current Medicare projections assume we will have an amelioration in inflationary pressures on this program just as the baby boomers begin to bring on tremendous levels of new demand.

The point of this discussion is that the potential rededication of 2 percent of GDP to rebalance OASDI might be tenable if that were the only imbalance that the government were facing. But it is not. As we look for policy options to deal with Social Security, we have to consider rebalancing it in the larger context of the total federal government's claim on the economy and within the context of other entitlements that must be financed out of total government revenues.

## SOCIAL SECURITY REFORM OPTIONS

Social Security is financed largely by the earmarked payroll tax, and promised benefits are defined in current law. The problem of insufficient revenues to meet the promised benefit stream can be addressed in a number of ways. One would be to simply raise the payroll tax by the necessary amount to meet benefit

*Figure 2*

**Current and Projected Levels of Entitlement Program Operations as a Percent of GDP**

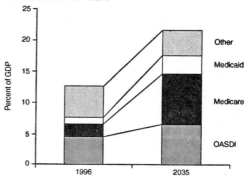

Source: Congressional Budget Office, *Long-Term Budgetary Pressures and Policy Options* (Washington, DC: The Congress of the United States, March 1997), Executive Summary, Table 2.

promises. There is very little support for this option even among the staunchest supporters of the current system.[4] An alternative way would be to reduce benefits by a sufficient amount to live within the current payroll tax rates. The Advisory Council actually considered a proposal along these lines, but no one on the Council was willing to support the proposal because of the resulting low levels of benefits that would be provided by the program and because of the relatively low rates of return that future generations of workers would receive under this approach to reform.[5]

Given the reluctance to address the shortfalls explicitly through straightforward tax increases or benefit reductions, a number of Advisory Council members opted to impose a set of implicit charges on workers and beneficiaries to cover actuarial shortfalls under the auspices of the "Maintenance of Benefits" (MB) option. They advocated: (1) increasing the number of years of earnings used in determining benefits from 35 to 38;(2) diverting income tax revenues on Social Security benefits now going to the Medicare HI trust fund to the OASDI funds; (3) taxing all benefits above workers' own lifetime nominal payroll tax contributions—i.e., their own basis in benefits; (4) investing 40 percent of the trust funds in the private equity markets to get a higher rate of return than that provided by current investments; and (5) raising the payroll tax rate by 1.6 percentage points in 2045. While only the last of these could be characterized as an explicit tax increase, each of the others would implicitly increase taxes or reduce benefits for program participants.

The majority of the Advisory Council members opposed the MB option largely because of its last two elements. The proposal to invest Social Security trust funds in the private equity markets would make the federal government by far the largest owner of private capital in our economy. Such a policy might result in politically motivated investment of such capital for reasons other than the economic interests of the program's participants. Even as the Advisory Council's debate was unfolding, Secretary of Labor Robert Reich was advocating that some of the assets in employer-based pensions should be used for "economically-targeted investment" purposes. At the height of the debate within the Advisory Council over this proposal, the Clinton Administration actually tapped federal workers' pension funds to avoid debt ceiling limits that were being exceeded during the budget battle with Congressional Republicans early in 1996. Concerns about the political use of retirement funds held by the federal government is not a pipe dream; it has already been a reality. An OASDI

trust fund holding more than a trillion dollars worth of equities in today's dollars would be much more tempting for such uses than the relatively small existing federal retirement funds that hold only a few billion dollars today. There are many cases, from California to Kansas to New York where the investment of assets in public retirement plans at the state and local levels has been influenced or dictated by political rather than economic considerations. Around the world, there are also cases from Singapore to Sweden where the assets in partially funded national retirement systems have been used for social investing purposes. While the advocates of Social Security becoming our economy's largest private investor dream up ways to insulate the investing from political directives, there is no way that a current Congressional limitation in this regard could preclude future Congresses from undoing it.

In addition to the problems of politicizing investment decisions, the MB proposal would also raise conflict of interest questions as the government reconciled its role as a fiduciary responsible for protecting the economic value of its portfolio while at the same time fulfilling its responsibility as a regulator of businesses in the interest of public welfare. Finally, it would raise issues of corporate governance. The advocates of this proposal suggest that the government would not vote its shareholder interests in proxy voting matters. Such a policy would change the relative balance of other stockholders on proxy votes and would be contrary to the government's own position on employer-based retirement program fiduciaries voting their ownership position for shares in their pension programs. Some members of the Advisory Council found it ironic that

U.S. policymakers would be considering a massive governmental buy-up of our economy's private capital as we enter the 21st century while many other governments around the world are moving in exactly the opposite direction because of lessons learned from the U.S. experience during the 20th century. The majority of the Advisory Council members opposed the proposed tax increase in 2045 because they felt it was patently unfair to propose tax rates on our grandchildren that we were not willing to pay ourselves.

Those Advisory Council members opposed to the MB proposal, 7 out of the total 13 members on the Council, proposed substantial reform of the current structure of Social Security as the means to salvage the system. They recommended that part of the solution include some funding of benefits through individual accounts. Two members developed an "Individual Account" (IA) proposal where the individual accounts would be financed by an added employee contribution of 1.6 percent of covered payroll with the accounts being held and managed by the Social Security Administration. Although workers would be given some discretion in directing where the individual account funds would be invested under this proposal, the other five members of the Council felt that it was inappropriate to have Social Security managing the funds for the same set of reasons that they opposed the MB proposal.

These latter five members of the Council, including me, felt that the accounts should be financed by the workers' share of the payroll tax contributions now going to finance retirement benefits through Social Security—namely 5 percent of covered payroll. Under our proposal, workers would have considerable discretion in investing their retirement assets held

in the form of "Personal Security Accounts" (PSAs) just as they do in the investment of individual retirement accounts and 401(k) assets.[6] The PSA proposal raises a transitional financing issue because current benefits are largely financed by current payroll tax revenues. If workers are allowed to keep their portion of the payroll tax that finances retirement benefits, added revenues would be required to meet current benefit commitments.

Figure 3 indicates the magnitude of the transition costs under the PSA proposal if it were to be financed on a pay-as-you-go basis through a supplemental payroll tax. The top line in the figure is the combined employer and employee tax rates that would be required in each year of the transition. The lower line shows the current law rate of 12.4 percent of covered payroll. If the transition is financed on a pay-as-you-go basis, the payroll tax to support the non-Medicare portion of the total benefit package would have to increase to roughly 15.9 percent of payroll shortly after the transition begins. Under this transition approach, virtually all of the transitional costs would be paid off within the span of a regular working lifetime. Workers near the end of their careers when the plan was implemented would incur a relatively high cost for a few years at the end of their careers. Workers who were young when the proposal was adopted would bear the full burden of the transition costs throughout their lives. Those entering the work force near the end of the transition would bear little of the cost. While all generations might benefit from this proposal under the right circumstances, it seemed unfair to distribute the costs

*Figure 3*

**Pay-As-You-Go Payroll Tax to Fund Transition to Personal Security Accounts**

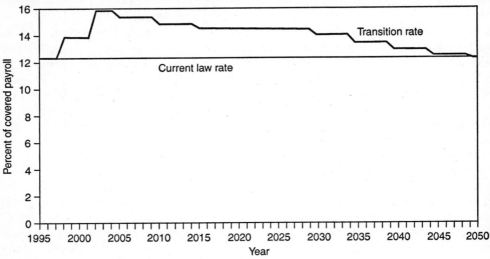

Source: Office of the Actuary, Social Security Administration.

of transition so heavily onto a single generation of workers.

To address the concerns about intergenerational fairness, we proposed that the transition not be financed purely on a pay-as-you-go basis. We proposed levying a flat 1.52 percent payroll tax over roughly 70 years with transitional borrowing when the transitional payroll tax supplement is insufficient to meet pay-as-you-go costs. Under this transition proposal, the burden on any single worker would not increase more than 12.3 percent (i.e., 1.52 percent payroll tax supplement divided by the base rate of 12.4 percent) in any given year. This compares with the pay-as-you-go transition where some workers would incur payroll tax increases of as much as 28.2 percent (i.e., 3.5 percent supplement divided by 12.4 percent). Spreading the transition costs over a larger number of cohorts of participants would make the transition less

onerous for those caught at the early part of the transition. Of course, it increases the cost for those at the end of the transition, but the workers adversely affected have the most to gain from the proposal under consideration.

Under the PSA proposal, the transitional federal borrowing would reach about 2 percent of GDP in 2007 and then gradually decline to zero around 2030 or so. The transitional borrowing would add to formal government debt. The added debt would peak at around 20 percent of GDP by 2020 and decline after that. At its peak, the present value of the added government debt would be equal to about $1.1 trillion. In the context of today's dollars, the borrowing would peak at $2.4 trillion. The added debt would be completely paid off by 2070 under the transition program.

Critics of the PSA proposal argue that the transitional costs are simply too great to be borne by workers and by the government. Their arguments seek to obfuscate the actual obligations that are implied by the current operations of Social Security and to confuse people about the financial transactions that would be involved in the various reform approaches. They argue that lower- and average-wage workers cannot afford to pay the extra cost of transitioning out of the current system. They argue that a government striving to balance its budget cannot afford to take on the transitional debt that would be involved in the PSA proposal. Both arguments are misleading.

If anyone disputes the Social Security's actuaries' estimates of the program's underfunding, they argue that the estimates are overly optimistic. They point to the continuous deterioration in the projections reported in Table 1 to support their case. Taking the actuaries' estimates as reasonable, however, even the MB proponents agree that the current system is underfunded over the next 75 years by about 20 percent. Their proposal would basically protect almost all of the benefits promised under current law. They would have us believe that they can accomplish this without increasing the payroll tax rate. From an economic perspective though, the 2.23 percent of payroll actuarial deficit can only be closed by imposing a real economic cost on the economy. Someone has to pay it regardless of whether it is borne through an explicit tax on workers, an explicit reduction in payments to beneficiaries, or some other hidden claim. The MB proposal would rely heavily on the latter route. Many analysts believe that the MB proposal would lead to higher interest rates on government borrowing because it would have the government buy up $1 trillion worth

of equities without creating significant new savings in the economy.[7] Such an increase in interest rates would undoubtedly carry over into increased interest rates on home mortgages, consumer debt, and other borrowing, directly affecting the well being of lower- and middle-wage workers. In short, there is no magic way to close this deficit without imposing costs on someone. The question is on whom we want to impose costs and how to impose them.

The confusion over the creation of "federal debt" under the PSA transition proposal arises because the government does its accounting purely on a cash basis. Under cash accounting the only governmental debt that is recognized in a given year is the difference in cash receipts and expenditures for the year. As such debt arises, the holders of the debt are issued government bonds. These bonds represent a claim on future revenue streams of the government and, as such, they represent obligations that will have to be met by future taxpayers. The cash accounting that recognizes the government's formal debt, however, only recognizes part of the true operations under federal financing and expenditure programs. It does not recognize the unfunded obligations that arise under various federal programs such as Social Security. For example, looking back to Table 1, the unfunded obligations in the OASDI programs have risen from zero at the end of 1984 to more than $3 trillion at the end of 1996. Just as in the case of formal federal debt, these obligations also represent a claim on future revenue streams of the government and, as such, they also represent obligations that will have to be met by future taxpayers. The only difference between them and the formal debt is that one is accounted for and the other is not when we calculate the annual budget flows and balances. Some analysts claim that there is a difference in the two forms of obligations because Congress can restructure Social Security, thus wiping out the statutory obligations under the program. While that is technically true, the thought of completely reneging on accrued benefits under the program has never been proposed by anyone. That means that much, if not most, of these statutory unfunded obligations will be every bit as burdensome to future taxpayers as the servicing of the formal debt obligations will be. Indeed, the MB proposal would have us cover virtually all of Social Security's current unfunded obligations.

When the total economic costs of the various proposals developed by the Social Security Advisory Council are considered, the proposed borrowing in the PSA plan can be seen in an appropriate perspective. Table 2 shows the estimated present value of the 75-year total federal obligations under the three proposals put forward by Council members. The PSA plan, including the full cost of transition financing cuts the obligations to future taxpayers by significantly more than either of the other proposals. The formal debt that would be created under the PSA would arise because of a restructuring of total federal obligations in a way that would ultimately reduce those obligations.

Table 2 is quite clear that either the PSA or IA proposals would significantly reduce the "entitlement" obligations of the federal government through reformation of Social Security. While some people believe that would be inadvisable policy, they have failed to address the issues raised by the projected growth in federal entitlement claims on the economy that

were discussed earlier. The only way we can keep Social Security, Medicare, and other federally sponsored retirement programs from making a larger claim on the economy than historical levels of total government funding is by constraining them. In that regard, the MB proposal and others like it are a total failure. It is likely that we can only accomplish the kinds of reductions in costs necessary to maintain Social Security's future viability by significantly restructuring it to meet the needs of workers and retirees in the 21st century.

## SHIFTING FROM A DEFINED BENEFIT TO A PARTIAL DEFINED CONTRIBUTION REGIME

The individual account approaches included in the IA and PSA plans would change the defined benefit nature of Social Security. Once again, some people see this as an undesirable change to the existing system. They raise the specter of individual financial risk and argue that exposing workers to such risk would be bad public policy. What they fail to address in their arguments is that the current system is fraught with risks that are not accounted for in their analysis. The implications of these risks are clear when the last two major policy adjustments to the Social Security Act are considered.

During the early 1970s the Social Security system faced a severe short-term financing crisis because of rapid growth in new retirees' benefit levels. The 1977 Amendments addressed this problem by reducing by about 25 percent the benefits of workers who would become eligible to retire five years after the implementation date of the Amendments. Despite the severe benefit reductions they imposed, the 1977 Amendments failed to completely

Table 2

## Present Value of OASDI's 75-Year Obligations under Alternative Policy Options

|  | Obligations | Change from current law | Percent change |
|---|---|---|---|
|  | (dollar amount in billions) | | |
| Present law | $ 21,345 | — | — |
| PSA flat benefit plus transition tax | 16,487 | 4,858 | 22.8 |
| OASDI benefit under IA proposal | 18,867 | 2,478 | 11.6 |
| MB proposal | 21,177 | 228 | 1.1 |

Source: Derived from tables prepared by the Social Security Administration, Office of the Actuary for 1994–1996 Social Security Council.

address the short-term financing problem and by the early 1980s the program faced trust fund insolvency. In addition, by the early 1980s there was growing awareness of the long-term financing problems facing the program. The 1983 Amendments were meant to address both of these by further curtailing benefits. While the 1983 Amendments supposedly "fixed" Social Security's financing problems for at least the next 80 years, here we are again less than 15 years later worrying about the system's underfunding. In a little over a decade, Social Security will begin to run a cash flow deficit, and it is projected to be facing insolvency before the youngest members of the baby boom generation are eligible to receive full benefits.

The risks that we face under the current system are that benefits are going to be cut significantly or that the taxes on workers are going to be increased significantly. Implicitly, if not explicitly, one or the other has to happen because the system is 20 percent out of actuarial balance today and is projected to be much further out of balance in the future.

If current law benefits were secure, we would not be carrying on a national debate about how to fix Social Security. The fact is that current law benefits are significantly under-financed for the majority of people that are contributing to the system today. While policymakers have not been willing to address this issue yet, those that have been willing to put proposals on the table have tended toward benefit reductions in their recommendations to rebalance the system. And these proposals are not all coming from the libertarian end of the political spectrum whose devotees would like to see the current program significantly curtailed on philosophical grounds alone.

Contemporary proposals to reduce Social Security benefits are coming from policymakers anchored in the political mainstream. Before he retired in 1994, Representative Jake Pickle, a Democrat from Texas and Chairman of the Social Security Subcommittee of the House Ways and Means Committee, proposed to rebalance the system virtually completely through benefit reductions. Senator Bob Kerrey, a Democrat from Nebraska, has reached across party lines to cosponsor a proposal to reduce benefits in the traditional Social Security program in order to finance the creation of individual accounts that would be held by workers. And as mentioned earlier, within the

Advisory Council there was virtually no support for a straightforward payroll tax increase to deliver future Social Security benefits defined by current law. Maybe some proposals advocating tax increases to deliver currently promised benefits will ultimately be tabled by policymakers but general reluctance to increase tax rates in this society suggests that such proposals will face major opposition in the legislative process.

Virtually all of the members of the Advisory Council sought to improve the rates of return in the Social Security system for younger cohorts of workers. In addition, the majority of the members of the Council were also concerned about the implications of reform proposals on national savings rates. As Bosworth and Burtless point out, both of these goals can conceivably be achieved either within the current defined benefit system or outside it through the creation of individual accounts.[8] As they note, from an economic perspective the important factor in achieving the goals of improved returns and higher national savings is the prefunding of benefits, not how those funds are held. But they also note that many people involved in the debate about Social Security reform are skeptical that the two different approaches are equivalent from a political perspective. The ultimate question that we face is whether the government can be the accumulator of a vast pool of private economic wealth and can be expected to invest it in a fashion that is neutral to the performance of financial markets and the independent operations of business. The supporters of the PSA plan within the Advisory Council thought that the government could not accumulate the pools of wealth in question nor remain neutral in the operations of a free economy if it held the large pools of private assets implied by the MB or IA proposals. While economic considerations were extremely important to this group, it was ultimately political considerations that drove them to suggest the individual account option that they did. They simply did not believe the economic goals that they thought were important could be achieved within our political framework through any mechanism other than individual accounts managed outside government.

The creation of individual accounts, of course, would expose workers to greater financial market risks in the accumulation of their base pensions than the financial market risks they currently face. But it is not clear that their overall risks would be any greater than they are in the current environment. If policymakers are reluctant to increase payroll taxes at all to simply sustain the current structure of benefits, the political probability of the Maintain Tax Rate Benefit (MTR), the benefit that could be provided to a worker if benefits were scaled back to live within the tax rate levels in current law, approaches one. In this regard, the Advisory Council's unwillingness to advocate a straightforward increase in payroll tax rates to deliver currently promised benefits is important.

The advocates of the MB plan sought to secure current benefit promises and the current benefit structure by crafting a proposal that would minimize the explicit costs of doing so to workers. But as we pointed out earlier, there is no way to cover the real deficit that exists in the current system without incurring real costs. If the only way policymakers can get society to bear these costs is to hide them, the proposal itself acknowledges that there is tremendous political risk that the public will be unwilling to deliver on current promises. The advocates of the individual account options developed by the Advisory Council believed that policymakers might be willing to explicitly increase the cost of providing benefits under the proviso that the added levies go into individual accounts. If they are correct, the political probability of a benefit greater than MTR increases significantly, but it would only do so at the expense of the worker taking on some investment risk.

A simulation approach has been used to determine benefit levels for selected birth cohorts of average age workers.[9] The simulation results suggest that there are tradeoffs between political risks and market investment risks that might make the choice between the two difficult for the older birth cohorts, especially the baby-boom birth cohorts. For those birth cohorts born after the baby boom, however, the advantages of prefunding a portion of the benefits through individual accounts are much clearer. And this does not take into account the added improvements in economic welfare that should result from the added savings that would be stimulated by the IA or PSA plans.

Critics of the PSA proposal argue that it would be costly if not impossible to administer. In this regard, the experience of the employer-based 401(k) system is instructive. Although this system is completely voluntary, it has experienced explosive growth over the period since it was first made available to workers in the early 1980s. The system went from virtually nothing to accounting for more than half the total contributions going into private employer-sponsored retirement programs in 1993. Under current law, these programs allow young and old workers alike to contribute from a few dollars a week or up to nearly $200 per week into them. In the aggregate, workers pour more than $1 billion per week into private 401(k) plans. Most workers are free to direct the investment of their own retirement savings in these plans, and they do so on a fully accounted basis that costs much less than 1 percent per year.

Critics also argue that the PSA plan is flawed because it does not require the annuitization of the benefit at retirement. While the PSA proposal did not call for forced annuitization, it did not preclude it either. Indeed, its authors suggested that it might make sense to require retirees to show that they had a lifetime annuity income that would equal 1.5 times the poverty line, or some other similar multiple of the poverty level income before they could liquidate their PSA accumulation at retirement. At some level of income that protects taxpayers from having injudicious consumers demanding welfare support, however, it is not the government's business how private consumers choose to distribute their lifetime savings.

Finally, critics of Social Security reform proposals that include an individual account element argue that Congress would be unlikely to force workers to keep the money in the accounts until they reach retirement. They suggest that our political leaders could not withstand the pressure to allow workers to tap retirement savings in cases of personal and financial hardship. The fact is that a wide range of countries around the world have adopted Social Security reforms of the sort recommended under the PSA proposal. Such reforms have swept across Latin America. A much larger, fully funded individual account program is being phased in currently in Australia. A similar approach is used in Singapore and is being considered by a number of other Asian countries including China. Sweden, the mother of all social welfare states, is moving toward a system very similar to the one recommended by the authors of the IA proposal. The UK has allowed workers to "contract out" of the second tier of their national retirement program for some years, essentially allowing voluntary PSAs in their national retirement system. The UK is beginning to discuss moving further down this path in the direction that Australia has gone. A wide range of other countries around the world are carrying on similar deliberations.[10] If our political system or our national policymakers are so politically incontinent that they cannot do what a wide range of countries around the world have been able to achieve, we may have a much larger problem to resolve than figuring out how to secure the retirement benefits of today's workers at a cost that future workers will be able to bear.

Possibly the most amazing aspect of what is going on all around the world is the range of other countries that have recognized the downstream perils of payroll tax financed pay-as-you-go retirement security systems. These countries are paying attention to the predictable demographics they face and changing the course of their national retirement programs—often much older than ours —generally by adopting some form of individual account program. They are amending existing systems to avoid the perils that taxpaying workers and dependent retirees face from retirement security systems that are not sustainable for aging populations. What is going on elsewhere in the world is not incompatible with the early direction of our own Social Security program.

The father of the U.S. Social Security system, Franklin D. Roosevelt, felt strongly that a significant portion of the system's promises should be funded. When he discovered that the original proposal submitted to Congress by his Committee on Economic Security did not provide for such funding, he made the Committee revise the legislative package to include it. While his proposed funding was included in the original Social Security Act, the levels of funding that FDR had insisted upon for his beloved Social Security program were never achieved, largely for two reasons. The first was Congressional worries that the accumulated funds would be used to buy up significant shares of private capital, a move many in Congress thought was incompatible with the nature of our government and the private ownership of capital. The second was that it was always easier for Congress to delay tax increases that would have led to the trust fund build-up that FDR envisaged than to bear the pain of imposing the necessary taxes; or it was more politically expedient to use excess tax revenues as they arose to raise benefits than to allow the trust fund to accumulate.

FDR was right; a healthy fund backing our national retirement system would be good for the economy and its participants' economic security. What more than 60 years of experience has told us, however, is that we can only achieve FDR's vision by significantly reforming the current system. We were among the last of the countries in the Western Hemisphere to adopt a Social Security program. We should not be the last to reform it.

# NOTES

1. *The 1997 Annual Report of the Board of Trustees of the Federal Old-Age and Survivors Insurance and Disability Insurance Trust Funds* (Washington, DC: US Government Printing Office, April 1997), p. 24.

2. Henry Aaron, "Is a Crisis Really Coming? (Social Security and . . .)," *Newsweek* (December 9, 1996).

3. For a full discussion of those issues, see Roland D. McDevitt and Sylvester J. Schieber, *From Baby Boom to Elder Boom: Providing Health Care for an Aging Population* (Washington, DC: Watson Wyatt Worldwide, 1996).

4. For example, the members of the 1994–1996 Social Security Advisory Council who advocated maintaining the current system and benefit structure to the maximum extent possible argued that any increase in the payroll tax should be largely devoted to supporting the Medicare program. See Robert M. Ball, et al., "Social Security for the 21st Century: A Strategy to Maintain Benefits and Strengthen America's Family Protection Plan," *Report of the 1994–1996 Advisory Council on Social Security*, vol. 1, Findings and Recommendations, p. 64.

5. Transcript of the Public Meeting of the Social Security Advisory Council, December 14, 1995 (Social Security Administration).

6. For a complete description of this proposal and its financing and benefits implications, see Sylvester J. Schieber and John B. Shoven, "Social Security Reform Options and Their Implications for Future Retirees, Federal Fiscal Operations, and National Savings," a paper prepared for a public policy forum, "Tax Policy for the 21st Century," sponsored by the American Council for Capital Formation, Washington, DC, December 1996. Copies available from the author on request.

7. For example, see Alan Greenspan, speech at the American Enterprise Institute's Public Policy Conference, January 1997, Joan T. Bok et al., "Restoring Security to Our Social Security Program," and Edward M. Gramlich and Marc M. Twinney, "The Individual Accounts Plan," in *The Report of the 1994–1996 Advisory Council on Social Security*, vol. 1, pp. 128, 155.

8. Gary Burtless and Barry Bosworth, "Privatizing Social Security: The Troubling Tradeoffs," *Brookings Policy Brief* (March 1997), No. 14.

9. For a full discussion of the simulation approach and the results of simulations for lower- and higher-wage workers, see Gordon P. Goodfellow and Sylvester J. Schieber, "Social Security Reform: Implications of Individual Accounts on the Distribution of Benefits," Pension Research Council Working Paper, Philadelphia: The Wharton School, University of Pennsylvania, May 1997.

10. For a more in-depth discussion of what is going on in the international arena, see Sylvester J. Schieber and John B. Shoven, "Social Security Reform: Around the World in 80 Ways," *The American Economic Review* (May 1996), vol. 86, no. 2, pp. 373–377.

# POSTSCRIPT

## Is Our Current Social Security Program Securely Anchored?

Ball believes Social Security is basically in good shape and that financing can easily be brought into long-range balance. He identifies the sources of the projected deficits: 50 percent from changes in actuarial methods and new sources of data and 50 percent from changes in assumptions. The problem is to eliminate the projected deficit of 2.23 percent of covered payroll. Ball's solution, which would maintain the basic structure of OASDI as a completely defined benefits program, involves six elements: increase taxation of benefits, change the cost of living adjustment, extend Social Security coverage, increase the wage-averaging period, increase the overall tax rate, and allow the investment of trust fund balances in equities. Ball rejects the two partial privatization proposals— individual accounts and private savings accounts —for a number of reasons: they require too drastic a reduction in basic benefits; they require too high an increase in current taxes; they increase risk; they are too complex; they are too costly; and they are politically unstable. In conclusion, Ball argues that his position on Social Security reform is consistent with community solidarity and the proper role of government in a market economy.

Schieber, unlike Ball, believes that the projected underfunding is a very serious problem that requires a fundamental restructuring of OASDI. He rejects the solution favored by Ball; in particular Schieber rejects the investment of trust funds in equities by government officials on the grounds that such an arrangement will politicize investment decisions, create conflicts of interest, and lead to problems of corporate governance. Moreover, Ball's Maintenance of Benefits Option, because it requires a 1.6 percent increase in the payroll tax in 2045, shifts the tax burden to future generations. As an alternative, Schieber proposes transforming Social Security from a completely defined benefits program to a partially defined benefits program through the partial privatization of OASDI. In defending his alternative, the Personal Savings Account Option, Schieber argues that it will actually reduce risk, and that it is consistent with reforms that are occurring in a number of countries across the globe. But, most importantly, he believes that his proposal of partial privatization is the only way in which important economic goals can be achieved within a democratic political framework.

Additional readings on this issue include "How Not to Fix Social Security," by Mark Weisbrot, *Dollars and Sense* (March/April 1997); "The Great Social Security Scare," by Jerry L. Mashaw and Theodore R. Marmor, *The American Prospect* (November/December 1996); "A Secure System," by Robert Ball,

*The American Prospect* (November/December 1996); "Different Approaches to Dealing With Social Security," by Edward M. Gramlich, *Journal of Economic Perspectives* (Summer 1996); and "Proposals to Restructure Social Security," by Peter A. Diamond, *Journal of Economic Perspectives* (Summer 1996). Also see three issues of *Economic Commentary, Federal Reserve Bank of Cleveland*: "Should Social Security Be Privatized?" by Jagadeesh Gokhale (September 1995); "Social Security: Are We Getting Our Money's Worth?" by Jagadeesh Gokhale and Kevin J. Lansing (January 1, 1996); and "A Simple Proposal for Privatizing Social Security," by David Altig and Jagadeesh Gokhale (May 1, 1996).

# ISSUE 10

## Does the Consumer Price Index Overstate Changes in the Cost of Living?

**YES: Michael J. Boskin et al.,** from "The CPI Commission: Findings and Recommendations," *American Economic Review* (May 1997)

**NO: Dean Baker,** from "The Inflated Case Against the CPI," *The American Prospect* (Winter 1996)

### ISSUE SUMMARY

**YES:** Michael J. Boskin et al., members of the Advisory Commission to Study the Consumer Price Index, (the Boskin Commission), believe that changes in the Consumer Price Index overstate changes in the cost of living by approximately 1.1 percent, and this has led to widespread overindexing of a number of government programs.

**NO:** Dean Baker, an economist with the Economic Policy Institute, argues that it is impossible to determine the overall direction and magnitude of bias in the Consumer Price Index because the Boskin Commission overstates the upward biases in the index and fails to consider factors that suggest downward bias.

Each month the Bureau of Labor Statistics releases a new estimate of the Consumer Price Index (CPI). This release usually merits front page attention in the nation's newspapers because changes in the CPI are interpreted as changes in the cost of living of Americans. If nominal income does not keep pace with increases in the cost of living, as determined by increases in the CPI, then real income falls.

Because of this connection between changes in the CPI and changes in the cost of living, a number of monetary arrangements in the economy are altered when the CPI changes; that is, they are indexed. For example, some private sector collective bargaining agreements tie wages to changes in the CPI. If the CPI increases, then wages automatically rise by the same percentage. But indexing is not limited to the private sector of the economy; the federal government has resorted to indexing in a variety of areas. In counting the number of poor persons, the poverty thresholds (the income levels that separate poor from nonpoor) are adjusted upward each year by the percentage increase in the CPI. With the individual income tax, the dollar value of the personal exemption is adjusted to reflect changes in the cost of living as determined by changes in the CPI. Social Security benefits are also adjusted each year to reflect changes in the cost of living and the CPI. So from the government's perspective, if changes in the CPI overstate changes in the cost of living, then its tax receipts will be lower than they should be and its Social Security payments will be higher than they should be. This, in turn, means federal government budget deficits and the national debt will be higher than they should be.

It is clearly important, then, to measure changes in the CPI and in the cost of living accurately. This issue addresses the question of the extent to which this accuracy is achieved. As a first step in understanding this debate it is important to understand how the CPI is calculated. The CPI, in technical terms, is a Laspeyres fixed-weight index. Accordingly, the first step in the calculation of the CPI is to determine the fixed weights—the goods and services that consumers purchase at a particular point in time known as the base period. This is known as the market basket and is accomplished by surveys of consumer purchasing behavior. The market basket can be considered the expenditure pattern of the typical consumer. The market basket currently used in the CPI was determined by surveys conducted in the early 1980s; that is, the base period for the CPI is the 1982–84 period. The second step is to gather information regarding the prices of the goods and services in the market basket, and this is done every month. The price information is necessary to determine the cost of the market basket. The cost of the market basket changes as prices change, but the market basket itself does not (it is fixed). If the cost of the market basket increases, then it costs the typical consumer more to buy an unchanged bundle of goods and services, that is, the cost of living has increased. The ratio of the cost of the market basket in the current period to the cost of the market basket in the base period (multiplied by 100) provides the current numerical value of the CPI. The percentage change in the CPI between any two periods represents the rate of inflation in consumer prices between those two periods and, by extension, the percentage change in the cost of living between those two periods.

The Advisory Commission to Study the Consumer Price Index was constituted by the Senate Finance Committee. The commission's final report, "Toward a More Accurate Measure of the Cost of Living," was submitted early in 1996. A summary of this report represents one side of the debate on this issue—Michael J. Boskin was the chair of the commission while Ellen R. Dulberger, Robert J. Gordon, Zvi Griliches, and Dale W. Jorgenson were the other members. The commission's report has generated a great deal of interest because its conclusions are so important—affecting everything from calculation of poverty rates to efforts to balance the budget. Some of the responses by economists are highly critical of the commission's basic finding that the CPI overstates changes in the cost of living. Dean Baker provides an excellent example of this criticism.

# YES

## Michael J. Boskin et al.

# THE CPI COMMISSION: FINDINGS AND RECOMMENDATIONS

Measuring prices and their rate of change accurately is central to almost every economic issue, from the conduct of monetary policy to measuring economic progress over time and across countries to the cost and structure of indexed spending and taxes. In the first external extensive evaluation of the nation's price statistics since the Stigler Commission in 1961, the CPI Commission (see Boskin et al., 1996) concluded that the change in the Consumer Price Index (CPI) overstates the change in the cost of living by about 1.1 percentage points per year (the range of plausible values is 0.8–1.6 percentage points). That is, if inflation as measured by the percentage change in the CPI is running 3 percent, the true change in the cost of living is about 2 percent. This bias might seem small, but when compounded over time, the implications are enormous. Over a dozen years, the cumulative additional national debt from overindexing the budget would amount to $1 trillion. The implications of overstating inflation for understanding economic progress are equally dramatic. Instead of falling, average real earnings have risen, and instead of stagnating, real median income has grown, over the last quarter century. The poverty rate would be smaller. And because the CPI component price indexes are inputs into the national income accounts, real GDP growth is also understated.

Why is inflation so hard to measure? Despite numerous improvements that have been made historically and continue to be made by government statisticians in all countries, including the U.S. Bureau of Labor Statistics (BLS), many of them laboring under inadequate human and financial resource constraints, it is difficult to keep up with the dynamic change in the economy. New products are being introduced all the time, and existing ones improved, while others leave the market. Relative prices of different goods and services change frequently, for example, in response to technological and other factors affecting costs and quality, which leads consumers to change their buying patterns. There are literally hundreds of thousands of goods and services available in rich industrialized modern market economies. A single supermarket may contain 30,000 differently priced items, and a Wal-Mart store over 40,000. As we have become richer, demand has increasingly

From Michael J. Boskin, Ellen R. Dulberger, Robert J. Gordon, Zvi Griliches, and Dale W. Jorgenson, "The CPI Commission: Findings and Recommendations," *American Economic Review*, vol. 87, no. 2 (May 1977). Copyright © 1997 by *American Economic Review*. Reprinted by permission.

shifted to services away from goods, and to characteristics of goods and services such as enhanced quality, more variety, and greater convenience. Technology and entrepreneurship provide them. But all these factors, plus others, mean that a larger fraction of what is produced and consumed in an economy is harder to measure than decades ago, when a larger fraction of economic activity consisted of easier-to-measure items such as tons of steel and bushels of wheat.

## I. FINDINGS

How to obtain information on who is buying what, where, when, why, and how in an economy, and then to aggregate it into one or a few measures of price change raises a host of complex analytical and practical problems. The mathematics of aggregating changes in the prices of different goods and services are complex and subtle (see Irving Fisher, 1922; Erwin Diewert, 1976). Despite decades of analytical and empirical research, some of it recently done in statistical agencies such as the BLS the statistical agencies around the world still primarily rely on fixed-weight indexes which do not account for consumer substitution among commodities. Thus, these Laspeyres measures of inflation are inherently upper bounds, and empirical studies led the Commission to conclude that this source of substitution bias —failing to catch that consumers substitute chicken for beef when beef prices go up (upper-level substitution bias), or Delicious for Macintosh apples under similar circumstances (lower-level substitution bias)—leads to an overstatement in the U.S. Consumer Price Index of about 0.4 percentage points.[1]

Likewise, there has been a fundamental change in the nature of retailing, perhaps most pronounced in the United States, but spreading virtually everywhere with the advent of superstores and discount chains. The same VCR available for $200 in a local appliance store may be only $160 at Circuit City. Since price data are collected *within* outlets, the shift of consumers to purchasing from discounters does not show up as a price decline, even though consumers reveal by their purchases that the price decline more than compensates for the potential loss of personal services. Thus, in addition to substitution bias among commodities there is an outlet substitution bias. In the United States, this adds another 0.1 percentage point of upward bias.

Another problem is that price data tend to be collected during the week. In the United States, about 1 percent of price quotes are collected on weekends, despite the secular trend of an increasing share of purchases made on weekends and holidays (probably reflecting the increasing prevalence of two-earner couples). Since some outlets emphasize weekend sales, there may be a "when" bias as well as a "what" and a "where" bias. Recent research suggesting that prices rise less rapidly in data collected by scanners rather than price-takers may be partly explained by this phenomenon.

These types of problems account for just a little under half of the 1.1 percentage points identified by our commission. Slightly over half results from the difficulty of adjusting fully for quality change and the introduction of new products. Economists have known since John Hicks (1940) that the introduction of a new product should be dealt with in a cost-of-living index by using its reservation price and including the consumer surplus attributable to the introduction of the product. Noting this, our commission took the more cautious approach of primarily including estimates of explicit dimensions of quality change and the very late introduction of major new products into the index. In the U.S. CPI, VCRs, microwave ovens, and personal computers were included a decade or more after they had penetrated the market and their prices had fallen 80 percent or more. Cellular telephones will not be included in the U.S. CPI until 1998, despite the facts that there are more than 40 million cellular subscribers in the United States today and that well over 100 million Americans receive calls on land-line phones initiated on cellular phones. Jerry Hausman of MIT estimates that the quality-adjusted price of cellular services has declined by 90 percent since 1989. The advent of personal communication services (PCS) competition and deployment of digital technology will have substantially occurred by the time cellular services begin to get priced. Correspondingly, the pace of quality change in some important areas, such as health care and consumer electronics, has been breathtaking, and our statistics are not keeping up.

When economists try to define the change in the cost of living it is to answer the question "How much more income will consumers need to be just as well off with the new set of prices as the old?" In addition to the substitution issue raised above, this clearly involves measuring *quality-adjusted* prices. One would not want to count a major improvement in quality that greatly enhances well-being as inflation. Hence, the Commission examined an exhaustive set of 27 subcomponents of the CPI, and based on empirical research findings and common-sense observation, estimated (we believe conservatively) a quality-change and new-product bias in the CPI of 0.6 percentage point per year.

Thus, the total bias is estimated at 1.1 percentage points per year, as detailed in Table 1.

## II. RECOMMENDATIONS

Our commission made a variety of recommendations that form guideposts for statistical agencies to improve the quality of their statistics. (Many of the world's statistical agencies, including the BLS in the United States, are planning to make progress on at least some of these fronts already.) These include changing from fixed-weight formulas to mathematical formulas that account for consumer substitution in the aggregation of prices of goods and services. Also important are reweighting the consumption basket more frequently and increasing the pace of sampling so that new products enter more quickly and the prices of new products, the commodity mix, and the outlet mix are adjusted more rapidly, and so that the prices collected are more representative of current market activity.[2] Finally, more use should be made of hedonic statistical methods to adjust for quality change.

More specifically, the Commission's first and overarching recommendation is that the BLS should establish a cost-of-living index as its objective in measuring consumer prices. All of the other specific recommendations are aimed toward achieving this goal. In its publications, the BLS has explicitly recognized that the CPI is not a cost-of-living-index for decades. Still, its most common and pervasive use and interpretation is as a cost-of-living index. We believe a more funda-

*Table 1*
**Estimates of Biases in the CPI-Based Measure of the Cost of Living (Percentage Points per Annum)**

| Sources of bias | Estimate |
| --- | --- |
| Upper-level substitution | 0.15 |
| Lower-level substitution | 0.25 |
| New products/quality change | 0.60 |
| New outlets | 0.10 |
| Total | 1.10 |
| (Plausible range) | (0.80–1.60) |

mentally sound cost-of-living index can and should be developed. In order to achieve this objective, the Commission recommends the publication of two indexes: one which is published monthly on a timely basis and is designed to maintain the spirit of the cost-of-living index yet accommodate the inconsistent timing schedules of the required information; and a second index which is published and updated annually and revised historically to introduce improvements arising from new information and new research results. The purpose of having two indexes is to accommodate the complex issues that must be addressed and the time delay in obtaining all of the necessary data.

We divided our recommendations into three time horizons. First, short-run recommendations include those we think can be implemented immediately, with little in the way of additional resources or new data-collection initiatives. These center on changing the current CPI computation, primarily to make it more current, and on computing an annually updated and subsequently revised cost-of-living index. Second, the intermediate-run reforms are those that are currently feasible but would require new data collection, reorganization of activities, or changes in the detail of the various subindexes produced by the CPI. And third, longer-run recommendations emphasize topics in areas that need additional research and attention....

Moving to a notion of a new "basket" each year will allow a faster introduction of new items and new outlets. Moving to a national sample for most such items would allow expansion of the number of specific items (models, varieties, types) sampled within a particular ELI and reduce thereby the number of forced substitutions. Also, this would allow for the use of new sources of data, such as scanner data on prices, and industry-wide information on sales of specific items (for more detailed weights), leading to a quicker identification of new goods and their faster incorporation into the index. This is also the level at which more extensive quality adjustments and "comparable" substitutions could be made, recognizing the appearance of new outlets and new versions of services that provide consumers, effectively, with cheaper sources for the same or similar items consumed previously.

A number of additional specific explicit and implicit recommendations are made in the report, such as creating a more permanent mechanism for bringing outside information, expertise, and research results to the BLS; converting the price of durables, such as cars, to a price of annual services analogous to that for owner-occupied housing; changing the treatment of insurance to an *ex ante* consumer price rather than an *ex post* profits-based measure; and determining whether collecting more price data on weekends and holidays would make a difference.

Longer-run considerations include examining the ramifications of the assumptions of price equilibrium, developing research programs to look beyond the current "market basket" framework, perhaps eventually to be able to publish supplementary information on non-market issues. The BLS should also develop a number of new data-collection initiatives, in particular, health status surveys to obtain more information on various quality-of-life issues. Most importantly, efforts should be made to gather data on time use from a large sample of consumers in order to deal with search and related issues.

Of the 1.1-percentage-point bias in the United States we have identified, we believe that about 0.4–0.5 percentage points, from the substitution bias, could be dealt with in relatively short order (a year or so) by the statistical agencies. Dealing with quality change and new products will be harder, but use of the appropriate statistical techniques and getting more up-to-date sampling should enable the statistical agencies to get another 0.2–0.3 percentage points over the intermediate run of several years (although exactly for which products, when, is impossible to say). Even with the widespread use of scanner data, it is likely that there will remain an irreducible minimum of quality-change and new-products bias. But the overstatement can be substantially reduced.

The Commission made a variety of recommendations to Congress, such as providing additional resources necessary to expand the Consumer Expenditure Survey sample and the detail collected, to make the Point-of-Purchase Survey (POPS) more frequent, and to acquire additional commodity detail from alternative national sources such as industry surveys and scanner data. Congress should establish a permanent rotating independent committee of experts to review progress in this area every few years, and to provide advice on the appropriate interpretation of the then-current statistics. Congress should also enact legislation necessary for the Department of Commerce and the Department of Labor to share information in the interests of improving the accuracy and timeliness of economic statistics and to reduce the resources consumed in their development and production. In particular, substantial progress can and should be made in reducing the time from survey collection to implementation in the price program. Other countries appear to be able to do this in less than half the time that it takes in the United States.

## III. CONCLUDING REMARKS

While the CPI is the best measure currently available, it is not a true cost-of-living index. It suffers from a variety of conceptual and practical problems as the vehicle for measuring changes in the cost of living. Despite important BLS updates and improvements, it is likely that changes in the CPI have substantially overstated the actual rate of price inflation. Moreover, revisions have not been carried out in a way that can provide an internally consistent series on the cost of living over an extended span of time. More importantly, changes in the CPI are likely to continue to overstate the change in the true cost of living for the foreseeable future. This overstatement will have important unintended consequences, including overindexing government outlays and tax brackets and increasing the federal deficit and debt. If the intent of such indexing is to insulate recipients and taxpayers from changes in the cost of living, use of the CPI substantially overcompensates (on average) for changes in the true cost of living.

The analytical and econometric research done over recent decades has heightened economists' understanding of these issues. The time has come for governments in the United States and elsewhere to recognize these problems and act accordingly. That involves providing enhanced support for the statistical agencies to improve the price statistics with all deliberate speed in a nonpoliticized manner. It may well require additional resources. Virtually every major private firm in the world is spending heavily on information technology (hardware, software, and human capital), and we should not expect better statistics from our government agencies without a corresponding investment.

Finally, the President and Congress must decide whether they wish to continue the widespread overindexing of their government programs. If the purpose of the indexing is to compensate recipients of the indexed programs or taxpayers for changes in the cost of living, no more and no less, they should move to wholly or partly adjust the indexing formulas. Such changes will have profound ramifications for our fiscal futures, but these changes should be made even if the budget were in surplus and there were no long-run entitlement cost problem. They should be made first and foremost in the interest of accuracy, not only for the budget and the programs, but for the economic information upon which citizens depend.

## NOTES

1. A similar bias occurs in most other countries (although Statistics Canada has fixed about half of this problem, and statistical agencies in other countries are working on it.)
2. The United States is ahead of most countries in its sampling procedures; some others do not yet sample.

## REFERENCES

Boskin, Michael J.; Dulberger, Ellen R.; Gordon, Robert J.; Griliches, Zvi and Jorgenson, Dale W. *Toward a more accurate measure of the cost of living*, Final Report to the Senate Finance Committee from the Advisory Commission to Study the Consumer Price Index. Washington, DC: Senate Finance Committee, 1996.

Boskin, Michael J. and Jorgenson, Dale W. "Implications of Overstating Inflation for Indexing Government Programs and Understanding Economic Progress." *American Economic Review*, May 1997 *(Papers and Proceedings)*, 87(2), pp. 89–93.

Diewart, Erwin. "Exact and Superlative Index Numbers." *Journal of Econometrics*, May 1976, 4(2), pp. 115–45.

Fisher, Irving. *The making of index numbers*. Boston, MA: Houghton-Mifflin, 1922.

Gordon, Robert J. and Griliches, Zvi. "Quality Change and New Products." *American Economic Review*, May 1997 *(Papers and Proceedings)*, 87(2), pp. 84–88.

Hicks, John. "The Valuation of the Social Income." *Economica*, May 1940, 7(2), pp. 105–40.

# NO

Dean Baker

# THE INFLATED CASE AGAINST THE CPI

There is now the appearance of an expert consensus that the government's most important measure of inflation, the consumer price index (CPI), seriously overstates the true increase in the cost of living. This sudden enlightenment is less the result of new research than political convenience. A cut in the CPI would reduce government payouts and ease the path to deficit reduction. Even better, it would do so via a technical adjustment that left few political fingerprints.

Tax brackets and government benefit programs such as Social Security are indexed to the CPI. If the CPI overstates inflation by 1 percent, as the Senate Finance Committee's Boskin panel has proposed, and the index is adjusted accordingly, this would reduce benefits and the deficit by a cumulative total of $634 billion over 10 years. Not bad for a technical fix.

Doubtless, the way we measure inflation requires continuous refinement. The Bureau of Labor Statistics (BLS) takes this task seriously, and has made myraid small adjustments over the past three decades. For years, there was a nuanced and relatively obscure debate about how to fine-tune the CPI. Lately, there has been a politically driven frenzy, as a small group of economists has labored to uncover—and exaggerate—all the ways in which the CPI might overstate inflation. Many claims have been advanced based on very little real evidence. There has also been virtually no effort to examine the ways in which the CPI might understate inflation.

The immediate protagonists are the five-member panel appointed by the Senate Finance Committee, chaired by former Bush economic advisor Michael Boskin, to make recommendations on revisions in the CPI. Though the group includes some eminent economists, all had previously testified on the CPI's supposed bias. All were chosen as known quantities who could be reliably counted upon to recommend a downward revision. Other eminent economists such as former BLS Commissioner Janet Norwood, who took the opposite view, were ignored. The panel was appointed in June 1995 and announced its 1 percent solution in mid-September. It conducted no original research. Instead, it used rough rules of thumb to reach its conclusions.

# THE CASE FOR SHRINKING THE CPI

Five factors are usually cited by those claiming an upward bias in the CPI. Each provides some basis for claiming the index overstates inflation. However, the size of any resulting overstatement is far smaller than what is being claimed, and may well be offset by the sources of understatement in the CPI.

**Substitution Effects.**   This is the most frequently cited source of bias, perhaps because so many reporters learned about it in their introductory economics classes. Most goods have close substitutes. If oranges are $1.99 a pound, consumers switch to apples. The CPI measures the prices of a fixed basket of goods and services. When the price of some goods in this basket rises temporarily, thrifty consumers shift to substitutes. By holding the basket fixed, the CPI then overstates the true increase in the cost of living for most consumers. This is a fair criticism.

However, most studies that have tried to measure the size of this bias find it to be very small, between 0.1 percent and 0.2 percent annually. (The Boskin panel scored it as 0.3 percent.) Moreover, one might fairly argue that even a close substitution "choice" dictated by a price rise entails an offsetting loss to quality. Presuming the substitute to be identical is like comparing, well, apples and oranges.

**The Wal-Mart Effect.**   Over the last several decades discount stores have displaced many traditional retailers. As a result, consumers purchase many goods at far lower prices. The CPI does base its local samples on where consumers actually shop, but the CPI does not record the switch from a traditional department store to a discount store as a price decline. Rather, the price differential is treated as offsetting the lower quality of service in the discount store. Clearly this treatment misses a cost saving. Since discount stores have grown rapidly at the expense of traditional retailers, many consumers must consider the cheaper price well worth the lower quality service.

However, the importance of this difference for the CPI has been vastly overstated. Only about 15 percent of the index consists of goods that could potentially be sold in discount stores (primarily apparel, appliances, and household furniture). The share of consumers who patronize discounters versus full-price retailers simply does not change much from year to year. Moreover, even if the true price difference is as much as 10 percent (after adjusting for differences in service quality), this would lead to a bias of just 0.015 percent a year. This compares to a figure of 0.2 percent to 0.4 percent often cited by those claiming a substantial CPI overstatement of inflation. The Boskin panel used a figure of 0.2 percent.

**Quality Bias.**   One of the largest sources of alleged overstatement of inflation is the failure of the consumer price index to fully account for the improvements in product quality. Clearly, a $2,000 computer today is a far superior machine to a $2,000 computer bought as recently as 1994. Most products are continuously improving in quality. But in fact, the consumer price index already includes extensive adjustments for product quality. It may even overstate the improvement in quality in some cases.

For example, the price index for new cars has increased approximately 150 percent from 1970 to the present, although the average price of an actual new car has increased about fourfold. Based on the CPI's price adjustment, it should be possible to purchase a car today for approximately 2.5 times what a comparable car cost in 1970. In 1970, a new Volkswagen Beetle cost about $2,000. But no new car is on the market today for anything close to $5,000, as would be implied by the new car index. The bottom-of-the-line new car available today for $9,000 is doubtless a significantly better car than a Volkswagen Beetle, but there are probably many consumers who would prefer to purchase a new Beetle at $5,000 rather than pay more for a better car.

This is the general problem with the quality adjustments in the index. Price increases attributed to quality adjustments are not counted as price increases in the index, even though many consumers might not pay for them if they had the choice.

There are also many areas where quality has plainly deteriorated. For example, many consumers have to spend more time fighting with health insurance companies over the processing of claims than 20 years ago, but this deterioration is not picked up in the index. Airline service has declined—less legroom, more changes of planes and missed connections, fewer meals, more convoluted fares. Other examples include longer waits in traffic and time spent waiting on hold or navigating voicemail instructions. None of these quality deteriorations are recorded in the CPI. Given the very limited research on quality adjustments in the CPI (the most frequently cited work is now twelve years out of date), it is impossible to reach any conclusive judgment about the size, or direction, of quality bias in the present index.

**New Products.**    New goods are typically not included in the index until several years after they first appear on the market. During this time, they often undergo large price reductions—which are not picked up in the index. The inclusion of these price declines would lead to a lower measure of inflation. The classic example of this problem is the hand calculator. When it first appeared on the market it cost over $1,000. Within a couple of years its price had fallen to under $100. This huge decline in price was not picked up in the CPI.

But wait. Most people don't buy very expensive new products. Such products only find mass markets after their price has come down dramatically. (How many people bought thousand-dollar hand calculators?)

The CPI is an "expenditure-weighted index," meaning that each dollar of consumer expenditure is weighted equally. This means that if Donald Trump spends 1,000 times what the average consumer spends, his expenditures count 1,000 times as much as those of the average consumer. Of course, it is the Donald Trumps who buy the expensive new products.

However, it is possible to construct the index in a different way, which would count each consumer's expenditures equally. Under this system 1 percent of my budget would count the same as 1 percent of Donald Trump's budget in determining the weighting of a particular item. Such an approach is clearly more appropriate for the purposes the CPI is intended for. There is no reason that Social Security recipients should get a smaller cost of living adjustment because a few wealthy people experience huge savings on hand calculators. Nor does it make sense that such a bonanza for the wealthy should affect wage contracts that use the CPI as a point of reference.

A "person-weighted" index that counted each individual's expenditures equally would provide a much better gauge of the increase in the cost of living experienced by most of the population—and it would virtually eliminate the problem of new goods as a source of bias in the index. Here is a case crying out for a genuine technical adjustment, but one that cuts in the opposite direction from the Boskin panel.

**Formula Bias.** This is the most technical issue (sorry). Suppose the price of a good rises from $1.00 to $1.10. This is a 10 percent increase in price. Suppose it then falls back from $1.10 to $1.00; this is a 9 percent decrease in price. If these changes were just added together it would imply a 1 percent increase in price even though the price had not changed at all. BLS was never so foolish as to construct the CPI in such a way that it would be generally subject to this bias. But there are other such technical problems. BLS has researched this issue extensively, and uncovered and corrected several such areas. It is possible that problems of this sort may still exist in places, but the impact is likely to be extremely small, almost certainly less than 0.1 percent annually.

Let's give the critics the benefit of the doubt. Adding all of these possible biases together, a plausible estimate of inflation overstatement in the CPI would be 0.4 percent—not the one full percentage point estimated by the Boskin panel. But this is a gross adjustment, not a net one: It revises only those elements of the CPI that apparently overstate inflation. To be accurate, one needs to offset this adjustment with factors that suggest the CPI may be too low.

## A DOWNWARD BIAS?

The possibility that the CPI understates inflation has received little attention, since it won't help cut the deficit. Indeed, if the CPI errs on the low side, then Social Security pensioners should be getting bigger checks. Consider three distinct sources of downward bias:

**Health Insurance Costs.** The CPI does not include most increases in insurance premiums for individual health insurance, or increases in copayments or deductibles on employer-purchased insurance. This has been a major drain on household budgets in recent years, as employers have shifted more of the cost of health insurance back to their employees. Nor does the CPI include increases in required payments by beneficiaries of government programs such as the proposed increases in the Medicare Part B premium. This exclusion would lead to an enormous understatement in the cost of living of an elderly household. Even under the Clinton Medicare proposal, the premium is scheduled to rise by approximately $500 per beneficiary over the next seven years. This increase will consume nearly 5 percent of the annual income of a couple with an income of $20,000, the midpoint of the income distribution for families over 65. Under the Gingrich proposal, the total increased costs to consumers would be substantially higher.

Today's basket of health services is in many respects superior to that of, say, two decades ago—thanks to new technologies, drugs, and lifesaving procedures. It's also true that under managed care, many doctors are more harried and patients are often rushed out of hospitals. Some of the higher cost of today's health care reflects not better service, but dead-weight losses—the cost of claims processing, risk selection, mergers, and acquisitions. Spending on health care has quintupled in three decades, but it's not at all clear that the quality has. It would take a great deal more research to determine how to net out the improvements and degradations to quality, and then weigh them against the unambiguously higher cost.

**Personal Business Expenditures.** This category of expenditures, which includes items such as lawyers' and brokerage fees, has been rising at the rate of 0.2 percent a year for the past 20 years as a share of disposable income. This is a category of spending that may not provide direct benefits to consumers but rather is often a cost of maintaining a standard of living threatened by deteriorating external circumstances. Suppose, for example, that I have to hire a lawyer in order to resolve a dispute with my health insurance company, because health insurers are becoming more aggressive. Compared to a situation where the insurance company deals with me honorably, this is a needless expense. I am worse off in direct proportion to the amount of money that I have to spend on my lawyer, regardless of the quantity of quality of legal services provided.

Similarly, if I have to rely on a private financial counselor to ensure a secure retirement, instead of receiving a company pension, I am worse off in direct proportion to the amount of money I must pay the counselor, not the fee per financial transaction. Likewise the cost of divorce lawyers and security consultants. Since the CPI only measures the change in the price of these services, rather than the change in the overall need for the services or genuine benefit derived, it is understanding the true increase in the cost of living.

**Quality of Life Factors.** Many factors that affect the quality of life are not picked up in the CPI. An obvious example is crime. If people have to spend more money in order to live in a safe neighborhood—say on security alarms—it is not captured by the CPI. Nor is a deterioration in the quality of public schools and therefore an increased need for spending on private schools or personal tutors. Nor is the cost of joining a private exercise club because the local public facility has closed or become unsafe. Many of these issues are quite complex and cannot be easily quantified in any meaningful way, but this doesn't make them any less real. Anyone attempting to make conclusive statements about changes in the "true" cost of living must be prepared to address such issues.

Given the very limited amount of research on the biases in the CPI, it is impossible at this point to reach any conclusive judgment about the magnitude or direction of the overall bias in the index. While the claim that "the CPI overstates inflation" has become a virtual mantra of the Washington punditry, honest proponents of this view acknowledge that it is based on very little evidence. The best solution would be to provide the professional statisticians at BLS with the resources they need to improve the CPI. This is clearly preferable to bending economic statistics in whatever direction is politically expedient.

## UNEXPECTED TWISTS

One striking thing about this whole debate is that conservatives try to have the argument both ways. Supposedly, a lower CPI would cut the deficit; and cutting the deficit would stop us from "robbing our grandchildren." But if the Boskin panel is right and the CPI is overstated by 1 percent per year, then real median wages are rising at 2 percent per year. This means that they will double in approximately 35 years, so that the average real wage will be approximately $50,000 a year (in 1995 dollars) in the year 2030. If so, our grandchildren will do just fine and there's no need to slash the Social Security of their grandparents.

As overstated CPI also means that people had been much poorer in the recent past than we realized. If the CPI was overstated by 1.5 percent in the past, as suggested by the Boskin Commission, then the average annual wage in 1960 was just $11,215 measured in 1995 dollars. In 1960, today's 70-year-olds were 35. It is hard to justify taking Social Security benefits from these people in order to make the 35-year-olds of 2030 better off.

In addition, the critics have ignored the implications of a significant CPI revision for monetary policy and growth. Alan Greenspan, chairman of the Federal Reserve, has testified that the CPI overstates inflation by as much as 1.5 percent. But if the official inflation rate is lowered, it undermines the entire rationale of Greenspan's tight money policy. So politicizing the CPI leads to some unexpected implications. It would be far better to return the question of CPI revision to intellectually honest technicians, where it belongs, and to argue deficit reduction on its merits.

# POSTSCRIPT

## Does the Consumer Price Index Overstate Changes in the Cost of Living?

The Boskin Commission states, firstly, that because of certain biases, changes in the CPI overstate changes in the cost of living by approximately 1.1 percent. The commission contends that this overstatement has created a number of other problems: the national debt is higher, estimates of economic growth are lower, and the official count of the number of poor persons is higher. The commission identifies four biases. The first is upper-level substitution bias. This bias arises because the CPI does not allow for the tendency of consumers to switch from products that have increased in price to similar commodities that have not, such as switches from beef to pork when beef prices increase. The second is lower-level substitution bias—the tendency of consumers to switch from steak to hamburgers when the price of steak increases. The third is new products/quality change bias; that is, the CPI does not sufficiently discriminate between an increase in the price of a product whose quality has increased and an increase in the price of a product whose quality is unchanged. The fourth is outlet bias. This is a reflection of a fundamental change in retailing with the growth of superstores and discount outlets that has taken place since the 1982–84 period. The CPI fails to capture this change in consumer shopping patterns. The Boskin Commission also makes a number of recommendations that it believes will lead to more accurate estimates of changes in the cost of living. These include the introduction of a new market basket every year, new data collection methods, and new research initiatives.

Baker begins with a charge of bias against the Boskin Commission itself: it was composed of individuals whose views on the upward bias of the CPI were well known; it did not conduct any new research; and it released its findings in less than four months. With respect to the specific findings of the Boskin Commission, Baker estimates that the upward bias of the CPI is probably closer to 0.4 percent rather than 1.1 percent. He then considers the notion that the CPI understates changes in the cost of living. Baker believes there are three sources of understatement. One source involves health insurance costs —the CPI does not include most increases in health insurance premiums paid by individuals or increases in copayments and deductibles associated with employer-provided health insurance. A second source is personal business expenditures. Lawyer and brokerage fees have been rising, and these expenditures may not provide direct benefits to consumers. Baker claims that it would be more appropriate to consider these increasing fees as an increasing cost of maintaining a given standard of living. The third source of downward bias involves quality of life factors. Baker offers several examples of quality of life factors ignored by the use of the CPI as a measure of the cost of living; one example is spending by consumers to protect themselves from crime. Combining a lower estimate of upward bias and the possibility of downward bias, he concludes that it is impossible to pinpoint the direction, let alone the magnitude of the overall bias in the CPI.

Additional readings on this issue include "The Overstated CPI—Can It Really Be True?" by Dean Baker, *Challenge* (September/October 1996); "Presto Change-O! On the Consumer Price Index," by Audrey Freedman, *Challenge* (March/April 1996); "The Downside of Bad Data," by Everett Ehrlich, *Challenge* (March/April 1997); "How Right Is the Boskin Commission—Interview With Janet Norwood," *Challenge* (March/April 1997); "Quality Changes in the CPI: Some Missing Links," by Charles Hulten, *Challenge* (March/April 1997); "The Boskin Commission's Trillion Dollar Fantasy," by Wynne Godley and George McCarthy, *Challenge* (May/June 1997); and "Bias in the Consumer Price Index: What Is the Evidence?" by Brent R. Moulton, *Journal of Economic Perspectives* (Fall 1996). For additional perspectives from the members of the Boskin Commission, see "Quality Change and New Products," by Robert J. Gordon and Zvi Griliches, *American Economic Review* (May 1997) and "Implications for Overstating Inflation for Indexing Government Programs and Understanding Economic Progress," by Michael J. Boskin and Dale W. Jorgenson, *American Economic Review* (May 1997). For an interesting discussion regarding the actual collection of price data for CPI computations, see "Is the CPI Accurate? Ask the Sleuths Who Get the Numbers," by Christina Duff, *Wall Street Journal* (January 16, 1997). For a discussion of the planned revision in the CPI, see "Overview of the 1998 Revision of the Consumer Price Index," by John S. Greenlees and Charles C. Mason, *Monthly Labor Review* (December 1996).

# ISSUE 11

## Is There a Need for a Constitutional Amendment to Balance the Budget?

**YES: Martin A. Regalia,** from "Should the Senate Pass a Balanced Budget Amendment to the U.S. Constitution? Pro," *Congressional Digest* (March 1997)

**NO: Robert Rubin,** from "Should the Senate Pass a Balanced Budget Amendment to the U.S. Constitution? Con," *Congressional Digest* (March 1997)

### ISSUE SUMMARY

**YES:** Martin A. Regalia, chief economist for the U.S. Chamber of Commerce, argues in favor of a constitutional amendment to balance the budget for three reasons: a balanced budget would have favorable economic effects; such an amendment is appropriate for the Constitution; and the amendment would not needlessly involve the court system in its enforcement.

**NO:** Robert Rubin, secretary of the treasury in the Clinton administration, believes that an amendment to the Constitution is not an appropriate mechanism for the achievement of this goal because it would effectively eliminate the ability of the government to respond to economic problems as they arise.

The Full Employment and Balanced Growth Act of 1978 lists a number of economic goals for the federal government. Besides the familiar objectives of full employment, price stability, and increased real income, the act specifically mentions the goal of a balanced federal budget. This means that the government is to collect in taxes an amount equal to its expenditures. Despite this legislative call to action, the federal government has failed to balance its budget, and recent deficits, at least in terms of dollar size, have been of record proportions. For example, between the years 1940 and 1975, there were only two instances when the deficit was in excess of $50 billion. For the years 1980 through 1990 the deficit averaged about $140 billion. In spite of legislative efforts to reduce budget deficits, the deficit reached a level of $290 billion in 1992. Although declining since then, deficits are projected to continue at least through fiscal year 2002. In its *Economic Report of the President 1997*, the Clinton administration projects deficits of at least $100 billion through fiscal year 1999.

When the federal government runs a deficit it sells securities—treasury bills, notes, and bonds. In this respect the government is just like a business firm that sells securities to raise funds, and the public debt increases by the amount of the deficit. The public or national debt represents the total value of outstanding government securities. Accordingly, the public debt at any point in time is a summary of all prior deficits (offset by the retirement of securities if the government chooses to repurchase its securities when it has a budget surplus). By September 1996 the gross federal debt was approximately $5.2 trillion. The debt is owned by (that is, the government securities have been purchased by) different groups, including individuals, commercial banks, pension funds, life insurance companies, federal government agencies, state and local governments, and corporations. Some securities are also sold to foreign individuals, businesses, and governments.

Following the elections in November 1996, there seemed to be general agreement that the government needed to balance the budget by the year 2002. Within this consensus, there were two areas of disagreement between the Democratic Clinton administration and the Republican Congress. One involved the various changes in spending and taxes that would be necessary to achieve the goal. The second was whether or not a constitutional amendment was necessary to ensure the attainment of the goal and to eliminate future deficit problems.

The balanced budget constitutional amendment considered by the 105th Congress would have required Congress to balance the budget by the year 2002 or two years after ratification (whichever is later) and every year thereafter. A three-fifths vote of both the House and the Senate could rescind the requirement. A waiver would also apply in times of military engagement. To become part of the Constitution a proposal must be approved by a two-thirds vote of both the House and the Senate and then ratified by three-fourths of the states. The whole process came to a grinding halt, at least for 1997, when the amendment failed by a single vote to secure the necessary two-thirds majority in the Senate.

As just stated, the proposed amendment was not approved by the Senate in 1997. What was agreed to by the Congress and the president in 1997 was a series of spending and tax changes, which, if everything works according to plan, will lead to a balanced budget by 2002. But without a constitutional amendment, this agreement could easily unravel. For this reason there is no doubt that there will be future efforts to pass a balanced budget constitutional amendment. So we can expect still another debate on this issue with the arguments following the basic points raised by Regalia and Rubin.

# YES

**Martin A. Regalia**

# SHOULD THE SENATE PASS A BALANCED BUDGET AMENDMENT TO THE U.S. CONSTITUTION? PRO

The [U.S.] Chamber [of Commerce] strongly supports a balanced budget amendment to the Constitution. Our members and their employees... have long felt the effects of Federal fiscal mismanagement. Large, persistent Federal deficits reduce saving and investment, stymie income and job growth, and reduce our standard of living. They ultimately lead to increased taxes, bigger government, and higher interest rates, all of which reduce the global competitiveness of U.S. firms.

The balanced budget amendment would prohibit Federal outlays from exceeding revenues, unless Congress approved a deficit by a three-fifths vote of both the Senate and House. The amendment would require the same three-fifths vote to increase the Federal debt limit and would require a "constitutional majority"—51 votes in the Senate and 218 in the House—to raise Federal taxes.

The Chamber is convinced that the balanced budget amendment will place renewed emphasis on fiscal discipline, forcing Congress to slow government spending while constraining its ability to raise taxes. In restoring the proper balance between spending and taxes, the balanced budget amendment also would force government officials to prioritize difficult spending choices.

The balanced budget amendment has been challenged on various grounds, including its economic effects, its appropriateness for the Constitution, and the contention that it would needlessly involve the court system in its enforcement. I would like to address each of these issues, and share with the committee the conclusions reached by the Chamber.

Critics of the balanced budget amendment contend that the negative effects of deficits are overblown, that deficits really do not matter. Others admit to some of the negative effects, but point to recent "improvements" in the deficit, claiming that we have adequately addressed the problem. Still others acknowledge the serious long-term ramifications of deficits, but claim that correcting this situation carries too high a social and political price.

From Martin A. Regalia, "Should the Senate Pass a Balanced Budget Amendment to the U.S. Constitution? Pro," in "Reducing the Deficit: The Ongoing Balanced Budget Debate," *Congressional Digest*, vol. 76, no. 3 (March 1997). Copyright © 1997 by The Congressional Digest Corporation, Washington, DC, (202)333-7332. Reprinted by permission.

Chronic government deficits, and the resulting accumulation of government debt, reduce the level of savings and investment, lower productivity growth, raise the specter of inflation, put upward pressure on interest rates, encourage trade deficits, and lower our standard of living.

Since the 1960s, we have seen the net national savings fall from about 10 percent of GDP [Gross Domestic Product] to consistently below 4 percent—too low to support the investment required for high productivity growth. Because long-term productivity growth is the key to rising standards of living, skimping on investment is dangerous.

First, chronic government borrowing tends to put upward pressure on interest rates. Businesses seeking to raise capital and households applying for mortgages have to compete with the Federal Government in securing loanable funds. This increase in demand pushes interest rates up. Consequently, fewer loans are made to the private sector, and those that are made carry a higher interest rate. This is known as "crowding out," since government borrowing displaces some private borrowing.

Second, because our economy is increasingly linked to the global market, there are important international impacts related to the budget deficit. Higher interest rates tend to precipitate an overvalued dollar, meaning that our goods and services cost more to our trading partners. This lowers our exports and pushes up our trade deficit. Many contend that one of the major forces behind the huge trade deficits of the 1980s was the Federal budget deficit.

Third, the amount we are paying to service our national debt has grown since 1969—from $43 billion to $240 billion

in 1996. As a share of total government outlays, interest payments on the debt have more than doubled, from about 7 percent during the early 1970s to over 15 percent currently. That means that for the same amount of revenue there is less money for other government programs, whether for national defense, our court system, Head Start, or environmental clean-up. No matter what the budget priorities are, fewer funds are available.

Large persistent deficits and the accumulation of debt can also have severe consequences for future generations. To the extent that government debt is held by foreigners—currently about 15 percent—there will be a net transfer from these future generations to foreign bond holders to service or retire the debt. Even more important, shifting funds from current private savings and investment to current government consumption via government deficits can leave future generations with inadequate investment, sluggish productivity growth, poor wage growth, and lower living standards.

Some critics charge that these negative effects of government are largely overblown and that much government spending is really investment. Some government spending can be regarded as "investment spending," meaning that funds spent now will generate stronger economic growth later. Spending on infrastructure—highways, bridges, dams, and mass transit, for example—and other programs such as education are often thought of that way because they provide benefits over a longer period of time. But the bulk of government spending goes to projects and programs that instead represent "current consumption." While many of these programs are desirable, we need to recognize that we should pay for them out of current income.

Many critics of the balanced budget amendment will acknowledge the problem but claim that such a "drastic" solution is unnecessary. They point to the 1993 OBRA [Omnibus Budget Reconciliation Act] legislation and recent deficit reduction as evidence that we have solved the problem. Unfortunately, this is an extreme form of denial. We need only look to history and current CBO [Congressional Budget Office] projections to see the fallacy in this argument.

Until about 1960 or so, running a balanced budget over time was an "unwritten" constitutional amendment. The U.S. government ran deficits during the War of 1812, the severe recession of 1837–43, the Civil War, and the Spanish-American War, to name a few episodes. But in other periods, the Federal Government ran surpluses to reduce its outstanding debt. On the whole, only emergencies justified running a deficit.

But since 1960, this informal rule apparently has gone by the wayside. In the past 36 years, the United States has avoided a deficit only once, when in 1969 there was a surplus of $3 billion. Given the chronic deficits we have grown to expect, it is time to make explicit through a constitutional amendment the old implicit principle of government living within its means.

While it is true that a combination of factors has lowered the current deficit, the impact is likely to be transitory. The Congressional Budget Office estimates that after bottoming out in 1966, the deficit will begin to rise once again both in absolute terms and as a percentage of GDP. What is even more discouraging is that despite all the rhetoric, neither the Congress nor the Administration have been able to agree on a statutory plan to balance the budget.

Some commentators have argued that a balanced budget requirement is a mere rule of accounting, incompatible with the broad principles in the Constitution. It is worth noting that the Constitution already contains several narrowly focused economic and fiscal provisions, including the Article I, Section 9 requirement of "a regular statement and account of the receipts and expenditures of all public money" and the Article I, Section 8 requirement that "duties, imports and excises . . . [be] uniform throughout the United States."

Moreover, the balanced budget amendment embodies two principal themes of the Constitution: limitation on Federal power, and protection of politically under-represented groups against majoritarian abuse. Thomas Jefferson, who perceived the inherent expansionist tendency of central government, supported a constitutional prohibition of Federal borrowing as a means of protecting individual liberty.

As I noted earlier, our Federal Government embraced the practice of holding government spending in check to avoid deficits, except during war or recession. In recent times, the erosion of this principle has created persistent structural deficits, removed the need to limit and prioritize programs, and led to an excessively large Federal sector. The balanced budget amendment requirement that Federal operations be funded from current revenues restores an important principle of fiscal responsibility and limited government.

Statutory attempts to impose fiscal discipline upon the Federal Government have failed, largely because Congress was able to change the rules in mid-game.

The ambitious deficit-reduction targets of the 1985 Gramm-Rudman-Hollings law were repeatedly modified when they conflicted with Congress's spending ambitions. Likewise, big-ticket items such as unemployment compensation payments and disaster relief are customarily designated as "emergency" spending, which exempts them from spending caps. Between 1980 and 1990, each year's actual spending exceeded the targets of that year's budget resolution by an average of $30 billion (the excess was $85 billion in 1990).

Each statutory response to the deficit has shown the same vulnerability: hard-won budget rules can be waived or modified by a simply majority vote. Not surprisingly, a majority can usually be assembled to support more spending. The key advantage of a constitutional amendment is that tough budgetary rules can be placed beyond the reach of simple congressional majorities.

Some lawmakers and commentators have raised questions about the enforcement of a balanced budget amendment. A primary concern is that congressional efforts to meet the balanced budget requirement would be challenged in the courts, and the judiciary would be thrust into a nonjudicial role of weighing policy demands, slashing programs, and increasing taxes.

On the other hand, there is a legitimate and necessary role for the courts in ensuring compliance with the amendment. Congress could potentially circumvent balanced budget amendment requirements through unrealistic revenue estimates, emergency designations, off-budget accounts, unfunded mandates, and other gimmickry. It is our view that the need to proscribe judicial policymaking can be reconciled with a constructive role for the courts in maintaining the integrity of the balanced budget requirement.

In general, the courts have shown an unwillingness to interject themselves into the fray of budgetary politics. The New Jersey Supreme Court observed that "it is a rare case. . . in which the judiciary has any proper constitutional role in making budget allocation decisions." The judiciary has remained clear of most budget controversies.

A strong framework of accounting guidelines will emerge from implementing legislation. Supporters in both the House and Senate have indicated their intention that implementing legislation embrace stringent accounting standards that will minimize the potential for litigation. Should legitimate questions arise concerning the methods by which Congress balances the budget, these standards will also provide objective criteria which meet constitutional standards for judicial intervention.

The implementing package is also likely to establish guidelines for judicial involvement, defining those issues appropriate for litigation and which parties have standing to litigate them. State budget officers, for example, could be given standing to contest unfunded Federal mandates. These enforcement procedures, coupled with budget process and accounting guidelines, will operate against a backdrop of traditional legal principles to rationally limit judicial action. The effect should be to prevent judicial over-reaching into legislative functions, while providing a check on congressional attempts to evade the requirements of the balanced budget amendment through procedural and numerical gimmickry.

For most of our Nation's history, the growth of the Federal Government was held in check by an implicit policy against deficits, except during war or recession. In recent times, the erosion of this principle has created persistent structural deficits, removed the need to limit and prioritize programs, and led to an excessively large Federal sector. Our Federal borrowing has created economic distortions that will result in less investment, lower productivity, and a lower standard of living for all Americans. The balanced budget requirement that Federal operations be funded from current revenues restores a critical principle of fiscal responsibility and limited government. It will help return this country to sound economic principles and provide for our continued growth and prosperity.

Finally, I would like to emphasize the Congress's role in this procedure. Congress is not being asked to enact a balanced budget amendment—it cannot. What we are asking is that the Congress allow the American people the opportunity to adopt this provision. If sufficient States refuse to ratify it, the amendment will, and should, die, but the American people should be given the chance to vote.

# NO
## Robert Rubin

# SHOULD THE SENATE PASS A BALANCED BUDGET AMENDMENT TO THE U.S. CONSTITUTION? CON

I spent 26 years on Wall Street before joining the Administration four years ago, and I have a deep and abiding belief in the profound importance of fiscal responsibility to our national economy. I have an equally strong conviction that a balanced budget amendment is a threat to our economic health, will expose our economy to unacceptable risks, and should not be adopted. I also believe that such an amendment is not necessary to achieve the critical objective of balancing our budget.

Throughout our history, with the exception of wartime, budget deficits —when they existed at all—were generally small. In the 1970s and 1980s, they began to rise and the Federal debt grew sharply. But after experiencing this period of fiscal indiscipline, I believe the atmosphere in Washington has changed.

This process of change began in 1990 with the passage of the Omnibus Budget Reconciliation Act signed into law by President Bush. We then took an enormous step forward with the deficit reduction program enacted in 1993, which has led to a reduction in the size of the deficit from 4.7 percent to 1.4 percent of GDP [Gross Domestic Product]. Last year, both the Administration and the Congress proposed budgets that would eliminate the deficit by 2002, and both are expected to do so again this year.

Not only has the atmosphere in Washington changed, but there is also a new enforcing factor at work, which is the emergence of global markets that are highly sensitive to a nation's degree of fiscal responsibility. A nation that does not address fiscal matters will be severely punished by markets with high interest rates that could impair or even severely impair its economy.

The sum total is that politically, historically, and economically, the forces are in place to balance the budget. Now we need to get the job done.

However, there is a distinction between balancing the budget and passing a constitutional amendment. When we contemplate an action as significant as amending the Constitution to require a balanced budget, we owe it to

From Robert Rubin, "Should the Senate Pass a Balanced Budget Amendment to the U.S. Constitution? Con," in "Reducing the Deficit: The Ongoing Balanced Budget Debate," *Congressional Digest*, vol. 76, no. 3 (March 1997). Copyright © 1997 by The Congressional Digest Corporation, Washington, DC, (202)333-7332. Reprinted by permission.

the American people to understand exactly what its consequences would be. And those consequences are serious. I believe the balanced budget amendment proposal would subject the Nation to unacceptable economic risks in perpetuity.

As Secretary of the Treasury, I am deeply concerned that a balanced budget amendment could turn slowdowns into recessions, mild recessions into worse ones, and bad recessions into depressions. A balanced budget requirement in the Constitution would make recessions longer and more painful, first by eliminating automatic stabilizers that protect people during a downturn and, second, by instead requiring measures to cut spending or increase taxes during slowdowns and recessions when the economy is already suffering from lack of demand.

Since World War II, we have made immense progress in reducing the toll of the boom and bust cycle through the introduction of automatic fiscal stabilizers and effective use of counter-cyclical fiscal policy. Under current law, for example, if unemployment rises, unemployment insurance payments rise as well, moderating the economic impact of recessions on companies, workers, and their families.

The extremes of the business cycle have declined sharply over the postwar period compared with the pre-era. A balanced budget amendment would undo this progress by turning off these stabilizers and actually require measures that could exacerbate a recession.

To take just one example, without automatic stabilizers, Treasury has estimated that unemployment in 1992 might have hit 9 percent instead of 7.7 percent, in excess of one million more jobs lost. Even were a three-fifths vote to waive the provisions of an amendment obtainable, slowdowns and recessions are hard to anticipate, and congressional action would almost surely be, at the very least, months late, by which time critical damage to the economy would already have been done.

A balanced budget amendment would also prevent us from dealing quickly and effectively with crises, from a second S&L [savings and loan] crisis to a second Hurricane Hugo to an escalating military threat.

For example, in September 1989, Hurricane Hugo struck the Carolinas, causing billions of dollars of damage. After President Bush declared a major disaster, Congress took action by appropriating $2.7 billion in emergency supplemental assistance to help the area rebuild. Under the balanced budget amendment, if the budget were otherwise in balance, this could not be done until after a vote of 60 percent of both houses.

As Secretary of the Treasury, I am also highly concerned that limits on our flexibility would increase the risk of default on the Federal debt. The possibility of default should never be on the table. Our creditworthiness is an invaluable national asset that should not be subject to question.

Default on payment of our debt would undermine our credibility with respect to meeting financial commitments, and that in turn would have adverse effects for decades to come, especially when our reputation is most important, that is, when the national economy is not healthy. Moreover, a failure to pay interest on our debt could raise the cost of borrowing not only for government, but for private borrowers, from companies to homeowners making payments on an adjustable mortgage.

It is also worth remembering that interest payments are only one type of obligation. If we are not able to meet our obligations, members of our armed forces, retirees receiving Social Security, those who depend on Medicare, and many others could suffer as well. The risk of this happening must not be increased.

The history of debt limit shows that raising the statutory debt limit is never an easy process. We all remember the enormous difficulties that surrounded this issue in 1995 and 1996. A requirement for a supermajority vote in both houses could make it far harder. Proponents argue that the constitutional amendment is needed to stiffen our resolve to balance the budget. But they also assume that, when necessary, Congress will waive its provisions by obtaining a three-fifths majority vote.

It is true that 60 votes are usually required for cloture in the Senate. Even more fundamentally, the Senate has long honored the rights of a minority to express its views and influence legislation. Nevertheless, recognizing that certain essential matters should not be held up by a minority, Senate rules permit a reconciliation bill which can be a vehicle for passing a budget or increasing the debt limit, to be passed by a simply majority. In contrast, this amendment would require a three-fifths majority to increase the debt limit or obtain a waiver from its provisions and would extend this supermajority requirement to such votes in the House. Thus, for example, 41 senators or 175 congressmen could throw the government into default; 41 senators could stop Social Security checks from going out or could advance a special agenda. In effect, a minority in either house could put the economic health of our Nation at risk by refusing to waive the balanced budget requirement or refusing to increase the debt limit unless that minority's agenda—which could

be budget-related or related to social policy or any other matter—was satisfied.

Let me add that a balanced budget amendment would also limit our ability to deal with national economic downturns in which only some regions were suffering, because most Members would not be experiencing the economic problems, making a 60 percent waiver more difficult to obtain. We cannot predict the political environment 10, 20, or 30 years from today, and we should not create enormous minority leverage in the face of uncertainty about future political conditions.

A balanced budget amendment may well be unenforceable. There is no way to compel Congress and the President to enact legislation to cut spending or raise taxes to balance the budget. Yet there is also no way to compel enactment of legislation to waive provisions of the amendment. It is not hard to imagine a situation in which a two-fifths minority of Congress opposes tax increases, a different two-fifths minority opposes spending cuts, and another two-fifths opposes a waiver of the balanced budget amendment to raise the debt limit. The amendment provides no method for resolving such an impasse.

Some proponents have suggested that, under these circumstances, the President would stop issuing checks, including those for Social Security benefits. Alternatively, judges might become deeply involved in determining whether Social Security or Medicare checks would be stopped. The President might also impound funds of his choosing. Or, the amendment might just prove to be unenforceable and therefore a nullity, reducing respect for the Constitution. All of these potential outcomes are extremely undesirable.

Let me mention, finally, two other problems. First, by requiring that a majority of the whole Congress approve a revenue increase, the amendment could make it more difficult to close special interest loopholes and eliminate obsolescent deductions and credits. Over time, this would reduce the fairness and efficacy of our tax code.

Second, unforeseen events could lead to a large end-of-the-year shortfall that could only be met in a very short period of time. Such shortfalls happen in many years. In Fiscal Year 1990, for example, CBO [Congressional Budget Office] re-estimated the deficit upward by $60 billion in the last nine months of the fiscal year. In such a case, huge cuts would be needed in those programs that happen to have payments late in the year, or where cuts can be made quickly, regardless of the consequences.

These are just two examples of why it would be a mistake to enshrine economic policy in the Constitution. We have no idea what economic conditions will be like in 10, 20, 30, or 40 years, and creating policy inflexibility is extremely unwise.

As I said at the beginning of my testimony, I have a deep commitment to the importance of deficit reduction and fiscal discipline to our Nation's economic health, and I believe that we can put in place balanced budget legislation this year. But I have an equally strong conviction that a balanced budget amendment poses real dangers for our Nation's economic future and, for this reason, must not be adopted.

# POSTSCRIPT

## Is There a Need for a Constitutional Amendment to Balance the Budget?

Regalia structures his argument for a constitutional amendment to balance the budget around three themes. The first theme is that chronic budget deficits create macroeconomic problems that can lead to lower living standards. The second theme is the appropriateness of the amendment for the Constitution. Regalia believes that the amendment is appropriate because it is consistent with two constitutional themes: limiting the power of the federal government and the protection of political minorities from abuse by the political majority. The third theme is the extent to which the courts would become involved in budget issues that are the responsibility of the Congress. On this point, Regalia argues that the implementing legislation that would be passed subsequent to the ratification of the amendment would "prevent judicial overreaching into legislative functions."

Rubin supports the goal of a balanced budget and asserts that historical, political, and economic forces that are now in place will lead to the attainment of this objective. Consequently, an amendment is unnecessary. But Rubin's opposition is more fundamental; the amendment is bad economics. In this regard he makes several points. First, such an amendment is likely to increase rather than decrease macroeconomic instability by eliminating automatic stabilizers. Second, it would impede the ability of the government to respond quickly and effectively to unexpected problems. Third, it may increase default risk on government securities. Fourth, it might be very difficult to enforce. Fifth, it might lead to actions that would reduce the fairness and efficacy of the tax code. Finally, events affecting the budget can occur quickly and, therefore, rapid response might be necessary regardless of consequences.

Although there seems to be a political consensus regarding the desirability of a balanced budget, it remains a contentious issue among economists. Useful information is presented in an annual series entitled *The Guide to the Federal Budget* by Stanley E. Collender (The Urban Institute Press). For a more specific discussion on the need for a constitutional amendment to balance the budget, see "The BBA: A Spent Idea," by Robert Eisner, *The Nation* (February 24, 1997); "Balancing Act," by Stephen Moore, *National Review* (February 10, 1997); and "The Balanced Budget Trap" by Karen M. Padget, *The American Prospect* (November/December 1996). For additional statements for and against the amendment, see *Congressional Digest* (March 1997). For a description of the 1997 legislative plan to balance the budget, see "Fight Looms Over Budget Plan's Detail" by Christopher Georges, *Wall Street Journal* (May 27, 1997).

# ISSUE 12

## Is the Federal Reserve the Cause of Poor Macroeconomic Performance?

**YES: Lester Thurow,** from "The Crusade That's Killing Prosperity," *The American Prospect* (March/April 1996)

**NO: Matthew Miller,** from "Grow Up," *The New Republic* (May 13, 1996)

### ISSUE SUMMARY

**YES:** Lester Thurow, an economics professor at Massachusetts Institute of Technology, believes that two major macroeconomic problems, a disguised high rate of unemployment and stagnating living standards, are due to Federal Reserve policies to limit economic growth to 2.5 percent or less per year.

**NO:** Matthew Miller, senior editor for the *New Republic*, believes that asking the Federal Reserve to raise aggregate demand above the economy's potential growth rate will create very few jobs and lead to systemic inflation.

In December 1913 the Federal Reserve Act became law. It created the Federal Reserve System (Fed), which began operations early in 1914. The Fed was designed as an institution that would counter the periodic financial panics that had plagued the U.S. economy. Indeed, the financial panic of 1907 led Congress to establish the National Monetary Commission. Following the Commission's studies, several proposals were advanced and, after extensive debate, the Fed was born.

As originally designed, the Fed had three purposes: "to give the country an elastic currency, provide facilities for discounting commercial credits, and improve the supervision of the banking system." Over time there have been many changes in the Fed. For example, the structure of the Board of Governors of the Fed, whose prime function is the formulation of monetary policy, was changed during the 1930s. Perhaps more important than changes in structure have been changes in its goals. From the original three purposes, the Fed has extended its purview to include "stability and growth of the economy, a high level of employment, stability in the purchasing power of the dollar, and reasonable balance in transactions with foreign countries." In moving from narrow financial goals to broader macroeconomic goals, the Fed has responded to legislative demands, primarily the Employment Act of 1946 and the Full Employment and Balanced Growth Act of 1978. While the Fed is usually described as an independent agency of the federal government, its structure, goals, operations, and, indeed, its very existence are determined by Congress and the president.

The conventional interpretation of the Fed is that it uses its tools—open market operations, discount rate changes, and changes in legal reserve requirements—to engage in countercyclical monetary policy. Thus, the Fed will purchase government securities, lower the discount rate, and/or lower legal reserve requirements to increase the money supply and lower interest rates, in order to stimulate an economy operating at less than full employment. But this conventional interpretation has been under attack for some time. Conservatives, led by monetarists such as Milton Friedman and Anna Schwartz, have argued that the Fed has hurt rather than helped the cause of economic stability. The monetarists point to a number of instances in U.S. economic history where the Fed has made things worse and not better. The moral of U.S. economic history, according to the monetarists, is that the economy would be more stable if the Fed did not engage in countercyclical monetary policy; the Fed should be passivist rather than activist.

More recently the debate has turned to the execution of activist policy. Some liberal economists as well as some conservatives believe that the Fed has been too concerned with inflation and in the process has restricted economic growth and tolerated too much unemployment. That is, the Fed has kept the money supply too low and interest rates too high. Other economists disagree; they believe that the Fed and other central banks cannot be all things to all people and that it should concentrate its efforts on achieving one macroeconomic goal: price stability. These economists think the Fed has followed the right course. If money supply growth had been higher and interest rates lower, the result would not have been higher growth and lower unemployment, but more inflation. Both sides of this disagreement are admirably presented by Lester Thurow and Matthew Miller. Although Thurow and Miller presented their arguments in 1996, the basic disagreement extended into 1997 when the Fed took action to increase interest rates in what was called a "preemptive strike" against inflation.

# YES

**Lester Thurow**

# THE CRUSADE THAT'S
# KILLING PROSPERITY

The great untold story of the American economy in the 1990s is the disguised high rate of unemployment and its direct impact on stagnating living standards. Properly calculated, our rate of joblessness is well into double digits. No wonder workers have no bargaining power to get their share of an increasingly productive economy.

Among economists, a debate rages on why earnings inequalities began to rise rapidly and real median wages started to fall a quarter century ago. Some blame a technological shift that cut demand for uneducated labor while boosting the demand for those with greater education and skills. Others identify global "factor price equalization"—in an open global economy overseas workers with comparable skills but lower wages are forcing the wages of Americans down.

What's left out of this lengthy, if inconclusive, debate is the role played by the slack economic environment in which these two forces have been operating. While each is real, their impacts would have been very different if they had operated in an environment of labor shortages rather than one of vast labor surplus. The U.S. economy has been celebrated for creating tens of millions of jobs during the past two decades. But properly counted, our true unemployment rate is no better than Europe's. And nothing keeps wages from rising like a large pool of idle or underemployed workers.

Today's slack labor markets were produced by the war against inflation— declared in the early 1970s and still underway 25 years later. Inflation began, with the mis-financing of the Vietnam War in the late 1960s, accelerated with the OPEC oil shock and food shocks of the early 1970s, expanded across the economy in the mid-1970s because of the widespread use of cost-of-living indexes in both labor and supplier contracts, and was rekindled by the second OPEC oil shock at the end of the 1970s.

While other remedies such as wage and price controls were initially tried, none seemed to work. Eventually all of the world's major governments came to the conclusion that the only cure for inflation was to use higher interest rates and tighter fiscal policies (higher taxes or lower expenditures) to restrain

From Lester Thurow, "The Crusade That's Killing Prosperity," *The American Prospect* (March/April 1996), pp. 54–59. Copyright © 1996 by The American Prospect, P.O. Box 383080, Cambridge, MA 02138. Reprinted by permission. All rights reserved.

prices by deliberately slowing growth to push unemployment up and to force real wages down. Excess capacity and surplus labor became the key players in the anti-inflationary game.

In the end the strategy for braking the world economy worked. The world's real economic growth rate slid from 5 percent per year in the 1960s to 3.6 percent per year in the 1970s. The double-digit inflation of the early 1980s led to another round of monetary tightening, and growth further decelerated to 2.8 percent per year in the 1980s. Actions such as Federal Reserve Chairman Alan Greenspan's seven interest rate hikes between early 1994 and early 1995 and the Bundesbank's very restrictive policies in Germany slowed the world's growth rate even further, and in the first half of the 1990s world growth has averaged just 2 percent per year. Today the Federal Reserve Board designs policies to limit American economic growth to a maximum of 2.5 percent or less. Anything more is believed to be inflationary. In its annual policy recommendations, the Organization for Economic Cooperation and Development (OECD) subscribed to the view that America's maximum non-inflationary growth rate was 2.5 percent.

*  *  *

Like a real war that has gone on far too long, all of the original reasons for the war —the mis-financing of the Vietnam War, OPEC oil shocks, food shocks, indexed wage and supply contracts, inflationary expectations—are long gone. As the war continues year after year, the negative side effects of the war, falling real wages and rising inequalities, have become far more corrosive than the original reasons for joining the battle. The battle continues even though the war against inflation has

been won. The combatants have gotten so used to "fighting on" that they cannot even recognize that they have won.

Slow growth cured inflation because it directly pushed real wages down—creating very slack labor markets. Indirectly, it created an environment where factor price equalization, a skill-intensive technological shift, and other factors could generate enormous downward pressures on real wages.

Restrictive monetary and fiscal policies have produced unemployment rates not seen since the Great Depression. Today, more than 10 percent of the European workforce is officially unemployed and in three countries (Spain, Ireland, and Finland) unemployment has been above 20 percent at some point in the first half of the 1990s. Spain and Italy have youth unemployment rates of over 60 percent. While it is very fashionable to blame Europe's high unemployment rates on "rigid labor markets," which is to say unions and welfare state protections, the real culprit is macroeconomic austerity. Most of the same protections existed before 1973, and coexisted nicely with high growth, full employment, and rising wages. Japan's official unemployment rate is near 3 percent, but Japan essentially has a system of private unemployment insurance where workers who would be fired in the United States remain on private payrolls. Even the Japanese admit that if their firms acted as American firms do, their unemployment rate would be over 10 percent.

## THE REAL UNEMPLOYMENT RATE

In the fall of 1995, America's official unemployment rate was hovering around 5.7 percent. But like an iceberg that is mostly invisible below the waterline, officially unemployed workers are just a small part of the total number of workers looking for more work.

If we combine the 7.5 to 8 million officially unemployed workers, the 5 to 6 million people who are not working but who do not meet any of the tests for being active in the workforce and are therefore not considered unemployed, and the 4.5 million part-time workers who would like full-time work, there are 17 to 18.5 million Americans looking for more work. This brings the real unemployment rate to almost 14 percent.

Slow growth has also generated an enormous contingent workforce of underemployed people. There are 8.1 million American workers in temporary jobs, 2 million who work "on call," and 8.3 million self-employed "independent contractors (many of whom are downsized professionals who have very few clients but call themselves self-employed consultants because they are too proud to admit that they are unemployed). Most of these more than 18 million people are also looking for more work and better jobs. Together these contingent workers account for another 14 percent of the workforce. In the words of *Fortune* magazine, "Upward pressure on wages is nil because so many of the employed are these 'contingent' workers who have no bargaining power with employers, and payroll workers realize they must swim in the same Darwinian ocean." Like the unemployed, these contingent workers generate downward wage pressures.

In addition there are 5.8 million missing males (another 4 percent of the workforce) 25 to 60 years of age. They exist in our census statistics but not in our labor statistics. They have no obvious means of economic support. They are the right age to be in the workforce, were once in the workforce, are not in school, and are not old enough to have retired. They show up in neither employment nor unemployment statistics. They have either been dropped from, or have dropped out of, the normal working economy. Some we know as the homeless; others have disappeared into the underground illegal economy.

Put these three groups together and in the aggregate about one-third of the American workforce is potentially looking for more work than they now have. Add in another 11 million immigrants (legal and illegal) who entered the United States from 1980 to 1993 to search for more work and higher wages, and one has a sea of unemployed workers, underemployed workers, and newcomers looking for work.

These millions of job-hunters lead to a more human-scale result that everyone can understand. At 5 p.m. a midsized metal-ceramic firm posts job openings for 10 entry-level jobs on its bulletin board. By 5 a.m. 2,000 people are waiting in line to apply for those 10 jobs.

## WHY WAGES FALL

While the economy has been generating about 2 million jobs per year since the end of the 1990–1991 recession, these gains are just barely large enough to hold even with migration and the normal internal rate of growth of the working-age population. However rapid, job growth cannot lead to wage increase, unless it is faster than the growth rate of those looking for work.

If one believes even marginally in the power of supply and demand, surplus labor of these magnitudes has to lead to falling real wages. Wages rise roughly with productivity growth only if there are labor shortages. Since slow growth throws the bottom 60 percent of the workforce into unemployment far more than it does the top 20 percent, the earnings of the bottom 60 percent should be expected to fall sharply relative to the top 20 percent in a period of high unemployment—as they have.

These direct negative effects on wages were compounded by several indirect effects. American economists used to talk about something called "efficiency wages." One of the mysteries of the post–World War II era was wages that rose even when there were unemployed qualified American workers who would have been glad to do those jobs for less. This anomaly was explained by arguing that firms deliberately paid incumbent workers above-market wages to secure a high degree of cooperation, commitment, and effort that they could not have gotten if their workforces could have quit and easily gotten equal wages elsewhere.

But in a world where there are always millions of unemployed and underemployed workers, firms do not have to pay efficiency wages. The same degree of cooperation, commitment, and effort can be achieved by using the motivation factor called "fear"—the fear of being thrown into this enormous sea of unemployment and underemployment. In the last five years examples abound of profitable firms that simply marched in and dramatically lowered the wages of their existing workforces by 20 to 40 percent. Workers complain but they don't quit.

Similarly, two decades of surplus labor have broken linkage between productivity gains and wage increases. The early 1990s demonstrated that no government would come running to the rescue with large fiscal and monetary packages designed to stimulate demand during recessions. Instead, recessions would be allowed to run their course and governments would simply wait for a recovery—or as happened in 1994 in the United States, adopt monetary policies to actually slow what was already by historical standards a very weak recovery.

Knowledge that governments won't shorten recessions radically changes expectations. If downturns are sharper and longer, business firms have to reduce prices if they wish to survive. As a result, in the 1990s more of America's productivity gains are showing up as falling prices and fewer are showing up as rising wages. Higher labor productivity doesn't lead to higher labor wages as it used to. Wages can fall while productivity rises—as has happened in the last 20 years.

The best example is the computer industry—an industry that pays very low wages for its production workers. Productivity is growing very rapidly, but all of that productivity gain shows up in lower prices or higher profits for chipmakers or software firms. None shows up as higher wages as used to occur in industries such as automobiles or steel. This sea of excess labor accentuates the downward pressures of a skill-intensive technology shift and global factor price equalization. Tight labor markets would offset much if not all of the impact on the bottom 60 percent of the wage distribution, but they don't exist.

A skill-intensive technological shift should raise the wages of the skilled and lower the wages of the unskilled, but in the context of vast supplies of excess labor the expected higher wages even for skilled workers don't appear. The upward wage pressures that should be seen are more than offset by the downward pressures from surplus unemployed skilled laborers. For males, real wages are now falling at all education levels, even for those with graduate degrees. For the unskilled the downward wage pressures that flow from this technological shift are magnified because of the surplus labor that already exists.

\* \* \*

The war on inflation has also intensified the downward wage pressures coming from a number of other sources. Some capitalists certainly plotted to kill America's labor unions. President Reagan's firing of all of America's unionized air traffic controllers legitimized a deliberate strategy of de-unionization. In the private sector, consultants were hired who specialized in getting rid of unions, decertification elections were forced, and legal requirements to respect union rights were simply ignored—firms simply paid the small fines that labor law violations brought and continued to violate the law. The strategy succeeded in shrinking union membership to slightly more than 10 percent of the private workforce (15 percent of the total workforce). And even where unions still existed they lost much of their power to influence wages or negotiate working conditions. Combined with corporate compensation committees who in the past 25 years have escalated CEO salaries from 35 to 157 times that of entry-level workers, one could argue that the capitalists had declared class warfare on labor—and were winning.

While the economics literature is inconclusive as to whether unions affect average wages (equally productive companies with and without unions tended to pay the same wages in the past), there is no doubt that unions affect the distribution of wages. Wage distributions are much more equal where unions exist.

High school-college wage differentials, for example, have always been smaller in the union sector than in the nonunion sector. As a result, with the demise of unions as a force in the American economy, wage differentials should be expected to rise. In addition, as company worries about unionization have waned, the gap between union and nonunion wages has doubled. Higher wages no longer need to be paid in nonunion firms to keep unions out.

The attack on unions could not have succeeded in an environment of tight labor markets. But in this sea of surplus labor, unions have little negotiating power to offer prospective members.

Deregulation has also led to some wage reductions. In regulated industries such as trucking and airlines, workers collected some of the excess profits—what economists call "rents"—that accrued from regulation. Truck driver wages and the wages of some airline employees fell dramatically with deregulation. In the case of truck drivers, wages fell three times as fast as elsewhere. The rents that had been built into their wages were transferred back to the consumer or to corporate profits. But in a world of tight labor markets more of those rents would have stayed with workers.

Since wages in the many advanced industrial countries are now above those in the U.S., most of the factor price equalization flowing from other First World countries is behind us. But ahead lies the integration of the Second World into the First World and a very different Third World. The communist countries did not run effective civilian economies but they ran excellent education systems. The Soviet Union was a high-science society with more engineers and scientists than anyone other than the United States. China is capable of quickly generating hundreds of millions of medium-skill workers. The end of communism and the success of the "little tiger" countries on the Pacific Rim have led the Third World to junk import substitution as a route to economic development, and to become export oriented. Where countries with only a few million workers used to be export oriented (Singapore, Hong Kong, Taiwan, and South Korea), Third World countries containing billions of people now want to be export oriented (Indonesia, India, Pakistan, Mexico). As a result, exports from low-wage Third World countries are apt to be much larger in the years ahead. Whatever one believes about how much of real wage declines and increases in wage dispersion can be blamed on globalization in the past, the forces of factor price equalization are going to grow enormously. If they continue to operate in a world of slack labor markets inside the United States, the rate of decline in real wages will accelerate.

## THE REAL INFLATION RATE

Inflation itself has already ended. But as long as the policymakers are convinced that the ghost of inflation will at any minute reappear, they will operate their policies as if inflation were a real threat.

It is possible, in fact, that inflation is even lower than its low official rate. The broadest measure of inflation, the implicit price deflator for the gross domestic product, fell from 2.2 percent in 1993 to 2.1 percent in 1994, and in the third quarter of 1995 inflation was running at the rate of 0.6 percent.

Having fallen during the previous recession, the producer's price index for finished consumer goods in December 1994 was below where it had been in April 1993 and annual rates of increase decelerated from 1.2 percent in 1993 to 0.6 percent in 1994. In 1994 and 1995 labor costs rose at the slowest rate since records had been kept and the core rate of inflation (the rate of inflation leaving out volatile energy and food prices) was the lowest rate recorded since 1965.

Officially the rate of inflation in the consumer price index (CPI) fell from 3 percent in 1993 to 2.6 percent in 1994, and to 2.5 percent in 1995, but Chairman Greenspan had himself testified to Congress that the CPI exaggerated inflation by as much as 1.5 percentage points since it underestimated quality improvements in goods (in computers, for example, it has performance rising at only 7 percent per year) and since it gives no credit at all for quality improvements in services. The Boskin Commission, appointed by the Senate Finance Committee, has estimated the upward bias in the CPI at between 1 and 2.4 percentage points. If one is willing to assume that the sectors where quality improvements are hard to measure are in fact improving quality at the same pace as those sectors where quality is easy to measure, the over-measurement of inflation may be closer to 3 percentage points.

Health care is a sector whose inflationary dynamics have little to do with macroeconomic pressures. Since health care accounts for 15 percent of GDP and health care prices were rising at a 5 percent annual rate in 1994, mathematically another 0.75 percentage points of inflation can be traced to health care (more than one-third of 1994's total inflation).

Put all of these factors together and it is clear that the rate of inflation in the sectors where inflation is controllable with slower growth is certainly very low and probably actually negative.

While some economists argue that the CPI does not in fact overstate inflation it is bizarre that Alan Greenspan is among those who think that inflation is significantly below its officially measured rate since it undercuts his arguments for contractionary monetary policy.

\* \* \*

Left to their own devices, those who operate central banks are never going to declare a permanent victory over inflation. The reasons are simple. If the battle against inflation is primary, central bankers will be described as, and actually be, the most important economic players in the game. Without inflation, they run rather unimportant institutions.

It is important to remember that in 1931 and 1932 as the United States was plunging into the Great Depression, economic advisers such as Secretary of the Treasury Andrew Mellon were arguing that nothing could be done without risking an outbreak of inflation —despite the fact that prices had fallen 23 percent from 1929 to 1932 and would fall another 4 percent in 1933. The fear of inflation was used as a club to stop the actions that should have been taken. Central banks are prone to see inflationary ghosts since they love to be ghostbusters. While it is true that no human has ever been hurt by a real ghost, it is equally true that ghostbusters have often created a lot of real human havoc.

Central bankers will of course tell us that when they gain anti-inflationary credibility," rapid noninflationary growth will resume. But this is a mirage shimmering in the hot desert air. If any central bank has anti-inflationary credibility, it should be the German Bundesbank, yet Germany has one of the industrial world's lowest real growth rates. If the Bundesbank has not yet achieved anti-inflationary credibility, no central bank ever will obtain this exalted status.

As a result, if policies are to change it will require a change in political perceptions. Rising inequalities and falling real wages have to come to be seen as more important problems than the ghost of inflation when it comes to getting elected or reelected. Social welfare programs for the poor are not politically viable as long as the poor do not vote for the politicians who support the programs that benefit them. Tight labor markets are equally politically unviable unless voters reward the politicians who are willing to reverse the macroeconomic policies that have been in place for the past 25 years.

The long-run answer to falling wages is a much better-skilled bottom three-quarters of the American workforce, but without a reversal in our macroeconomic policies no set of human-capital investment policies can hope to work.

# NO

## Matthew Miller

## GROW UP

It's no surprise in a campaign year to find a clamor for more growth and a penchant for sloppy economic arguments. In the primaries, it was tax-cutting supply-siders Steve Forbes and Jack Kemp egged on by their allies at *The Wall Street Journal*'s editorial page, who took up the chorus. Now it's liberal economists Lester Thurow and Robert Eisner, Wall Street pooh-bah Felix Rohaytn and manufacturing CEOs like Tenneco's Dana Mead and General Electric's Jack Welch. The Federal Reserve and its chairman, Alan Greenspan, we're told, are strangling the economy in the misguided belief that growth in excess of 2.5 percent will spark inflation. Worse, the claim goes, because this slow-growth conspiracy permeates officialdom—both the Congressional Budget Office and the Clinton administration, for example, forecast such anemic growth over the next seven years—it's sure to be self-fulfilling. If the Fed would just take its foot off the brakes and lower interest rates, the dissenters say, the economy would roar like it did in the 1960s, when we grew more than 4 percent yearly with 2.5 percent inflation. With five consecutive years of inflation at 3 percent or less, the Fed is chasing a ghost.

Are the Fed bashers right? To answer that question, let's first assume that almost everyone wants more economic growth, just as almost everyone wants world peace. Let's also admit that one powerful constituency in our midst represents an exception: the wealthy, who are hurt far more by a little extra inflation than by a little extra unemployment and thus flex their muscle (via the bond markets) in favor of the latter. Whether you're a cheerleader for growth or one of its secret opponents, the case against the Fed still comes down to two questions. First, in the short term, is there enough slack in the economy to allow the Fed to boost spending and increase output and employment without triggering an inflationary spiral? Second, is there reason over the long term to think our economy can "sustainably" grow faster than 2 to 2.5 percent yearly—that is, without risking an outsized inflation that can be exorcised only by a repeat of the bruising recession the Fed put us through in the early 1980s?

The unhappy answer, for someone like me who's dissatisfied with our economic performance, is that the Fed demonizers are mostly wrong: they overstate their case and are often incoherent in their arguments. This means we'll have to look somewhere other than the Fed to solve the wage stagnation and growing inequality that plague us.

To see why, take the short-term complaint first. For all their squabbles, economists generally agree that there's a rate of unemployment beneath which we can go only at the risk of accelerating inflation. They call this, with typical lyricism, the "non-accelerating inflation rate of unemployment," or NAIRU. Think of it as a way for the dismal science to avoid saying explicitly that a certain level of human misery is "natural." The intuition behind it is straightforward. Workers lose jobs or enter the market where suitable new work is unavailable; because it takes time, training and even relocation to find their next opportunities, they may remain unemployed for months. Pumping the economy beyond such "normal" levels of slack has proven to be a reliable predictor of inflation for twenty years, as the proverbial situation of "too much money chasing too few goods" translates into price hikes. Alan Blinder, the former Fed vice chairman who recently returned to Princeton, calls the NAIRU theory the "clean little secret of macroeconomics."

Economists peg the NAIRU today at between 5.5 and 6 percent. With unemployment now at 5.5 percent (down from 7.4 percent in 1992), there's little reason to hope for bold new progress. It's true that some economists debate whether the NAIRU is really 5.5 or a little less. And getting the rate down another half a point means jobs for 600,000 more people. There's a case to be made, therefore, that the Fed could probe a little further, inching down interest rates to see what happens.

* * *

But here's the point: saying we might be able to get a fraction of a percent more jobs today is different from implying we can stamp out unemployment. It's also different from saying the economy can grow at 3 or 4 percent in perpetuity as the growth propagandists urge. Even today's Fed bashers acknowledge there's a limit to how far you can push down unemployment without fueling inflation; they simply argue, without specifics, that it's lower than we think. But, as Stanford University's Paul Krugman points out, acknowledging this limit means conceding that the extra growth they're screaming for can only last a year or two at best.

Why? For the last two decades (in another empirical relationship so sturdy it's called Okun's Law), every percentage point the economy has grown annually beyond 2.5 percent has reduced the unemployment rate by half a point. You can get higher growth for a while when you're starting from the bottom, say, of the Reagan recession, with its 10.7 percent jobless rate. But, even if the noninflationary level of unemployment is as low as 4.5 percent, getting there from today's 5.5 percent would give you just two years of 3.5 percent growth. That's it. To believe that you can grow this fast in perpetuity, you'd have to believe we can get unemployment down to an unprecedented 3 percent five years from now or toward zero (and beyond!) after a decade. It's just not credible.

To be sure, even a year or two of an extra point of growth is nothing to sneeze at; I'll take a $70 billion lift in GDP [Gross Domestic Product] wherever we can find it. But the truth is that short-term demand management by the Fed can't deliver millions of new jobs, nor bring us anywhere close to our golden days of growth or the booms enjoyed by the Asian "tigers" today. Which brings us to the long-term question: Can anything get us back to those glory days?

\* \* \*

The economy's long-run potential rate of growth is a function of two things: the growth of the labor force and the growth in productivity (or output per worker). Arguments about growth have to work through one or both of these factors to be credible. Growth was faster in the 1960s, for example, because our working-age population was growing more rapidly, women were joining the workforce, and productivity was rising at more than 2 percent yearly. Countries like Taiwan and Indonesia grow at enviable rates today for similar reasons.

Here, however, things have changed. American women have completed their historic transition toward work outside the home; their labor force participation rate of 38 percent in 1960 has expanded and finally stabilized at 58 percent in the 1990s. Along with a post-baby boom drop in fertility rates, this helps explain why our labor force overall now grows at just over 1 percent a year. The great but mysterious post-1973 productivity slowdown, meanwhile, has left annual output per worker rising at a little over 1 percent as well. Together, these rates produce today's "gloomy" view of potential growth of 2.2 to 2.5 percent. It's not rocket science or conspiracy. It's math.

And it isn't just theory. In 1994, for example, still coming back from recession, the economy grew at 3.5 percent. As Alan Greenspan testified in February, if 3.5 percent was the true rate of increase in the economy's long run capacity, we should have seen no change in the economy's unused resources, or "slack," over that year. Instead, the "slack" tightened: measures of capacity use rose by 3 percent, and the unemployment rate dropped a full point. Greenspan correctly noted other signs of strain as well: deliveries of materials slowed, for example, and factory overtime rose.

Asking the Fed to pump aggregate spending or demand beyond the economy's potential growth rate is a recipe for systemic inflation. That doesn't mean we shouldn't try to raise potential growth through improving our infrastructure or investing more in research and development; indeed the search for productivity-boosting strategies is the heart of what economic policy debate should be about. But monetary policy is only one piece of economic policy. Its aim should be to promote a sustainable growth (and jobs) trajectory that avoids the kind of price spiral that takes a costly recession to excise.

In the face of this analysis—offered by such Democratic economists as Krugman, former Carter Council of Economic Advisers chairman Charles Schultze and Alan Blinder, whose agreement with Greenspan on these matters got lost in the media hype over their supposed differences—how does the growth chorus respond? Basically with a grab bag of sophistries. Since they sound good the first time you hear them, it's worth shooting down the big ones.

*Inflation is really lower.* Lester Thurow argues in the current *American Prospect* that "inflation itself has already ended," citing, among other things, Alan Greenspan's own assertions that the Consumer Price Index may overstate price hikes by up to 1.5 percent. With the official CPI coming in at 2.5 percent last year, he says, "real" inflation may be only 1 percent, so it's time the Fed stopped worrying and stepped on the gas pedal.

There's only one problem. If inflation is overstated, then economic growth is already a lot higher, since it's calculated by subtracting out inflation from observed nominal growth. On Thurow's logic, we're already growing at 4 percent, so what's his beef? Of course, at other times Thurow is happy to use the overstated CPI to argue that real wages are falling. It's hard to avoid the conclusion that he's trying to have it both ways—the tell-tale sign of a propagandist.

*Productivity is really higher.* Felix Rohaytn and assorted CEOs say productivity growth is higher than the official measure of 1 percent or so, meaning the potential growth the Fed is targeting is too low. The trouble with this argument is its reliance on anecdotes from manufacturing firms, like the kind Rohaytn advises. It's true that manufacturing productivity has undergone a resurgence, growing at 3.5 percent yearly since early 1993. But manufacturing only represents 20 percent of the economy.

*Wages are falling.* Thurow rightly argues that you can't possibly have an inflationary threat if it's not translated into higher wages. But economy-wide wages are actually rising 2 to 3 percent yearly.

Yes, some people's wages, particularly those with less education, are falling, and we urgently need to figure out how to reverse this. But, again, that's not an argument that inflation is dead.

*Divine intervention.* "Suppose God came to the Pentagon and said, 'There's never going to be another war,'" Thurow said to me, "You think the generals would tell us? Now suppose God came to Alan Greenspan and said, 'There's never going to be inflation again.' The head of the Federal Reserve Board will never declare victory on inflation." Thurow may be right there. And the oath Greenspan takes before testifying may not be enough to smoke him out. But for now I'm comfortable leaving that between Greenspan and the Big Central Banker upstairs. The Fed's institutional interest in inflation-busting isn't proof that the Fed is lying.

Saying the Fed can't solve our growth problems doesn't equal complacency about lousy economic performance. It simply means that scapegoating the Fed is a feel-good diversion from the tougher search for policies—fixing our schools, funding new technologies, raising savings and investment—that would actually boost productivity, wages and long-term growth. Let's agree that Greenspan and Company could usefully probe for a few hundred thousand more jobs. Then let's get back to the real work.

# POSTSCRIPT

## Is the Federal Reserve the Cause of Poor Macroeconomic Performance?

Thurow argues that preoccupation with a war against inflation, which has already been won, has led to substandard macroeconomic performance. That is, the Fed's anti-inflation policy of limiting economic growth to 2.5 percent or less per year has led to a true unemployment rate at least twice as high as the official unemployment rate, falling real wages, and stagnating living standards. As for differences between the official unemployment rate and the true unemployment rate, Thurow contends that the official unemployment rate ignores discouraged workers and involuntary part-time employment. So even though there has been a substantial increase in the number of jobs, the surplus labor market has prevented increases in real wages. To support his position that the war against inflation has already been won, Thurow cites a number of statistics and asserts that the Consumer Price Index may overstate inflation by as much as 3 percent per year.

Miller states that attacks on the Fed's monetary policies have come from the right as well as from the left: both ends of the political and economic spectrum want faster economic growth. To determine whether the criticisms of the Fed are correct, Miller poses two questions: Can the Fed accelerate economic growth without accelerating inflation? Can the economy sustain a growth rate faster than 2.5 percent per year? In answering the first question, Miller argues in terms of the nonaccelerating inflation rate of unemployment (NAIRU); he believes that the evidence is strong that faster growth will lead to accelerating inflation. As for the second question, Miller makes a number of points: to get and sustain a growth rate of 3.5 percent would require that the unemployment rate be down to 3 percent in five years and to zero in ten years; both the growth rate of labor force and productivity are now lower than they have been; and, if Thurow is right about overestimates of inflation, the actual growth in the economy is greater than the measured growth in the economy.

Additional reading on this issue includes "Monetary Policy: Goals and Strategy," by Janet Yellen, *Business Economics* (July 1996); "Inflation and Money Supply," by Alan Greenspan, *Vital Speeches of the Day* (March 15, 1997); "Low Inflation or No Inflation: Should the Federal Reserve Pursue Complete Price Stability?" by George Akerlof, William Dickens, and George Perry, *Challenge* (September/October 1996); "Missing the Turn," by James Medoff and Andrew Harles, *Challenge* (March/April 1997); and "Gains in Productivity, Profits Curb Inflation Despite Pay Increases," by Jacob M. Schlesinger, *Wall Street Journal* (May 21, 1997).

# ISSUE 13

# Is the Nonaccelerating Inflation Rate of Unemployment a Useful Guide for Macroeconomic Policy?

**YES: Joseph Stiglitz,** from "Reflections on the Natural Rate Hypothesis," *Journal of Economic Perspectives* (Winter 1997)

**NO: James K. Galbraith,** from "The Surrender of Economic Policy," *The American Prospect* (March/April 1996)

## ISSUE SUMMARY

**YES:** Joseph Stiglitz, chairman of the Clinton administration's Council of Economic Advisers, argues that the nonaccelerating inflation rate of unemployment (NAIRU), because it is useful in both understanding the causes of inflation and in predicting changes in the rate of inflation, is also useful as a guide for the execution of macroeconomic policy.

**NO:** James K. Galbraith, professor of economics at the LBJ School of Public Affairs at the University of Texas, believes that the shocks that have increased the rate of inflation have occurred both when the unemployment rate has been high and when it has been low, and, therefore, the NAIRU is useless as a guide for the conduct of macroeconomic policy.

There seems to be very little disagreement regarding macroeconomic goals—the outcomes the national economy needs to achieve. They are (1) economic growth—the output of goods and services expand over time; (2) full employment—all those seeking employment are successful in their job search; and (3) price stability—the average level of prices remains constant. While there is widespread agreement on the macroeconomic goals, there are significant differences regarding what should be done when the national economy fails to achieve them.

Noninterventionists believe that the macroeconomy is self-correcting and government action is unnecessary; indeed, they argue that government action may make macroeconomic conditions worse. Activists believe that the government must intervene if the macroeconomy is not performing as desired; policy action can be useful in improving macroeconomic performance.

But the activists may not agree about everything. There are any number of examples. Consider first the choice of government actions. One option is fiscal policy—changes in government transfer payments, changes in government purchases of goods and services, and changes in taxes. Fiscal policy requires the cooperation of the executive and congressional branches of government because these types of changes require the passage of legislation. The second option is monetary policy, which involves changes in the money supply and interest rates. Monetary policy does not require executive-congressional cooperation; it is entrusted to the Federal Reserve System, an independent agency of the federal government. In this context, activists may agree that there is a need for government action to correct a macroeconomic problem but disagree on whether the appropriate response involves monetary policy or fiscal policy.

A second example of disagreement among activists is the usefulness of the NAIRU as a guide for policy action. To understand the nature of this disagreement, it is necessary to review some basic definitions. The rate of inflation is the rate of increase in the average level of prices as measured by the Consumer Price Index, for example. Over time the rate of inflation can be accelerating (increasing from 3 percent in one year to 5 percent in the next year); decelerating (decreasing from 3 percent in one year to 1 percent in the next year), or nonaccelerating (constant at 3 percent in both years). The unemployment rate is defined as the percentage of the labor force that is unemployed—the percentage of those who are seeking work but are unable to find jobs.

The natural rate hypothesis suggests that there is a particular unemployment rate consistent with constant or nonaccelerating inflation; this unemployment rate is the NAIRU. If the unemployment rate falls below the NAIRU then prices begin to rise more rapidly; inflation begins to accelerate. If the unemployment rate is above the NAIRU then prices begin to rise less rapidly; inflation begins to decelerate. In this fashion the NAIRU can be used as a policy guide. A simple application can be stated as follows: if the unemployment rate is above the NAIRU, then engage in expansionary fiscal or expansionary monetary policy action because such actions will serve to reduce the unemployment rate without making inflation worse. This simple application can be extended: once the unemployment rate reaches the NAIRU, it is appropriate to terminate expansionary policy. Further action to reduce the unemployment rate may lower the unemployment rate, but only at the cost of accelerating inflation.

Both Joseph Stiglitz and James K. Galbraith can be considered activists in the sense that both believe that government action can improve macroeconomic performance. They disagree, however on the usefulness of the NAIRU as a guide to policy action. Stiglitz believes that it is a useful guide for policy actions even though its actual numerical value may change over time. Galbraith disagrees. He believes that the use of the NAIRU as a guide for macroeconomic policy has led to more unemployment than was necessary to maintain price stability. He argues that if we really want full employment, we need to abandon the use of the NAIRU and adopt what he calls a full employment policy.

# YES

## Joseph Stiglitz

# REFLECTIONS ON THE NATURAL RATE HYPOTHESIS

Few concepts in economics with an acronym as unpleasant as NAIRU have attained as much public prominence in the past 10 years. Who, 10 years ago, would have thought that White House economic press conferences would begin with a question concerning the administration's estimate of the NAIRU? The issue typically posed is not whether there is a NAIRU, but what its level actually is.

I have become convinced that the NAIRU is a useful analytic concept. It is useful as a theory to understand the causes of inflation. It is useful as an empirical basis for predicting changes in the inflation rate. And, it is useful as a general guideline for thinking about macroeconomic policy. But these points are controversial within the profession....

Let me begin my defense of the NAIRU by asserting that it is a very well defined concept. In fact, the main advantage of using the somewhat ugly term NAIRU instead of its more euphonious synonym, the natural rate, is that each time we use the term we are reminded of its meaning. The NAIRU is defined as the nonaccelerating inflation rate of unemployment; that is, the rate of unemployment consistent with an unchanging inflation rate. When unemployment is below the NAIRU, there is pressure for the inflation rate to rise; contrarily, when unemployment is above the NAIRU, there is pressure for the inflation rate to fall....

I think of the theory behind the NAIRU essentially as a description about how the economy behaves out of equilibrium. When unemployment is below the NAIRU, real wage demands are greater than the amount firms are willing to pay (at prevailing prices and price expectations).... Equilibrium—defined in this case as inflation stable at a level equal to its expectation—is only achieved when unemployment rises to the NAIRU, making the behavior of wage setters compatible with the behavior of price setters. In other words, the natural rate hypothesis views changes in the inflation rate as a labor market phenomenon whose magnitude can be proxied by a particular measure of labor market slack: the unemployment rate.

In this paper, I want to elaborate on three criteria for evaluating whether the NAIRU is useful for academics and policymakers.... The following sections discuss the natural rate hypothesis in the context of these three criteria: its ability to explain changes in the inflation rate, our ability to explain why the NAIRU changes, and the usefulness of these ideas for policy discussions.

## THE EMPIRICAL SUCCESS OF THE PHILLIPS CURVE

The most basic implication of the natural rate hypothesis is that changes in the inflation rate are (in large part) a labor market phenomenon whose magnitude can be proxied by a particular measure of labor market slack—the unemployment rate. I believe the data support the view that unemployment is a good predictor of the direction that inflation will move. One nonparametric way to approach this issue is to compare the direction of the change in inflation (as measured by the core experimental CPI) with the level of demographically adjusted unemployment.[1] Since 1960, inflation rose in 26 of the 32 quarters when the unemployment rate was below 5 percent, but inflation fell in 24 of the 27 quarters when unemployment was above 7 percent This empirical regularity is very strong. It also suggests an upper bound on our uncertainty about the NAIRU: it looks as if it has been contained within 5 and 7 percent for the period from 1960 to the present. Note that this is the NAIRU for the demographically adjusted unemployment rate; mapping it into a concept that we can compare to the actual history of unemployment would widen the band somewhat....

I want to go beyond these tests to discuss some tentative conclusions we have reached in our more structural research at the CEA [Council of Economic Advisers], many of which are consistent with the empirical research in this area, as exemplified by some of the papers in this symposium. When we regress changes in the inflation rate on past values of unemployment, regardless of the precise specification or other variables included, we get t-statistics on lagged unemployment on the order of 4 or 5.... Such results make us just about as certain that unemployment has predictive power for changes in the inflation rate as we can ever be in empirical research.

Just saying that unemployment matters, however, is not enough. To defend my thesis that the NAIRU is a useful concept, I need to demonstrate how much it matters. In our regressions, we find that keeping the unemployment rate one percentage point below the NAIRU for one year will result in the inflation rate increasing by between 0.3 and 0.6 of a percentage point. That magnitude is definitely large enough to command the attention of policymakers. Finally, our analysis indicates that at least 20 percent of the variation in the inflation rate can be explained by unemployment alone. This figure serves as a reminder that the actual inflation process—and the policy decisions that must be made based on it—is much more complicated than a simple link between the NAIRU and inflation. However, economists should not readily surrender any parsimonious concept that can explain 20 percent of something important.

## WHAT DO ECONOMISTS KNOW ABOUT CHANGES IN THE NAIRU?

The second criterion for the NAIRU being a useful concept is that we can explain why it changes over time, predict those changes to some degree, and possibly even identify policies that might alter it. When Milton Friedman first proposed the natural rate hypothesis in his presidential address to the American Economic Association in 1968, it sounded like royal edict had established the natural rate as another one of the universe's invariant constants. Today, there is general recognition that if a NAIRU exists, it must be changing over time.

A few years, ago the typical estimates of the NAIRU ranged from 6.0 to 6.2 percent. If this natural rate remained operative today, the below 6 percent unemployment from August 1994 through the latter part of 1996 should have increased inflation. For example, if the natural rate were 6.2 percent and we assume that each year the unemployment rate is a percentage point below the NAIRU inflation rises by 0.5 of a percentage point, then the average unemployment rate of 5.6 percent from August 1994 to August 1996 would have led to a 0.6 point increase in the inflation rate. Instead, inflation, as measured by the yearlong increase in the core CPI, fell from 2.9 percent to 2.6 percent over that period.[2]

Through 1995 and 1996, inflationary pressures have been milder than in previous periods when unemployment was this low. For adherents to the NAIRU approach, the reason is clear: the natural rate of unemployment has fallen.... Our own preliminary finding is that the NAIRU has fallen by around 1.5 percentage points since its peak in the early 1980s. I should caution, however, that the uncertainty surrounding this estimate, both the formal standard errors and the uncertainty over whether we are estimating the correct model, is very large.

The three main forces in this decline are the changing demographics of the labor force, the fact that productivity growth has become more in line with worker expectations and the general increase in the competitiveness of the labor and product markets. Accounting for demographic change is straightforward. Imagine that each demographic group has its own unchanging natural rate of unemployment: higher for teenagers than adults, higher for women than for men, and so on.[3] Then imagine that the only source of changes in the NAIRU are changes in the proportion of these different groups in the labor force. If we assume that demographic changes had about the same effect on the NAIRU as they have had on observed unemployment, then about one-third of the 1.5 percentage point decline in the NAIRU can be attributed to demographic changes. The single most important demographic change is the aging of the baby boomers—we now have a more mature labor force, with greater representation of age groups that have traditionally had lower unemployment rates.

The second explanation for the change in the NAIRU, which is linked to productivity growth, can be called the "wage-aspiration effect." Although neither the level or rate of change of productivity has any long-run effect on the unemployment rate—witness the fact that unemployment has been about the same over the course of a century of massive productivity growth and large shifts in its trend growth rate—changes in the productivity growth rate can have temporary effects on the natural rate of unemployment. The intuition is that workers' demands for increased real wages depend on their past rate of change, possibly because of the psychological fact that people get accustomed to a certain rate of increase in their standard of living. Thus, after a fall in the productivity growth rate, workers will initially demand real-wage growth based on their previous experience and thus faster than the increase in productivity, which puts upward pressure on the inflation rate and requires a higher level of unemployment for the economy to stay in equilibrium. But this increased NAIRU is only temporary, either because the productivity shock itself is temporary, or because workers will eventually moderate their demands in response to permanently lower productivity growth. Either way, the NAIRU can return to its preshock level. This effect, called the wage-aspiration effect, surely contributed to a rising NAIRU in the 1970s and early 1980s, in the aftermath of the productivity slowdown. However, workers have now had a lot of time to adjust their real-wage aspirations down to reflect the slower productivity growth, which should be helping the NAIRU rebound to its earlier, lower rate.

... Our estimates at the CEA indicate the wage-aspiration effect has lowered the NAIRU by around 0.5 percentage point since the early to mid-1980s. However, I want to emphasize that there is a lot of uncertainty in this estimate.

The most likely suspects for the remaining decline in the NAIRU all fall under the heading of increased competitiveness of the product and labor markets. This is partly the consequence of the increased opening of markets at home and abroad through regulatory reform and trade-opening agreements. Although trade is still a relatively small part of our economy—around 10 percent —the fact that much of the U.S. manufacturing sector faces potential competition is enough to deliver wage restraint. Changes in labor markets, such as decreasing rates of unionization, have also had some salutary effects on inflation, regardless of their other impacts. Although quantifying these general notions of competitiveness and the institutional structure of the labor market is extremely difficult, it is not implausible to think that they account for the remaining 0.5 percentage point decline in the NAIRU since the early 1980s.

In addition to demography, wage aspiration and competitiveness, a fourth factor might currently be affecting the NAIRU and might affect it even more in the near future: hysteresis. The idea that sustained high unemployment will gradually raise the natural rate of unemployment is perhaps most familiar in the European context. The intuition behind the claim emphasizes that high sustained unemployment decreases both the work and job-search skills of the unemployed (outsiders) at the same time that those who remained employed (insiders) want to maintain wages at the expense of expanding employment. The reverse of these forces might be at work in the U.S. labor market today. Research has not conclusively shown that hysteresis is one of the forces that has lowered the NAIRU in the American economy. But if it does, then high unemployment is even worse than we thought, because it raises the NAIRU, and lower unemployment is even better than we thought, because it reduces the NAIRU.[4]

These trends may continue to reduce the NAIRU in the future. Demography will continue to lower the natural rate of unemployment as the current bulge of workers in the 35–49 age bracket move into the even lower unemployment 50 plus age bracket, although this effect will be partly offset by the increase in teenagers resulting from the so-called "baby-boom echo." If hysteresis does work in reverse, the current spell of low unemployment should help to generate a lower NAIRU in the next few years. The other two factors affecting the natural rate are harder to predict, although the competitiveness of the economy seems likely to increase with the process of increased opening of international trade and continued reforms in the U.S. regulatory structure.

## THE NAIRU AND MACROECONOMIC POLICY

The third criterion that the natural rate hypothesis has to pass if it is to maintain its claim to an important place in the analytic toolkit of economists is that it be useful for discussing and analyzing policy even when there is uncertainty about its current and future level. In a sense, it is hard to think about macroeconomic policy without the concept of the NAIRU. Clearly, we would like to get unemployment as low as possible, without inflation accelerating. If there is no clear, systematic relation between inflation and unemployment, why wouldn't policymakers simply keep trying to push unemployment lower and lower?

Thus, policymakers must base their actions on some perceptions about the consequences of changed levels of economic activity on the rate of inflation. The more subtle question, put roughly, is, "Should policymakers 'target' the NAIRU?" To answer that, we need to know what are the consequences of basing policy on a mistaken estimate of the NAIRU.

There is a famous dictum of Alfred Marshall that the world is continuous, and I think this applies to macroeconomic policy as well: if the economy heads a little below the NAIRU, then we can expect a little more inflation. This view stands in opposition to the view, more common in nonacademic circles, that the NAIRU is like a precipice: take one step over it, and you fall into a spiral of rapidly accelerating inflation. The evidence simply does not support this view. In fact, the evidence suggests that we can go even further than Marshall and say that in this case the world is not only continuous but approximately linear: if you hold the unemployment rate below the NAIRU for a year, the inflation rate rises by about 0.3 to 0.6 of a percentage point per year. Contrary to the accelerationist view, not only does the economy not stand on a precipice—with a slight dose of inflation leading to ever-increasing levels of inflation—but the magnitude by which inflation rises does not increase when the unemployment rate is held down for a prolonged period of time.[5] Thus, small mistakes have only small consequences.

What if macroeconomic policymakers do make the mistake of holding unemployment below the NAIRU for a period of time, and inflation rises as a result? What is required to reverse this type of a mistake? The traditional view was that the Phillips curve was convex—the costs of a disinflation in terms of lost employment were viewed as substantially higher than the benefits of greater employment from a similarly sized inflation. The underlying intuition was that contractions decreased output by creating more slack in the economy, thus raising unemployment, while expansions ran into capacity constraints, quickly resulting in higher prices with little employment gain. In this environment, a risk-neutral policymaker would be averse to experimenting with the unemployment rate. In contrast, if the Phillips curve is linear, then experimentation has zero expected cost—the cost of a deflation in terms of temporarily increased unemployment is exactly equal to the benefit of the lower unemployment that caused the inflation in the first place.

I want to go even further and suggest that there is some evidence that the Phillips curve might be concave. This concavity is consistent with the literature on asymmetric price adjustment, which shows that in monopolistically competitive markets, producers might adjust prices down to avoid being undercut by a rival but will be more reluctant to raise prices even in the face of generally rising prices. Our empirical research at the CEA has found that when we run Phillips curve regressions allowing for a kink at the NAIRU, we find that the best fit is with a concave function. Although this concavity is relatively mild, it is statistically significant. This particular nonlinearity, if in fact it holds up in future research, suggests that even risk-averse policymakers might want to engage in moderate experiments with the unemployment rate. If, hypothetically, they then discovered that the unemployment rate had fallen 0.5 percentage points below the NAIRU for a six-month period, then with a concave Phillips curve it would take less of a rise in unemployment, possibly 0.4 of a percentage point above the NAIRU for six months, to wring the consequent inflation back

out of the system. If the hysteresis effect proves important, then these conclusions are reinforced.[6]

## CONCLUSION

When I discuss the NAIRU with the press or in public, I am usually asked about what I think the Federal Reserve will or should do. The answer I and other members of the Clinton administration give is always the same: we do not comment on Fed policy. This stance has served the economy well by contributing to a sense of confidence that our economy is well managed. But there are also good economic reasons to avoid being pinned down to a particular NAIRU. The NAIRU can be moving. Unemployment explains only a portion of changes in inflation, and there are a variety of other economic goals besides simply fighting inflation. The analytic framework connecting NAIRU to inflation is only one of many ingredients that go into the formulation of macroeconomic policy. Moreover, there are broader concerns of macroeconomic policy: if we can understand better the determinants of the NAIRU and the inflationary process, perhaps we can better design policies that reduce the NAIRU and alter the tradeoffs.

The natural rate hypothesis passes all three tests I have outlined. Unemployment is an empirically successful way to predict changes in the inflation rate. Economists have good explanations for the now undeniable fact that the NAIRU has fallen in the last 15 years, and forces like demography and hysteresis will continue to put downward pressure on the natural rate. Finally, the natural rate provides a useful framework for thinking about policy questions even if there is considerable uncertainty about its exact magnitude. In particular, although no one knows exactly where the NAIRU is, these results suggest that in testing the waters, we do not risk drowning. If need be, we can always reverse course. But by experimenting, and showing some hesitation about restraining the economy through higher interest rates or other methods as the NAIRU draws nigh, we might learn a little more about the depth of the waters and possibly become better swimmers in the process.

## NOTES

1. The demographically adjusted unemployment rate takes the actual unemployment rates for different demographic groups and weights them by their labor force shares in a given year, in this case, 1993.

2. The weakness of inflationary pressures is also illustrated by the fact that in August 1996, wage growth was still lagging behind the sum of inflation and trend productivity growth. As noted in the text, inflation can be taken as 2.6 percent, and I consider trend productivity growth to be 1.1 percent, for a total of 3.7 percent. However, even after the fairly strong growth in earnings in the August 1996 unemployment report, average hourly earnings were growing at 3.6 percent annually. The broader-based Employment Cost Index shows that compensation increased only 2.9 percent over last year's level.

3. There are reasons why these groups might have different "natural rates." New entrants to the labor force (teenagers) typically are involved in more search, in order to find a good "match"; hence, there is likely to be a higher level of frictional unemployment.

4. In proposing the concept of the natural rate of unemployment, Milton Friedman separated the demand-management choices of policymakers from the constraints on those choices. While the argument here agrees with Friedman that supply-side labor market factors like demography are of primary importance, the concept of hysteresis suggests that rather than macroeconomic policymakers being faced with a NAIRU given to them solely by the supply side of the economy, the natural rate also depends on the evolution of aggregate demand. In short, Friedman's dichotomy may be overstated.

5. One way to test this hypothesis is to estimate accelerationist models that nest nonaccelerationism as a restricted case. We have found that the coefficients on the acceleration terms are insignificant; in other words, the restricted model fits the data almost as well as the accelerationist model. This is true in a variety of specifications.

6. With hysteresis effects, policymakers face a complicated dynamic programming problem, in which policy today must take into account the impacts on the future NAIRU. This discussion has analyzed only some of the aspects of macroeconomic policymaking. A fuller discussion would take into account factors such as costs of adjustment and of variability in output and unemployment, and dynamic learning effects; for example, are there policies that can affect the degree of uncertainty about the value of the NAIRU or of policy tradeoffs?

# NO

James K. Galbraith

# THE SURRENDER OF ECONOMIC POLICY

There is a common ground on economic policy that now stretches, with differences only of degree, from the radical right to Bill Clinton. Across the spectrum, all declare that the main job of government is to help markets work well. On the supply side, government can help, up to a point, by providing education, training, infrastructure, and scientific research—all public goods that markets undervalue. But when it comes to macro economic policy, government should do nothing except pursue budget balance, and leave the Federal Reserve alone.

To accept a balanced budget and the unchallenged monetary judgment of the Federal Reserve is, by definition, to remove macroeconomics from the political sphere. Thus, the remaining differences between Clinton and the Congress are over details. Should we head for budget balance in seven years, eight, or ten? Should we cut (or impose) this or that environmental regulation? Do Head Start, the AmeriCorps, and technology subsidies justify their cost? And so on, in long litanies that no one believes will make a fundamental difference in American lives. Even if there were substantial gains to be made by public investments on the supply side, the conservative fiscal consensus precludes them by denying the resources.

We have now seen two Democratic presidents—Carter and Clinton—deeply damaged because they did not dispute this orthodoxy in good time and therefore could not control the levers of macro policy. Macroeconomics, not microeconomics, is the active center of power. Practical conservatives understand this. It is no accident that conservatives always seek to control the high ground of deficit and interest rate policy, nor any surprise that liberals defeat themselves from the beginning when they concede it.

Yet, the economics behind this consensus is both reactionary and deeply implausible. It springs from a never-never-land of abstract theory concocted over 25 years by the disciples of Milton Friedman and purveyed through

From James K. Galbraith, "The Surrender of Economic Policy," *The American Prospect* (March/April 1996), pp. 60–67. Copyright © 1996 by The American Prospect, P.O. Box 383080, Cambridge, MA 02138. Reprinted by permission. All rights reserved.

them to the whole profession. Liberals —and anyone else concerned with economic prosperity—should now reject this way of looking at the world.

## THE RIGHT-WING CONSENSUS ON EMPLOYMENT AND INFLATION

The conservative macroeconomic creed is built on three basic elements. They are, first, *monetarism*—the idea that the Federal Reserve's monetary policy controls inflation, but has little effect on output and employment except perhaps in the very short run. Second, there is *rational expectations*, which is the idea, for which Robert Lucas just won the Nobel Prize, that individual economic agents are so clever, so well informed, and so well educated in economics that they do not make systematic errors in their economic decisions, especially the all-important choices of labor supply. And third, there is *market clearing*: the idea that all transactions, including the hiring and firing of workers, occur at prices that equate the elemental forces of supply and demand.

Taken together, these assumptions conjure an efficient labor market that yields appropriate levels of employment and wages. The employment level generated by this abstraction is the core policy concept of mainstream macroeconomics, known as the natural rate of unemployment.[1] If unemployment is above the natural rate, the theory dictates that prices and wages will fall. If unemployment is below the natural rate, the theory dictates that inflation will rise. Sustainable, noninflationary employment growth occurs only at the natural rate.

Among most economists these ideas are amazingly noncontroversial. The only dispute is over a narrow point of policy

—whether there is any value in attempts to steer the economy toward the natural rate if it happens to be, for a time, either above or below it. To the strictest natural-raters, doing nothing is always and everywhere the right prescription, because the economy will always return to the natural rate on its own. Policy cannot help, and the very instruments of macro policy should be abandoned.

The self-described "New Keynesian," a breed found throughout the Clinton administration, believes a vestigial role for macro policy can be preserved. Unemployment may persist above the natural rate because wages take more time than other prices to adjust to changes in supply and demand, leading to failure of the labor market to "clear." That being so, there may be no harm in policy measures—a little stimulus now and then when there is a serious recession—to speed the return to the natural rate so long as a "soft landing" is carefully engineered.

Alas, the location of the natural rate is not actually observed. Worse, the damn thing will not sit still. It is not only invisible, it moves! This is no problem for the never-do-anything crowd. But it poses painful difficulties for would-be intervenors, those few voices in the administration who call, from time to time, for summer jobs, public works programs, and lower interest rates. How can one justify a dash to the goalposts, if you don't know where they are? New Keynesians obsessively estimate and reestimate the location of the natural rate, in order to guide their policy judgments. Sadly, they have never yet been able to predict its location, which may be one reason why there has never yet been a successful "soft landing."

## WHERE IS THE NATURAL RATE?

To the (questionable) extent that the Federal Reserve has any coherent macroeconomic theory, it tends to be implicitly New Keynesian on this issue. That is, the Federal Reserve Board is an inveterate intervenor, raising interest rates when unemployment is too low, and lowering them, grudgingly, to end or sometimes to avoid recessions. And so the Federal Reserve also spends a good deal of time and effort trying to pin down the phantom and elusive natural rate.

In 1994, with the natural rate estimated by numerous astrologers at about 6 percent, monetary policymakers faced an interesting problem. Actual unemployment, now at 5.8 percent, had fallen below the estimated natural rate. So how then to interpret the rest of the data, which contrary to theory showed no evidence of accelerating inflation? Did the apparent lack of inflationary acceleration mean that the natural rate had perhaps fallen, and if so to what value? Or, had the barrier been broken and, in Robert Solow's phrase, was inflation "acceleration just around the corner"? Or again, was the whole theory rotten and fit for the garbage?

The Federal Reserve proved unwilling to change its estimate of the natural unemployment rate. So it tightened monetary policy from February 1994 through early 1995, as the economy broached the 6 percent unemployment barrier. But then the Federal Reserve shifted course and started cutting interest rates in July 1995, even though unemployment remained below 6 percent. Why? It will be interesting to learn, when the full minutes are released, whether the Federal Reserve formally changed its estimate of the natural rate in July of 1995, and if so, on

what ground and to what number. Or we may learn that the Federal Reserve doesn't really have a natural rate theory anymore, but is only holding on to the rhetoric of these ideas, for want of any alternative that ideological conservatives might accept.

\* \* \*

The components of today's low inflation rate are not at all consistent with the natural rate theory. No part of present inflationary pressure, such as it is, stems from wages. Wage compensation, two-thirds of all costs, remains flat. The whole of today's modest inflation stems from a boom in profits and investment income, and from the effects of this boom on commodity prices and other incidentals of the inflation process. There has also been some contribution from the rising interest costs imposed since February 1994 by the Federal Reserve's own policy.

This problem is illustrated in "What's Driving Inflation?" (Figure 1). The old relationship between inflation and labor costs really has busted up since Reagan fired the air traffic controllers and he and Volcker overvalued the dollar. Prices may be rising at 2.7 percent annually, but real wages are scarcely moving. Indeed we find that all inflation accelerations after 1960, with the sole exception of that following Richard Nixon's election campaign in 1972 (when price controls were in force), were led by prices and not by wages.

## THE NOMADIC AIRU

How is all of this to be reconciled with a theory of inflation acceleration based exclusively on the natural rate of unemployment in an aggregate labor market? It can't be done. If there is excess

*Figure 1*
## What's Driving Inflation?

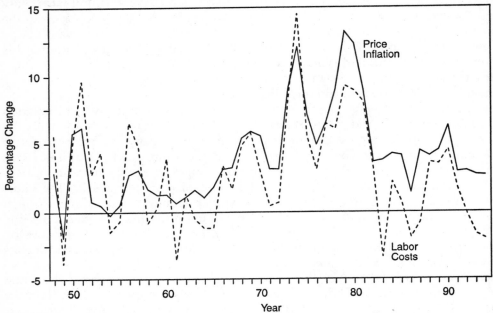

This graph shows that wages have lagged behind prices for more than 20 years—good evidence that labor markets are not tight.

demand for labor, surely a good (new) classical economist must insist that real wages are rising. But they aren't—and haven't been in 20 years. Something must be wrong with the natural rate model. (Good economists at the Federal Reserve know this, and it bothers them, as it should.) In fact, something is more than wrong with the model. The model is junk, as we should have known long ago.

This is nicely shown by the two graphs in Figure 2 ("Follow the Bouncing Natural Rate"). The first shows how the unemployment rates at which inflation accelerated have changed over the last 40 years. In the 1950s they were low, in the 1970s, quite high. But recent data rather resemble the 1950s again, which would indicate that there is room for

unemployment to come down without kicking off inflation. Depending on how you factor in the high-inflation decade of the 1970s, an honest estimate of the natural rate—even if you believe it—might be 6 percent or much lower.

But the second graph shows how fruitless the search for a natural rate really is. The graph employs centered 12-month moving averages of monthly data for both inflation and unemployment. It illustrates that rising inflation is essentially unpredictable: The shocks that cause it sometimes happen at high unemployment, sometimes not until unemployment is quite low. There is no sign in recent data of rising inflation as unemployment falls.

## Figure 2
## Following the Bouncing Natural Rate

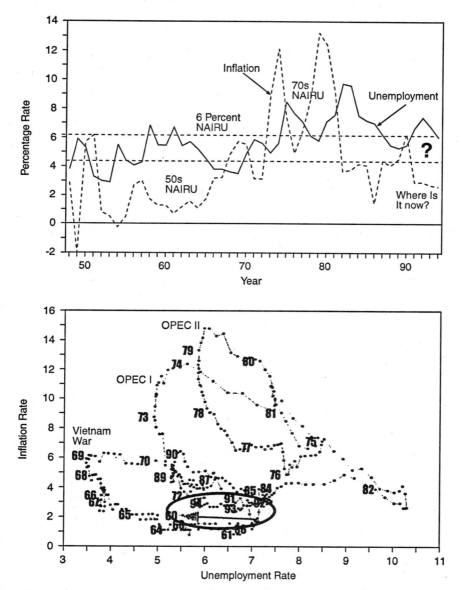

The graph at the top shows how estimates of the natural rate can change over time. Recent data resemble the 1950s, indicating that an honest estimate of the natural rate today might be far lower than 6 percent.

The graph at the bottom shows how unpredictable shocks (like OPEC) have pushed around the relationship between inflation and unemployment. Since a shock can hit at a high unemployment rate as well as at a low one, why not go for full employment?

Indeed, the pattern of widening gyres reversed itself after the deep recession of 1982. Through the rest of the 1980s, unemployment fell without wage pressures and without sharp rises in inflation. The recession of 1989 hit while inflation was low by historic standards. And in the past four years, 1992 through 1995, there has been falling unemployment with falling unit labor costs and no rise whatever in inflation (see the horizontal ellipse). We do not know where the nomadic accelerating inflation rate of unemployment (AIRU) is today—because we don't know when the next shock might hit us. So why not go for full employment? . . .

## MACRO POLICY IN A STRUCTURALIST WORLD

Conservatives employ the myth of the market to oppose political solutions to distributive problems. But to leave things to the market is no less a political choice than any other.

Suppose the concept of an aggregate labor market and the associated metaphor of a natural rate of unemployment could be wiped away with a stroke from the professional consciousness (as it deserves to be). The policy notion that controlling the reduction of unemployment is the principal means of fighting inflation would lose its power. It would then become intellectually possible to revive the idea of giving a job to everybody who wants one. The issue becomes not how many jobs but rather who to employ and on what terms?

**Investment and Consumption.** Creating jobs is a matter of finding things for people to do. Investment of all kinds creates jobs, and stabilization of private investment demand is the traditional macroeconomic issue. Low and stable interest rates are essential here—more on that later. Public investment can step in where private investment will not go, and should be designed and pursued for its direct benefits, not its imaginary indirect ones. But *consumption* is also an important and much maligned policy objective. People should have the incomes they need to be well fed, housed, and clothed—and also to enjoy life. Public services can help: day care, education, public health, culture, and the arts all deserve far more support than they are getting.

**Technology.** Technological renewal should be understood as part of a strategy of maintaining investment demand. It makes sense progressively to shut down the back end of the capital stock, for environmental, safety, energy efficiency, and competitive reasons. Properly designed regulation can help, and this will open up investment opportunities for new technologies. At the same time, a flatter wage structure and bigger safety net, including retraining but also more generous early retirement for older displaced workers, would reduce the cost of job loss and the resistance from affected workers. Again, this is an adjunct of high-growth macro policy, not a substitute for it.

**Inflation.** Inflation policy would not go away. But the pursuit of relative price stability, rather than being the result of sluggish growth and tight money, would become concerned with the management of particular elements of cost, as the economy got closer to full employment. This includes wage pressures, and also materials prices, rent, and interest. Management of aggregate demand—an undoubted force on nonwage prices—could operate through channels with less effect on employment (a variable tax on excess profits, for example). Since wages are a major element in costs, inflation policy would be concerned with the institutional mechanisms of wage bargaining.

**Distribution.**  This exercise returns us to the real, inevitably political questions obscured by technical mumbo jumbo about natural unemployment rates: our overall structure of incomes and opportunities. What should be the distribution of incomes? How much range, between the bottom and the top? Between capital and labor? Between skilled and not? In my view, the present course of rising inequality must be reversed, and liberals should frankly support the political steps required for this purpose. Trade unions should be strengthened and the aggressive new organizing campaigns of the AFL-CIO strongly supported. Minimum wages should be raised. And liberals should strongly defend the progressive income tax, as well as support proposals for wealth taxation.

Once the basic distribution of income has been set right, further gains in real wages can only happen, on average, at the rate of productivity growth. But to keep the distribution from getting worse again, these gains should be broadly distributed, substantially social and only slightly industrial or individual. In other words, we need to return to the principle of solidarity—that the whole society advances together.

Higher minimum wages are especially important for this purpose. In their book, *Myth and Measurement*, David Card and Alan Krueger argue that raising the minimum wage within a reasonable range would not cost jobs. In fact, higher minimum wages may increase employment by reducing job

turnover. This is a doubly important work, once for its direct policy relevance and again because it flatly contradicts, and deeply undercuts, standard models of the aggregate labor market.

**Interest Rates.**  Low and stable has to be the watchword. Interest rates should lose their present macroeconomic function, which has been to guarantee stagnation. They should serve instead to arbitrate the distribution of income between debtors and creditors, financial capital and entrepreneurship. As a first approximation, real rates of return on short-term money should be zero. And there is no reason why long-term rates of interest in real terms should exceed the long-term real growth rate of the economy. Indeed they should lie below this value, effecting a gradual redistribution of wealth away from the creditor and toward the debtor class and a long-term stabilization of household and company balance sheets. Speculation in asset markets should be heavily taxed.

**Deficits.**  Ironically, the budget deficit hardly comes up in this discussion. During the postwar boom, we were a high-employment, low-inflation, low-interest-rate society with a progressive tax structure. Such societies do not have structural-deficit problems. A peacetime military budget would also greatly help. At any rate, the present fixation on balancing the budget is nonsense, as all serious economists should loudly declare.

The above, all taken together, would be a macroeconomic policy to fight for! The liberal microeconomic supply-siders can do some useful things—or think they can—by getting a little money into education, training, infrastructure. But the point is to raise living standards, to increase security and leisure, and to provide jobs that are worth having. And that requires us to reclaim macroeconomics as a major policy tool.

## NOTES

1. Some economists prefer the term nonaccelerating inflation rate of unemployment or NAIRU. The idea is essentially the same. The natural rate/NAIRU was introduced to supplant the older Phillips Curve idea of a static trade-off between inflation and unemployment, and to suggest that inflation would not only rise, but inevitably accelerate, if unemployment falls too low.

# POSTSCRIPT

## Is the Nonaccelerating Inflation Rate of Unemployment a Useful Guide for Macroeconomic Policy?

Stiglitz argues the NAIRU can be a useful guide in the formulation of macroeconomic policy if it satisfies three criteria. The first criterion is a robust empirical relationship between unemployment or the natural rate of unemployment and changes in the rate of inflation. The second criterion concerns the ability to explain and predict changes in the NAIRU. Stiglitz believes that the NAIRU has been declining and that causes of this decline have been identified as the changing labor force demographics, closer correspondence between productivity growth and worker expectations, increased competition in product and labor markets, and sustained lower unemployment. The third criterion involves the consequences of policy actions if an incorrect value of the NAIRU is employed. Stiglitz believes that the consequences of policy actions under these conditions will be minor. Therefore, because all three criteria are satisfied, he concludes that the NAIRU is a useful guide for macroeconomic policy.

Galbraith begins his analysis by stating his belief that macroeconomic policy has been removed from the political sphere. That is, the Democratic Clinton administration and the Republican Congress have reduced fiscal policy to balancing the budget and have left monetary policy to an unchallenged Federal Reserve. Focusing on the NAIRU, Galbraith makes two important claims. First, since 1960 all accelerations in inflation except one were led by prices and not wages. Second, rising inflation is essentially unpredictable. Both of these points convince Galbraith that the NAIRU is useless as a policy guide. He argues, instead, for a full employment macroeconomic policy.

For a series of more technical discussions of the natural rate of unemployment, see the *Journal of Economic Perspectives* (Winter 1997). This issue contains the complete essay by Stiglitz as well as another essay by Galbraith attacking the natural rate concept, "Time to Ditch the NAIRU." Other articles in this issue are "The Time-Varying NAIRU and Its Implications for Economic Policy," by Robert J. Gordon; "The NAIRU, Unemployment and Monetary Policy," by Douglas Staiger, James H. Stock, and Mark W. Watson; "What Do We Know and Do Not Know About the Natural Rate of Unemployment?" by Olivier Blanchard and Lawrence F. Katz; and "Theory Ahead of Language in the Economics of Unemployment," by Richard Rogerson. Also see "Our NAIRU Limit: The Governing Myth of Economic Policy," by Robert Eisner, *The American Prospect* (Spring 1995).

# ISSUE 14

## Would Adopting Wisconsin's Welfare Reforms End Welfare As We Know It?

**YES: Robert Rector,** from "Wisconsin's Welfare Miracle," *Policy Review* (March/April 1997)

**NO: Michael Wiseman,** from "Welfare Reform in the United States: A Background Paper," *Housing Policy Debate* (1996)

### ISSUE SUMMARY

**YES:** Heritage Foundation senior policy analyst Robert Rector claims that Wisconsin has already won more than half the battle against Aid to Families with Dependent Children (AFDC) dependence and is proceeding with the other half with breathtaking speed.

**NO:** University of Wisconsin economist Michael Wiseman concludes that not even the governor of Wisconsin has found the key to welfare savings by means other than cutting benefits and active broad-based efforts at job placement and training.

Given American society's traditional commitment to a market system and its fundamental belief in self-determination, Americans are generally uncomfortable enacting social welfare legislation that appears to give someone "something for nothing," even if that individual is clearly in need. Thus, when we trace the roots of the existing U.S. social welfare system back to its origins in the New Deal legislation of President Franklin D. Roosevelt during the Great Depression of the 1930s, we see that many of the earliest programs linked jobs to public assistance. One exception was Aid to Families with Dependent Children (AFDC), which was established as part of the 1935 Social Security Act. This program provided money to families in which there were children but no breadwinner. In 1935, and for many years thereafter, this program was not particularly controversial. Two reasons explain this: the number of beneficiaries was relatively small, and the popular image of an AFDC family was that of a white woman with several young children whose husband had died as the result of an illness or an industrial accident.

In the early 1960s, as the U.S. economy prospered, poverty—and what to do about it—captured the attention of the nation. The Kennedy and Johnson administrations declared a War on Poverty: major legislative initiatives focused social welfare programs on the plight of the poor, who represented about one-fifth of the population and were white by a ratio of two to one. This pattern is often overlooked because the incidence of poverty among African Americans exceeded 50 percent of that community.

The policies of the Kennedy and Johnson administrations were designed to address the needs of those trapped in "pockets of poverty," a description popularized in the early 1960s by Michael Harrington (1929–1989), a political theorist and prominent socialist. Between 1964 and 1969 the number of AFDC recipients increased by more than 60 percent, and the costs of the program more than doubled. The number of AFDC families grew throughout the 1970s and 1980s, and the program became increasingly controversial.

The controversy grew for several reasons: the increase in the number of recipients, the increase in costs, and a change in perceptions. During the Reagan years, a welfare mother was characterized as a woman in a big-city public housing project whose children had been deserted by their father, or as an unmarried woman who bore more children only to get more financial assistance through welfare. By the late 1980s and early 1990s, AFDC had become one of the most controversial social welfare programs.

Social critics used this negative image of the welfare mother to attack AFDC. Charles Murray, for example, charged AFDC with encouraging welfare dependency, teenage pregnancies, the dissolution of the traditional family, and an erosion of the basic American work ethic. Such criticism set the stage for the first major reforms in AFDC in 25 years. In 1988 the Family Support Act was passed. The intent of this legislation was to develop state-run programs that would help individuals who receive welfare assistance to break away from their dependency through work, training, and education.

Within a few short years, most states had nearly 20 percent of their welfare caseload either working or in a work training program. The use of waivers became widespread. These waivers, which allowed states to experiment with federal rules governing AFDC eligibility, work incentives, and work mandates, were either approved or pending in all but four states by mid-1996.

In the face of this sea change in public attitudes and state public policy, President Bill Clinton pledged to "end welfare as we know it." Within eight months of the start of his second term, Congress obliged. In a bold legislative move it passed the Personal Responsibility and Work Opportunity Act. This act abolished the AFDC entitlement that had guaranteed poor families a standardized set of welfare benefits for 60 years and replaced AFDC with a new block grant program entitled Temporary Assistance for Needy Families (TANF), which allowed individual states far more discretion in determining which families would be supported and how much each of these families would get.

No single state pursued these options more aggressively and with more apparent success than the state of Wisconsin. Both Robert Rector and Michael Wiseman agree that Wisconsin has ended "welfare as we know it." What they disagree on is what works and what does not in the Wisconsin waivers and more importantly, what the future holds for states that follow Wisconsin's lead.

# YES
**Robert Rector**

## WISCONSIN'S WELFARE MIRACLE

Everyone wants—or professes to want—to "end welfare as we know it." Despite such lofty proclamations, welfare is still thriving. [In 1996], federal and state governments spent $411 billion on means-tested welfare programs that provide cash, food, housing, medical care, and social services to poor and low-income Americans. This greatly exceeded the $324 billion spent in 1993, the first year of the Clinton presidency.

At the core of America's vast, dysfunctional welfare system is Aid to Families with Dependent Children (AFDC). At present, nearly one out of seven children in the United States receives AFDC, residing with a mother married to a welfare check rather than a working husband. The typical family now on AFDC will spend nearly 13 years in the program.

"Ending welfare" must begin with reform of AFDC. Congress enacted major new legislation last summer that will start this process. The new law promises three major changes. First, it eliminates the entitlement system of AFDC funding, under which states that increased their AFDC caseloads received automatic increases in federal funding, while states that reduced dependence faced a fiscal penalty.

Second, the new law establishes performance standards that will require each state to reduce its AFDC caseload, or at least, if the caseload does not decline, require some recipients to work in return for their benefits.

Third, the law sets a new goal of reducing illegitimacy and will reward states that reduce out-of-wedlock births without increasing the number of abortions.

Although the new federal legislation sets the proper framework for reform among the states, the liberal welfare establishment and its allies in the media incessantly warn that reform will prove to be difficult, if not impossible. But one state has already proven the naysayers wrong: Wisconsin. Wisconsin's experience with welfare reform provides an unparalleled model for implementing reform that other states would be wise to follow.

In the last 10 years, while AFDC caseloads in the rest of the nation were rising steeply, the caseload in Wisconsin has dropped by half. In inner-city Milwaukee, the caseload has fallen by 25 percent, but in the rest of the state, caseloads have fallen by nearly 70 percent. In 28 of Wisconsin's 77 counties, the welfare rolls have already dropped by 80 percent or more.

And if all this weren't remarkable enough, the pace of Wisconsin's reduction in welfare dependency is accelerating. In Milwaukee, the AFDC caseload is now shrinking 2 percent per month; in the rest of the state, 5 percent. Wisconsin's achievements are utterly unprecedented in the history of AFDC. Liberal welfare experts used to insist that a successful work program might reduce welfare caseloads by 5 percent over five years; in much of Wisconsin, the number of people on welfare is steadily falling by that amount every 30 days.

Wisconsin has thus won more than half the battle against AFDC dependence and is proceeding with the other half with breathtaking speed. This victory is crucial, since welfare dependency severely hampers the healthy development of children. In the long term, the greatest beneficiaries of Wisconsin's dramatic achievements in reforming welfare will be the children themselves.

## THE ROAD LESS TRAVELED

This remarkable story begins in 1987, when a major congressional debate on welfare culminated in the Family Support Act (FSA). Touted as yet another "end of welfare," the FSA was a complete bust. The Act did, however generate the expectation among voters that welfare recipients would be required to work. In the same year a second unheralded event occurred with far greater significance for the future of welfare: Tommy Thompson took office as governor of Wisconsin.

Following a gubernatorial campaign largely about welfare, Thompson entered office with a firm commitment to reform. Figure 1 tells the rest of the story. Despite the rhetorical promises of the Family Support Act, the nationwide AFDC caseload remained constant in the late 1980s and then grew by more than a third between 1990 and 1994. The nationwide caseload has eased downward over the last two years, but the majority of states still suffer higher levels of welfare dependency than before the Family Support Act became law.

Wisconsin has been the only clear exception to this pattern. Upon taking office, Thompson initiated a series of reforms that cut welfare dependency during the late 1980s and blocked any resurgence during the 1990–93 recession. Starting in 1994, a second round of more sophisticated work-related reforms has caused the caseload to nosedive further. But the raw figures understate Thompson's achievements. As noted, welfare rolls across the country ballooned by some 35 percent during the early 1990s. There is every reason to believe that, without Thompson's reforms, Wisconsin would have followed this national trend. If it had, its AFDC caseload would have surged from around 100,000 recipients in 1987 to a peak of 135,000 in 1993. It is reasonable to conclude that Thompson has not merely cut his state's caseload in half (from 98,295 recipients to 48,451) but has reduced it by some two-thirds relative to the potential peak in dependence that Wisconsin would have experienced in the early 1990s in the absence of reform.

Many states brag about their recent declines in welfare dependency. In the past 24 months, for example, Indiana has cut its caseload by 32 percent, Oregon by 30 percent, Maryland by 29 percent, Massachusetts by 25 percent, Oklahoma by 24 percent, and Michigan by 22 percent. But, in almost every case, these successes merely represent a pruning back of the explosive surge in welfare dependency of the early 1990s. In reality, other reforming states lag a half-decade behind Wisconsin; they are only now engaging in the initial stages of dependency reduction that Wisconsin accomplished in the late 1980s. We might say that the reforms in most states have merely blown the foam off the top of the beer mug, while Wisconsin has already drained the mug halfway to the bottom.

Having cut its caseload in half, Wisconsin's reformers are now grappling with a more difficult, less employable group of welfare recipients. Skeptics argued that after Wisconsin weaned the most employable recipients off the rolls in the early stages, the decline in the caseload would slow and then stop. Yet the opposite has occurred. As new reforms have been implemented over the last three years, the decline has accelerated sharply. Wisconsin continues to reduce dependency at a rate surpassing all other states.

## REFORM INITIATIVES

The general thrust of welfare reform in the Thompson administration has been to require reasonable behavior by recipients as a condition of receiving aid. An early example was *Learnfare*. Enacted in 1987, the *Learnfare* program required welfare recipients to ensure that their school-age children attended school regularly, and reduced welfare payments to families with truant children. Although *Learnfare* did not reduce the AFDC rolls directly, it did have a symbolic importance, sending a clear message to both the bureaucracy and the welfare clientele that, for the first time, the government seriously intended

to demand constructive behavior of welfare recipients and to sanction those who were derelict.

The centerpiece of reform, however was the requirement that a growing share of those on the AFDC rolls engage in employment-related activities such as training and tightly supervised job search. By the 1990s, many Wisconsin counties were operating sophisticated systems aimed at pushing welfare recipients quickly into the labor market. For example, a particularly effective program in Sheboygan County required most AFDC recipients to undertake closely supervised job search immediately after applying for benefits. Individuals who failed to find employment within a few weeks were required to perform community-service work until they could find a private-sector job.

Beginning in 1994, Thompson's staff initiated a more sophisticated and successful round of reforms. His administration instructed county welfare directors to de-emphasize education and job training in the classroom and to concentrate on activities leading to immediate work. The state created new incentives to guide the welfare bureaucracies: Counties would no longer be simply allocated work, training, and day-care funds but would be required to earn those funds by increasing the number of recipients placed in jobs or community-service work.

The governor's staff also understood that many applicants entering the welfare system had other options. The easiest way to break this group of the debilitating habit of dependency was to prevent it from forming in the first place, by reducing the number of new AFDC enrollments. The state began a pilot program based on this principle in 18 counties in 1994 (gradually expanded to

*Figure 1*

**AFDC Families: Wisconsin vs. the Nation**

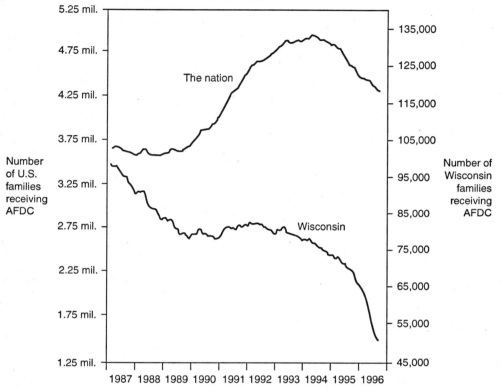

Source: U.S. Department of Health and Human Services.

cover 60 by early 1996). The program, *Work First,* provided new applicants with counseling on the negative effects of dependence, offered short-term aid (such as car repairs) that might eliminate the need to enroll in AFDC, and required most new applicants to begin working in private-sector jobs or community-service jobs almost immediately after enrolling in welfare. (Once a recipient starts a full-time job in the private sector AFDC benefits are eliminated; however AFDC benefits generally continue at a reduced level while the recipient works part time. By contrast, a recipient performing community-service work continues to receive full AFDC payments but must work for the benefits obtained.)

Another pilot program called *Work Not Welfare* (WNW) began in January 1995 in two counties, Fond du Lac and Pierce. WNW placed an absolute time limit of 24 months on receiving AFDC. Although this program obviously had no direct impact on dependency in most of the state, it did send a strong symbolic message to welfare recipients: Long-term dependence would no longer be tolerated. (Still, caseloads in those two counties have fallen only slightly more rapidly than in most other counties.)

In December 1995, the governor's staff instituted a radical new system for rewarding good performance in county welfare offices. The new system employed competitive bidding for the management of each county's welfare system. Governmental or private organizations currently running AFDC in each county were thus threatened with competition and could be replaced by outside organizations. The current welfare organizations, however could escape the competitive bidding process if they fulfilled new performance criteria specified by the state. Chief among these criteria was a requirement that each county reduce its AFDC caseload by roughly 15 to 25 percent (requirements varied by county) over the subsequent 12 months.

## DECISIVE NEW POLICIES

In April 1996, Wisconsin unveiled two more decisive reforms. *Work First* (renamed Self-Sufficiency First) went into effect in all counties including Milwaukee, and a new *Pay for Performance* (PFP) system was implemented statewide. For decades politicians have talked about making welfare recipients work while creating regulations that made this impossible. With *Pay for Performance*, Wisconsin closed the loopholes, creating for the first time a real work requirement for AFDC recipients. Prior to PFP, a recipient who failed to obtain a private-sector job might be required to perform community service. If the recipient failed to actually perform this service work, however, the state could only cut AFDC benefits slightly. Under PFP, a recipient would see his welfare check reduced in direct proportion to the number of hours of community work he fails to perform. An individual who performs no work would receive no AFDC or food stamps. Critically, the PFP principle was also applied to other constructive activities such as class attendance or supervised job search.

PFP effectively eliminated the freedom of most Wisconsin AFDC recipients to receive welfare without working. Caseloads, already in rapid decline, began to plummet. In the first seven months after the implementation of *Pay for Performance* and *Self-Sufficiency First*, the AFDC caseload dropped 14 percent in Milwaukee and 33 percent in the rest of the state. If the trends continue, the welfare rolls statewide will drop by an additional one-third over the next 12 months.

## REFORM SKEPTICS

Apologists for big welfare have naturally sought some pretext for ignoring or trivializing Wisconsin's achievement The most common ploy is to attribute the decline in AFDC caseload to a "good economy." Although Wisconsin has enjoyed low unemployment and healthy growth in jobs, it is ridiculous to claim that this has brought about a dramatic reduction in caseload. After all, over the past 40 years states have often experienced robust economic growth without any significant drop in the welfare rolls, let alone a drop of 50 percent.

The limited role of economics in Thompson's victory over dependence can be seen by comparing Wisconsin with the 13 states that have experienced lower levels of unemployment than Wisconsin over the past decade. In these states, the welfare rolls, on average, actually increased by some 20 percent. None produced a substantial decline in welfare

*Table 1*

## Wisconsin Leads the Nation

| Rank | State | Jan. 1987 | Sep. 1996 | Change in Caseload |
|---|---|---|---|---|
| 1. | Wisconsin | 98,295 | 49,930 | −49.2% |
| 2. | Michigan | 214,273 | 167,210 | −22.0% |
| 3. | Iowa | 39,697 | 31,010 | −21.9% |
| 4. | Louisiana | 85,047 | 66,540 | −21.8% |
| 5. | Mississippi | 57,082 | 44,840 | −21.4% |
| 6. | Alabama | 47,817 | 40,640 | −15.0% |
| 7. | South Dakota | 6,620 | 5,670 | −14.4% |
| 8. | Nebraska | 16,246 | 13,950 | −14.1% |
| 9. | Maryland | 66,248 | 57,130 | −13.8% |
| 10. | Ohio | 227,035 | 201,950 | −11.0% |
| 11. | Illinois | 240,764 | 217,130 | −9.8% |
| 12. | New Jersey | 117,694 | 106,500 | −9.5% |
| 13. | North Dakota | 5,069 | 4,660 | −8.1% |
| 14. | Kansas | 25,256 | 23,390 | −7.4% |
| 15. | Indiana | 53,156 | 49,500 | −6.9% |
| 16. | Massachusetts | 87,195 | 81,260 | −6.8% |
| 17. | South Carolina | 45,640 | 42,640 | −6.6% |
| 18. | Wyoming | 4,640 | 4,340 | −6.5% |
| 19. | Oregon | 30,368 | 28,530 | −6.1% |
| 20. | Pennsylvania | 187,946 | 179,880 | −4.3% |
| 21. | Arkansas | 22,797 | 22,060 | −3.2% |
| 22. | Montana | 9,410 | 9,490 | 0.9% |
| 23. | Maine | 19,329 | 19,700 | 1.9% |
| 24. | Utah | 13,720 | 14,030 | 2.3% |
| 25. | West Virginia | 36,485 | 37,470 | 2.7% |
| 26. | Minnesota | 54,699 | 57,150 | 4.5% |
| 27. | Virginia | 56,751 | 60,340 | 6.3% |
| 28. | Oklahoma | 32,653 | 35,230 | 7.9% |
| 29. | Colorado | 31,079 | 33,550 | 8.0% |
| 30. | Vermont | 7,678 | 8,660 | 12.8% |
| 31. | New York | 358,083 | 412,720 | 15.3% |
| 32. | Missouri | 67,690 | 78,980 | 16.7% |
| 33. | Kentucky | 59,579 | 69,840 | 17.2% |
| 34. | Dist. of Col. | 19,988 | 25,140 | 25.8% |
| 35. | Washington | 75,697 | 96,800 | 27.9% |
| 36. | Rhode Island | 15,843 | 20,420 | 28.9% |
| 37. | Delaware | 7,810 | 10,450 | 33.8% |
| 38. | Idaho | 6,215 | 8,500 | 36.8% |
| 39. | Georgia | 87,329 | 120,520 | 38.0% |
| 40. | Tennessee | 65,296 | 90,520 | 38.6% |
| 41. | Connecticut | 38,919 | 57,040 | 46.6% |
| 42. | California | 585,321 | 870,230 | 48.7% |
| 43. | Hawaii | 14,498 | 21,890 | 51.0% |
| 44. | Texas | 153,934 | 238,340 | 54.8% |
| 45. | North Carolina | 67,360 | 107,480 | 59.6% |
| 46. | Alaska | 7,163 | 12,320 | 72.0% |
| 47. | New Mexico | 18.207 | 32,970 | 81.1% |
| 48. | Florida | 102,013 | 200,290 | 96.3% |
| 49. | New Hampshire | 4,329 | 8,920 | 106.1% |
| 50. | Arizona | 29,114 | 61,790 | 112.2% |
| 51. | Nevada | 5,575 | 13,120 | 135.3% |
|  | **U.S. Total** | **3,735,386** | **4,267,926** | **14.3%** |

Change in number of families receiving Aid to Families with Dependent Children, January 1987 through September 1996, by state.

Source: U.S. Department of Health and Human Services.

caseloads. Although a robust economy has undoubtedly helped Wisconsin to reduce welfare dependency, it is far from the principal cause.

Another common dodge of the skeptics is to claim that reform has raised welfare costs. This charge is no surprise; defenders of the status quo have always claimed that taxpayers must "invest" more funds in order to "end welfare." But Wisconsin's reforms did not result in increased spending in either the short or long term. Although the state has increased its outlays on welfare administration, job training, and day care, these expenditures have been more than offset by the rapidly shrinking caseload. Wisconsin spends more per family on welfare now than in 1987, but it has half the number of families on welfare. The greatest expenditure increase has been for welfare administration; although day-care costs have also increased modestly, they still constitute only 6 percent of the total. Today Wisconsin's aggregate spending on AFDC benefits, administration, training, and day care, in current dollars, is some 5 to 10 percent lower than in 1986, the last year before Thompson became governor. But in the rest of the nation, similar expenditures have nearly doubled in the same period: Clearly, Wisconsin's reforms have produced huge de facto savings, not higher costs. In inflation-adjusted terms, Wisconsin's spending is actually down by a third since 1986.

## LESSONS LEARNED

The Wisconsin experience provides a cornucopia of lessons for the rest of the nation. In reforming welfare, Wisconsin has rediscovered a philanthropic philosophy once ubiquitous in American charities, but largely abandoned over the past 40 years. This philosophy regards dependence and idleness as harmful to the welfare recipient and insists that he perform useful labor in exchange for benefits he receives.

Thus a serious work requirement provides not only a sound moral foundation, but also performs a crucial gatekeeping function. A key problem for rational charity is separating those who truly need aid from those who do not but are willing to take a free handout if one is offered. Work requirements serve that purpose. For example, in the 19th century, religious organizations throughout the United States provided food and shelter to persons who would today be called "homeless." Before providing a free meal and a bed, however, the shelter would require the man seeking aid to perform some useful chore such as chopping firewood. Charity workers had discovered that such a requirement greatly reduced the numbers seeking aid. This "work test" winnowed out those who did not need aid and allowed the philanthropists to focus limited resources on the truly needy.

With one out of seven children enrolled in AFDC, the current system is so large that serious reform will be impossible. The initial task in transforming welfare is to shrink the AFDC caseload to manageable proportions. Culling those who do not truly need aid from the welfare rolls will allow the system to focus its efforts on those who have the most difficulty becoming self-sufficient, and will free up resources and energy needed to deal with the underlying problems, such as educational failure and illegitimacy, that promote future dependence.

Wisconsin's example provides nine clear rules on how to sharply reduce dependency:

**1. Set the right goal.** If the ultimate aim of reform is to reduce dependence, the official goal must be to reduce the welfare caseload. A large drop in caseload entails dramatic administrative change and threatens the financial self-interest of the welfare industry. Ingenious welfare bureaucrats will thus propose other performance criteria that allow them to claim success in reducing dependence while caseloads continue to rise. Such ersatz benchmarks generally include: the length of time spent on welfare; the number of recipients in training, part-time employment, or make-work jobs; or the number who leave welfare. Decisionmakers should not be fooled: It is the size of the caseload that matters.

**2. Focus on the size of the caseload, not welfare exits.** Measuring the number of recipients who leave welfare—or "exits" —is misleading. Large numbers of "exits" from welfare will occur even when welfare caseloads are rising. States with liberal welfare systems may have larger numbers of exits because they encourage highly employable persons to enroll in welfare. By contrast, a serious work requirement may actually reduce welfare exits since it will discourage the most employable persons from enrolling in welfare in the first place.

**3. Avoid education and training.** Government training and remedial education programs in general do not increase recipients' wage rates and do little to reduce dependence. A recent Labor Department study of the government's largest training program, the Job Training Partnership Act (JTPA), found that the program had little or no effect on the wages of trainees: The average hourly wage rate of female trainees rose 3.4 percent, while the hourly wages of males did not increase at all.

**4. Use work requirements to reduce welfare applications.** The most important effect of a work requirement is to reduce dramatically the number of persons who apply for welfare. This is called the "dissuasion" effect of work requirements. By operating programs such as Self-Sufficiency First and by requiring most new applicants to find private-sector employment or perform community-service work shortly after enrolling in welfare, Wisconsin has cut the number of new AFDC entrants almost in half over the last two years.

**5. Require continuous activity.** In the private sector, employees are expected to work continuously, not intermittently. This principle must be duplicated in welfare. Once a recipient begins supervised job search, training, or work, some activity should be required without interruption or lessened intensity until the recipient leaves AFDC. In order to reduce welfare recidivism, the work obligation should resume as soon as a former welfare recipient returns to the AFDC rolls.

**6. Establish a pay-after-performance benefits system.** Welfare should be based on "pay-after-performance": Recipients will not receive the welfare check until after they have performed work or other required activity. If they fail to perform the required number of hours of activity, the welfare check must be reduced on a pro-rata basis.

**7. Use community-service "workfare" as an enforcement mechanism.** Upon applying for welfare, employable recipients should be required to begin a supervised search for employment. If they have not found a private-sector job within six weeks, they should be required to perform community-service work. Of course, the real goal of reform is to see that recipients obtain private-sector employment, not to push them into make-work jobs. But in a conventional welfare system, large numbers of recipients will claim they cannot find private-sector jobs. If such "unsuccessful job seekers" are permitted to remain idly on the rolls, reform will fail. Instead, all individuals who fail to obtain private-sector jobs should be placed immediately in community service slots on a pay-for-performance basis.

This effectively eliminates any recipient's chance of receiving a welfare income without working, and pushes recipients into private-sector jobs while dissuading other individuals from entering welfare. Mandatory community service is thus the crucial backstop to a serious work requirement. Of course, this does not mean that large numbers of recipients will end up in make-work community service. In Wisconsin few do, but the threat of community work is the key to propelling recipients into the private sector.

**8. Impose work requirements on the most employable recipients first.** The initial goal of welfare reform should be to restrict welfare to those who truly need it and to eliminate from the rolls those who do not. In order to accomplish this goal and to shrink welfare caseloads, work requirements should be focused on the most employable welfare recipients first. These would include two-parent families (10 percent of the caseload in a typical state) and mothers who do not have preschool children (typically 50 percent).

This strategy may seem counterintuitive, but it is essential to reducing dependence. The number of crucial community-service work slots (where the recipient is required to work for benefits) in the first phases of reform will be quite small in relation to the overall caseload. If the least employable recipients occupy these slots, they will remain there for long periods, clogging up the system. When highly employable recipients, by contrast, are faced with the prospect of performing community-service work, most will respond by quickly leaving AFDC, freeing the work slots for others, who will in turn leave the rolls. Through this revolving process, the caseload will begin to shrink quickly. (A variant of this principle is to focus work requirements on recent applicants who are, in general, more employable than the rest of the caseload.)

**9. Establish bureaucratic incentives and competition.** Throughout the United States, most of the welfare industry is liberal, regards welfare recipients as victims of social injustice, and is threatened by reforms that will sharply reduce its welfare clientele. In order to ensure the faithful and efficient implementation of conservative reforms, decisionmakers must establish precise performance criteria linked to rewards and sanctions for the welfare bureaucracies. In Wisconsin, welfare offices were forced to compete with one another to earn funding, and ultimately each county office faced the threat of elimination if it failed to meet high performance standards set by the governor.

## LOOKING TOWARD THE FUTURE

The lessons from Wisconsin greatly influenced the national welfare reform enacted in Washington [in 1996]. The new federal law encourages states to pursue work policies similar to Wisconsin's. Among the specific features of the new federal law drawn from Wisconsin are the federal performance standards based on caseload reduction, the use of workfare to "dissuade" new applicants, and a requirement that states set up pay-for-performance systems.

Tommy Thompson has shown that state governments can overcome AFDC dependency. The greatest benefit will accrue to children. In the past, liberals have been mesmerized by the belief that "poverty" somehow harms children and that welfare, by "combating poverty," is therefore good for kids. Hence they are timid, if not outright adversarial, in their attitude toward serious efforts to reduce welfare dependency. But studies that compare children on welfare with poor children not on welfare show that it is actually welfare dependency, not poverty, that harms children. A childhood of welfare dependency lowers children's IQs, increases their likelihood of academic failure, and diminishes their future earnings as an adult. Welfare is a system of child abuse; by radically reducing dependence, Wisconsin's reforms will improve the future well-being of children.

There is, however, one very important shortcoming to Wisconsin's welfare achievement: The current reforms have not cut the state's illegitimate birth rate. Illegitimacy does much more harm to children's development than does welfare dependency. The ultimate goal of reform must be not only to reduce dependency but to rebuild marriage. One can only hope that over the next decade, Wisconsin's reformers will tackle the problem of out-of-wedlock births with the ingenuity and diligence they have already applied to the question of dependence.

Throughout his tenure as governor, Tommy Thompson has routinely accomplished what the welfare industry declared impossible. He has demolished many of the fables buttressing the welfare status quo. Among the venerable myths debunked by Wisconsin are the following: Recipients really want to work but jobs are not available; the lack of day care makes employment impossible; education and training are the key to reducing dependence; and it costs more to reform than to continue the status quo. Thompson has not only rewritten the rule book on fighting dependence; he has invented a new language in which future rules will be written.

Perhaps the most surprising aspect of Wisconsin's story is the extraordinary outcomes produced by mundane policies. There is nothing radical about initiatives like *Self-Sufficiency First* or *Pay for Performance*. Indeed, these policies are pretty much what most voters have in mind when they hear talk of making welfare recipients work. It is true that in the fall of 1997, Thompson will inaugurate a new set for reforms termed Wisconsin Works, or W2. This will abolish AFDC entirely and replace it with a pure employment-based system of assistance. Although great things are expected of W2, its arrival should not overshadow the fact that the current reforms will have already eliminated a vast portion of the Wisconsin AFDC caseload before W2 even begins.

Other states that are in early stages of reform need not leap as far as W2. Any state that will enact *Pay for Performance* and *Self-Sufficiency First*, and follow the nine principles outlined above, will dramatically reduce the welfare dependency of its citizens. Wisconsin has shown the way; it is now up to rest of the nation to apply the lessons learned.

# NO

# Michael Wiseman

# WELFARE REFORM IN THE UNITED STATES: A BACKGROUND PAPER

## INTRODUCTION

... This article surveys the major issues surrounding welfare reform, outlines the competing proposals for reform, reviews PRWORA [Personal Responsibility and Work Opportunity Reconciliation Act], and comments on the outlook for further reform. I argue that the likely outcome of the coming struggle over welfare reform is, at least over the next few years, increased hardship for the poor. Contrary to popular wisdom, however, I also argue that the new legislation is likely to produce a larger federal role in welfare and more difficulty for governors than would have been the case given continuation of the programs ended by welfare reform. Because so many poor families using public assistance are located in central cities, many of the consequences, both positive and negative, of the reform effort will be concentrated there. Welfare reform is in essence an urban policy issue....

By convention, the term welfare is applied to programs of public assistance that give aid to individuals or families on the basis of need and means. There are many such programs in the United States, including locally funded and state-funded general relief; various housing assistance programs; the Low-Income Home Energy Assistance Program; school lunch and breakfast programs; and the Special Supplemental Food Program for Women, Infants, and Children (WIC). The four means-tested programs most important to the national welfare reform debate are Aid to Families with Dependent Children (AFDC), food stamps, supplemental security income (SSI), and Medicaid. AFDC gives cash to needy families with children; food stamps are special coupons that indigent families and individuals can use to purchase food; SSI provides income to needy aged, blind, and disabled persons; and Medicaid provides health care for the poor. PRWORA replaced AFDC with block grants to states for Temporary Assistance for Needy Families (TANF) and altered eligibility standards for food stamps and SSI. The TANF block grant allows states to sustain the AFDC program for at least the coming fiscal year, and as a result the changes have yet to affect either programs or caseloads sig-

From Michael Wiseman, "Welfare Reform in the United States: A Background Paper," *Housing Policy Debate* (1996). Copyright © 1996 by *Housing Policy Debate*. Reprinted by permission. Notes and references omitted.

nificantly. Thus I begin with discussion of welfare before PRWORA. I then turn to predictions of how states will change the welfare system under block grants. . . .

I choose 1993, the year between the election of President Clinton and the landmark congressional election of 1994, as point of reference.

*Caseload trends.*    Political concern about welfare has been driven in part by exceptionally rapid recent caseload growth. Between 1980 and 1989, the AFDC caseload grew by about 5.5 percent (figure 1). Between 1989 and 1993, the caseload grew by 33 percent. Part of this acceleration is attributable to the recession of 1990 to 1992. However, the economic downturn at the beginning of this decade was by most measures no more severe than that of 1980 to 1982, when the caseload response was much less.

These trends produced a substantial increase in the proportion of American children living in families at least partly dependent on welfare. In a typical month in 1980, about 1 child in 10 lived in a family receiving AFDC; by 1993 the odds had increased to 1 child in 8. Almost 14 percent of American families with children received AFDC during an average month in 1993; a higher proportion received such benefits at some time during the year.

*Welfare costs.*    Between 1980 and 1993, the welfare caseload grew by 39 percent. Over the same interval, real outlays for the "big four" transfer programs grew by 116 percent, and the composition of welfare outlays changed in ways that affect both the state and federal share of outlays and the effect of the system on poverty. These changes have

had important consequences for welfare politics in the 1990s.

A number of observations can be made by examining constant-dollar expenditures on AFDC, food stamps, SSI, and Medicaid for 1980 through 1995:

1. *Effort has increased.* It is difficult to argue that the national antipoverty effort has diminished since President Carter's last year of office. In addition to outstripping the rate of growth in the AFDC caseload over this interval, the 116 percent growth in overall real outlays for public assistance substantially exceeded growth in population (13 percent), in real gross domestic product (36 percent), and in the number of poor children (29 percent). The rate of growth accelerated after 1985.

2. *Medicaid is the villain.* While national effort at public assistance may not have decreased, it has been redirected. Most (80 percent) of the increase in assistance outlays is attributable to rising costs of Medicaid. In 1980, Medicaid accounted for 45 percent of outlays in the four categories identified here; by 1993 this share had grown to 63 percent and was continuing to rise. While approximately 36 percent of Medicaid recipients are in AFDC households, this group accounts for only about 30 percent of Medicaid outlays. Costs for members of other served groups (the elderly, the disabled) are typically much greater. From 1980 to 1988, the share of payments on behalf of AFDC recipients in Medicaid costs fell. Between 1988 and 1993, the share grew by 25 percent. Thus, while AFDC-related Medicaid costs are slightly less than a third of Medicaid outlays, the growth of this segment during the period leading up

*Figure 1*

**AFDC Caseload, United States, 1980–1995 (Monthly Average)**

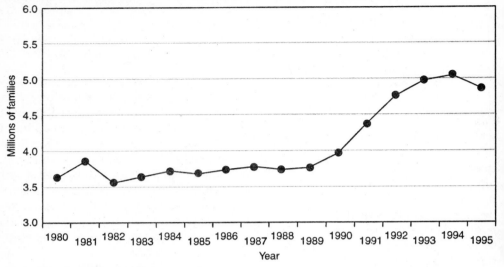

Note: Data for 1995 are preliminary.

Source: U.S. House Committee on Ways and Means (1994).

to the Contract with America was exceptionally rapid.

3. *AFDC is the loser.* Outlays for AFDC benefits grew more slowly than the number of AFDC recipients from 1980 to 1993 (a 14 percent increase compared with a 33 percent increase). Thus, real cash benefits received by individual families declined. States set the level of AFDC benefits. Between January 1985 and January 1994, the maximum AFDC grant for a family of three in the median state (based on benefits) fell from $461 to $367 (a 20 percent decrease) in constant (January 1994) dollars. . . .

The bottom line is that "spendable" welfare (i.e., food stamps and AFDC) has become increasingly federalized over the past 13 years as states have lowered AFDC benefits while food stamp benefits have been sustained.

4. *SSI lost, too.* The basic SSI benefit is wholly federally funded. The law permits (and, in some instances, requires) states to supplement the federal payment. Currently, all but eight states provide some type of supplement to the federal benefit. However over time state SSI supplements have not kept up with inflation, while the federal benefit has. The result is that the direct federal share in overall SSI costs has increased and food stamp benefits paid to SSI recipients have also gone up. This too has increased the federal share of the costs of aiding the SSI target population.

5. *The state share remains unchanged.* The federalization of spendable welfare cited above would be expected to increase the federal share in overall assistance payments. In fact, the federal share of the cost of AFDC, food

stamps, SSI, and Medicaid combined did not change at all over the 1980–95 interval. The... culprit has already been identified. Medicaid outlays grew much faster than food stamp and SSI benefits combined. The federal government still pays only slightly more than half the costs of Medicaid. The rapid growth in total Medicaid outlays kept the overall federal share at slightly less than two-thirds....

In sum, despite cutbacks, states have not found substantial fiscal relief in public assistance policy. Although the states were clearly attempting to reduce their fiscal contribution to social welfare costs, the rapid increase in Medicaid offset the attempt so that as late as 1995 the states' apparent share was virtually the same as it had been 13 years earlier. Given the failure of national health insurance reform, it was likely that states would seek fiscal relief in other ways. The fact that states do respond strategically to the incentives created by federal assistance policy is important, because PRWORA changes state incentives substantially.

*Welfare and poverty.* At the same time that outlays for public assistance were increasing, so too were poverty rates. In 1980, 18 percent of all children lived in families with reported incomes below the federal poverty standard (approximately $12,000 in current dollars for a family of three); by 1993, the proportion was 23 percent. The 1995 poverty rate among all persons, children and adults, was 13.8 percent; in 1980, it was 13 percent, and it has not fallen below that level since....

## THE PROBLEM OF REFORM

The litany of indictments suggests that the U.S. welfare system is a ripe target for government reinventing. The lesson of recent American history is that welfare reform is hard to accomplish, and as bad as some problems are, the system can be made worse by ill-considered fixes. There are several reasons for this.

### Poverty Is Complex
The welfare system in part mirrors the complexity of poverty in general. Simple solutions for many, if not most, poverty issues are elusive, and the enthusiasm of even the most zealous reformer often dims as special case after special case is identified. In general, the less experienced the author is with poverty and welfare operation and the farther the author is from the nearest welfare office, the simpler the solution proffered....

## WELFARE REFORM IN THE STATES

*The Bush initiative.* ... In 1991, the Bush administration made a strategic decision to encourage state welfare demonstrations [or experiments] as a means of establishing an initiative in this area at minimal federal cost.

In his 1992 State of the Union Address, President Bush encouraged states to continue efforts to "replace the assumptions of the welfare state and help reform the welfare system" and promised to make the waiver process "easier and quicker." The response was swift and substantial. Between the State of the Union message and the end of the Bush administration the following January, 22 state applications for waiver-based welfare reform demonstrations were received. Of these,

14 were approved and the remaining 8 proposals were carried over to the Clinton administration. None were denied.

Following precedents established by the Reagan administration's Interagency Low-Income Opportunity Advisory Board, the Bush administration applied two standards in dealing with these initiatives. To be approved, waiver-based demonstrations had to be cost neutral and rigorously evaluated. A demonstration was cost neutral if it would not add to federal welfare outlays. Rigorous evaluation meant, for the most part, evaluation by random assignment. The two criteria were linked: A demonstration's effects on costs were assessed by comparing costs between control and experimental groups. States were obligated to cover the difference between federal per-case costs for the controls and federal per-case costs for recipients in the experimental group. Content did not play a major role in waiver strategy.

*Clinton policy.* Since the ambitious waiver program was largely a Republican initiative, one might have expected the new Democratic administration to curtail waiver-based welfare demonstration activity. Instead, two weeks after his inauguration, President Clinton promised the National Governors' Association that his own administration would continue to support state demonstrations, as long as the results were "honestly evaluated." The result was rapid growth in the number of waiver applications and waiver-based demonstrations approved. In the interval between Clinton's inauguration and the 1994 congressional elections, the administration approved 21 more waiver demonstrations in 20 states. By mid-1996, on the eve of PRWORA's passage, it had approved waivers for 43 states and the District of Columbia.

These state initiatives featured an extraordinary collection and combination of interventions, ranging from benefit reductions to cash incentive schemes for encouraging inoculation of children against disease. Objective evaluation of this avalanche of novelties is difficult. A defensible summary is that few will ever produce any results usable in the process of policy development. In general, the interventions were too poorly planned, the number of program changes too large, and the evaluation schemes too limited in scope to encompass the range of possible program effects. In some ways this outcome was politically desirable. In state welfare reform initiatives, the political payoff from demonstration activism may be more important than the modest gain in knowledge that might be attained. Moreover, in most cases the political payoff seems to come early, while assessment is postponed virtually indefinitely.

*The waiver leader: Wisconsin.* A prime example of the difference in timing between political attention and demonstration outcomes is provided by Wisconsin's Work Not Welfare initiative. Proposed in early 1993 following President Clinton's address to the National Governors' Association, Work Not Welfare is an experiment designed to test the impact of a time limit for welfare receipt. The program was approved by HHS [U.S. Department of Health and Human Services] in November; it began in two small Wisconsin counties in January 1995 with a target number of experimental cases under 1,000. The final report is scheduled for the year 2006.

Work Not Welfare is one of nine Wisconsin welfare reform demonstrations initiated since Governor Tommy Thompson took office in January 1987. Overall, Thompson's record on welfare has been extraordinary: Between his inauguration and January 1994, the AFDC caseload in Wisconsin fell by 21 percent. The Thompson administration is understandably willing to attribute this decline to the welfare reform initiatives. However, most of the reduction was accumulated before the state's waiver-based initiatives were under way, and like Work Not Welfare, some of the more celebrated of the Thompson initiatives have involved only a small proportion of the caseload. Contrary to the image of the Thompson administration beyond the state's borders, a significant proportion of the Wisconsin waiver-based demonstrations have actually increased the generosity of the welfare system by improving services and extending eligibility to two-parent families without application of the 100-hour rule. It is the Thompson administration's benefit strategy and income tests that have been restrictive.

While definitive assessments are complicated, it appears that at least through 1994 the overall Wisconsin achievement is attributable to the combination of a robust economy (the September 1994 unemployment rate in Wisconsin was 4.5 percent, compared with 5.9 percent for the nation), a gradual tightening through inflation of the welfare eligibility standard in the state, a freeze on welfare benefits, and aggressive use of the funds for recipient job assistance provided by FSA [Family Support Act of 1988]. In 1994, *Rising Tide*, the Republican National Committee's news magazine, reported that Thompson considered the JOBS program his "favorite" in the welfare arena. *Rising Tide* failed to note that JOBS [Job Opportunities and Basic Skills] is a product of FSA, not the waiver process.

Since 1994, both Wisconsin's unemployment rate and its welfare caseload have continued to decline. The state has launched two additional initiatives—Self Sufficiency First and Pay for Performance—intended to increase efforts by local operating agencies to move persons applying for assistance into employment and to facilitate penalizing recipients who fail to participate in JOBS programs. Between December 1994 and mid-1996, the AFDC caseload fell an additional 29 percent. The state is conducting an evaluation of these initiatives based on comparison of outcomes for cases subject to the Self Sufficiency First–Pay for Performance initiative with outcomes for a set of cases selected at random to be exempt, but results are not yet available. The evaluation may be terminated as the state moves to its latest initiative, Wisconsin Works, to be discussed later.

*Conclusion: Image and reality.* Perhaps the most important conclusion to be drawn from the plethora of state initiatives is that no one, not even Thompson, has really found the key to welfare savings by means other than cutting benefits and active and broad-based efforts at job placement and training. As politically significant as the state initiatives may be, both the content and the scale of implementation of most have been modest, and states like Wisconsin that have undertaken more ambitious efforts have done so in an exceptionally favorable economic context. Governors know that political hyperbole is one thing, budget consequences another. An index of real state commitment to welfare-to-work efforts is provided by the JOBS program. While most states appeared eager to pursue welfare demonstrations, as of March 1996 only 12 states (including Wisconsin) had claimed all federal funds available for the JOBS operation, even though such funds required very little in state matching expenditure.

The record of the Thompson administration and the panoply of state initiatives spawned by Bush and Clinton waiver policy were important elements of the politics of welfare in the aftermath of the 1994 election. Wisconsin's achievement was generally cited as representative of what states could do when not hampered by federal regulation. In 1995, Thompson became chairman of the National Governors' Association, and he used this position to promote award of even greater latitude to states to structure their welfare programs. This gubernatorial effort might have been cast as the leading alternative to the strategy set forth in the Clinton administration's WRA [Work and Responsibility Act], were it not for the emergence on the stage of welfare reform of a third set of players, the House Republicans, led by Speaker Newt Gingrich. Since the congressional Republican initiative was originally aimed at the Clinton reform, it is the Clinton plan that is discussed first.

## THE CLINTON PLAN

Welfare politics caused the Clinton administration's WRA to be pitched as "ending welfare as we know it." This characterization was disingenuous, since much of the proposal was a continuation of the reform trajectory established by FSA. What was new, of course, was the time limit. But the significance of even this centerpiece, as proposed by Clinton, should not be exaggerated. Its billing had more to do with the political strategy of the 1992 presidential campaign than with the substance of the program.

### The Time Limit

Prior to assuming national office, President Clinton was actively involved in welfare reform, both in Arkansas and as part of a task force of the National Governors' Association. During the presidential campaign, Bruce Reed (then a volunteer speech-writer) brought the work of Harvard scholar David Ellwood to Clinton's attention. With the support of the Ford Foundation, Ellwood had recently published a book, *Poor Support* (Ellwood 1988), that offered a plan for welfare reform.

*Poor Support* called for a divide-and-conquer antipoverty strategy that combined a substantial increase in services and payments to the poor with different approaches to be fashioned for different subgroups (recall the "tagging is appropriate" welfare reform principle). Ellwood argued that with such a strategy in place, the nation might limit welfare payments to a period ranging from 18 to 36 months; adults still without jobs by the end of that period could be required to accept some form of public employment. Ellwood's time-limit proposal was based in part on his earlier research with a Harvard colleague, Mary Jo Bane, on the duration of spells of welfare receipt. That research indicated that a substantial share (in the original version almost half) of welfare cases close within two years of opening. If this result was correct, the implication was that more costly interventions could be avoided for many recipients by waiting for nature to take its course....

## Work and Responsibility Act

As released, WRA built on the strategy established by FSA by increasing federal and state efforts to obtain child support from noncustodial parents, changing JOBS, continuing the process of eliminating the distinction between the regular (single-parent) and the unemployed-parent (two-parent) subprograms in AFDC, and developing national performance standards for agencies involved in delivering welfare services. The legislation went beyond FSA in developing a National Teen Pregnancy Prevention Initiative to "encourage responsible behavior." The act responded to the recommendations of the Welfare Simplification and Coordination Advisory Committee by proposing streamlining of eligibility procedures and standards across the AFDC and Food Stamp programs. State flexibility in welfare program design was to be increased to allow states greater latitude in setting program parameters without waivers. In particular, states were to be allowed to vary work incentives incorporated in payment computation and to eliminate welfare benefit increases for children conceived after their mothers began receiving assistance. Finally, new state demonstrations were proposed in such areas as payment procedures for the EITC [earned income tax credit], methods of job search assistance, and effects of state assumption of responsibility for ensuring that child support awards are paid on schedule. Thus while WRA increased state latitude in welfare program operation, it also took steps toward establishing an agenda for reform-oriented experimentation. . . .

The welfare reform group recognized that the WORK innovation could be costly and could be difficult to implement on an adequate scale. Indeed, the lesson of experience, including that of Governor Reagan in California in the early 1970s, is that subsidized employment is difficult to do, and no state experiment with welfare work requirements has yet to attain the scale contemplated by WRA. But while certainly difficult to implement, a work assignment incorporated as a scheduled feature of JOBS case management had many attractive features. There is some evidence that work experience increases the chances that recipients will obtain unsubsidized employment. A work requirement is a way out of the problems posed by the design of financial incentives for work. A common work requirement provides more leeway for unifying the treatment of single- and two-parent families in AFDC; WRA offered states the option of eliminating the 100-hour employment restriction for two-parent families. Above all, a timed work requirement might assist in making the entire welfare-to-work process "time conscious." . . .

## Summary

WRA was a creditable effort at welfare reform. The problem is that there was little in it that would not have been there had the same task force produced draft legislation a year earlier. By delaying, the administration fueled expectation that something entirely different was in the wings, an expectation that WRA did not fulfill. By appearing to deliver its own initiative stillborn, the administration devalued it, thus opening the field for less thoughtfully constructed congressional and state alternatives. At least when viewed in terms of media attention, states have been responsible for far more action on the welfare reform front since 1992 than the federal government, and the administration's delay encouraged

Congress, governors, and, apparently, voters to fill the gap.

## REPUBLICAN ALTERNATIVES

The major Republican congressional response to the Clinton administration's failure to deliver welfare reform was the Personal Responsibility Act (PRA). Wisconsin produced the boldest of the plans advanced by Republican governors.

**Personal Responsibility Act**
Originally championed by the new Speaker of the House, Representative Newt Gingrich of Georgia, PRA was a follow-up on the promise of welfare reform included in the Republican Contract with America introduced in August 1994 and was built on a reform scheme proposed in November 1993 by 160 House Republicans. As originally formulated, the plan tackled WRA and the underlying administration strategy for welfare reform virtually point by point. Everything was made tougher; the most important provisions involved the JOBS/WORK program, time limits teen pregnancy, illegitimacy, program consolidation, federal and state financing, and aid to immigrants....

**Legislative Changes**
Many of the changes incorporated in the original PRA were modified during the first six months of the new Congress. The House of Representatives version of the law (H.R. 4) was passed in March 1995 and retained the "Personal Responsibility Act" title. The Senate Finance Committee passed a substitute bill, the Family Self-Sufficiency Act, later in the year....

Despite substantial conformity, important differences arose. The House legislation followed the original PRA in banning cash payments for children born to families already receiving assistance, to unwed mothers under 18 years of age, and to most noncitizens. The Senate legislation banned no children from assistance and let states determine whether aid was to be given to noncitizens. The House bill ended the JOBS program; the Senate bill kept JOBS, but in modified form. The House bill gave states the option of operating a simplified Food Stamp program using the same eligibility rules that are applied under TANF. In contrast, the Senate bill did not address the Food Stamp program. Both the House and Senate bills left Medicaid eligibility untouched. Indeed, eligibility for Medicaid would continue to be evaluated on the basis of the rules applied in the old AFDC program....

These differences were hardly insurmountable. But before they could be addressed, welfare reform was sidetracked by conflict between the White House and Congress over the federal budget. When Congress reconvened early in 1996, the outlook for welfare reform was clouded by the presidential campaign. In the meantime, the number of states involved in waiver-based welfare reform demonstrations continued to grow.

**Wisconsin Works**
The most ambitious of the state initiatives was produced in Wisconsin as a follow-up to the two-year time limit experiment described earlier. To conduct his Work Not Welfare experiment, Governor Tommy Thompson needed to obtain approval from the Wisconsin state legislature as well as from the federal government. The legislature approved the initiative but attached a provision

calling for the state's social service agency to submit by 1995 "a proposal for welfare reform in this state" that would replace most public welfare programs by 1999. The proposal was to guarantee income support to needy persons who could not work, guarantee employment to those who could work but could not find jobs, and assure low-income persons "affordable child care" and "affordable health care."

The legislature's "end welfare" requirement was a boon to Governor Thompson. In the context of the national debate over welfare reform, the requirement allowed him to use state resources to develop and advertise a comprehensive reform scheme. The Hudson Institute, a conservative policy analysis organization, set up an office in Madison and organized foundation funding for technical support for a task force appointed to draft a plan. The proposal, called Wisconsin Works and nicknamed W-2, was completed in early spring of 1995. It was formally announced by Governor Thompson on August 3 of that year, following a Vermont meeting of the National Governors' Association. Enabling legislation was passed by the state legislature in March 1996.

Viewed from both state and national perspectives, W-2 is an extremely important development. It is the first fully articulated plan for what a state welfare system might look like in an era of block grants. For citizens concerned about the direction of public assistance policy under something like PRA, Wisconsin Works provides a picture of one direction that states might go should they be freed of the program restrictions previously contained in the Social Security Act.

W-2 is a strategy realized in a program. The strategy has six major features:

1. Virtually all cash assistance is linked to some form of employment.
2. The variety of situations and capabilities of persons seeking public assistance is addressed by tagging and case management.
3. The connection between benefits and dependence is reduced by decoupling cash assistance from access to health insurance and child care assistance.
4. State administrative control and incentives for efficiency are enhanced by allowing public and private agencies to compete for designation as local program operators.
5. The change in the orientation of public assistance as well as agency culture is dramatized by a shift in responsibility for public assistance from the state's social service agency to the employment service agency, the Department of Workforce Development.
6. The "end of welfare" is taken seriously: The state is committed to rapid and complete implementation, with all components in place by September 1997.

... In sum, W-2 is dramatic in ambition, scope, and detail. Once again, Governor Thompson challenged the Clinton administration, this time by demonstrating that a state could develop a comprehensive welfare reform package in far less time than had been required for the WRA. If implemented, W-2 would genuinely end welfare, as Wisconsin's legislature had required. Moreover, like most of the state's initiatives, W-2 involved considerable financial commitment, especially given the state's promise of universal means-tested access to child care and insurance for families with children.

The program appears to be a dramatic refutation of the arguments of some that states would respond to the fiscal incentives produced by a change to block grant funding with a "rush to the bottom." W-2 seems to be better characterized as a rise to the challenge.

Drama in scope and ambition notwithstanding, the W-2 announcement attracted little public attention outside the state, perhaps partly because the media had become inured to years of Wisconsin welfare reform hyperbole. Few appreciated the difference between W-2 and earlier programs. More important, however, was the shift of national attention to the struggle between Congress and the president over the budget. It began to appear that action on welfare reform would await another election. For Thompson, this outcome was galling. W-2 was not intended as just another waiver-based demonstration. Given the breadth of the proposal, something akin to the authorization contained in PRA was believed essential. By spring 1996 it began to appear that resolution would await the outcome of the coming presidential election.

### President Clinton's Announcement and the End of the Impasse

However, the politics of welfare reform took a new turn the following May when President Clinton used his weekly radio address to claim credit for state welfare reform initiatives and to challenge Congress to act on welfare reform. "There are bipartisan welfare reform plans sitting in the House and Senate right now," he said, "that do what the American people agree welfare reform must do: They require welfare recipients to work; they limit the time people can stay on welfare; they toughen child support enforcement and they protect our children. So I say

to Congress: Send me a bill that honors these fundamental principles; I'll sign it right away. Let's get the job done."

The president congratulated Wisconsin for adding momentum to the "quiet revolution" in welfare reform with the W-2 proposal, which "has the makings of a solid, bold welfare reform plan." He then appeared to endorse the plan by pledging that his administration "would work with Wisconsin to make an effective transition to a new vision of welfare based on work." This endorsement was extraordinary given that the state had not even applied for waivers for W-2. Governor Thompson's staff scrambled to complete a waiver proposal, which the governor delivered personally to HHS.

This episode was a clear short-term victory for the president on the welfare reform issue. If Congress did not act, the president would respond to any Republican campaign challenge on welfare policy by claiming that it was Congress, and not he, that had prevented the accomplishment of welfare reform in 1996. Congress did indeed respond, and after reconciliation of House and Senate versions of reform legislation, the result was PRWORA (Public Law 104-193). Despite last-minute protests from various members of his administration and others, the president signed the bill in August.

### PERSONAL RESPONSIBILITY AND WORK OPPORTUNITY RECONCILIATION ACT

PRWORA is the most substantial welfare reform legislation since establishment of the SSI program and revision and expansion of the Food Stamp program in the 1970s. The most significant change is the termination of entitlement by families to cash assistance provided under Title

IV-A of the Social Security Act (the authorizing legislation for AFDC). In place of the matching grant program, PRWORA creates block grants to cover TANF and related services. The new law restricts or eliminates provision of public assistance to most noncitizens, families that have received aid for more than five years, and children previously made eligible on certain criteria for SSI. The law contains major new policies aimed at reducing the rate of nonmarital births as well as substantial revisions in the Federal-State Child Support Enforcement Program, in the Food Stamp program, and in child nutrition programs.

The heart of PRWORA is replacement of AFDC, JOBS, and Emergency Assistance with a block grant for TANF. (The Emergency Assistance program provides matching funds for use by states to support families with children at immediate risk of destitution or homelessness.) Each state receives a fixed amount based on federal payments received for the three supplanted programs in fiscal year 1994, payments for fiscal year 1995, or the average for fiscal years 1992 to 1994, whichever is largest. Given that for most states caseloads have declined (see Figure 1), the TANF block grant results in a net increase in federal funds over what would have been received under pre-PRWORA regulations. The TANF block grant is supplemented with a substantial increase in federal funding for child care. A contingency fund is established for support of states with exceptional unemployment rates, and states with either exceptional population growth rates or very low benefits are eligible for supplemental grants.

TANF funds are to be used to help needy families with children, assist parents in moving to self-support through work and marriage, prevent and reduce out-of-wedlock births, and "encourage the formation and maintenance of two-parent families." In general, how states are to do this is left open, but the law includes certain restrictions and performance requirements. States are required to sustain spending of state funds on the replaced programs plus child care at 75 percent of the spending done in fiscal year 1994. Eligibility for federally funded TANF is denied families with members who have received assistance for five years or more (states are allowed to exempt 20 percent of their caseloads from this requirement).

As in the original Clinton plan, adults receiving TANF assistance must "engage in work" after two years (or less at state option). The criteria for satisfying the work engagement requirement are left to states to define. However, in addition to the two-year work engagement requirement for individuals, the law follows PRA by requiring states to have a specific and increasing fraction of their entire caseload involved in certain work activities identified by the legislation. The required level of participation for single parents is 25 percent in 1997 and rises five percentage points a year to 50 percent in 2002. For adults in two-parent families, the required participation rate begins at 75 percent in 1997 and jumps to 90 percent in 1999. "Participation" initially means 20 hours per week for single parents; for parents with no children under six, the requirement rises to 30 hours by 2000. Adults in two-parent families must work 35 hours per week. States are allowed some variation in these standards, but the end result will still be a much higher level of activity required from recipients and more monitoring to enforce these requirements than under AFDC. . . .

## REFLECTIONS

Put another way, PRWORA has initiated change, but we are uncertain of the direction....

**Seeing Consequences Will Be Difficult**
... One possible consequence of the elimination of entitlement by TANF is that states will attempt to cut costs by making it more difficult to apply for aid. Wisconsin is already experimenting with a system, Self Sufficiency First, that requires persons seeking assistance to complete 60 hours of employment search before the state even begins processing their aid applications. Other states may practice more subtle means of dissuasion, and it is likely that some people in need will lose access to assistance altogether. This "entry effect" will never be captured by agency information systems because such systems cover only the status of persons approved for assistance. Under AFDC, persons meeting standards of need but denied access to assistance could and did seek legal aid. Careful attention needs to be paid to the way state systems come to accommodate, or dissuade, applicants.

**Equity Is a Problem**
Under AFDC, federal assistance was distributed to states on the basis of state expenditure effort, per capita income, and need—that is, the number of eligible families applying for assistance. While the details of the formula actually used may be difficult to justify, the principle seems sound. The lion's share of PRWORA funds will be distributed for the next five years on the basis of circumstances at the beginning of the decade. These circumstances were established in part by a recession that varied substantially across states in impact. In contrast, PRA proposed allocation of funds across states based on trends in population and numbers of poor households. It is likely that before long losers under the new system will demand redress.

**Large-Scale Workfare Will Be Costly**
As politically attractive as they may be in the abstract, welfare employment programs are costly to operate and difficult to manage. The reasons are clear: Even bad jobs require capital and some management (at minimum, rakes and straw bosses), and unlike "real" employment, welfare employment programs encourage high turnover. The skills required for management of effective workfare operation are quite different from those sought elsewhere in government, and they do not come cheaply. PRWORA requires an unprecedented level of participation in work and work-related activities, and the funds for meeting these standards come out of the same aggregate appropriation as basic benefits. The consequence may be expanded state costs, reduced benefits, or both....

**The Bottom Still Looms**
Regardless of motivation or dedication of governors, PRWORA creates substantial incentives for reduction in benefits. While the law includes some safeguards for maintenance of effort, the standard is set low (75 percent of 1994 expenditures if the state meets the work participation requirement) and the range of expenditure states are allowed to count as part of "effort" is broad. Moreover, states are permitted to set aside any amount of their TANF grants they like in a contingency fund to meet demand in the event of a recession or other development that increases need. For every state, the shift

from AFDC to TANF at least doubles the cost to the state's general fund of financial assistance to the poor.

In the near term, the expansion of funds provided by caseload decline and the new block grant is likely to prevent any retreat on benefits. By the next budget cycle, however, the extent of reduction permitted under maintenance-of-effort requirements and the range of outlays that can be tallied to establish effort will be well understood. At this point, legislators will begin to appreciate the new terms of trade between public assistance and other state activities that PRWORA establishes. Likewise, the cost of meeting activity requirements will be better understood. Pressure will be felt to reduce welfare expenditures and shift the expenditure level that is sustained in the direction of supporting work programs. Spendable income for welfare recipients will, under this scenario, decline.

Earlier I argued that interstate variation in welfare benefits has in the past been reduced by incentives created by the matching grant formula. Those incentives are eliminated, or at least reduced, by PRWORA. Disparity in benefit levels is therefore likely to grow as some states drop benefits faster than others. This in turn may create incentives for high-benefit states to reduce outlays to discourage migration. It should be emphasized that these effects are hypothetical, but such predictions are not unwarranted. As evidence already cited indicates, states do respond to the incentives created by grant allocation procedures.

Again, the outcome of this process remains to be seen. But if CBO projections are accepted, PRWORA will result in only a $3^1/2$ percent decline in federal outlays on public assistance between 1997 and 2003. Any decline in state outlays in excess of this amount will increase the federal share in social assistance, and such effects will be magnified if benefit reduction leads to greater costs for food stamps. The nearly inevitable outcome will be a greater federal fiscal role at the same time that federal administrative control is curtailed.

## Cities Are Where Much Will Happen

For reasons rooted in the Constitution, negotiations over welfare reform have been almost exclusively a matter between states and Washington, DC. This emphasis on states obscures the likely concentration of effects of welfare reform in urban areas. A rough sense of this concentration can be gained from a recent study of public assistance receipt by the U.S. Bureau of the Census (1995). In 1991, 29 percent of the U.S. population lived in central cities of metropolitan areas. In contrast, 44 percent of recipients of AFDC, General Assistance (public assistance without federal contribution), and SSI did. PRWORA restrictions have their greatest effect on long-time recipients. The same study reported the geographic distribution of persons who reported receipt of public assistance for every month over the 1991–92 interval. *Half* of all persons reporting continuous receipt of AFDC lived in central cities. This allocation of population does not match the allocation of employment, so agencies charged with assisting people to find the employment required by TANF will have to reach beyond city and across county borders.

## Many of the Poor Are Indeed Needy

It is easy to generate political support for abstractions like "eliminating fraud and abuse" or "illegal immigrants." But most polls indicate continuing public support for government assistance to people who really look needy—those who appear to make valiant efforts at self-support but, because of bad fortune or other circumstances, fail. Inevitably, the restrictions imposed by states because of PRWORA will produce and publicize tragic cases of deprivation because of government fiat. People who lose welfare after running up against the time limit, children abandoned, aliens claiming risk of death or worse at home—all will attract media attention, and all will be state responsibilities. PRWORA does not preclude aiding such folk; in some instances it just precludes using federal dollars to do so. To the extent that such cases, when given faces, reveal true need, local and state government will feel pressure to respond....

### Medicaid Is Still a Problem

Despite the importance of Medicaid to state budgets, welfare reform left the program largely untouched. Indeed, eligibility for Medicaid continues to be determined on the same basis as before. Congress thereby avoided a bruising battle with the health care industry, but it also left untouched one of the principal problems in the social assistance system.

### Wisconsin Waits

The new law gives states the option of continuing operation of welfare demonstrations operated under federal waiver. Initial reports indicate that many will not do so, in part because of disinterest in sustaining evaluation programs based on random assignment and because some program features previously permitted only under waivers are allowable under new federal law. Ironically, the W-2 program still cannot be fully imple-

mented without waivers, for the proposal involves changes in Medicaid and food stamps, as well as changes in treatment of child support payments in benefit computation, that are not permitted under the new law. Despite the president's commitment to "work with Wisconsin to make an effective transition to a new vision of welfare based on work," the state's proposal has been rejected, and its offer to work with the federal government to develop a satisfactory evaluation scheme has been largely ignored. State budgeting for W-2 was in part based on claims established in prior years on federal savings generated by earlier innovations. It is now the federal position that such claims have been superseded by the TANF block grant....

## CONCLUSION

Here, then, is where we are. The nation has achieved interim relief for states for public assistance expenditures. This relief has been accomplished in substantial part by restricting access to welfare. The federal share of public assistance expenditures has been increased, while the federal role in managing the core of the program, now called TANF, has been reduced. The problem of developing and implementing a research agenda for studying program management and effects has yet to be addressed. The consequences of PRWORA are difficult to predict because they involve response to the program by both states and actual and potential assistance recipients. What is certain is that while the new legislation may have ended AFDC, it has most certainly not ended the struggle for welfare reform.

# POSTSCRIPT

## Would Adopting Wisconsin's Welfare Reforms End Welfare As We Know It?

The public policy we adopt to address the needs of those who have been left outside the economic mainstream will dramatically shape the world in the near future. Will the new work incentives and disincentives associated with staying on welfare create a whole new generation of middle-income families, or are we in the process of creating a new generation of dropouts who will live in the dark shadows of society?

It must be remembered that we are dealing with a large number of lives. The latest statistics on poverty indicate that more than 36 million persons suffered the effects of poverty in 1995. Although this poverty rate for white Americans was lower than any other racial group, the vast majority (67 percent) of poor people are white. What is even more startling is the fact that more than one in five children live in poverty, and if we look at children in single-parent families, the rate soars well above 50 percent.

Consequently, whether the post-AFDC era is a boom or a bust has immediate implications for those who are least able to defend themselves—children who live in poverty. One place to start reading in this area is an essay by Daniel R. Meyer and Marian Cancian entitled "Economic Well-Being of Women and Children After AFDC," *La Follette Policy Report* (Winter 1997). Meyer and Cancian are colleagues of Wiseman at the University of Wisconsin. Another policy analyst who warns of the dire prospects associated with the new welfare reform is Peter Edelman. Edelman has long been a vocal critic of the AFDC system, yet when President Clinton signed the new welfare bill Edelman resigned in protest from his position of assistant secretary for planning and evaluation at the Department of Health and Human Services. See his article "The Worst Thing Bill Clinton Has Done," *The Atlantic Monthly* (March 1997).

For the opposing viewpoint see M. Tanner, S. Moore, and D. Hartman, "The Work vs. Welfare Trade-off," *Cato Policy Analysis* (1995). See also William A. Niskamen's article "Welfare and the Culture of Poverty," *Cato Journal* (Spring/Summer 1996). " For a very strong indictment of antipoverty programs, read Walter E. Williams's "The Economics of Poverty," *Vision and Values* (January 1997).

Discussions of welfare reform are found in numerous places, from policy journals—see Gary Burtless and Kent Weaver, "Reinventing Welfare—Again," *The Brookings Review* (Winter 1997)—to articles in popular magazines such as Adam Cohen's, "The Great American Welfare Lab," *Time* (April 21, 1997).

# On the Internet . . .

http://www.dushkin.com

### European Union (EU)
This site of the European Union in the United States has everything from history to current status, as well as Web links and a search capability.
*http://www.eurunion.org*

### OECD Online
The Organization for Economic Cooperation and Development resulted from the need to rebuild Europe after World War II, but it expanded to become truly international, with policies designed to expand world trade on a multilateral, nondiscriminatory basis.
*http://www.oecd.org*

### International Monetary Fund (IMF)
The home page of the IMF links to Information About Its Purpose and Activities, Special Drawing Rights, What's New, the 1997 Annual Meeting, and to other organizations and publications.
*http://www.imf.org/*

### International Trade Administration
The U.S. Department of Commerce is dedicated to helping U.S. businesses compete in the global marketplace, and at this site it offers assistance through many Web links under such headings as Trade Statistics, Cross-Cutting Programs, Regions and Countries, and Import Administration.
*http://www.ita.doc.gov/*

### Social Science Information Gateway (SOSIG)
Project of the Economic and Social Research Council (ESRC). It catalogs 22 subjects and lists more URL addresses from European and developing countries than many U.S. sources.
*http://sosig.esrc.bris.ac.uk/*

### World Bank
At this home page of the World Bank you can click on News, Topics in Development, Countries and Regions, Doing Business with the Bank, and more, as well as use its search feature.
*http://www.worldbank.org*

# PART 3

## The World Around Us

*For many years America held a position of dominance in international trade. That position has been changed by time, events, and the emergence of other economic powers in the world. Decisions that are made in the international arena will, with increasing frequency, influence our lives. In the global marketplace trade relations are influenced by swings in the economies of trading partners. The environment is also a major concern for economists and other analysts today.*

■ Should the United States Protect Domestic Industries from Foreign Competition?

■ Does Free Trade Make the Poor, Poorer?

■ Does Global Warming Require Immediate Government Action?

■ Should Pollution Be Put to the Market Test?

■ Has the North American Free Trade Agreement Been a Success?

# ISSUE 15

## Should the United States Protect Domestic Industries from Foreign Competition?

**YES: Robert Kuttner,** from "The Free Trade Fallacy," *The New Republic* (March 28, 1983)

**NO: Michael Kinsley,** from "Keep Free Trade Free," *The New Republic* (April 11, 1983)

### ISSUE SUMMARY

**YES:** Columnist Robert Kuttner alleges that David Ricardo's eighteenth-century view of the world does not "describe the global economy as it actually works" in the twentieth century. He says that, today, "comparative advantage" is determined by exploitative wage rates and government action; it is not determined by free markets.

**NO:** Social critic Michael Kinsley replies that we do not decrease American living standards when we import the products made by cheap foreign labor. He claims protectionism today, just as it did in the eighteenth century, weakens our economy and only "helps to put off the day of reckoning."

The basic logic of international trade has not changed over time. The villains change, the winners and losers change, but the theory remains the same. Thus, do not be alarmed that the readings that follow refer to 15-year-old editorials that appeared in the *Wall Street Journal*, the *New York Times*, or the *Village Voice*. The pleadings made in these articles are almost identical to those that are now being made in the newspapers of the 1990s. As the saying goes, "The more things change, the more they stay the same." It is because of the timelessness of the free trade versus protectionism debate that we have included the Kuttner/Kinsley selections, even though these essays first appeared in print over a decade ago. Not only does the basic logic of international trade not change over time, it is indistinguishable from domestic trade: Both domestic and international trade must answer the fundamental economic questions: "*What* to produce?" "*How* to produce it?" and "*For whom* to produce?" The distinction is that the international trade questions are posed in an international arena. This is an arena filled with producers and consumers who speak different languages, use different currencies, and are often suspicious of the actions and reactions of foreigners.

If markets work the way they are expected to work, free trade simply increases the extent of a purely domestic market and, therefore, increases the advantages of specialization. Market participants should be able to buy and consume a greater variety of inexpensive goods and services after the establishment of free trade than they could before free trade. You might ask, Then why do some wish to close the borders and deny Americans the benefits of free trade? The answer to this question is straightforward. These benefits do not come without a cost.

There are two sets of winners and two sets of losers in this game of free trade. The most obvious winners are the consumers of the less expensive imported goods. These consumers are able to buy the low-priced color television sets, automobiles, or steel that is made abroad. Another set of winners are the producers of the exported goods. All the factors in the export industry, as well as those in industries that supply to the export industry, experience an increase in their market demand. Therefore, their income increases. In the United States, agriculture is one such export industry. As new foreign markets are opened, farmers' incomes increase, as do the incomes of those who supply the farmers with fertilizer, farm equipment, gasoline, and other basic inputs.

On the other side of this coin are the losers. The obvious losers are those who own the factors of production that are employed in the import-competing industries. These factors include the land, labor, and capital that are devoted to the production of such items as U.S.–made color television sets, U.S.–made automobiles, and U.S.–made steel. The less expensive foreign imports displace the demand for these products. The consumers of exported goods are also losers. For example, as U.S. farmers sell more of their products abroad, less of this output is available domestically. As a result, the domestic prices of these farm products and other export goods and services rise.

The bottom line is that there is nothing "free" in a market system. Competition—whether it is domestic or foreign—creates winners and losers. Historically, we have sympathized with the losers when they suffer at the hands of foreign competitors. However, we have not let our sympathies seriously curtail free trade. Robert Kuttner argues that we can no longer afford this policy. He maintains that U.S. workers face "unfair foreign competition" and that the international rules of the game have changed. Michael Kinsley replies that this is pure, unadorned protectionism. He concludes that "each job 'saved' will cost other American workers far more than it will bring the lucky beneficiary."

# YES

Robert Kuttner

# THE FREE TRADE FALLACY

In the firmament of American ideological convictions, no star burns brighter than the bipartisan devotion to free trade. The President's 1983 Economic Report, to no one's surprise, sternly admonished would-be protectionists. An editorial in *The New York Times*, midway through an otherwise sensibly Keynesian argument, paused to add ritually, "Protectionism might mean a few jobs for American auto workers, but it would depress the living standards of hundreds of millions of consumers and workers, here and abroad."

The Rising Tide of Protectionism has become an irresistible topic for a light news day. Before me is a thick sheaf of nearly interchangeable clips warning of impending trade war. With rare unanimity, the press has excoriated the United Auto Workers for its local content legislation. *The Wall Street Journal*'s editorial ("Loco Content") and the *Times*'s ("The Made-in-America Trap") were, if anything, a shade more charitable than Cockburn and Ridgeway in *The Village Voice* ("Jobs and Racism"). And when former Vice President Mondale began telling labor audiences that America should hold Japan to a single standard in trade, it signaled a chorus of shame-on-Fritz stories.

The standard trade war story goes like this: recession has prompted a spate of jingoistic and self-defeating demands to fence out superior foreign goods. These demands typically emanate from overpaid workers, loser industries, and their political toadies. Protectionism will breed stagnation, retaliation, and worldwide depression. Remember Smoot-Hawley!

Perhaps it is just the unnerving experience of seeing *The Wall Street Journal* and *The Village Voice* on the same side, but one is moved to further inquiry. Recall for a moment the classic theory of comparative advantage. As the English economist David Ricardo explained it in 1817, if you are more efficient at making wine and I am better at weaving cloth, then it would be silly for each of us to produce both goods. Far better to do what each does best, and to trade the excess. Obviously then, barriers to trade defeat potential efficiency gains. Add some algebra, and that is how trade theory continues to be taught today.

To bring Ricardo's homely illustration up to date, the economically sound way to deal with the Japanese menace is simply to buy their entire

From Robert Kuttner, "The Free Trade Fallacy," *The New Republic*, vol. 188, no. 12 (March 28, 1983). Copyright © 1983 by The New Republic, Inc. Reprinted by permission of *The New Republic*.

cornucopia—the cheaper the better. If they are superior at making autos, TVs, tape recorders, cameras, steel, machine tools, baseballs, semiconductors, computers, and other peculiarly Oriental products, it is irrational to shelter our own benighted industries. Far more sensible to buy their goods, let the bracing tonic of competition shake America from its torpor, and wait for the market to reveal our niche in the international division of labor.

But this formulation fails to describe the global economy as it actually works. The classical theory of free trade was based on what economists call "factor endowments"—a nation's natural advantages in climate, minerals, arable land, or plentiful labor. The theory doesn't fit a world of learning curves, economies of scale, and floating exchange rates. And it certainly doesn't deal with the fact that much "comparative advantage" today is created not by markets but by government action. If Boeing got a head start on the 707 from multibillion-dollar military contracts, is that a sin against free trade? Well, sort of. If the European Airbus responds with subsidized loans, is that worse? If only Western Electric (a U.S. supplier) can produce for Bell, is that protection? If Japan uses public capital, research subsidies, and market-sharing cartels to launch a highly competitive semiconductor industry, is *that* protection? Maybe so, maybe not.

Just fifty years ago, Keynes, having dissented from the nineteenth-century theory of free markets, began wondering about free trade as well. In a 1933 essay in the *Yale Review* called "National Self-Sufficiency," he noted that "most modern processes of mass production can be performed in most countries and climates with almost equal efficiency." He won-

dered whether the putative efficiencies of trade necessarily justified the loss of national autonomy. Today nearly half of world trade is conducted between units of multinational corporations. As Keynes predicted, most basic products (such as steel, plastics, microprocessors, textiles, and machine tools) can be manufactured almost anywhere, but by labor forces with vastly differing prevailing wages.

With dozens of countries trying to emulate Japan, the trend is toward worldwide excess capacity, shortened useful life of capital equipment, and downward pressure on wages. For in a world where technology is highly mobile and interchangeable, there is a real risk that comparative advantage comes to be defined as whose work force will work for the lowest wage.

In such a world, it is possible for industries to grow nominally more productive while the national economy grows poorer. How can that be? The factor left out of the simple Ricardo equation is idle capacity. If America's autos (or steel tubes, or machine tools) are manufactured more productively than a decade ago but less productively than in Japan (or Korea, or Brazil), and if we practice what we preach about open trade, then an immense share of U.S. purchasing power will go to provide jobs overseas. A growing segment of our productive resources will lie idle. American manufacturers, detecting soft markets and falling profits, will decline to invest. Steelmakers will buy oil companies. Consumer access to superior foreign products will not necessarily compensate for the decline in real income and the idle resources. Nor is there any guarantee that the new industrial countries will use their burgeoning income from American sales to buy American capital equipment (or computers, or even coal), for they are all striving to develop their own advanced, diversified economies.

Against this background of tidal change in the global economy, the conventional reverence for "free trade" is just not helpful. As an economic paradigm, it denies us a realistic appraisal of second bests. As a political principle, it leads liberals into a disastrous logic in which the main obstacle to a strong American economy is decent living standards for the American work force. Worst of all, a simple-minded devotion to textbook free trade in a world of mercantilism assures that the form of protection we inevitably get will be purely defensive, and will not lead to constructive change in the protected industry.

The seductive fallacy that pervades the hand-wringing about protectionism is the premise that free trade is the norm and that successful foreign exporters must be playing by the rules. Even so canny a critic of political economy as Michael Kinsley wrote in these pages that "Very few American workers have lost their jobs because of unfair foreign trade practices, and it is demagogic for Mondale and company to suggest otherwise." But what is an unfair trade practice? The Common Market just filed a complaint alleging that the entire Japanese industrial system is one great unfair trade practice!

To the extent that the rules of liberal trade are codified, they repose in the General Agreement on Tariffs and Trade (stay awake, this will be brief). The GATT is one of those multilateral institutions created in the American image just after World War II, a splendid historical moment when we could commend free trade to our allies the way the biggest kid on the block calls for a fair fight.

The basic GATT treaty, ratified in 1947, requires that all member nations get the same tariff treatment (the "most favored nation" doctrine), and that tariffs, in theory at least, are the only permissible form of barrier. Governments are supposed to treat foreign goods exactly the same as domestic ones: no subsidies, tax preferences, cheap loans to home industries, no quotas, preferential procurement, or inspection gimmicks to exclude foreign ones. Nor can producers sell below cost (dumping) in foreign markets....

In classical free trade theory, the only permissible candidate for temporary protection is the "infant industry." But Japan and its imitators, not unreasonably, treat every emerging technology as an infant industry. Japan uses a highly sheltered domestic market as a laboratory, and as a shield behind which to launch one export winner after another. Seemingly, Japan should be paying a heavy price for its protectionism as its industry stagnates. Poor Japan! This is not the place for a detailed recapitulation of Japan, Inc., but keep in mind some essentials.

The Japanese government, in close collaboration with industry, targets sectors for development. It doesn't try to pick winners blindfolded; it creates them. It offers special equity loans, which need be repaid only if the venture turns a profit. It lends public capital through the Japan Development Bank, which signals private bankers to let funds flow. Where our government offers tax deductions to all businesses as an entitlement, Japan taxes ordinary business profits at stiff rates and saves its tax subsidies for targeted ventures. The government sometimes buys back outdated capital equipment to create markets for newer capital.

The famed Ministry of International Trade and Industry has pursued this essential strategy for better than twenty years, keeping foreign borrowers out of cheap Japanese capital markets, letting in foreign investors only on very restricted terms, moving Japan up the product ladder from cheap labor intensive goods in the 1950s to autos and steel in the 1960s, consumer electronics in the early 1970s, and computers, semiconductors, optical fibers, and just about everything else by 1980. The Japanese government also waives antimonopoly laws for development cartels, and organizes recession cartels when overcapacity is a problem. And far from defying the discipline of the market, MITI encourages fierce domestic competition before winnowing the field down to a few export champions....

The Japanese not only sin against the rules of market economics. They convert sin into productive virtue. By our own highest standards, they must be doing something right. The evident success of the Japanese model and the worldwide rush to emulate it create both a diplomatic crisis for American trade negotiators and a deeper ideological crisis for the free trade regime. As Berkeley professors John Zysman and Steven Cohen observed in a careful study for the Congressional Joint Economic Committee last December, America, as the main defender of the GATT philosophy, now faces an acute policy dilemma: "how to sustain the open trade system and promote the competitive position of American industry" at the same time.

Unfortunately, the dilemma is compounded by our ideological blinders. Americans believe so fervently in free markets, especially in trade, that we shun interventionist measures until an industry is in deep trouble. Then we build it half a bridge.

There is no better example of the lethal combination of protectionism plus market-capitalism-as-usual than the steel industry. Steel has enjoyed some import limitation since the late 1950s, initially through informal quotas. The industry is oligopolistic; it was very slow to modernize. By the mid-1970s, world demand for steel was leveling off just as aggressive new producers such as Japan, Korea, and Brazil were flooding world markets with cheap, state-of-the-art steel.

As the Carter Administration took office, the American steel industry was pursuing antidumping suits against foreign producers—an avenue that creates problems for American diplomacy. The new Administration had a better idea, more consistent with open markets and neighborly economic relations. It devised a "trigger price mechanism," a kind of floor price for foreign steel entering American markets. This was supposed to limit import penetration. The steelmakers withdrew their suits. Imports continued to increase.

So the Carter Administration moved with characteristic caution toward a minimalist industrial policy. Officials invented a kind of near-beer called the Steel Tripartite. Together, industry, labor, and government would devise a strategy for a competitive American steel industry. The eventual steel policy accepted the industry's own agenda: more protection, a softening of pollution control requirements, wage restraint, new tax incentives, and a gentlemen's agreement to phase out excess capacity. What the policy did not include was either an enforceable commitment or adequate capital to modernize the industry. By market standards, massive retooling was not a rational course, because the return on steel investment was well below prevailing yields on other investments. Moreover, government officials had neither the ideological mandate nor adequate information to tell the steel industry how to invest. "We would sit around and talk about rods versus plate versus specialty steel, and none of us in government had any knowledge of how the steel industry actually operates," confesses C. Fred Bergsten, who served as Treasury's top trade official under Carter. "There has never been a government study of what size and shape steel industry the country needs. If we're going to go down this road, we should do it right, rather than simply preserving the status quo." . . .

The argument that we should let "the market" ease us out of old-fashioned heavy industry in which newly industrialized countries have a comparative advantage quickly melts away once you realize that precisely the same nonmarket pressures are squeezing us out of the highest-tech industries as well. And the argument that blames the problem on overpaid American labor collapses when one understands that semiskilled labor overseas in several Asian nations is producing advanced products for the U.S. market at less than a dollar an hour. Who really thinks that we should lower American wages to that level in order to compete?

In theory, other nations' willingness to exploit their work forces in order to provide Americans with good, cheap products offers a deal we shouldn't refuse. But the fallacy in that logic is to measure the costs and benefits of a trade transaction only in terms of that transaction itself. Classical free-trade theory assumes full employment. When foreign, state-led competition drives us out of indus-

try after industry, the costs to the economy as a whole can easily outweigh the benefits. As Wolfgang Hager, a consultant to the Common Market, has written, "The cheap [imported] shirt is paid for several times: once at the counter, then again in unemployment benefits. Secondary losses involve input industries . . . machinery, fibers, chemicals for dyeing and finishing products."

As it happens, Hager's metaphor, the textile industry, is a fairly successful example of managed trade, which combines a dose of protection with a dose of modernization. Essentially, textiles have been removed from the free-trade regime by an international market-sharing agreement. In the late 1950s, the American textile industry began suffering insurmountable competition from cheap imports. The United States first imposed quotas on imports of cotton fibers, then on synthetics, and eventually on most textiles and apparel as well. A so-called Multi-Fiber Arrangement eventually was negotiated with other nations, which shelters the textile industries of Europe and the United States from wholesale import penetration. Under M.F.A., import growth in textiles was limited to an average of 6 percent per year.

The consequences of this, in theory, should have been stagnation. But the result has been exactly the opposite. The degree of protection, and a climate of cooperation with the two major labor unions, encouraged the American textile industry to invest heavily in modernization. During the 1960s and 1970s, the average annual productivity growth in textiles has been about twice the U.S. industrial average, second only to electronics. According to a study done for the Common Market, productivity in the most efficient American weaving operations is 130,000 stitches per worker per hour—twice as high as France and three times as high as Britain. Textiles, surprisingly enough, have remained an export winner for the United States, with net exports regularly exceeding imports. (In 1982, a depressed year that saw renewed competition from China, Hong Kong, Korea, and Taiwan, exports just about equaled imports.)

But surely the American consumer pays the bill when the domestic market is sheltered from open foreign competition. Wrong again. Textile prices have risen at only about half the average rate of the producer price index, both before and after the introduction of the Multi-Fiber Arrangement.

Now, it is possible to perform some algebraic manipulations and show how much lower textile prices would have been without any protection. One such computation places the cost of each protected textile job at several hundred thousand dollars. But these static calculations are essentially useless as practical policy guides, for they leave out the value over time of maintaining a textile industry in the United States. The benefits include not only jobs, but contributions to G.N.P., to the balance of payments, and the fact that investing in this generation's technology is the ticket of admission to the next.

Why didn't the textile industry stagnate? Why didn't protectionism lead to higher prices? Largely because the textile industry is quite competitive domestically. The top five manufacturers have less than 20 percent of the market. The industry still operates under a 1968 Federal Trade Commission consent order prohibiting any company with sales of more than $100 million from acquiring one with sales exceeding $10 million. If an industry competes vigorously domestically, it can innovate and keep prices low, despite being sheltered from ultra-low-wage foreign competition—or rather, thanks to the shelter. In fact, students of the nature of modern managed capitalism should hardly be surprised that market stability and new investment go hand in hand.

The textile case also suggests that the sunrise industry/sunset industry distinction is so much nonsense. Most of America's major industries can be winners *or* losers, depending on whether they get sufficient capital investment. And it turns out that many U.S. industries such as textiles and shoes, which conventionally seem destined for lower-wage countries, can survive and modernize given a reasonable degree of, well, protection.

What, then, is to be done? First, we should acknowledge the realities of international trade. Our competitors, increasingly, are not free marketeers in our own mold. It is absurd to let foreign mercantilist enterprise overrun U.S. industry in the name of free trade. The alternative is not jingoist protectionism. It is managed trade, on the model of the Multi-Fiber Arrangement. If domestic industries are assured some limits to import growth, then it becomes rational for them to keep retooling and modernizing.

It is not necessary to protect every industry, nor do we want an American MITI. But surely it is reasonable to fashion plans for particular key sectors like steel, autos, machine tools, and semiconductors. The idea is not to close U.S. markets, but to limit the rate of import growth in key industries. In exchange, the domestic industry must invest heavily in modernization. And as part of the bargain, workers deserve a degree of job security and job retraining opportunities.

Far from being just another euphemism for beggar-thy-neighbor, a more stable trade system generally can be in the interest of producing countries. Universal excess capacity does no country much of a favor. When rapid penetration of the U.S. color TV market by Korean suppliers became intolerable, we slammed shut an open door. Overnight, Korean color TV production shrank to 20 percent of capacity. Predictable, if more gradual, growth in sales would have been preferable for us and for the Koreans.

Second, we should understand the interrelationship of managed trade, industrial policies, and economic recovery. Without a degree of industrial planning, limiting imports leads indeed to stagnation. Without restored world economic growth, managed trade becomes a nasty battle over shares of a shrinking pie, instead of allocation of a growing one. And without some limitation on imports, the Keynesian pump leaks. One reason big deficits fail to ignite recoveries is that so much of the growth in demand goes to purchase imported goods.

Third, we should train more economists to study industries in the particular. Most economists dwell in the best of all possible worlds, where markets equilibrate, firms optimize, the idle resources re-employ themselves. "Microeconomics" is seldom the study of actual industries; it is most often a branch of arcane mathematics. The issue of *whether* governments can sometimes improve on markets is not a fit subject for empirical inquiry, for the paradigm begins with the assumption that they cannot. The highly practical question of *when* a little protection is justified is ruled out *ex ante*, since neoclassical economics assumes that less protection is always better than more.

Because applied industrial economics is not a mainstream concern of the economics profession, the people who study it tend to come from the fields of management, industrial and labor relations, planning, and law. They are not invited to professional gatherings of economists, who thus continue to avoid the most pressing practical questions. One economist whom I otherwise admire told me he found it "seedy" that high-wage autoworkers would ask consumers to subsidize their pay. Surely it is seedier for an $800-a-week tenured economist to lecture a $400-a-week autoworker on job security; if the Japanese have a genuine comparative advantage in anything, it is in applied economics.

Fourth, we should stop viewing high wages as a liability. After World War II, Western Europe and North America evolved a social contract unique in the history of industrial capitalism. Unionism was encouraged, workers got a fair share in the fruits of production, and a measure of job security. The transformation of a crude industrial production machine into something approximating social citizenship is an immense achievement, not to be sacrificed lightly on the altar of "free trade." It took one depression to show that wage cuts are no route to recovery. Will it take another to show they are a poor formula for competitiveness? Well-paid workers, after all, are consumers.

# NO                                    Michael Kinsley

## KEEP FREE TRADE FREE

Free trade is not a religion—it has no spiritual value—and Bob Kuttner is right to insist, as he did in TNR two weeks ago, that if it is no longer good for America in practical terms, it is not a sensible policy for liberals anymore. He and I would also agree that a liberal trade policy ought to be good for working people in particular (including people who would like to be working but aren't). The question is whether free trade is just a relic from two happier eras—the period of liberal clarity two centuries ago when Adam Smith and David Ricardo devised the theories of free enterprise and free trade, and the period of American hegemony after World War II when we could dominate world markets—or whether it is still a key to prosperity.

Kuttner argues that Ricardo's theory of "comparative advantage"—that all nations are better off if each produces and exports what it can make most efficiently—no longer applies. Local factors such as climate and natural resources don't matter much anymore. As a result, "most basic products . . . can be manufactured almost anywhere" with equal efficiency. This means, Kuttner says, that the only ways one nation (e.g., Japan) gains comparative advantage over another (e.g., us) these days are through low wages or "government action." Either of these, he says, makes nonsense of Ricardo's theory. In addition, Kuttner says, Ricardo didn't account for the problem of "idle capacity"—expensive factories sitting unused.

"Idle capacity" is an argument against any competition at all, not just from abroad, and has a long history of being carted out whenever established companies (the airlines, for example) want the government to prevent newcomers from horning in on their turf. If you believe in capitalism at all, you have to believe that the temporary waste of capital that can result from the turmoil of competition is more than outweighed by the efficiency of competition in keeping all the competitors on their toes. A capitalist who builds a plant knowing (or even not knowing) that it is less efficient than a rival abroad deserves whatever he gets. As for older plants that are already built—that capital is sunk. If the cost of running those plants is higher than the cost of buying the same output from abroad, keeping them running is more wasteful than letting them sit idle.

From Michael Kinsley, "Keep Free Trade Free," *The New Republic*, vol. 188, no. 14 (April 11, 1983). Copyright © 1983 by The New Republic, Inc. Reprinted by permission of *The New Republic*.

This brings us to the real problem; not sunk capital but sunk lives. The middle-class living standard achieved by much of the United States working class is one of the glories of American civilization. Yet Kuttner says, "semi-skilled labor overseas is producing advanced products for the U.S. market at less than a dollar an hour. Who really thinks that we should lower American wages to that level in order to compete?"

We shouldn't, of course. But importing the products of cheap foreign labor cannot lower American living standards as a whole, and trade barriers cannot raise living standards. This is not a matter of morality: it is a matter of mathematics. If widgets can be imported from Asia for a price reflecting labor costs of $1 an hour, then an hour spent making widgets adds a dollar of value to the economy. This is true no matter what American widget makers are being paid. If foreign widgets are excluded in order to protect the jobs of American widget makers getting $10 an hour, $1 of that $10 reflects their contribution to the economy and $9 is coming out of the pockets of other workers who have to pay more for widgets. Nice for widget makers, but perfectly futile from the perspective of net social welfare.

After all, if this economic alchemy really worked, we could shut our borders to all imports, pay one another $1,000 an hour, and we'd all be rich. It doesn't work that way. In fact, as a society, we're clearly better off taking advantage of the $1 widgets. The "comparative advantage" of cheap Asian labor is an advantage to *us* too. That's why trade is good.

But what about the poor widget makers? And what about the social cost of unemployment? If former widget makers aren't working at all, they aren't even adding a dollar's worth to the economy. Protectionism is, in effect, a "make work" jobs program—but a ridiculously expensive one, both directly and indirectly. The direct cost, in this example, is $9 an hour. The indirect cost is in reducing the efficiency of the economy by preventing international specialization.

If the disparity between American and foreign wages is really that great, Americans just shouldn't be making widgets. We could pay widget workers at $8 an hour to do nothing, and still be better off. We could put them to work at their current wage doing anything worth more than a dollar an hour. We could spend the equivalent of $9 an hour on retraining. And we owe it to widget workers to try all these things if necessary, because they are the victims of a change that has benefited all the rest of us by bringing us cheaper widgets (and because, as Lester Thurow points out, doing these things will discourage them from blocking the needed change). To protect them while they keep on making widgets, though, is insane.

These suggestions are, of course, overt tax-and-spend government programs, compared to the covert tax-and-spend program of protectionism. In a period of political reaction, the covert approach is tempting. But hypocrisy is not a sensible long-term strategy for liberals, nor is willfully ignoring the importance of economic productivity.

In many basic industries, American wages are not all that far out of line, as Bob Kuttner seems to acknowledge in the case of autos. Modest wage adjustments can save these jobs and these industries for America. It is uncomfortable for a well-paid journalist to be urging pay cuts for blue-collar workers. On the other hand, steelworkers (when they are working) make more than the median American income. Protectionism to preserve wage levels is just a redistribution of national wealth; it creates no new wealth. Nothing is wrong with redistribution, but in any radical socialist redistribution of wealth, the pay of steelworkers would go down, not up. So it's hard to see why the government should intervene to protect steelworkers' wages at the expense of general national prosperity. This is especially true when millions are unemployed who would happily work for much less, and there is no jobs program for them.

But Bob Kuttner believes that protection can be good for general national prosperity even apart from the wage question, in an age when other nations' "comparative advantage" comes from government policies that include protectionism. It is important to separate different strands in the common protectionist argument that we have to do it because Japan does it. Many politicians of various stripes, and William Safire in a recent column, argue (on an implicit analogy between trade war and real war) that only by threatening or building trade barriers of our own can we persuade the Japanese to dismantle theirs and restore free trade. Kuttner, by contrast, thinks that the idea of free trade is outmoded; that the Japanese are *smart* to restrict imports and we would be smart to do the same as part of an "industrial policy."

Both Safire and Kuttner assume incorrectly that free trade needs to be mutual. In fact, the theory of free trade is that nations benefit from their own open borders as well as the other guy's. This may be right or wrong, but the mere fact that Japan is protectionist does not settle the question of what our policy should be.

Certainly, it's worth looking at Japan for clues about how to succeed in the world economy, and certainly one key to Japan's success seems to be a government-coordinated industrial policy. (The current vogue for "industrial policy" is assessed by my colleague Robert Kaus in the February *Harper's*—forgive the plug.) But why must such a policy include trade barriers? One reason Japan thwarts imports is a conscious decision to reduce workers' living standards in order to concentrate national resources on industrial investment. I presume this isn't what Kuttner and other liberal trade revisionists have in mind. Kuttner and others include protectionism in their "industrial policy" for two other reasons. First, as a sort of bribe to get unions to go along with sterner measures—possibly necessary, but not a case for protection on its own merits. Second, to give promising industries a captive market in which to incubate and gather strength before taking on the world.

The trouble with this "nurture" argument is that there's no end to it. Kuttner himself says that it's "not unreasonable" to "treat every emerging technology" this way, and also says that "most of America's major industries can be winners" with the right treatment. After you add the few hopeless loser industries where we must allegedly create barriers to save American wages, you've got the whole economy locked up, and whether this will actually encourage efficiency or the opposite is, at the very least, an open question. And if every major country protects every major industry, there will be no world market for any of them to conquer.

Kuttner's model for "managed trade" is the Multi-Fiber Arrangement, an international agreement that restricts imports of textiles. This, according to Kuttner, permitted the American textile industry to modernize and become productive, to the point where exports exceeded imports— a less impressive accomplishment if you recall that the M.F.A. *restricts* imports.

Kuttner concedes that, despite the productivity gains, textile prices are higher than they would be without protection from cheap foreign labor. (Indeed, the current situation in the textile industry, as Bob Kuttner describes it, seems to vindicate Luddites, who got their start in textiles; human beings could do the work more efficiently, but machines are doing it anyway.) So what's the point? According to Kuttner, "The benefits include not only jobs, but contributions to G.N.P., to the balance of payments, and the fact that investing in this generation's technology is the ticket of admission to the next." Yet Kuttner does not challenge the "algebraic manipulations" he cites that show how each job saved costs the nation "several hundred thousand dollars" in higher textile prices. The only "contribution to G.N.P." from willful inefficiency like this can be the false contribution of inflation. The balance of payments is a measure of economic health, not a cause of it; restricting imports to reduce that deficit is like sticking the thermometer in ice water to bring down a feverish temperature. As for the suggestion that the *next* generation of technology will bring the *real* payoff— well, they were probably promising the same thing two decades ago when the Multi-Fiber Arrangement began.

Kuttner also worries that "without some limitation on imports," Keynesian fiscal policies don't work. This is like the monetarists who worry that financial advances such as money market funds will weaken the connection between inflation and the money supply. Unable to make their theory accord with life, they want the government to make life accord with their theory. There *is* a world economy—which Bob Kuttner seems to recognize as a good thing— and this means Keynesian techniques will increasingly have to be applied internationally....

There can be no pretense that domestic content legislation has anything to do with "industrial policy"—improving the competitive ability of American industry. It is protectionism, pure and unadorned, and each job "saved" will cost other American workers far more than it will bring the lucky beneficiary. Like most protectionist measures, far from aiding America's adjustment to world competition, it just helps put off the day of reckoning.

# POSTSCRIPT

## Should the United States Protect Domestic Industries from Foreign Competition?

The desirability of free trade is one of few issues on which a large majority of professional economists agree. Survey after survey confirms this: Economists are ardent supporters of free trade. In spite of this general consensus, protectionism is hotly debated. This certainly is the case in these two essays.

Kuttner argues two basic points in his essay. First, he contends that the world that English economist David Ricardo modeled in 1817 is starkly different than the world we know today. He describes our world as "a world of learning curves, economies of scale, and floating exchange rates." It is a world where comparative advantage "is created not by markets but by government action." Second, he maintains that although free markets will lead to factor price equalization—that is, wage rates in developing countries will rise and U.S. wage rates will fall as long as there is a differential—we should not, and cannot, allow this to happen. He asks: Do we want wage levels in the United States to fall to a dollar an hour?

Kinsley does not believe that free trade is a relic from the past. After looking at the simple mathematics of Kuttner's proposal, Kinsley contends, "Protectionism is, in effect, a 'make work' jobs program—but a ridiculously expensive one, both directly and indirectly." He believes we can achieve the same end without sacrificing the benefits of "international specialization." Kinsley goes on to argue that when "every major country protects every major industry"—the natural consequence of Kuttner's national industrial policy—"there will be no world market for any of them to conquer." He contends that we will return to the isolationists' world, a world that is poorer than it need be.

Since the majority of economists support the notion of free trade, readings supporting this position are very easy to identify. However, if you would like to read an extreme position paper, you might try Paula Stern's "Ronald Reagan: The International Bad Boy on Trade," *The International Economy* (July/August 1991). In this essay she argues that "the essence of Reagan's trade policy became clear: Espouse free trade, but find an excuse on every occasion to embrace the opposite." For a more scholarly discourse, you might read Douglas Irwin's "Retrospectives: Challenges to Free Trade," *Journal of Economic Perspectives* (Spring 1991). Irwin concludes that when all is said and done, the charges leveled at free trade "will not fundamentally challenge the belief of economists in free trade."

# ISSUE 16

# Does Free Trade Make the Poor, Poorer?

**YES: William Greider,** from "Global Warning: Curbing the Free Trade Free-fall," *The Nation* (January 13, 1997)

**NO: Gary Burtless,** from "Worsening American Income Inequality: Is World Trade to Blame?" *The Brookings Review* (Spring 1996)

## ISSUE SUMMARY

**YES:** Columnist and social critic William Greider warns that blind acceptance and promotion of "free-market doctrine" must inevitably lead to deepening inequality and deterioration at home.

**NO:** Gary Burtless, a senior fellow at the Brookings Institution, concedes that the demand for and relative wages of less skilled workers have plunged, but he maintains that this dramatic shift is not confined to the traded-goods sector.

Many claim that the United States is in the midst of a radical redistribution of income. The rich are getting richer and the poor, poorer. This is indicated in the data, which measures the share of "real income" received by families ranked from lowest income to highest income and then separates the population into five equal groups or "quintiles."

Income distributional patterns are markedly different before and after 1979. Prior to 1979, economic growth benefited all income groups. That is, whether you were poor (part of the first quintile), middle class (part of the second, third, or fourth quintile), or affluent (part of the fifth quintile), the average real income in your income group increased. True, some groups gained more than others over time, but nevertheless, in the words of John F. Kennedy, "a rising tide raises all boats."

After 1979 this pattern changed. The tide of economic growth raised the yachts of the rich, just as it did in the pre-1979 period; but apparently the row-boats of those with meager or moderate means were washed into the "stagnant backwaters" of the economy. The real income, or purchasing power income, of the bottom 40 percent of all American households fell (the bottom 20 percent falling by 8.8 percent), while the real incomes of the top 40 percent rose (the real income of the top 5 percent rising by 45.5 percent). This represents a redistribution of income, but it is a redistribution from the poor to the rich. This is not an expected pattern in this land of "equal opportunity," where public policy has attempted to level the playing field for all, rather than provide a few in society an unsurmountable lead in the race to the top of the mountain.

Much has been written about the underlying cause or causes of this radical shift in the distribution of income in the United States. (Note that the 1995 quintile shares reported in 1997 indicated a possible reversal of this pattern. For the first time since 1979, the most affluent households in the United States —the top 20 percent and the top 5 percent—experienced a very modest decline in their share of income. The share of all income received by the top 5 percent fell from 21.1 percent to 21.0 percent in the 1995 data compared to the 1994 data, while the top 20 percent share fell from 46.9 percent to 46.5 percent.) The disturbing pattern that characterizes the post-1979 period has been variously attributed to (1) the influx of unskilled immigrants—both documented and undocumented; (2) changes in age composition of the population—where 15-to-24-year-olds are a larger proportion of the potential workforce; (3) the marked rise in the percentage of the workforce with a college education, resulting in a wage gap when compared to those without advanced education; (4) the decline in the economic influence of the labor union movement; (5) the shift from an industrial-based economy to a service-based economy; (6) the rapidly rising skill levels required for employment in all sectors of the economy; (7) changing public policy—reducing the progressivity of federal taxes and curtailing the magnitude and extent of the "safety net"; (8) the growing presence of female-headed households; and (9) the globalization of the world economy.

It is the latter issue that is debated by William Greider and Gary Burtless. Greider takes the position that the "freefall" in the incomes of middle-class Americans can be traced to the blind acceptance of free markets and free trade without the mediating influence of government. Burtless, on the other side, argues that there are many reasons for the "widening income gap" and none of them are linked to liberalizing international trade.

# YES
William Greider

## GLOBAL WARNING: CURBING THE FREE-TRADE FREEFALL

The global system of finance and commerce is in a reckless footrace with history, plunging toward a dreadful reckoning with its own contradictions, pulling everyone along with it. Responsible experts and opinion leaders, of course, do not generally share my sense of alarm. Nor do most political authorities, who, in any case, seem thoroughly intimidated by economic events. Some important voices in business and finance do occasionally express similar anxieties, but multinational enterprise is preoccupied with its own imperatives, finance capital consumed by its own search for returns. Public opinion may be uneasy, even angry, but people generally are confused and rudderless.

The destructive pressures building up within the global system are leading toward an unbearable chaos that, even without a dramatic collapse, will likely provoke a harsh, reactionary politics that can shut down the system. This outcome is avoidable if nations will put aside theory and confront what is actually occurring, if they have the courage to impose remedial changes before it is too late.

If the positive energies of this revolutionary process are to be preserved, it has to be slowed down, not stopped, and redirected on a new course of development that is more moderate and progressive, that promises broader benefits to almost everyone. The economic problem requires governments to discard the hollow abstractions of financial accounting and begin rebuilding the tangible foundations for balanced prosperity, for work and wages, and for greater social equity—not only for older, wealthier nations but for the aspiring poor in the emerging "one world." It is far easier to describe some ways this might be achieved than to imagine that governing elites will act upon them.

The first priority is to reregulate finance capital. Governments will have to reimpose some of the control discarded during the last generation, both to stabilize financial markets and to make capital more responsive to the needs of producing economies. Measures like transaction taxes on foreign exchange would be a beginning. Such controls would take some of the profit out of currency trading and other speculative activities but would not inhibit long-term flows of capital for foreign investment and trade.

The popular belief that governments lack the power to control international fiance is simply wrong: to disarm the exaggerated power and random follies of the global bond market, they can tighten terms for easy credit; in some arenas of credit, ceilings on interest rates can be reimposed; prohibitions on accepting transfers of offshore funds could shut down the banking centers where capital hides from securities laws and income taxes. Governments, in essence, must reclaim the ruling obligations of the nation-state from private markets.

The central economic problem of our present Industrial Revolution, not so different in nature from our previous one, is an excess of supply—the growing, permanent surpluses of goods, labor and productive capacity. The supply problem is the core of what drives destruction and instability: accumulation of redundant factories as new ones are simultaneously built in emerging markets, mass unemployment and declining wages, irregular mercantilist struggles for market entry and shares in the industrial base, market gluts that depress prices and profits, fierce contests that lead to cooperative cartels among competitors, and other consequences.

* * *

The shocking lesson of economic history —experience that now seems largely forgotten—is that vast human suffering and random destruction of productive capacities are unnecessary. From the crisis and turmoil of the early twentieth century, nations painfully discovered that there is nothing inevitable about these market forces or the social convulsions they sow if societies will act to counter them. A shared prosperity emerges, as Keynes taught, only when people throw off passivity and learn to take control of their fate.

Governments can counter the disorders and ameliorate losses mainly by stimulating consumption, creating more buyers for unsold goods—the rising market demand that activates idle factories and workers. The present regime is fundamentally pathological because it destroys consumer incomes while creating a growing surfeit of goods. Many different measures can push the global system in the opposite direction, but the underlying problem, bluntly stated, requires shifting returns from capital to labor, reversing the maldistribution of incomes generated by the marketplace under the rentier system.

Greater social equity is not only consistent with but required by a sound and expanding economy: When rising incomes are broadly distributed, it creates mass purchasing power—fueling a virtuous cycle of growth, savings and new investment. When incomes are narrowly distributed, as they are now, the economic system feeds upon itself, eroding its own energies for expansion, burying consumers and business, even governments, in impossible accumulations of debt. A relative few become fabulously wealthy, but a healthy economy is not sustained by manic investing. Nothing about modern technologies or the "information age" has altered these ancient fundamentals.

* * *

The genuine meaning of "one world" will be tested by how nations answer this question: Can the global system be turned toward a less destructive path without throwing poor people over the side? Older economies may be tempted to revert to insular, self-protective remedies, but this will destroy the promise of the globalizing revolution and could even produce its own implosion of commerce —balkanized struggles for markets that substitute political conflict for the economic disorders. The challenge of "one world" is to create the standards for a progressive system that everyone can trust, that does not leave anyone out.

The imperatives for a new world order can be boiled down to a series of mutually reinforcing propositions, each of which would help to redress the economic imbalances of supply and demand. They include the following ideas:

*1. Tax capital instead of labor.* Even a modest shift in tax structures can stimulate the creation of new jobs and wage incomes while it creates the mechanism for making investors and corporations more accountable for their behavior. The tax codes of most of the advanced industrial nations are tilted against work, focusing regressive payroll taxes on wage earners and their employers, thus raising the real cost for a company that expands its work force. By comparison, financial wealth is lightly taxed and, at least in the United States, is not subject to the property taxes that people pay on real-property assets like homes and businesses.

Reducing the tax barrier to employment can be done in a progressive manner that favors work for the less skilled —lower payroll tax rates on jobs at the lower end of the wage scale, higher taxes at the high end. That would provide a discreet incentive to multiply jobs for those who need them most—a cheaper and more effective approach than social

programs that try to help people after they are already poor or unemployed. The same principle could target the common practice, at least among U.S. companies, of escaping the social overhead of doing business by marginalizing workers in piecemeal jobs—the "temporary" or "contract" work that lacks decent wages or benefits. The supposed efficiency of these measures actually involves pushing the social costs—health care or income support for indigent retirees—onto others, mainly the general public.

Direct taxation of financial capital could also create a mechanism for rewarding the firms and investors who take responsibility for broader economic and social consequences while punishing the free riders. Globalizing corporations, which move jobs offshore and arbitrage tax concessions from different governments, ought to be treated less favorably than the enterprises that are conscientiously increasing their domestic employment. Capital investors, likewise, have a financial obligation to the commonweal that protects them.

A direct tax on wealth is not as radical as it may sound to Americans, since eleven other nations in the Organization for Economic Cooperation and Development, including Germany, already have modest versions. The principle is not different from ordinary property taxes or business-license taxes on merchants or professionals, since capital owners benefit from the public domain. For instance, Edward Wolff has proposed that the United States follow the model of Switzerland and adopt a system of modest, graduated rates that would start by exempting the first $100,000 of financial assets, tax the next $100,000 at a rate of only .05 percent and rise to a rate of 0.3 percent about $1 million. He calculates that such a system would have raised only $40 billion in 1994—a lot of money but hardly an onerous burden on the wealthy, nor a solution to the fiscal disorders.

A central purpose of taxing capital, however, is to establish the means for defining the responsibility of capital owners to each nation and its people. If capital wants to enjoy record returns from the global system, it must help pay for the economic and social wreckage it leaves behind. Once that principle is established, the tax code can begin to make distinctions among both corporations and investors, based upon their civic behavior.

"The emerging modern system gives a larger share of income and power to capital, yet the burdens of government and community have steadfastly been shifted to labor," as one financial economist explained to me. "At some point, we have to ask whether utterly free capital is a benefit to everyone. Free capital is certainly a benefit to the people who own the capital. But they couldn't exist if these governments did not exist to protect them. No one wants to locate the Chicago Board of Trade in Bangkok or Jakarta. They want to be in the United States or maybe five or six other countries, where their transactions and their wealth will be safe."

Similar logic could change the strategic calculations of multinational corporations as they disperse production, perhaps by making preferential distinctions in the tax code. If the national objective is to stimulate domestic employment, then capital or corporate stocks might get a reduction or even exemption from capital gains taxation if the corporate balance sheet confirms that the enterprise is increasing jobs by investing at home. Capital should be taxed at the full rate if

it is doing the opposite. The global dispersal of industry would not be stopped, but firms and shareholders would have to help pay for what they left behind.

This approach inevitably favors domestic companies over multinationals, but it also discards the fraudulent proposition that any tax break or subsidy to business automatically translates into a benefit for society at large. If that assumption was ever sound, it is clearly suspect in the era of globalizing corporations. Governments promoting the trading fortunes of multinationals have not yet answered the gut question: Who in the nation benefits from this process, owners or workers, capital or citizens?

2. *Reform the terms of trade to insure more balanced flows of commerce, compelling exporting nations to become larger consumers of global production.* The present system is propped up by the persistent trade deficits of wealthier nations, mainly the United States, a condition that cannot endure for much longer. Rhetorical promises notwithstanding, global agreements like the General Agreement on Tariffs and Trade (GATT) and the endless rounds of trade disputes have failed utterly to redress trade imbalances. Indeed, prospects are worsening as China and other major new industrial powers prepare to enter the world market. A fundamental principle, therefore, must be established: An industrial economy cannot expect to construct a vast oversupply of production for export while refusing to accept equivalent volumes of imports from others.

The system, in effect, has to provoke a meaningful showdown with the Japanese model of wealth accumulation—the mercantilist practices that exact zero-sum advantage at the expense of trading partners. Those economies that persist in accumulating huge trading surpluses should lose their cost-free access to foreign markets through emergency tariffs or other measures. On the other hand, nations that practice genuine reciprocity of buying and selling, including the aspiring poor nations, should be rewarded with preferences. In short, Japan and other Asian nations like China that follow Japan's strategic path would face an unsentimental choice: Either expand imports or expect to be stuck with excess productive capacity.

The objective of temporary trading barriers would not be to protect domestic industrial sectors but to force everyone to confront the underlying crisis of surpluses. Every trading nation, including poor nations hoping to become less poor, has a tangible stake in solving the supply problem because it poses a principal obstacle to adopting a pro-growth regime for the world. Under the current system, older economies may actually suffer from faster growth if their rising consumption simply generates a deluge of imports and larger trade deficits, while the foreign markets remain closed to their production. Until this zero-sum condition is corrected, the potential for greater growth will remain stymied. Emergency tariffs to correct a nation's financial disorders are an extreme measure, but not prohibited by GATT. If the United States threatened such measures, other nations might at last face up to the larger global problem of oversupply.

3. *Bring the bottom up—raising wages on the low end as rapidly as possible—by requiring trading nations to honor labor rights.* By defending human freedom, the trading system can establish that the collective right of workers to bid up their wages is sanctioned and protected. Morality aside, the economic objective is straightforward: Raising wages at the bottom enlarges the base of consumption for everyone's goods. Even in the best of circumstances, the downward pressures on high-wage labor markets will not abate soon, given the vast sea of available low-wage workers. But every gain in wage levels at the bottom, even a modest gain, translates into immediate economic benefit for the global system: more purchasing power.

At present, the system functions in reverse, eroding consumption by replacing high-wage labor with cheap labor. To be sure, the new industrial workers in Asia and Latin America have new wage incomes to spend, but overall the system experiences a net loss in the potential for mass consumption. The challenge, roughly speaking, is to create a global system that functions most energetically by pulling the bottom up instead of the top down. Many poorer nations are naturally hostile to the suggestion, fearing that they will lose the comparative advantage of cheap labor or political control over their work forces. But companies or nations that rely on repression and exploitation of the weak for trading advantage are not truly ready for membership in a "one world" economy. They should be penalized, even excluded.

The easiest way to accomplish this reform is to insert an enforceable "social clause" in the global trade agreements requiring all trading nations to honor long-established international rules for labor rights. As a practical matter, that is unlikely to happen at the level of GATT and the World Trade Organization, since both developing countries and multinational corporations are opposed to any labor reform.

The political opening lies in negotiating regional or nation-to-nation compacts that establish networks of social standards and extend trading preferences to those who honor them (the opportunity Bill Clinton failed to act upon when pushing NAFTA). Reciprocal trade agreements that link several rich nations with several poor nations could establish a working model that demonstrates the positive economic energies that flow from labor reform. As participants benefit on both ends, other nations, rich and poor, may see the wisdom of emulating the reform.

Nations are, of course, entitled to their sovereignty—the power to set domestic social standards free of foreigners' interference—but that does not require foreigners to buy their goods. Advanced economies need not meddle in other nation's domestic politics, since they can regulate the behavior of their own multinationals, both at home and abroad. If the national interest lies in bringing up wages worldwide, then governments may withdraw subsidies and tax preferences from companies that, like the U.S. electronics industry in Malaysia, actively seek to block labor rights of their foreign workers.

4. *Forgive the debtors—that is, initiate a general write-off of bad debts accumulated by poorer nations.* Extinguishing failed loans issued by international agencies such as the International Monetary Fund and the World Bank would free desperately poor economies, especially in Africa, to pursue more viable strategies for domestic development. The liquidation of debt obligations is fundamentally a stimulative economic measure since it frees cash for other pursuits, including active consumption, and it is socially enlightened because it eases global poverty.

Writing off these debts is probably inevitable, in any case, since most of the loans can never be repaid. Right now, the interest costs simply bleed the poor nations further each year and often require new loans so they can keep up payments on old loans. Liquidation would free their meager cash flows for genuine development and at least the possibility that they may someday become significant consumers in the global system.

To accompany the debt forgiveness, however, the operating purposes of the international lending institutions must also be reformed. The I.M.F. and World Bank must develop greater respect for indigenous strategies for growth, promoting a more patient development of domestic economies instead of simply enforcing the financial imperatives of the global system. To cite the most obvious contradiction, these institutions routinely use their power to suppress wages and consumption in the developing countries when the advanced nations that finance their lending have an interest in achieving the opposite. If the lending institutions are unable to change direction, then sponsoring governments should withdraw funding and abolish them, writing off their loan portfolios in the process.

5. *Reform the objectives of central banks so they will support a pro-growth regime instead of thwarting it.* The purposes of monetary policy have to be returned to a more balanced and democratic perspective—an understanding that growth, employment and wages are crucial to a sound economy, no less important than the prerogative of stored wealth. So long as the Federal Reserve and the central banks of

other nations stand in the way of more vigorous growth that might allow a reinflation of wages, the problem of weakening consumption and oversupply is sure to increase, accompanied by compounding debt burdens.

The policy choices embedded in the regulation of money and credit always involve difficult trade-offs between different risks—recession or inflation, idle capacity or overheated activity, failed debtors or financial speculation. But the consequences of these choices are not distributed evenly throughout society, especially when policy is always skewed toward the interests of wealth holders. Most of the leading central banks are ostensibly independent of politics, yet this does not prevent them from adhering faithfully to the narrow constituency of finance capital. Their prejudices are unlikely to change until the competing interests—labor, manufacturing and other sectors—organize counter-pressures demanding a more generous policy of economic growth. To make central banks yield, they should be reconstituted as open and accountable governing institutions.

Unfortunately, central banks are stuck in the past, still fighting the last war against inflation when the global system now faces the opposite danger—a massive deflation of prices, economic activity and debt. The trade-offs surrounding monetary policy have been profoundly altered by globalized finance and production. Yet central bankers continue to operate in the traditional manner, as if they were still regulating self-contained domestic economies. This anomaly leads them to err repeatedly on the downside—discouraging domestic economic activity and new investment in the name of stability—even as markets respond to global influences of supply and demand. If a new era of growth is to occur, new theoretical understandings must replace the traditional rules of central banking.

6. *Refocus national economic agendas on the priority of work and wages, rather than trade or multinational competitiveness, as the defining issue for domestic prosperity.* Obviously, these objectives are intertwined and interacting, but it makes a great difference as to which to put first. If advanced nations, especially the United States, concentrate on promoting employment and more equitable incomes, they can make a great contribution to the global system, in addition to domestic well-being, by boosting mass consumption. If governments continue to be preoccupied with globalization and promotion of the free-market doctrine, then they must inevitably accept the consequences of deepening inequality and deterioration at home.

The actions that governments could take will require new spending, but should focus less on government social aid programs and more on wage realities in private-sector labor markets. Many such measures are traditional forms of intervention: raising minimum wages, strengthening labor laws to encourage companies to share productivity gains with workers, restoring progressive taxation to redistribute income, curbing the luxurious corporate subsidies embedded in the tax code and government programs, underwriting major works projects like high-speed rail systems or urban housing rehabilitation.

If it is true that global pressures will drag down wages and employment for at least another generation, then the economic imperative for large-scale subsidized employment is inescapable. If people cannot find jobs that promise a living wage for families, then all the various social interventions that government undertakes will be futile. Instead, societies will accumulate another generation of dispossessed and alienated citizens.

The same essential question has to be asked of every public measure: Does it genuinely promise to enhance work and wages? In debating that question, people will discover that much of what government currently does is useless or even harmful to broadly shared prosperity. But the answers may also begin to bring the economic future into clearer focus, defining potential new pillars for domestic economic activity. Financial reform, for instance, might direct credit subsidies to sectors like housing or small-scale busi-

ness enterprises or a national child-care system—new business activity that becomes a significant employer while filling real needs. Every such step, of course, tends to distribute the economic returns more broadly through society and thus creates more buyers for the world's surplus production.

If people can get beyond passivity and insecurity, an era of economic experimentation lies ahead—ventures that explore new social and economic arrangements, projects that can be encouraged by government, not managed by it. Among rich and poor, people are already exploring ideas that may change their destiny, social invention that needs not wait upon market forces.

# NO

## Gary Burtless

# WORSENING AMERICAN INCOME INEQUALITY: IS WORLD TRADE TO BLAME?

Since 1970 American incomes have become strikingly less equal. Living standards of poor and lower middle-class Americans have fallen while those of affluent Americans have continued to improve. And the trend toward inequality has not been confined to the United States. Nations throughout the industrialized world have seen income disparities rise since the late 1970s.

Many people blame rising income inequality on the growing importance of trade, especially trade with nations in the developing world, in the past quarter century. In *The Trap*, a bestseller in Western Europe, Sir James Goldsmith argues that free trade with low-wage countries has harmed and threatens to impoverish low-skilled and middle-class workers in the advanced industrial countries. A similar argument was used by Ross Perot and other U.S. opponents of the North American Free Trade Agreement, who warned that freer trade with Mexico would eliminate industrial jobs and reduce the wages of semi-skilled U.S. workers. More recently, Republican presidential aspirant Patrick Buchanan has called for an "equalization tax" on imports from third world countries to protect American workers against competition from Asian and Latin American workers who may be paid one-tenth the U.S. industrial wage. How well does the case against free trade stand up to the facts?

## TRENDS IN U.S. INCOME INEQUALITY

There is no disputing the worsening trend in U.S. income inequality. Figure 1 documents the rate of change in income for Americans divided into five quintiles of the income distribution. Income changes are calculated after taking account of changes over time in the price level and changes in the size of families in different parts of the income distribution. (Average family size shrank after 1969, so it took less income to support families at the same standard of living.) The black bars represent income changes during 1969–79, the gray bars, changes between 1979 and 1993. During 1969–79, Americans in all quintiles made income gains, though people in the lowest income quintile made the smallest percentage gains. After 1979, incomes fell in each of the three bottom quintiles while continuing to grow in the top two. Compounded over the 24-year period, the differences in the rate of change in income imply dramatic movements in relative well-being. At the 5th percentile, income fell 34 percent; at the 95th percentile, it rose 43 percent. In 1969, income at the 95th percentile of adjusted personal income was a little less than 12 times income at the 5th percentile. By 1993, income at the 95th percentile was more than 25 times income at the 5th percentile.

Several developments lie behind the widening income gap, and most of them have little direct or indirect link to liberalized international trade. Significant gains in capital income during the decade of the 1980s, for example, caused unearned income to grow strongly in the top part of the income distribution. And at the same time, changes in the pattern of government transfers—with growing cash transfers going to the elderly, many of whom tend to be well up the income distribution, and shrinking cash transfers to the poor—reduced the effectiveness of those transfers in combating poverty. Changes in the structure of U.S. households also added to income inequality. Single-parent families are more likely to be poor than families that have two parents, and a much higher percentage of Americans now lives in single-parent families. Finally, the dramatic increase in paid employment among American women has tended to boost inequality since the late 1970s. In the 1950s and 1960s, families with a well-paid male earner were less likely than average to have a well-paid female earner. By 1993, families with a highly paid male earner were *more* likely than average to have a highly paid female earner. These non-trade-related economic and demographic trends account for more than half the growth in overall U.S. income inequality since 1969.

## EARNINGS INEQUALITY

Even if trade is not to blame for trends in unearned income or changes in the composition of American households, it could still be an important source of growing *wage* inequality. Figure 2, based on annual earnings reports in the Census Bureau's Current Population Survey, shows that between 1969 and 1993, earnings fell for men in the bottom 40 percent of the earnings distribution, remained unchanged for men in the middle quintile, and rose for men at the top. The disparate trends in wage earnings became more pronounced after 1979. Earnings fell sharply in low-wage groups, and wage disparities between well-paid and poorly paid men widened at an accelerated pace. Although overall wage trends have been much healthier for women (gray bars in Figure 2), women have also experienced widening earnings disparities, especially in recent years. After 1979 women in the top quintile saw their earnings climb more than 25 percent. For women at the bottom, annual earnings fell after 1979.

## DOES TRADE HARM UNSKILLED U.S. WORKERS?

The argument that trade is to blame for U.S. earnings inequality rests on the assumption that trade hurts U.S. workers with skills similar to those of workers in developing countries. The intuition

*Figure 1*

## Change in Adjusted Real Personal Income, by Quintile, 1969–93

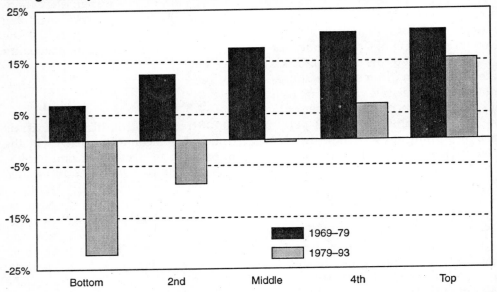

*Note:* Personal incomes are "adjusted" to reflect differences in family size. The top quintile extends only through the 97th percentile.

*Source:* Author's tabulations of the March 1970, 1980, and 1994 Current Population Survey files.

behind this view is straightforward: very poorly paid unskilled workers overseas take away job opportunities and drive down the wage of unskilled American workers.

It is easy to see in theory how surging exports from developing countries could harm less-skilled U.S. workers in the trade-affected industries. To counter the competition from cheap unskilled labor abroad, American employers must reduce the wages, or make less intensive use, of unskilled labor if they wish to remain in business. Presumably, some employers who continue to rely heavily on unskilled workers will go bankrupt, others will move production overseas, others will adopt new technologies that permit them to dismiss some unskilled work-

ers, and still others will specialize in new products where relative wages and factor prices favor production in the United States. No matter which alternative they choose, the demand for less-skilled workers in the traded-goods industries will fall. Shrinking demand will reduce the relative wage of less-skilled workers in comparison with highly skilled workers.

But if trade is the main factor behind the growing woes of unskilled workers in the traded-goods industries, then firms that do not produce internationally traded goods and services should take advantage of the shrinking wage of less-skilled workers by hiring more of them. If, instead, they also begin to pare back use of unskilled labor, it must be something other than (or in addition to)

*Figure 2*

## Changes in Real Earnings, by Gender and Earnings Quintile, 1969–93

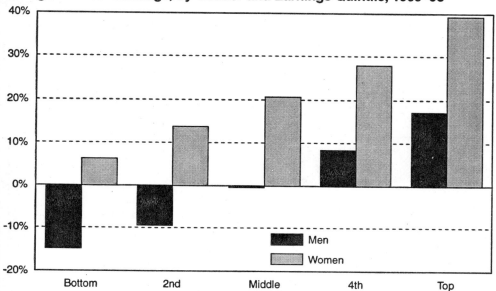

*Note:* Annual earnings of full-time, year-round wage and salary workers. Top quintile extends only through the 96th percentile for men and the 99th percentile for women.

*Source:* Author's tabulations of the March 1970, 1980, and 1993 Current Population Surveys.

trade that is lowering the demand for less-skilled workers.

Figure 3 helps show whether trade is behind the drop in relative demand for less-skilled labor. It compares wage inequality trends among male workers in two broad classes of U.S. industries— one (including manufacturing, mining, and agriculture) that is highly trade-affected and another (including construction, retail trade, personal services, and public administration) that is not trade-affected. (An excluded group of industries, including transportation, wholesale trade, finance, and insurance, falls in an intermediate category.) Earnings inequality is calculated as the ratio of annual earnings at the 90th percentile of the earnings distribution to earn-

ings at the 10th percentile. Male inequality is growing in both the most and the least trade-affected industries, and it is growing at the same rate— 47 percent between 1969 and 1993. Although wages are more equal among women in trade-affected industries than among women in the least-affected industries, wage inequality among women has grown faster in the nontrade industries since 1979—the very period in which U.S. trade problems and manufactured imports were concentrated. When the data for men and women are combined, the earnings ratio in the most trade-affected industries rose 29 percent between 1969 and 1993—exactly the same as the rise in inequality across all industries.

*Figure 3*

**Ratio of Earnings of Male Workers at 90th Percentile to Earnings at 10th Percentile, 1969–93**

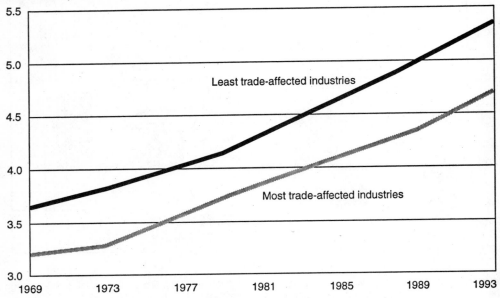

*Note:* Annual earnings of full-time, year-round wage and salary workers.
*Source:* Author's tabulations of selected Current Population Surveys.

The same pattern of relative earnings change is apparent in trends among workers with different levels of schooling. Educational pay premiums have risen since 1969 for every industry and for both sexes. But the premiums have not risen any faster in the industries most affected by trade than they have in other industries. For working men as a group, the premium for post-college education rose 36 percent between 1969 and 1993; for men in trade-affected industries, the premium rose 33 percent. And the gap in pay between high school dropouts and men with some college rose exactly as fast among men in trade-affected industries as it did among men as a whole. Women in the trade-affected industries had a somewhat larger rise in the post-college pay premium than women in other industries, but the difference is comparatively small.

Even though wage inequality and educational pay premiums moved in the same pattern across different industries, liberalized trade may still explain the pronounced shift toward greater inequality. In a competitive and efficient labor market, pay premiums for skill and education should eventually rise and fall together across industries, whatever the reason for the change in pay premiums.

But if the trade from newly industrializing countries in Asia and Latin America is placing special pressure on producers in trade-affected industries, we would expect these industries to shed low-wage workers *faster* than industries where com-

*Figure 4*

**Percentage of Full-time Equivalent Male Workers without a High School Diploma, 1969–93**

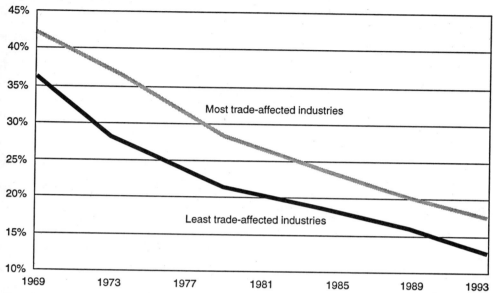

*Source:* Author's tabulations of selected Current Population Surveys.

petitive pressure comes exclusively from other domestic firms. To what extent was this the experience in the United States?

Between 1969 and 1993, trade-affected industries did indeed reduce the percentage of less educated workers on their payrolls (Figure 4). In 1969, 42 percent of male and 45 percent of female workers in trade-affected industries had no high school degree. By 1993, those figures had fallen to 18 percent for men, 17 percent for women. These trends certainly seem consistent with the view that liberal trade has deprived less-skilled workers of job opportunities in the traded-goods sector. But employment patterns in industries unaffected by trade moved in exactly the same direction. The percentage of male workers without a high school degree in the industries *least* affected by trade fell

from 36 percent in 1969 to 13 percent in 1993. If anything, industries unaffected by trade cut their use of low-skill workers even faster than trade-affected industries—a pattern that is extremely hard to square with the claim that foreign trade is the main factor behind soaring wage inequality.

**BESET ON ALL SIDES**

Over the past quarter century, the nation has seen a dramatic shift in the pattern of demand for workers with different levels of skill. Job opportunities for the less-skilled have shrunk, and relative wages for unskilled and semi-skilled workers have plunged. But these trends are not confined to the traded-goods sector. They are also apparent in industries, such as construction and retail trade, where international trade is a minor concern. International trade, it seems, has not been the decisive factor in the trend toward greater earnings inequality. Other developments have been at least as influential, if not more so.

Among economists, the leading explanation for increased wage inequality is changes in the technology of production. Such innovations as the personal computer or new forms of business organization have favored workers with greater skill and reduced the value of unskilled labor.

But other developments are also at work. Economic deregulation, new patterns of immigration into the United States, declining minimum wages, and the dwindling influence of labor unions have also contributed to the job woes of unskilled and semi-skilled workers. Liberal trade with the newly industrializing countries of the world has certainly played a part in worsening the job prospects of America's unskilled workers. But if we follow the advice of Ross Perot and Patrick Buchanan and erect a new wall of trade protection, we would do little to ease the plight of less-skilled workers. Too many other forces are conspiring to push their wages down.

# POSTSCRIPT

## Does Free Trade Make the Poor, Poorer?

Perhaps no single issue in this book will affect you more directly than this issue on income distribution. It is not that you will end up in the bottom 60 percent of the U.S. households that are trapped in the "stagnant backwaters of our economy." Quite the contrary. You are far more likely to be college graduates or soon-to-be college graduates and you will be the winners in any future economic "competitions."

In spite of this, you should be concerned. Unless this pattern is moderated, we will become a country of the "haves" and the "have nots." Many see the process well underway. The "haves" are increasingly becoming isolated in their exclusive communities and the "have nots" are increasingly concentrated in their deteriorating inner-city neighborhoods. The less movement that occurs between these two extremes, as the middle class disappears and the extremes are stretched farther and farther apart, the more distrust will grow and the seeds of social unrest sown.

The cause of this perverse distribution of income is unclear. Greider would have us return to the pre-Reagan days when the federal government was active in the American economy. For more on Greider's views, read his column that regularly appears in *Rolling Stone* or check out one of his recent books: *One World, Ready or Not: The Manic Logic of Global Competition* (Simon and Schuster, 1997); *Who Will Tell the People: The Betrayed of American Democracy* (Simon and Schuster, 1992); or *How the Federal Reserve Runs the Country* (Simon and Schuster, 1992). Greider is not alone in his views. Hines and Lang in their essay "The New Protectionism," *The Nation* (July 15 and 22, 1996) assert that "globalization unquestionably leads to lower wage economics." Jerry Mandur in "The Dark Side of Globalization," in the same issue of *The Nation*, tell us that "the only boats that will be lifted are those of the owners and managers of the process; the rest of us will be on the beach, facing a rising tide."

There is much written on the other side of this issue. Conservatives such as John O. McGinnis are horrified at the prospect of limited markets. See "Restraining Leviathan," *National Review* (March 11, 1996). For a more sophisticated reflection of Greider's thesis, refer to Norman S. Fieleke's "Is Global Competition Making the Poor Even Poorer?" *New England Economic Review* (November/December 1994). Finally, there is another strongly worded essay opposing government intervention, by James A. Dorn, entitled "Trade and Human Rights: The Case of China," *Cato Journal* (Spring/Summer 1996).

# ISSUE 17

## Does Global Warming Require Immediate Government Action?

**YES: Cynthia Pollock Shea,** from "Protecting Life on Earth: Steps to Save the Ozone Layer," *Worldwatch Paper 87* (1988)

**NO: Lester B. Lave,** from "The Greenhouse Effect: What Government Actions Are Needed?" *Journal of Policy Analysis and Management* (vol. 7, no. 3, 1988)

### ISSUE SUMMARY

**YES:** Cynthia Pollock Shea, a senior researcher with the Worldwatch Institute, pleads with governments and industries to initiate a "crash program" designed to halt emissions of chemicals such as chlorofluorocarbons, which deplete the ozone, before irreparable damage is done to world agriculture, marine life, and human health.

**NO:** Professor of economics Lester B. Lave warns against drastic solutions that could themselves be harmful or, at a minimum, "costly if the greenhouse consequences are more benign than predicted."

Few of us can forget the heat wave of the summer of 1988. Electric bills skyrocketed as air conditioners ran day and night. Bright green lawns turned yellow-brown. Lakes, streams, and reservoirs fell to critically low levels; car washing was discouraged, lawn sprinkling was banned, and toilets were bricked. Citizens and policymakers alike were concerned that the world was entering the long-predicted and much-feared period of global warming associated with the greenhouse effect.

As summer turned to fall, then–presidential candidate Bush promised vot_ ers that if he were elected, he would become the "environmental president." He would protect the environment from the advancing global warming— at least he would attempt to slow its progress. Once elected he joined other heads of state in a Paris environmental summit. This, in turn, led to the policy prescriptions that he introduced in a speech delivered at Georgetown University in early February 1990. Four broad policies were detailed in this speech:

1. *Increase the information base.* He proposed a sharp increase in U.S. expen ditures on studies focused on "global climate change."
2. *Redirect and increase expenditures on basic energy research and development from $16.4 billion to $17.5 billion.* This represented a modest 6.4 percent

increase in the Department of Energy's budget and some redistribution of funds from civilian applied research and development programs to grants for basic research.

3. *A phaseout of most chlorofluorocarbons.* In line with a 1987 international agreement, the Montreal Protocol, President Bush proposed a 50 percent cut in the production of these powerful greenhouse gases that attack the ozone layer.

4. *A "plant-a-tree" program.* The Bush administration proposed planting a billion trees each year at a cost of $170 million annually.

The question we must ask is whether or not these presidential initiatives are appropriate in light of the costs and benefits of public action to slow or reverse the progress of global warming. Once again we must turn to our marginal analysis to determine how aggressive public policy should be in slowing the progress of global warming. We can anticipate that alternative policies will have increasing marginal costs and decreasing marginal benefits as more ambitious programs are employed. Two views of these costs and benefits are provided in the following essays. Cynthia Pollock Shea warns that if decisive action is not taken immediately to protect the ozone layer, we will face serious health hazards, reduced crop yields, decreased fish populations, and industrial damage. Lester B. Lave, on the other hand, argues that there is too much uncertainty to rush forward with sweeping policy action. He preaches moderation.

Since the consequences of these policy decisions may be irreversible and not fully felt for many decades in the future, extreme care must be taken. Older generations may be totally immune from the consequences. It is the younger generations that will pay for the mistakes made in the early 1990s.

# YES

## Cynthia Pollock Shea

# PROTECTING LIFE ON EARTH:
# STEPS TO SAVE THE OZONE LAYER

When British scientists reported in 1985 that a hole in the ozone layer had been occurring over Antarctica each spring since 1979, the news came as a complete surprise. Although the theory that a group of widely used chemicals called chlorofluorocarbons (CFCs) would someday erode upper atmospheric ozone had been advanced in the mid-1970s, none of the models had predicted that the thinning would first be evident over the South Pole—or that it would be so severe.

Ozone, the three-atom form of oxygen, is the only gas in the atmosphere that limits the amount of harmful solar ultraviolet radiation reaching the earth. Most of it is found at altitudes of between 12 and 25 kilometers. Chemical reactions triggered by sunlight constantly replenish ozone above the tropics, and global air circulation transports some of it to the poles.

By the Antarctic spring of 1987, the average ozone concentration over the South Pole was down 50 percent. Although the depletion was alarming, many thought that the thinning was seasonal and unique to Antarctica. But an international group of more than 100 experts reported in March 1988 that the ozone layer around the globe was eroding much faster than models had predicted. Between 1969 and 1986, the average concentration of ozone in the stratosphere had fallen by approximately 2 percent.

As ozone diminishes, the earth receives more ultraviolet radiation, which promotes skin cancers and cataracts and depresses the human immune system. As more ultraviolet radiation penetrates the atmosphere, it will worsen these health effects, reduce crop yields and fish populations, damage some materials such as plastics, and increase smog. Compounds containing chlorine and bromine, which are released from industrial processes and products, are now widely accepted as the primary culprits in ozone depletion. Most of the chlorine comes from CFCs; the bromine originates from halons used in fire extinguishers.

Spurred to action by the ozone hole, 35 countries have signed an international agreement—the Montreal Protocol—aimed at halving most CFC emissions by 1998 and freezing halon emissions by 1992. But the agreement is so riddled with loopholes that its objectives will not be met. Furthermore, scientific findings subsequent to the negotiations reveal that even if the treaty's goals were met, significant further deterioration of the ozone layer would still occur.

New evidence that a global warming may be under way strengthens the need to further control and phase out CFC and halon emissions. With their strong heat-absorbing properties, CFCs and halons are an important contributor to the greenhouse effect. Currently available control technologies and stricter standards governing equipment operation and maintenance could reduce CFC and halon emissions by some 90 percent. But effective government policies and industry practices to limit and ultimately phase out chlorine and bromine emissions have yet to be formulated. Just as the effects of ozone depletion and climate change will be felt worldwide, a lasting remedy to these problems must also be global.

## THE OZONE DEPLETION PUZZLE

As a result of the efforts of many scientists, the pieces of the ozone depletion puzzle have gradually been falling into place. During the long, sunless Antarctic winter—from about March to August—air over the continent becomes isolated in a swirling polar vortex that causes temperatures to drop below -90 degrees Celsius. This is cold enough for the scarce water vapor in the dry upper atmosphere to freeze and form polar stratospheric clouds. Chemical reactions on the surface of the ice crystals convert chlorine from nonreactive forms such as hydrogen chloride and chlorine nitrate into molecules that are very sensitive to sunlight. Gaseous nitrogen oxides, ordinarily able to inactivate chlorine, are trans-

formed into frozen, and therefore nonreactive, nitric acid.

Spring sunlight releases the chlorine, starting a virulent ozone-destroying chain reaction that proceeds unimpeded for five or six weeks. Molecules of ozone are transformed into molecules of ordinary, two-atom oxygen. The chlorine emerges unscathed, ready to attack more ozone. Diminished ozone in the vortex means the atmosphere there absorbs less incoming solar radiation, thereby perpetuating lower temperatures and the vortex itself.

Paradoxically, the phenomenon of global warming encourages the process. Higher concentrations of greenhouse gases are thought to be responsible for an increase in the earth's surface temperature and a decrease in the temperature of the stratosphere. In addition, methane, one of the primary greenhouse gases, is a significant source of stratospheric water vapor. Colder temperatures and increased moisture both facilitate the formation of stratospheric clouds.

While many of the meteorological and chemical conditions conducive to ozone depletion are unique to Antarctica, ground-based research in Greenland in the winter of 1988 found elevated chlorine concentrations and depressed ozone levels over the Arctic as well. Although a strong vortex does not develop there and temperatures are not as low, polar stratospheric clouds do form.

The theories on how chlorine interacts on the surface of particles in polar stratospheric clouds are leading to worries that similar ozone-depleting reactions may occur around the globe. If chemicals such as sulfate aerosols from volcanoes and human-made sulfurs are capable of hosting the same catalytic reactions, global ozone depletion may accelerate even more rapidly than anticipated.

Consensus about the extent of ozone depletion and its causes strengthened with the release of the NASA Ozone Trends Panel report on March 15, 1988. Ozone losses were documented around the globe, not just at the poles. The blame was firmly placed on chlorofluorocarbons. The panel reported that between 30 and 64 degrees north latitude, where most of the world's people live, the total amount of ozone above any particular point had decreased by between 1.7 and 3 percent in the period from 1969 to 1986 (Table 1). The report further stated that while the problem was worst over Antarctica during the spring, "ozone appears to have decreased since 1979 by 5 percent or more at all latitudes south of 60 degrees south throughout the year." The hole alone covers approximately 10 percent of the Southern Hemisphere.

Within a matter of weeks the report's conclusions were widely accepted, and public debate on the issue began to build. Ozone depletion is occurring far more rapidly and in a different pattern than had been forecast. Projections of the amount and location of future ozone depletion are still highly uncertain. Although the fundamental mechanisms of ozone depletion are generally understood, the effect of cloud surface chemistry, the rate of various chemical reactions, and the specific chemical pathways are still in doubt. According to Sherwood Rowland, one of the first to sound a warning, policy decisions now and for at least another decade must be made without good quantitative guidelines of what the future holds.

Table 1

### Global Decline in Atmospheric Ozone, 1969–1986*

| Latitude | Year-round decrease (percent) | Winter decrease (percent) |
|---|---|---|
| 53–64° N | −2.3 | −6.2 |
| 40–53° N | −3.0 | −4.7 |
| 30–40° N | −1.7 | −2.3 |
| 19–30° N | −3.1 | n.a. |
| 0–19° N | −1.6 | n.a. |
| | | |
| 0–19° S | −2.1 | n.a. |
| 19–29° S | −2.6 | n.a. |
| 29–39° S | −2.7 | n.a. |
| 39–53° S | −4.9 | n.a. |
| 53–60° S | −10.6 | n.a. |
| 60–90° S | −5.0 or more | n.a. |

*Data for the area 30 to 64 degrees north of the equator are based on information gathered from satellites and ground stations from 1969 to 1986. Data for the area from 60 degrees south to the South Pole are based on information gathered from satellites and ground stations since 1979. All other information was compiled after November 1978 from satellite data alone.

Sources: U.S. National Aeronautics and Space Administration, Ozone Trends Panel; Cass Peterson, "Evidence of Ozone Depletion Found Over Big Urban Areas," *The Washington Post*, March 16, 1988.

## EFFECTS OF ULTRAVIOLET RADIATION

At present, ozone absorbs much of the ultraviolet light that the sun emits in wavelengths harmful to humans, animals, and plants. The most biologically damaging wavelengths are within the 290- to 320-nanometer band, referred to as UV-B. But according to uncertain projections from computer models, erosion of the ozone shield could result in 5 to 20 percent more ultraviolet radiation reaching populated areas within the next 40 years—most of it in the UV-B band.

In light of the findings of the NASA Ozone Trends Panel, the U.S. Environmental Protection Agency (EPA) damage projections cited in this section are conservative. Although the EPA ranges are based on current control strategies, they assume ozone depletion levels of 1.2 to 6.2 percent. Yet all areas of the globe have already suffered depletion beyond this lower bound.

Globally, skin cancer incidence among Caucasians is already on the rise, and it is expected to increase alarmingly in the presence of more UV-B. Some 600,000 new cases of squamous and basal cell carcinoma—the two most common but rarely fatal skin cancer types—are reported each year in the United States alone. Worldwide, the number of cases is at least three times as high. Each 1 percent drop in ozone is projected to result in 4 to 6 percent more cases of these types of skin cancer. The EPA estimates that ozone depletion will lead to an additional 31,000 to 126,000 cases of melanoma—a more deadly form of skin cancer—among U.S. whites born before 2075, resulting in an additional 7,000 to 30,000 fatalities.

Under the same EPA scenarios, from 555,000 to 2.8 million Americans born before 2075 will suffer from cataracts of the eyes who would not have otherwise. Victims will also be stricken earlier in life, making treatment more difficult.

Medical researchers also fear that UV-B depresses the human immune system, lowering the body's resistance to attacking micro-organisms, making it less able to fight the development of tumors, and rendering it more prone to infectious diseases. In developing countries, particularly those near the equator that are exposed to higher UV-B levels, parasitic infections could become more common. The response may even decrease the effectiveness of some inoculation programs, such as those for diphtheria and tuberculosis.

Terrestrial and aquatic ecosystems are also affected. Screenings of more than 200 plant species, most of them crops, found that 70 percent were sensitive to UV-B. Increased exposure to radiation may decrease photosynthesis, water-use efficiency, yield, and leaf area. Soybeans, a versatile and protein-rich crop, are particularly susceptible. One researcher at the University of Maryland discovered that a simulated ozone loss of 25 percent reduced the yield of one important soybean species by as much as 25 percent. He also found that plant sensitivity to UV-B increased as the phosphorus level in the soil increased, indicating that heavily fertilized agricultural areas may be the most vulnerable.

Aquatic ecosystems may be the most threatened of all. Phytoplankton, the one-celled microscopic organisms that engage in photosynthesis while drifting on the ocean's surface, are the backbone of the marine food web. Because they require sunlight, they cannot escape incoming ultraviolet radiation and continue to thrive. Yet if they remain at the water's surface, studies show that a 25 percent reduction in ozone would decrease their productivity by about 35 percent. A significant destruction of phytoplankton and its subsequent decomposition could even raise carbon dioxide levels, speeding the warming of the atmosphere.

Zooplankton and the larvae of several important fish species will be doubly strained: Their sole food supply, phytoplankton, will be scarcer. For some shellfish species, a 10 percent decrease in ozone could result in up to an 18 percent increase in the number of abnormal larvae. Commercial fish populations already threatened by overharvesting may have more difficulty rebuilding due to effects of increased UV-B. Some species will undoubtedly be more vulnerable to increased ultraviolet radiation than others, and the changes are likely to be dramatic. Ultimately, entire ecosystems may become more unstable and less flexible.

Increased UV-B levels also affect synthetic materials, especially plastics, which become brittle. Studies conducted for the EPA estimated that without added chemical stabilizers, the cumulative damage to just one polymer, polyvinyl chloride, could reach $4,700 million by 2075 in the United States alone.

Ironically, as more ultraviolet radiation reaches the ground, the photochemical process that creates smog will accelerate, increasing ground-level ozone. Studies show that ground-level ozone retards crop and tree growth, limits visibility, and impairs lung functions. Urban air quality, already poor in most areas of the world, will worsen. In addition, stratospheric ozone decline is predicted to increase tropospheric amounts of hydrogen peroxide, an acid rain precursor.

Despite the many uncertainties regarding the amount of future ozone depletion, rising UV-B levels, and their biological effects, it is clear that the risks to aquatic and terrestrial ecosystems and to human health are enormous. The central conclusion of the EPA studies is that "the benefits of limiting future CFC/halon use far outweigh the increased costs these regulations would impose on the economy."

## CHEMICAL WONDERS, ATMOSPHERIC VILLAINS

Chlorofluorocarbons are remarkable chemicals. They are neither toxic nor flammable at ground levels, as demonstrated by their discoverer, Thomas Midgley, Jr., in 1930, when he inhaled vapors from a beaker of clear liquid and then exhaled to extinguish a candle. A safe coolant that was inexpensive to produce was exactly what the refrigeration industry needed. E.I. du Pont de Nemours & Company marketed the compound under the trademark Freon. (In chemical shorthand, it is referred to as CFC-12). International production soared, rising from 545 tons in 1931 to 20,000 tons in 1945. Another use for the chemical, as a blowing agent in rigid insulation foams, was discovered in the late 1940s.

Over time, the versatility of the various CFCs seemed almost endless. CFC-11 and CFC-12 were first used as aerosol propellants during World War II in the fight against malaria. In the postwar economy, they were employed in aerosol products ranging from hairspray and deodorant to furniture polish. By the late 1950s, a combination of blowing agents CFC-11 and carbon dioxide was used to make softer furniture cushions, carpet padding, and automobile seats.

Many social and technological developments in recent decades were assisted by the availability of CFCs. Air conditioners made it possible to build and cool shopping malls, sports arenas, high-rise office buildings, and even automobiles. Artificial cooling brought comfort, business, and new residents to regions with warm climates. And healthier, more interesting diets are now available because food can be refrigerated in the production and distribution chain.

Even the computer revolution was aided by CFCs. As microchips and other components of electronic equipment became smaller and more sophisticated, the need to remove the smallest contami-

Table 2

## Global CFC Use, by Category, 1985

| Use | Share of total (percent) |
|---|---|
| Aerosols | 25 |
| Rigid-foam insulation | 19 |
| Solvents | 19 |
| Air conditioning | 12 |
| Refrigerants | 8 |
| Flexible foam | 7 |
| Other | 10 |

Source: Daniel F. Kohler and others, *Projections of Consumption of Products Using Chlorofluorocarbons in Developing Countries*, Rand N-2458-EPA, 1987.

Table 3

## Per Capita Use of CFC-11, CFC-12, and CFC-113, 1986 (Kilograms Per Capita)

| | CFC-11 | CFC-12 | CFC-113 | Total* |
|---|---|---|---|---|
| United States | .34 | .58 | .31 | 1.22 |
| Europe | .47 | .34 | .12 | .93 |
| Japan | .23 | .29 | .43 | .91 |

*Rows not completely additive due to trade.

Source: U.S. Environmental Protection Agency, *Regulatory Impact Analysis: Protection of Stratospheric Ozone*, 1987.

nants became critical. CFC-113 is used as a solvent to remove glue, grease, and soldering residues, leaving a clean, dry surface. CFC-113 is now the fastest growing member of the CFC family; worldwide production exceeds 160,000 tons per year.

An industry-sponsored group, the Alliance for Responsible CFC Policy, pegs the market value of CFCs produced in the United States at $750 million annually, the value of goods and services directly dependent on the chemicals at $28,000 million, and the end-use value of installed equipment and products at $135,000 million. Around the world, aerosols are still the largest user of CFCs, accounting for 25 percent of the total (Table 2). Rigid-foam and solvent applications, the fastest growing uses for CFCs, are tied for second place.

In 1987, global CFC production (excluding the People's Republic of China, the Soviet Union, and Eastern Europe) came close to 1 million tons. Combined production of CFC-11 and CFC-12 accounts for at least three-fourths of this total. Total per capita use of the three most common CFCs is highest in the United

States—at 1.22 kilograms—but Europe and Japan are not far behind (Table 3).

From 1931 through 1986, virtually all the CFC-11 and CFC-12 produced was sold to customers in the Northern Hemisphere. Since raw chemicals and products made with and containing CFCs were then exported, in part to developing countries, final usage was not quite as lopsided. Indeed, the Third World accounted for 16 percent of global CFC consumption in 1986 (Table 4). As populations, incomes, and the manufacturing base grow in developing countries, CFC use there is projected to rise.

Halons, which are used in fighting fires in both hand extinguishers and total-flooding systems for large enclosed areas, contain bromine, a more effective ozone destroyer than chlorine. Demand for halons, which were developed in the 1940s, quadrupled between 1973 and 1984 and is still growing at a rate of 15 percent annually.

Alarming though the latest ozone measurements are, they reflect only the responses to gases released through the early 1980s. Gases now rising through the lower atmosphere will take up to

*Table 4*

## CFC Consumption by Region, 1986

| Region | Share of total (percent) |
|---|---|
| United States | 29 |
| Other industrial countries* | 41 |
| Soviet Union, Eastern Europe | 14 |
| Other developing countries | 14 |
| People's Republic of China, India | 2 |

*The European Community accounts for more than half, followed by Japan, Canada, Australia, and others.

Source: "The Ozone Treaty: A Triumph for All," *Update from State*, May/June 1988.

eight years to reach the stratosphere. And an additional 2 million tons of substances containing chlorine and bromine are still on the ground, trapped in insulation foams, appliances, and fire-fighting equipment.

Chlorine concentrations in the upper atmosphere have grown from 0.6 to 2.7 parts per thousand million in the past 25 years. Under even the most optimistic regulatory scenarios, they are expected to triple by 2075. Bromine concentrations are projected to grow considerably faster. Without a complete and rapid phaseout of CFC and halon production, the real losers will be future generations who inherit an impoverished environment.

## REDUCING EMISSIONS

On September 16, 1987, after years of arduous and heated negotiation, the Montreal Protocol on Substances That Deplete the Ozone Layer was signed by 24 countries. Provisions of the agreement include a freeze on CFC production (at 1986 levels) by 1989, a 20 percent decrease in production by 1993, and another 30 percent cut by 1998. Halon production is subject to a freeze based on 1986 levels starting in 1992....

The means to achieve these reductions are left to the discretion of individual nations. Most signatory countries are responding with production limits on chemical manufacturers. Although this approach complies with treaty guidelines, it effectively ensures that only those willing to pay high prices will be able to continue using CFCs. It also places the onus of curbing emissions on the myriad industrial users of the chemicals and on the consumers of products that incorporate them. Moving quickly to protect the ozone layer calls for a different approach —one that targets the largest sources of the most ozone-depleting chemicals.

When concern about the ozone layer first emerged in the 1970s, some industrial country governments responded. Since 56 percent of combined CFC-11 and CFC-12 production in 1974 was used in aerosols, spray cans were an obvious target. Under strong public pressure, Canada, Norway, Sweden, and the United States banned CFC propellants in at least 90 percent of their aerosol products. The change brought economic as well as environmental benefits. Hydrocarbons, the replacement propellant, are less expensive than CFCs and saved the U.S. economy $165 million in 1983 alone. The European Community adopted a different approach. In 1980, the member countries agreed not to increase their capacity to produce these two CFCs and called for a 30 percent reduction in their use in aerosol propellants by 1982 (based on 1976 consumption figures).

Despite rapid growth, CFC-113 emissions may be some of the easiest and most economical to control. The chemical is only used to clean the final product and is not incorporated in it. Thus emissions are virtually immediate; three-fourths result from vapor losses, the remainder from waste disposal. A U.S. ban on land disposal of chlorinated solvents that took effect in November 1986, consideration of similar regulations elsewhere, the high cost of incinerating CFC-113 (because it contains toxic fluorine), and accelerating concern about ozone depletion have all created strong incentives for solvent recovery and recycling.

Since CFC-113 costs about twice as much as other CFCs, investments in recovery and recycling pay off more quickly. Recycling of CFC-113 is now practiced on-site at many large computer companies. Smaller electronics firms, for which in-house recycling is not economical, can sell their used solvents to commercial recyclers or the distributors of some chemical manufacturers.

Capturing CFC emissions from flexible-foam manufacturing can also be accomplished fairly quickly but requires investment in new ventilation systems. New suction systems coupled with carbon adsorption technologies are able to recover from 40 to 90 percent of the CFCs released.

Another area that offers significant savings, at a low cost, is improved design, operating, and maintenance standards for refrigeration and air conditioning equipment. Codes of practice to govern equipment handling are being drawn up by many major trade associations. Key among the recommendations are to require worker training, to limit maintenance and repair work to authorized personnel, to install leak detection systems, and to use smaller refrigerant charges. Another recommendation, to prohibit venting of the refrigerant directly to the atmosphere, requires the use of recovery and recycling technologies.

Careful study of the automobile air conditioning market in the United States, the largest user of CFC-12 in the country, has found that 34 percent of emissions can be traced to leakage, 48 percent occur during recharge and repair servicing, and the remainder happen through accidents, disposal, and manufacturing, in that order. Equipment with better seals and hoses would reduce emissions and result in less need for system maintenance.

Over the longer term, phasing out the use and emissions of CFCs will require the development of chemical substitutes that do not harm the ozone layer. The challenge is to find alternatives that perform the same function for a reasonable cost, that do not require major equipment modifications, that are nontoxic to workers and consumers, and that are environmentally benign. . . .

The time has come to ask if the functions performed by CFCs are really necessary and, if they are, whether they can be performed in new ways. If all known technical control measures were used, total CFC and halon emissions could be reduced by approximately 90 percent. Many of these control strategies are already cost-effective, and more will become so as regulations push up the price of ozone-depleting chemicals. The speed with which controls are introduced will determine the extent of ozone depletion in the years ahead and when healing of the ozone layer will begin.

## BEYOND MONTREAL

An international treaty to halve the production of a chemical feared responsible for destroying an invisible shield is unprecedented. But unfortunately, for several reasons, the Montreal Protocol will not save the ozone layer.

First, many inducements were offered to enhance the treaty's appeal to prospective signatories—extended deadlines for developing and centrally planned economies, allowances to accommodate industry restructuring, and loose definitions of the products that can legitimately be traded internationally. The cumulative effect of these loopholes means that, even with widespread participation, the protocol's goal of halving worldwide CFC use by 1998 will not be met.

Second, recent scientific findings show that more ozone depletion has already occurred than treaty negotiators assumed would happen in 100 years. A recent EPA report concluded that by 2075, even with 100 percent global participation in the protocol, chlorine concentrations in the atmosphere would triple. The agreement will not arrest depletion, merely slow its acceleration.

Third, several chemicals not regulated under the treaty are major threats to the ozone layer. Methyl chloroform and carbon tetrachloride together contributed 13 percent of total ozone-depleting chemical emissions in 1985. As the use of controlled chemicals diminishes, the contribution of these two uncontrolled compounds will grow.

The recognition that global warming may have already begun strengthens the case for further and more rapid reductions in CFC emissions. CFCs currently account for 15 to 20 percent of the greenhouse effect and absorb wavelengths of infrared radiation that other greenhouse gases allow to escape. Indeed, one molecule of the most widely used CFCs is as effective in trapping heat as 15,000 molecules of carbon dioxide, the most abundant greenhouse gas. In light of these findings, logic suggests a virtual phaseout of CFC and halon emissions by all countries as soon as possible. Releases of other chlorine and bromine-containing compounds not currently covered under the treaty also need to be controlled and in some cases halted.

The timing of the phaseout is crucial. Analysts at EPA examined the effects of a 100 percent CFC phaseout by 1990 and a 95 percent phaseout by 1998. Peak chlorine concentrations would differ by 0.8 parts per thousand million, some one-third of current levels. And under the slower phasedown, atmospheric cleansing would be prolonged considerably: Chlorine levels would remain higher than the peak associated with the accelerated schedule for at least 50 years.

As noted, it is technically feasible to reduce CFC and halon emissions by at least 90 percent. Sweden is the first country to move beyond endorsing a theoretical phaseout. In June 1988 the parliament, after extensive discussions with industry, passed legislation that includes specific deadlines for banning the use of CFCs in new products. Consumption is to be halved by 1991 and virtually eliminated by 1995. Environmental agencies in Britain, the United States, and the Federal Republic of Germany have endorsed emissions reductions of at least 85 percent. Chemical producers in these three countries account for over half the global output of controlled substances.

Levying a tax on newly manufactured CFCs and other ozone-depleting substances is one way governments can cut emissions and accelerate the adoption of alternative chemicals and technologies. If the tax increased in step with mandatory production cutbacks, it would eliminate windfall profits for producers, encourage recovery and recycling processes, stimulate use of new chemicals, and provide a source of funding for new technologies and for needed research. Encouraging investments in recycling networks, incinerators for rigid foams, and collection systems for chemicals that would otherwise be discarded could substantially trim emissions from existing products, from servicing operations, and from new production runs. Research on new refrigeration, air conditioning, and insulation processes is worthy of government support. Unfortunately, international funding for developing such technologies totals less than $5 million.

As mentioned in the text of the Montreal Protocol, results of this research, as well as new technologies and processes, need to be shared with developing countries. Ozone depletion and climate warming are undeniably global in scope. Not sharing information on the most recent developments ensures that environmentally damaging and outdated equipment will continue to be used for years to come, further eroding the Third World technology base. . . .

The scientific fundamentals of ozone depletion and climate change are known, and there is widespread agreement that both have already begun. Although current models of future change vary in their predictions, the evidence is clear enough to warrant an immediate response. Because valuable time was lost when governments and industries relaxed their regulatory and research efforts during the early 1980s, a crash program is now essential. Human health, food supplies, and the global climate all hinge on the support that can be garnered for putting an end to chlorine and bromine emissions.

# NO

**Lester B. Lave**

# THE GREENHOUSE EFFECT: WHAT GOVERNMENT ACTIONS ARE NEEDED?

Human beings are causing global-scale changes for the first time.... [A]rticles by Gordon MacDonald and Irving Mintzer document the "greenhouse" effect and give some indications of the environmental changes that will result. The possibility of such global changes rouses deep emotions in people: awe that humans have become so powerful, rage that we are tampering with the natural environment on a large scale, and fear that we might create an environment hostile to our progeny. Technologists tend to focus on the first emotion with the optimism that we can also find ways to head off or solve the problems. Environmentalists fix on the second, fearing that humans can only ruin nature. This article focuses on the third, asking what governmental or other social actions are possible and warranted. What should be done now and in the foreseeable future as a result of what is currently known about the atmospheric concentration of greenhouse gases, the resulting climate change, and the consequences for people?

## WHY DOES THE GREENHOUSE EFFECT RECEIVE SO MUCH ATTENTION?

Scientists have been giving great attention to the greenhouse effect for more than a decade, despite the vast qualitative and quantitative uncertainties. The public joins scientists in the concern that current activities could create a much less hospitable planet in the future. Congress has also directed its concern to these issues. Congress generally regards programs whose impact is more than three to ten years in the future as hopelessly long term; it seems bizarre that greenhouse effects, which are a century or so into the future, have received major Congressional attention....

Greenhouse effects have the attributes of being (1) global (in the sense that all regions are affected), (2) long term (in the sense that near-term effects are undetectable and important effects or people and their well being are perhaps a century in the future), (3) ethical (in the sense that they involve the preferences and well being of people who have not been born yet, as

From Lester B. Lave, "The Greenhouse Effect: What Government Actions Are Needed?" *Journal of Policy Analysis and Management*, vol. 7, no. 3 (1988). Copyright © 1988 by John Wiley & Sons, Inc. Reprinted by permission. Notes omitted.

well as plants, animals, and the environment more generally), (4) potentially catastrophic (in the sense that large changes in the environment might result, as well as massive loss of human life and property), and (5) contentious (in the sense that coming to decisions, translating these into agreements, and enforcing agreements would be difficult due to important "spillover" or external effects, uncertainty, the incentives for individual nations to cheat, the difficulty of detecting cheating, and the difficulty of enforcing agreements even after cheating is detected). In addition, many of the likely public investments such as attempts to substitute for carbon dioxide producing activities would be expensive and disruptive. In other words, this set of issues exercises almost all of the tools of policy analysis and poses deep problems to decision analysts. Below, I point out some particularly attractive research areas, such as behavioral reactions, crucial to formulating policy regarding greenhouse gases.

*Uncertainty.* A dominant question in formulating greenhouse policy is: What is the uncertainty concerning current statements about emissions, atmospheric accumulation, resulting climate changes, and resulting effects on the managed and unmanaged biospheres?...

The Department of Energy has put major resources over the past decade into understanding the carbon cycle, the current sources and sinks of carbon in the environment and the mechanisms that handle increasing carbon emissions into the environment. It is safe to say that the carbon cycle is not understood well, with uncertainty regarding perhaps 20% of total sources and sinks of carbon entering the environment. Controversies surround the importance of deforestation, the amount of carbon retained in the at-

mosphere, the amount being absorbed by the oceans, and the amount being taken up in plants.

The dynamics can be even more difficult to understand, because the oceans hold less carbon as they warm. Thus, there could be a destabilizing feedback of a warmer atmosphere leading to ocean warming, which induces release of carbon to the atmosphere. With the oceans becoming a net source rather than a sink, atmospheric concentrations would increase more rapidly, leading to rapidly increasing atmospheric temperatures, which induce ocean warming and carbon release. Is this scenario one that leads to disaster—or one where the ocean warming takes so long that fossil fuels are fully used and the increased carbon taken up by plants before the oceans warm enough to release appreciable carbon dioxide to the atmosphere? To what extent, and how quickly, would increased plant growth, due to a warmer climate, more rain, and higher atmospheric concentrations of carbon dioxide, absorb much more of the atmospheric carbon and slow or stop atmospheric warming?

The speed with which natural ecosystems can adapt to climate change is also a matter of concern. A large-scale climate change, comparable to a carbon dioxide doubling, has occurred over the last 18,000 years since the end of the last great ice age. While the temperature changes are comparable, the previous change occurred over 18,000 years while the change due to the greenhouse effect would occur over a century or so, perhaps one-hundred times faster. This rate of change could exceed the abilities of natural ecosystems to adapt. The amount of change is small, however, compared to what is currently experienced for the changes from day to night or season to season.

The issues related to carbon dioxide are much different from the issues related to other greenhouse gases. Neither of the two feedback mechanisms sketched above apply to CFC (chlorofluorucarbons) or methane. The Environmental Protection Agency estimates that about half of the atmospheric warming, after a century, would be attributed to gases other than carbon dioxide—an estimate that is markedly different from those of ten years ago. Much needs to be done to understand feedback mechanisms for the other greenhouse gases and to investigate possible interactions among the gases. For example, atmospheric warming is likely to increase the demand for air conditioning, which would lead to greater electricity use (resulting in increased carbon dioxide emissions) and to greater emissions of CFC from compressor leaks. The warming would also increase the demand for insulation, some of which would be foam insulation made with CFC, releasing much more of this gas to the atmosphere.

The current global circulation models are magnificent examples of technical virtuosity. The physical movements and energy fluxes of the atmosphere are described by partial differential equations that are too complicated to be solved explicitly. Thus the models depend upon expert judgment to decide what aspects of the problem should be treated explicitly within the model and how much attention each aspect should get. The current predictions of the consequences of doubling atmospheric carbon dioxide come mainly from models that treat the oceans as if little mixing occurred and there were no currents. The models also ignore many chemical reactions in the atmosphere.

Clearly, these models are "wrong" in the sense of being bad examples of reality. But the central question is whether failing to include these elements results in an error of 10% or whether the models could be wrong to the extent of predicting warming when these gases actually result in atmospheric cooling. . . .

As shown below, exploring the consequences of this warming requires detailed predictions or assumptions for each area about climate, storm patterns, and the length of the growing season. These predictions are little more than educated guesses. For the modelers, this uncertainty is a stimulus to do better. For the policy analyst, the uncertainty must be treated explicitly in deciding what actions are warranted now and in the future.

Even vast uncertainty need not preclude taking preventive action. Uncertainty should induce caution and prevent decision makers from rushing into actions and commitments, however. For example, precipitous action would have led to forbidding military and 747 flights in the stratosphere in the early 1970s. Then, in the late 1970s, precipitous action might have led to building aircraft to fly in the stratosphere as much as possible. Finally, today aircraft flights in the stratosphere are regarded as irrelevant to stratospheric ozone levels.

It is prudent to be concerned about potentially disastrous effects and to be willing to take some actions now, even given the uncertainty. For example, American regulators insisted on building strong containment vessels around civilian nuclear reactors, even though they regarded the chance of a mishap that would require the containment vessel as remote. The USSR regulators did not insist on such safeguards, with quite different results between the problems at Three Mile Island and the tragedy at Chernobyl.

While there is major uncertainty, the policy conclusions about CFC emissions are different today from those about carbon dioxide emissions, as I discuss below.

*Accounting for the Uncertainty.* The long-term effects of an increase in greenhouse gases are unknown and almost certainly unknowable. The physical changes, such as the gross increase in temperature for each latitude might be predicted, but it is unlikely that the dates of last frost and first freeze and detailed patterns of precipitation will be known for each growing area. Still more difficult to forecast is the adaptive behavior of individuals and governments. The accumulation of greenhouse gases could be enormously beneficial or catastrophic for humans. Or more likely, it would be beneficial at some times and places and catastrophic at others.

Preventive actions are akin to purchasing an insurance policy against potentially catastrophic greenhouse effects. Most people voluntarily purchase life insurance, even though the likelihood of dying in a particular year is very small. I suspect that people would be willing to pay a premium for a policy that would protect against an inhospitable Earth a century or so hence. But, the question is what type of insurance policy is most attractive and how much of a premium are people willing to pay.

Preventing all greenhouse effects is virtually impossible. If the climate changes and resultant human consequences are to be headed off, then heroic actions would be required immediately to reduce emissions of all the greenhouse gases throughout the world. For example, nuclear plants could be built to phase out all coal-burning plants within several decades. The decision to do that would be enormously expensive and disruptive. Such a decision would have to be agreed to in every country and enormous resources would be required to implement it. I would not support such a decision for many reasons.

Short of such heroic measures, are there any actions that might be taken now, even though uncertainty dominates the predictions of effects? Prudence would dictate that we should take actions that might prove highly beneficial, even if they are unlikely to be needed, if their cost is small. Proscribing coal use is not an attractive insurance policy, but we should give serious consideration to limiting the growth rate of coal use. The world discovered after 1974 that there was not a one-to-one coupling of energy use and economic activity. Since then, the developed countries have experienced a considerable increase in economic activity while most countries use little or no more energy than in 1974. Reducing the emissions of other greenhouse gases would be less difficult and disruptive than large reductions in coal use. In particular, it is not difficult or expensive to switch to CFC substitutes that are less damaging and to stop using these chemicals as foaming agents for plastics and in consumer products.

Thus, one of the best ways to deal with uncertainty is to look for robust actions, actions that would be beneficial in the worst case, not harmful in other cases, and not very costly to take. Emphasizing energy conservation is perhaps the best example of a prudent policy. Conservation makes sense without any appeal to greenhouse effects, given the deaths and disease associated with mining, transport, and air pollution from coal. The greenhouse effects simply underline what is already an obvious conclusion, but not one that is being pursued vigorously. So much energy could be saved by adjusting fully to current market prices that sufficient conservation might be attained merely by encouraging this adjustment. In particular, large subsidies to energy use distort resource-allocation decisions significantly.

A second example of an inexpensive insurance policy is switching to less damaging CFCs and using less of them.

Another approach is to develop a strategy of reevaluation at fixed intervals or as new information becomes available. Instead of viewing the current decision as the only opportunity to worry about greenhouse issues, one can attempt to clarify which particular outcomes would cause greatest concern. Then one could revisit the issues periodically to see if uncertainty has been resolved or at least substantially diminished.

## SOCIAL AND ECONOMIC CONSEQUENCES OF CLIMATE CHANGE

Announcement of an invention, such as a new drug, is generally greeted with public approval. Certainly there is recognition that innovations may bring undesired consequences, such as occurred with Thalidomide, and so premarket testing and technology assessment have been established and emphasized in many regulatory areas. An innovation seems to be defined in terms of the intent of the inventor to produce something that will make society better or at least to make him richer. On net, it is fair to say that such innovations are viewed positively, with the untoward consequences to be dealt with if they arise.

In contrast, an environmental change such as the greenhouse effect is viewed with horror. Such changes are generally not desired by anyone, but rather emerge as the unintended consequences of society's actions. Those who are horrified might admit that there are some changes that are likely to be beneficial, but they would still regard the overall effect as catastrophic. People tend to be more alarmed by large-scale, rapid environmental changes because the consequences would be important and uncontrollable.

Why are Americans such determined optimists about new technology and such determined pessimists about environmental changes? I suspect that much of the difference is explained by the good intent of the inventor versus the unintended nature of the environmental change. If so, this suggests that people have unwarranted faith in the good intentions of inventors, compared to the unintended changes from taking resources or using the environment as a garbage pail.

Deriving the social and economic consequences of climate change is more difficult than might appear. To be sure, if an area becomes so hot or dry that habitation is impossible, or if an area is under water, the consequences are evident. Thus, if sea level rose, the low-lying parts of Louisiana, Florida, Bangladesh, and the Netherlands would be drastically affected. The vast number of short-term effects are difficult to predict and evaluate. Furthermore, the long-term changes are likely to be less drastic (adjustment occurs to mitigate the difficulties, although this might take a long term for an ecosystem), and so the consequences will be even more difficult to infer.

In particular, a change in climate presents a challenge to farmers. If summers are hotter and drier in the corn belt, then a farmer growing corn in Illinois is going to experience crop failure more frequently, due both to droughts and to heat damage. As the climate changes, rare crop damage will give rise to occasional and then frequent damage. Will the Illinois farmer keep planting corn, surviving with the aid of ever-larger government subsidies? Or will he plant new crops that flourish under the hotter, drier climate?

Climate change also presents an opportunity. Sylvan Wittwer, a noted agronomist, observed that "... the present level of atmospheric carbon dioxide is suboptimal, and the oxygen level is supraoptimal, for photosynthesis and primary productivity in the great majority of plants." The increased atmospheric carbon dioxide concentrations would enhance growth and water-use efficiency, leading to more and faster growth. Charles Cooper remarks that a doubled atmospheric concentration of carbon dioxide "... is about as likely to increase global food, at least in the long run, as to decrease it. It is certain though, that some nations, regions, and people will gain and others will lose." A new climate regime with more precipitation and a longer growing season bodes well for agriculture—if we figure out what crops to plant and figure out generally how to tailor agriculture to the new climate regime, and how to deal with new pests.

The midcontinental drying, if it occurs, could mean the end of current agricultural practices in the midwest. This climate change might induce more irrigation, dry farming practices such as have been demonstrated in Israel, new cultivars, different crops, or even ceasing to cultivate this land. The increased rains might mean there was sufficient winter precipitation to provide water for summer irrigation; it would certainly mean that there was sufficient water elsewhere in the country to be transported to the midwest for irrigation. Large dams and canals might be required, but the technology for this is available. Certainly this water would be more expensive than that currently available, but there is no reason to be concerned about starvation or even large increases in food prices for the U.S. On net, food and fibers might be slightly more expensive or less expensive in the U.S. under the new climate, but the change is almost certain to be small compared to other economic changes.

For the U.S., there is no difficulty with finding the appropriate technology for breeding new crops that fit the climate, developing a less water-intensive agriculture, or for moving water for irrigation. The difficulty would be whether agronomists are given the right tasks, whether farmers give up their old crops and farming methods, and whether society can solve the myriad social problems associated with damming newly enlarged rivers and moving the water to where it is needed.

The "less managed" areas, including forests, grasslands, and marsh, might experience large changes and a system far from long-term equilibrium. These effects would be scarcely discernable in measured gross national product, but would be viewed as extremely important by many environmentalists.

Water projects and resources more generally might pose a greater problem. Large-scale water projects, such as dams and canals, are built to last for long periods. Once built, they are not easily changed. Thus, major climate change could lead to massive dams fed by tiny streams or dams completely inadequate for the rivers they are designed to control. Similarly, treaty obligations for the Colorado are inflexible and could pose major problems if there is less water flowing down the river. Similarly, the climate change would induce migration, both across areas in the U.S. and from other countries. The legal and illegal migration could pose major problems. Finally, Americans treasure certain natural resources, such as waterfalls. Climate change that stopped the flow at popular falls would be regarded seriously.

Commenting on energy modeling, Hans Landsberg wrote: "... all of us who have engaged in projecting into the more distant future take ourselves too seriously.... What is least considered is how many profound turns in the road one would have missed making 1980 projections in 1930! I am not contending that the emperor is naked, but we surely overdress him."

## REPRISE: WHY SO MUCH CONCERN FOR THE GREENHOUSE EFFECT?

It is the symbolic nature of the issues that has drawn attention to the greenhouse effect. Anyone who thinks he can see 100 years into the future is mad. If humans have now acquired the power to influence the global environment, then it is likely that we will cause changes even larger than those discussed here within the next century or so. Both the greenhouse effect and other global changes could be predominantly beneficial or harmful to humans and various aspects of the environment, although they are likely to be beneficial in some times and places and detrimental in others. But a large element of the public debate is almost scandalized at the notion

that the changes might be beneficial or made beneficial by individual actions and government policies.

The difficulty is public concern that global scale effects are now possible; we have had a "loss of innocence." In the past, if an individual ruined a plot of land, he could move on. If human actions caused major problems such as the erosion of the Dalmatian coast of Yugoslavia, there was always other inviting land. But, if the Earth is made inhospitable, there is no other inviting planet readily at hand.

I share this concern, but find it naive. Having acquired the power to influence the global environment, there is no way to relinquish it. No one intends to change the global environment by emitting greenhouse gases. Rather, the change is an inadvertent consequence of business as usual. The culprit is not a malevolent individual or rapacious company. Instead, it is the scope of human activities stemming from a large population, modern technology, and an unbelievable volume of economic activity. These culprits are not going to disappear, however much we might all wish that people did not have the ability to affect our basic environment. In this sense, the human race has lost its environmental innocence.

The symbolism is important because of the need to educate the public and government and gauge their reactions to this first global environmental issue. If people and governments show themselves to be concerned and willing to make sacrifices, the prospect for the future looks brighter. If instead, each individual and nation regards the effects as primarily due to others, and as someone else's problem, the increases in economic activity and advances in technology promise a future with major unintended changes in the Earth's environment.

Such changes could be dealt with by concerned global action to stop the stimulus and thus the response. Or they could be dealt with by individual and national actions to adapt to the consequences. However much I might wish for concerted action among countries, I do not believe this is likely to occur. There are too many disparate interests, too much to be gained by cheating, too much suspicion of the motives of others, and too little control over all the relevant actors. Thus, reluctantly, I conclude that mitigation through adaptation must be our focus.

For example, within the United States, federal environmental laws have been only a modest success in preventing environmental pollution. Ozone problems have worsened, ground water has become more polluted, and we seem no closer to dealing with radioactive and toxic wastes. When the scope of the problem becomes international, as with acid rain, there is little or no progress. Curtailing sulfur oxides emissions into the air necessarily involves promoting some interests while hurting others. Those who would be hurt are, not surprisingly, more skeptical about whether low levels of acid sulfate aerosols cause disease than those who believe that they would benefit. Getting agreement on action has proven essentially impossible for abating sulfur oxides. It is hard to imagine that a debate among 140 nations on the greenhouse effect would lead to an agreement to adopt binding programs to abate emissions.

A multinational agreement on controlling CFC has been negotiated in 1987. This is an extremely encouraging, and surprising development. There are many obstacles to effective implementation, however, from ratification by each country to best faith efforts to abide by the sense of the agreement.

## CONCLUSION

The greenhouse effect is the first of what are likely to be many long-term, global problems. Analysis is difficult because of the vast uncertainty about causes and effects, as well as of the consequences of the resulting climate change. The current uncertainties together with the costs of precipitous action imply that heroic actions to curtail the emissions of all greenhouse gases are not justified. Nonetheless, the current facts support a program of energy conservation, abatement, research, and periodic reconsideration that is far more activist than the current policy of the U.S. government.

I would like to thank Stephen Schneider and Jesse Ausubel for comments. This work was supported in part by the National Science Foundation (Grant No. SES-8715564).

# POSTSCRIPT

## Does Global Warming Require Immediate Government Action?

The harsh reality is that the environment is deteriorating. Very few, if any, physical scientists dispute this fact. What is disputed is the rate of decline in the global environment and whether or not citizens acting at the end of the twentieth century should try to alter this process. Do we have enough knowledge of the future to take dramatic steps today that will reshape the world of tomorrow? These are hard questions. If we answer incorrectly, our children and our children's children may curse us for our lack of resolve to solve environmental problems that were clear for all to see.

Shea and Lave both agree that there is a clear and present danger associated with ozone-depleting chemicals, such as chlorofluorocarbons, which are also the gases that contribute to the greenhouse effect. What they disagree upon is whether or not we know enough today to take immediate, decisive action. Do *you* know enough? If you do not, we suggest that you read further in this area. *It is your future that is being discussed here.*

A brief history of scientific concerns about the greenhouse effect, which stretches back to the late nineteenth century, is found in Jesse H. Ausubel, "Historical Note," in the National Research Council's *Changing Climate: Report of the Carbon Dioxide Assessment Committee* (National Academy Press, 1983). We should note that there are a number of other essays in *Changing Climate* that may be of interest to you. The Environmental Protection Agency (EPA) has published many studies you might want to examine. See, for example, the EPA's study entitled *The Potential Effects of Global Climate Change on the United States* (December 1989) or *Policy Options for Stabilizing Global Climate* (February 1989). An extensive analysis of the scientific, economic, and policy implications are also found in the *1990 Economic Report of the President.*

# ISSUE 18

## Should Pollution Be Put to the Market Test?

**YES: Alan S. Blinder,** from *Hard Heads, Soft Hearts* (Addison-Wesley, 1987)

**NO: David Moberg,** from "Environment and Markets: A Critique of 'Free Market' Claims," *Dissent* (Fall 1991)

### ISSUE SUMMARY

**YES:** Alan S. Blinder, a member of the Board of Governors of the Federal Reserve System, urges policymakers to use the energy of the market to solve America's environmental problems.

**NO:** Social critic David Moberg warns against giving businesses more flexibility and economic incentives, and he argues that clear public policy and direct government intervention will have the most positive effects on the environment.

Markets sometimes fail. That is, markets sometimes do not automatically yield optimum, economically efficient answers. This is because prices sometimes do not reflect the true social costs and benefits of consumption and production. The culprit here is the presence of externalities. Externalities are spillover effects that impact third parties who had no voice in the determination of an economic decision.

If, for example, my friend and coeditor Frank J. Bonello decided to "cut a few corners" to hold down the costs of his commercially produced banana cream pies, he might well create a *negative externality* for his neighbors. That is, if in the dark of night, Bonello slipped to the back of his property and dumped his banana skins, egg shells, and other waste products into the St. Joe River that borders his property, part of the cost of producing banana cream pies would be borne by those who live downstream from the Bonello residence. Since the full costs of production are not borne by Bonello, he can set a competitively attractive price and sell many more pies than his competitors, whom we assume must pay to have their waste products carted away.

If Bonello is not forced to internalize the negative externality associated with his production process, the price attached to his pies gives an improper market signal in regard to the true scarcity of resources. In brief, because Bonello's pies are cheaper than his competitors, demanders will flock to his doorstep to demand more and more of his pies, unknowingly causing him to dump more and more negative externalities on his neighbors downstream.

In this case, as in other cases of firms casting off negative externalities, the public sector may have to intervene and mandate that these externalities be internalized. This is not always an easy task, however. Two difficult questions must be answered: (1) Who caused the external effect? Was it only Bonello's banana cream pie production? and (2) Who bore the costs of the negative external, and what are their losses? These questions require detective work. We must not only identify the source of the pollution, but we must also identify the people who have been negatively affected by its presence and determine their "rights" in this situation. Once this has been achieved, the difficult task of evaluating and measuring the negative effects must be undertaken.

Even if this can be successfully negotiated, one last set of questions remains: What are the alternative methods that can be used to force firms to internalize their externalities, and which of these methods are socially acceptable and economically efficient? This is the subject of the debate that follows.

Alan S. Blinder warns against the limitations inherent in a market solution to this problem; however, he still supports harnessing the power of the market in order to rid the world of the harmful effects of pollution. David Moberg, on the other hand, takes care to note that private market solutions can be effective. But he maintains that, many times, old-fashioned regulation can be even more effective.

# YES

Alan S. Blinder

# CLEANING UP THE ENVIRONMENT: SOMETIMES CHEAPER IS BETTER

*We cannot give anyone the option of polluting for a fee.*

—Senator Edmund Muskie
(in Congress, 1971)

In the 1960s, satirist Tom Lehrer wrote a hilarious song warning visitors to American cities not to drink the water or breathe the air. Now, after the passage of more than two decades and the expenditure of hundreds of billions of dollars, such warnings are less appropriate—at least on most days! Although the data base on which their estimates rest is shaky, the Environmental Protection Agency (EPA) estimates that the volume of particulate matter suspended in the air (things like smoke and dust particles) fell by half between 1973 and 1983. During the same decade, the volume of sulfur dioxide emissions declined 27 percent and lead emissions declined a stunning 77 percent. Estimated concentrations of other air pollutants also declined. Though we still have some way to go, there is good reason to believe that our air is cleaner and more healthful than it was in the early 1970s. While the evidence for improved average water quality is less clear (pardon the pun), there have at least been spectacular successes in certain rivers and lakes.

All this progress would seem to be cause for celebration. But economists are frowning—and not because they do not prize cleaner air and water, but rather because our current policies make environmental protection far too costly. America can achieve its present levels of air and water quality at far lower cost, economists insist. The nation is, in effect, shopping for cleaner air and water in a high-priced store when a discount house is just around the corner. Being natural cheapskates, economists find this extravagance disconcerting. Besides, if we shopped in the discount store, we would probably buy a higher-quality environment than we do now....

## IS POLLUTION AN ECONOMIC PROBLEM?

.. Nothing in this discussion ... implies that the appropriate level of environmental quality is a matter for the free market to determine. On the contrary, the market mechanism is ill suited to the task; if left to its own devices, it will certainly produce excessive environmental degradation. Why? Because users of clean air and water, unlike users of oil and steel, are not normally made to pay for the product.

Consider a power plant that uses coal, labor, and other inputs to produce electricity. It buys all these items on markets, paying market prices. But the plant also spews soot, sulfur dioxide, and a variety of other undesirables into the air. In a real sense, it "uses up" clean air—one of those economic goods which people enjoy—without paying a penny. Naturally, such a plant will be sparing in its use of coal and labor, for which it pays, but extravagant in its use of clean air, which is offered for free.

That, in a nutshell, is why the market fails to safeguard the environment. When items of great value, like clean air and water, are offered free of charge it is unsurprising that they are overused, leaving society with a dirtier and less healthful environment than it should have.

The analysis of why the market fails suggests the remedy that economists have advocated for decades: charge polluters for the value of the clean air or water they now take for free. That will succeed where the market fails because an appropriate fee or tax per unit of emissions will, in effect, put the right price tag on clean air and water—just as the market now puts the right price tag on oil and steel. Once our precious air and water resources are priced correctly, polluters will husband them as carefully as they now husband coal, labor, cement, and steel. Pollution will decline. The environment will become cleaner and more healthful. . . .

## The Efficiency Argument

It is now time to explain why economists insist that emissions fees can clean up the environment at lower cost than mandatory quantitative controls. The secret is the market's unique ability to accommodate individual differences—in this case, differences among polluters.

Suppose society decides that emissions of sulfur dioxide must decline by 20 percent. One obvious approach is to mandate that every source of sulfur dioxide reduce its emissions by 20 percent. Another option is to levy a fee on discharges that is large enough to reduce emissions by 20 percent. The former is the way our current environmental regulations are often written. The latter is the economist's preferred approach. Both reduce pollution to the same level, but the fee system gets there more cheaply. Why? Because a system of fees assigns most of the job to firms that can reduce emissions easily and cheaply and little to firms that find it onerous and expensive to reduce their emissions.

Let me illustrate how this approach works with a real example. A study in St. Louis found that it cost only $4 for one paper-products factory to cut particulate emissions from its boiler by a ton, but it cost $600 to do the same job at a brewery. If the city fathers instructed both the paper plant and the brewery to cut emissions by the same amount, pollution abatement costs would be low at the paper factory but astronomical at the brewery. Imposing a uniform emissions tax is a more cost-conscious strategy. Suppose a $100/ton tax is announced. The paper company will see an opportunity to save $100 in taxes by spending $4 on cleanup, for a $96 net profit. Similarly, any other firm whose pollution-abatement costs are less than $100 per ton will find it profitable to cut emissions. But firms like the brewery, where pollution-abatement costs exceed $100 per ton, will prefer to continue polluting and paying the tax. Thus the profit motive will automatically assign the task of pollution abatement to the low-cost firms—something no regulators can do.

Mandatory proportional reductions have the seductive appearance of "fairness" and so are frequently adopted. But they provide no incentive to minimize the social costs of environmental clean-up. In fact, when the heavy political hand requires equal percentage reductions by every firm (or perhaps from every smokestack), it pretty much guarantees that the social clean-up will be far more costly than it need be. In the previous example, a one-ton reduction in annual emissions by both the paper factory and the brewery would cost $604 per year. But the same two-ton annual pollution abatement would cost only $8 if the paper factory did the whole job. Only by lucky accident will equiproportionate reductions in discharges be efficient.

Studies that I will cite later... suggest that market-oriented approaches to pollution control can reduce abatement costs by 90 percent in some cases. Why, economists ask, is it more virtuous to make pollution reduction hurt more? They have yet to hear a satisfactory answer and suspect there is none. On the contrary, virtue and efficiency are probably in harmony here. If cleaning up our air and water is made cheaper, it is reasonable to suppose that society will buy more clean-up. We can have a purer environment and pay less, too. The hardheaded economist's crass means may be the surest route to the soft-hearted environmentalist's lofty ends.

## The Enforcement Argument

Some critics of emissions fees argue that a system of fees would be hard to enforce. In some cases, they are correct. We obviously cannot use effluent charges to reduce concentrations of the unsightly pollutant glop if engineers have yet to devise an effective and dependable devise for measuring how much glop firms are spewing out. If we think glop is harmful, but are unable to monitor it, our only alternative may be to require firms to switch to "cleaner" technologies. Similarly, emissions charges cannot be levied on pollutants that seep unseen —and unmeasured—into groundwater rather than spill out of a pipe.

In many cases, however, those who argue that emissions fees are harder to enforce than direct controls are deceiving themselves. If you cannot measure emissions, you cannot charge a fee, to be sure. But neither can you enforce mandatory standards; you can only delude yourself into thinking you are enforcing them. To a significant extent, that is precisely what the EPA does now. Federal antipollution regulations are poorly policed; the EPA often declares firms in compliance based on nothing more than the firms' self-reporting of their own behavior. When checks are made, noncompliance is frequently uncovered. If emissions can be measured accurately enough to enforce a system of quantitative controls, we need only take more frequent measurements to run a system of pollution fees.

Besides, either permits or taxes are much easier to administer than detailed regulations. Under a system of marketable permits, the government need only conduct periodic auctions. Under a system of emissions taxes, the enforcement mechanism is the relentless and anonymous tax collector who basically reads your meter like a gas or electric company. No fuss, no muss, no bother—and no need for a big bureaucracy. Just a bill. The only way to escape the pollution tax is to exploit the glaring loophole that the government deliberately provides: reduce your emissions.

Contrast this situation with the difficulties of enforcing the cumbersome command-and-control system we now operate. First, complicated statutes must be passed; and polluting industries will use their considerable political muscle in state legislatures and in Congress to fight for weaker laws. Next, the regulatory agencies must write detailed regulations defining precise standards and often prescribing the "best available technology" to use in reducing emissions. Here again industry will do battle, arguing for looser interpretations of the statutes and often turning the regulations to their own advantage. They are helped in this effort by the sheer magnitude of the information-processing task that the law foists upon the EPA and state agencies, a task that quickly outstrips the capacities of their small staffs.

Once detailed regulations are promulgated, the real problems begin. State and federal agencies with limited budgets must enforce these regulations on thousands, if not millions, of sources of pollution. The task is overwhelming. As one critic of the system put it, each polluter argues:

(1) he is in compliance with the regulation; (2) if not, it is because the regulation is unreasonable as a general rule; (3) if not, then the regulation is unreasonable in this specific case; (4) if not, then it is up to the regulatory agency to tell him how to comply; (5) if forced to take the steps recommended by the agency, he cannot be held responsible for the results; and (6) he needs more time. . . .

**Other Reasons to Favor Emissions Fees**
Yet other factors argue for market-based approaches to pollution reduction.

One obvious point is that a system of mandatory standards, or one in which a particular technology is prescribed by law, gives a firm that is in compliance with the law no incentive to curtail its emissions any further. If the law says that the firm can emit up to 500 tons of glop per year, it has no reason to spend a penny to reduce its discharges to 499 tons. By contrast, a firm that must pay $100 per ton per year to emit glop can save money by reducing its annual discharges as long as its pollution-abatement costs are less than $100 per ton. The financial incentive to reduce pollution remains.

A second, and possibly very important, virtue of pollution fees is that they create incentives for firms to devise or purchase innovative ways to reduce emissions. Under a system of effluent fees, businesses gain if they can find cheaper ways to control emissions because their savings depend on their pollution abatement, not on how they achieve it. Current regulations, by contrast, often dictate the technology. Firms are expected to obey the regulators, not to search for creative ways to reduce pollution at lower cost.

For this and other reasons, our current system of regulations is unnecessarily adversarial. Businesses feel the government is out to harass them—and they act accordingly. Environmental protection agencies lock horns with industry in the courts. The whole enterprise takes on the atmosphere of a bullfight rather than that of a joint venture. A market-based approach, which made clear that the government wanted to minimize the costs it imposed on business, would naturally create a more cooperative spirit. That cannot be bad.

Finally, the appearance of fairness when regulations take the form of uniform percentage reductions in emissions, as they frequently do, is illusory. Suppose Clean Jeans, Inc. has already spent a considerable sum to reduce the amount of muck it spews into the Stench River. Dirty Jeans, Inc., just downriver, has not spent a cent and emits twice as much. Now a law is passed requiring every firm along the Stench to reduce its emissions by 50 percent. That has the appearance of equity but not the substance. For Dirty Jeans, the regulation may be a minor nuisance. To comply, it need only do what Clean Jeans is already doing voluntarily. But the edict may prove onerous to Clean Jeans, which has already exploited all the cheap ways to cut emissions. In this instance, not only is virtue not its own reward—it actually brings a penalty! Such anomalies cannot arise under a system of marketable pollution permits. Clean Jeans would always have to buy fewer permits than Dirty Jeans....

## OBJECTIONS TO "LICENSES TO POLLUTE"

Despite the many powerful arguments in favor of effluent taxes or marketable emissions permits, many people have an instinctively negative reaction to the whole idea. Some environmentalists, in particular, rebel at economists' advocacy of market-based approaches to pollution control—which they label "licenses to pollute," a term not meant to sound complimentary. Former Senator Muskie's dictum, quoted at the beginning of this chapter, is an example. The question is: Are the objections to "licenses to pollute" based on coherent arguments that should sway policy, or are they knee-jerk reactions best suited to T-shirts?* My own view is that there is little of the former and much of the latter. Let me explain.

Some of the invective heaped upon the idea of selling the privilege to pollute stems from an ideologically based distrust of markets. Someone who does not think the market a particularly desirable way to organize the production of automobiles, shirts, and soybeans is unlikely to trust the market to protect the environment. As one congressional staff aide put it: "The philosophical assumption that proponents of [emissions] charges make is that there is a free-market system that responds to ... relative costs.... I reject that assumption." This remarkably fatuous statement ignores mountains of evidence accumulated over centuries. Fortunately, it is a minority view in America. Were it the majority view, our economic problems would be too severe to leave much time for worry about pollution.

Some of the criticisms of pollution fees are based on ignorance of the arguments or elementary errors in logic. As mentioned earlier, few opponents of market-based approaches can even explain why economists insist that emissions fees will get the job done more cheaply.

One commonly heard objection is that a rich corporation confronted with a pollution tax will pay the tax rather than reduce its pollution. That belief shows an astonishing lack of respect for avarice. Sure, an obstinate but profitable company *could* pay the fees rather

---

*[Earlier in his book, Blinder warns his readers about simplistic answers to complex questions. He concludes that "if it fits on a T-shirt, it is almost certainly wrong."—Eds.]

than reduce emissions. But it would do that only if the marginal costs of pollution abatement exceed the fee. Otherwise, its obduracy reduces its profits. Most corporate executives faced with a pollution tax will improve their bottom lines by cutting their emissions, not by flouting the government's intent. To be sure, it is self-interest, not the public interest, that motivates the companies to clean up their acts. But that's exactly the idea behind pollution fees....

One final point should lay the moral issue to rest. Mandatory quantitative standards for emissions are also licenses to pollute—just licenses of a strange sort. They give away, with neither financial charge nor moral condemnation, the right to spew a specified amount of pollution into the air or water. Then they absolutely prohibit any further emissions. Why is such a license morally superior to a uniform tax penalty on all pollution? Why is a business virtuous if it emits 500 tons of glop per year but sinful if it emits 501? Economists make no claim to be arbiters of public morality. But I doubt that these questions have satisfactory answers.

The choice between direct controls and effluent fees, then, is not a moral issue. It is an efficiency issue. About that, economists know a thing or two.

Having made my pitch, I must confess that there are circumstances under which market-based solutions are inappropriate and quantitative standards are better. One obvious instance is the case of a deadly poison. If the socially desirable level of a toxin is zero, there is no point in imposing an emission fee. An outright ban makes more sense.

Another case is a sudden health emergency. When, for example, a summertime air inversion raises air pollution in Los Angeles or New York to hazardous levels, it makes perfect sense for the mayors of those cities to place legal limits on driving, on industrial discharges, or on both. There is simply no time to install a system of pollution permits.

A final obvious case is when no adequate monitoring device exists, as in the case of runoff from soil pollution. Then a system of emissions fees is out of the question. But so also is a system of direct quantitative controls on emissions. The only viable way to control such pollution may be to mandate that cleaner technologies be used.

But each of these is a minor, and well recognized, exception to an overwhelming presumption in the opposite direction. No sane person has ever proposed selling permits to spill arsenic into water supplies. None has suggested that the mayor of New York set the effluent tax on carbon monoxide anew after hearing the weather forecast each morning. And no one has insisted that we must meter what cannot be measured. Each of these objections is a debater's point, not a serious challenge to the basic case for market-oriented approaches to environmental protection....

## RAYS OF HOPE: EMISSIONS TRADING AND BUBBLES

There are signs, however, that environmental policy may be changing for the better. The EPA seems to be drifting slowly, and not always surely, away from technology-driven direct controls toward more market-oriented approaches. But not because the agency has been convinced by the logic of economists' arguments. Rather, it was driven into a corner by the inexorable illogic of its own procedures. Necessity proved to be the midwife of common sense.

The story begins in the 1970s, when it became apparent that many regions of the country could not meet the air quality standards prescribed by the Clean Air Act. Under the law, the prospective penalty for violating of the standards was Draconian: no new sources of pollution would be permitted in these regions and existing sources would not be allowed to increase their emissions, implying a virtual halt to local economic growth. The EPA avoided the impending clash between the economy and the environment by creating its "emissions-offsets" program in 1976. Under the new rules, companies were allowed to create new sources of pollution in areas with substandard air quality as long as they reduced their pollution elsewhere by greater amounts. Thus was emissions trading born.

The next important step was invention of the "bubble" concept in 1979. Under this concept, all sources of pollution from a single plant or firm are imagined to be encased in a mythical bubble. The EPA then tells the company that it cares only about total emissions into the bubble. How these emissions are parceled out among the many sources of pollution under the bubble is no concern of the EPA. But it is vital to the firm, which can save money by cutting emissions in the least costly way. A striking example occurred in 1981 when a DuPont plant in New Jersey was ordered to reduce its emissions from 119 sources by 85 percent. Operating under a state bubble program, company engineers proposed instead that emissions from seven large stacks be reduced by 99 percent. The result? Pollution reduction exceeded the state's requirement by 2,300 tons per year

and DuPont saved $12 million in capital costs and $3 million per year in operating costs.

Partly because it was hampered by the courts, the bubble concept was little used at first. But bubbles have been growing rapidly since a crucial 1984 judicial decision. By October 1984, about seventy-five bubbles had been approved by the EPA and state authorities and hundreds more were under review or in various stages of development. The EPA estimated the cost savings from all these bubbles to be about $800 million per year. That may seem a small sum compared to the more than $70 billion we now spend on environmental protection. But remember that the whole program was still in the experimental stage, and these bubbles covered only a tiny fraction of the thousands of industrial plants in the United States.

The bubble program was made permanent only when EPA pronounced the experiment a success and issued final guidelines in November 1986. Economists greeted this announcement with joy. Environmentalist David Doniger ... complained that, "The bubble concept is one of the most destructive impediments to the cleanup of unhealthy air." By now, many more bubbles have been approved or are in the works. Time will tell who was right.

The final step in the logical progression toward the economist's approach would be to make these "licenses to pollute" fully marketable so that firms best able to reduce emissions could sell their excess abatement to firms for which pollution abatement is too expensive. Little trading has taken place to date, though the EPA's November 1986 guidelines may encourage it. But at least one innovative state program is worth mentioning.

The state of Wisconsin found itself unable to achieve EPA-mandated levels of water quality along the polluted Fox and Wisconsin Rivers, even when it employed the prescribed technology. A team of engineers and economists then devised a sophisticated system of transferable discharge permits. Firms were issued an initial allocation of pollution permits (at no charge), based on historical levels of discharges. In total, these permits allow no more pollution than is consistent with EPA standards for water quality. But firms are allowed to trade pollution permits freely in the open market. Thus, in stark contrast to the standard regulatory approach, the Wisconsin system lets the firms along the river—not the regulators—decide how to reduce discharges. Little emissions trading has taken place to date because the entire scheme has been tied up in litigation. But one study estimated that pollution-control costs might eventually fall by as much as 80 percent compared to the alternative of ordering all firms along the river to reduce their discharges by a uniform percentage.

The state of Wisconsin thus came to the conclusion that economists have maintained all along: that applying a little economic horse sense makes it possible to clean up polluted rivers and reduce costs at the same time—a good bargain. That same bargain is available to the nation for the asking....

## A HARD-HEADED, SOFT-HEARTED ENVIRONMENTAL POLICY

Economists who specialize in environmental policy must occasionally harbor self-doubts. They find themselves lined up almost unanimously in favor of market-based approaches to pollution control with seemingly everyone else lined up on the other side. Are economists crazy or is everyone else wrong?

... I have argued the seemingly implausible proposition that environmental economists are right and everyone else really is wrong. I have tried to convey a sense of the frustration economists feel when they see obviously superior policies routinely spurned. By replacing our current command-and-control system with either marketable pollution permits or taxes on emissions, our environment can be made cleaner while the burden on industry is reduced. That is about as close to a free lunch as we are likely to encounter. And yet economists' recommendations are overwhelmed by an unholy alliance of ignorance, ideology, and self-interest.

This is a familiar story. The one novel aspect in the sphere of environmental policy is that the usual heavy hitter of this triumvirate—self-interest—is less powerful here than in many other contexts. To be sure, self-interested business lobbies oppose pollution fees. But, as I pointed out, they can be bought off by allowing some pollution free of charge. Doing so may outrage environmental purists, but it is precisely what we do now.

It is the possibility of finessing vested financial interests that holds out the hope that good environmental policy might one day drive out the bad. For we need only overcome ignorance and ideology, not avarice.

Ignorance is normally beaten by knowledge. Few Americans now realize that practical reforms of our environmental policies can reduce the national clean-up bill from more than $70 billion per year to less than $50 billion, and probably to much less. Even fewer understand the reasons why. If the case for market-based policies were better known, more and more people might ask the obvious question: Why is it better to pay more for something we can get for less? Environmental policy may be one area where William Blake's optimistic dictum —"Truth can never be told so as to be understood and not believed"—is germane.

Ideology is less easily rooted out, for it rarely succumbs to rational argument. Some environmentalists support the economist's case. Others understand it well and yet oppose it for what they perceive as moral reasons. I have argued at length that here, as elsewhere, thinking with the heart is less effective than thinking with the head; that the economist's case does not occupy the moral low ground; and that the environment is likely to be cleaner if we offer society clean-up at more reasonable cost. As more environmentalists come to realize that T-shirt slogans are retarding, not hastening, progress toward their goals, their objections may melt away.

The economist's approach to environmental protection is no panacea. It requires an investment in monitoring equipment that society has not yet made. It cannot work in cases where the sources of pollution are not readily identifiable, such as seepage into groundwater. And it will remain an imperfect antidote for environmental hazards until we know a great deal more than we do now about the diffusion of pollutants and the harm they cause.

But perfection is hardly the appropriate standard. As things stand now, our environmental policy may be a bigger mess than our environment. Market-based approaches that join the hard head of the accountant to the soft heart of the environmentalist offer the prospect of genuine improvement: more clean-up for less money. It is an offer society should not refuse.

# NO

David Moberg

# ENVIRONMENT AND MARKETS: A CRITIQUE OF "FREE MARKET" CLAIMS

The soot-darkened skies and fouled waters of Eastern Europe have given apologists for laissez-faire capitalism a new rallying cry: the "free market," far from being nature's enemy, is the environment's savior.

Some environmentalists have argued that there is no fundamental conflict between environmental responsibility and "free market" economics. Ecology, they contend, is ultimately sound, profitable business and environmental regulation must employ market forces if it is to succeed. They advocate giving business more flexibility and incentives, such as the right to buy and sell pollution rights, to increase efficiency and innovation so as to meet environmental goals.

Other environmentalists, however, continue to share a skepticism, with roots in both conservative and leftist traditions, about the compatibility of the market and the environment. This camp is also dissatisfied with the results of the first two decades of environmental regulation. Its advocates want a more aggressive democratic voice in what are usually private decisions. Ecological principles have become the basis for alternative models to capitalist markets, conflicting with or complementing the longstanding social class critiques. Ecologists have also opened another front criticizing not just the adequacy of market mechanisms but also market society in general and its exaltation of individual acquisitiveness and unbridled growth of commodity production.

All human societies have been shaped by interaction with nature, from the nomadism of hunters to the settled cultures of rich ecological niches, such as our own Northwest Coast or the slash-and-burn agriculture of tropical forests. Although earlier cultures undermined themselves by radically altering environments, stripping forests from the hills of Greece or raising the salinity of irrigated Mesopotamian soil, the worst depredation of the environment has come since the rise of capitalism. Now there is the prospect that human society has such an unsustainable relation with nature that both the future of humanity and the fate of thousands of other creatures is at stake.

From David Moberg, "Environment and Markets: A Critique of 'Free Market' Claims," *Dissent* (Fall 1991). Copyright © 1991 by David Moberg. Reprinted by permission.

But has capitalism itself been the cause of environmental damage or is the root problem industrial technologies or a growing population that consumes more and more goods?

Although the rapid growth of both population and global consumption magnifies every environmental impact, there are huge differences in environmental effects among nations, even the industrialized ones. The worst environmental insults are a result of modern industry, but not all industries degrade the environment equally. The nature of society, not just its size or technology, is largely responsible for the crisis in nature.

Obviously, the private market damages the natural environment because pollution is external to the balance sheets of private business. A factory owner doesn't pay to flush waste down the river or into the air; the costs are borne by nature as well as other people who share the environment. On the other hand, if a farmer preserves a marsh that cleans the stream's water, nourishes fish and wildlife, and prevents floods, he is paid nothing for those services. But if he sells it to be filled in for a shopping center, he will make money, and our accounting system evaluates this as economic growth, with no deductions for this loss of the wetland's natural functions. Likewise, nobody pays for the Amazon forest serving as "the lungs of the world" or preserving its diverse life forms for the future. So, the market doesn't adequately account for either negative or positive externalities.

If an ingenious entrepreneur devises a pollution-free production process that costs more than her competitor's, she will probably lose the market race: in most cases, nobody—except for a few generous souls—will pay the tab for her contribution to the common welfare. Now it is possible to level the playing field with taxes, fees, or penalties for the polluter, but it is difficult to assess the price of damage to the environment, especially if it is not a localized toxic spill but a global problem, like the greenhouse effect. Litigation over Exxon's Alaska oil spill or over compensation to the victims of Union Carbide's Bhopal disaster suggests the ethically and economically knotty problems.

## WHO DETERMINES THE LOSSES?

There are similar problems if more direct environmental regulations are subjected to cost-benefit analysis: how much is a human life worth? Some economists argue that it's the person's likely future lifetime earnings. That makes an Indian peasant pretty expendable compared to a Connecticut executive. Such cost-benefit analyses illegitimately import values of the marketplace to answer questions that arise because of fundamental flaws in that same market system.

How much is a sea otter worth?, *Business Week* asked. Surveying people about how much the animals are worth to them or measuring lost income if sea otters disappeared may keep a few economists employed, but it does not answer the question. If only one respondent said it was of infinite value, that would throw off the survey. If you limit the response to how much a person would be willing to spend, the result would obviously be affected by how much money people have, a standard flaw of market preference analysis.

Nobody asks the sea otter how much otters are worth. But the presumption that human-kind's use of the world is the sole measure of its value is arrogant. Nor can anyone survey future generations on their valuations of nature. And trying to measure the environment in terms of clean-up costs makes the neat presumption, easy in economics but questionable in nature, that all processes are reversible.

So, correctly pricing the environmental effects of human activities is at best rough guesswork, an attempt to squeeze profound issues of value into a Procrustean bed of price. Ultimately, despite imported trappings of economic analysis, the decision is social: what does society value?

\* \* \*

The market also fails to value adequately the depletion of nonrenewable resources. Again, future generations are largely ignored. How does the market allocate the right of a few generations in the twentieth and twenty-first centuries to use up most of the world's nonrenewable hydrocarbon resources? For a Brazilian gold miner or peasant, suffering in an economy burdened by huge external debts, short-term market rationality may dictate destroying the forest (just as the short-term rationality of the banks collecting their debts indirectly destroys the forest). But its resources of flora and fauna are lost, its land rendered useless. In different ways, then, the extreme inequities of income generated in the global market exhaust the planet —from the pressure of impoverished Third World masses on the land to the disproportionate consumption of nonrenewable resources and generation of waste in the richest countries....

Laissez-faire religion rests on the blind faith that maximizing profits will over time yield the most rational results. Yet even within a capitalist framework, far-sighted investment at the expense of current profits often makes sense. Critics

have charged, with compelling evidence, that the short-term preoccupations of American business have weakened the American economy. With regard to nature, myopic economic calculation is even more devastating. Given the scale and toxicity of human activity today, waiting for the market to signal a need for change may result in catastrophic, even irreversible damage, such as global warming or extinction of valuable species. There is a fundamental conflict, Daly and Cobb argue, between short-term profit maximization and the real needs and concrete resources of the whole community far into the future.

## DEFERRING GRATIFICATION

Again, the calculations of the market are inadequate. Economists often discount a future sum of money, figuring its present value as the amount that, if put in the bank at current interest rates, would yield the future sum. For the same reasons that bedevil other efforts to price nature, such discounting fails to assess the future value of the environment. From a free-market perspective, it may be rational for the private owner to kill the goose that lays the golden egg—if it can be sold now for more than its discounted future value and the proceeds invested. But thereby, Daly and Cobb argue, "society has lost a perpetual stream of golden eggs."

When we consider how long certain toxic substances and especially radioactive wastes are likely to remain threats, the problem is compounded: we rob the inheritance of future generations and leave them with a poisonous debt. If future people could be consulted, they would never sign the one-sided contract now being written. We can conclude that for several different reasons the market doesn't accurately price goods so as to take account of their environmental consequences. It ignores negative and positive externalities, ill accounts for depletion of natural resources, inappropriately measures income and welfare, and fails to take responsibility for future generations' welfare.

* * *

Since the defense of the market usually rests in large part on its ability to allocate resources efficiently and provide accurate information through prices, this failure to incorporate the environment is not a trifling flaw.

Can it be corrected? Increasingly some environmentalists argue for "green taxes" that would adjust prices upward to include uncounted environmental costs. U.S. energy users don't pay directly for as much as $300 billion a year in subsidies and tax credits (at least $50 billion a year, mainly to fossil fuels and nuclear power), environmental degradation, damage to health, military expenditures (the Gulf War alone would have added approximately $25 a barrel to imported oil), or employment effects of energy policies, according to Harold M. Hubbard, a scientist at Resources for the Future. By other calculations, we should now be paying more than $100 a barrel for oil if all costs were included. But Hubbard acknowledges that "calculating the actual cost of energy is not a simple matter.... The answers that economists derive may depend as much on social values as they do on analytical solutions to well-defined problems."

If consumers had to pay directly for the full price of energy, several things would happen. First, there would be economic shock and an increase in inequality. In general, the proportion of income spent on energy declines as income increases, although the use of energy increases (at the lowest income levels a decline in car ownership modifies this trend). Then there would be attempts to cope, by cutting back some use (much use is not very discretionary), and then, more important, by increasing efficiency. Also, other energy alternatives would become more competitive. And there would obviously be public clamor to do something—from unleashing nuclear power to promoting solar energy.

U.S. experience after the OPEC price increases of the 1970s illustrates the mixed record on market response to higher energy prices. Because the economy was ill-prepared to absorb the shocks, much of the stagflation of the decade can be attributed to everybody's efforts to pass on the costs to someone else. But the U.S. economy, with some governmental encouragement, also became more energy efficient. In little more than a decade after the first OPEC price increase, the energy intensity of the U.S. economy—energy per unit of GNP—dropped by about one-fourth. Energy production, including new sources of oil, increased in response to higher prices—but far less than mainstream economists predicted.

Much of the efficiency gain was driven by government regulation as well as by market factors. But what's remarkable is how limited the response was, considering the potential. After all, even before the OPEC price hikes, Germany and Japan used roughly half as much energy per unit of GNP as the United States and afterward still made efficiency gains nearly as great or greater than the United States did. Further, using technologies that are commercially available now, the United States could reduce its electric energy consumption by 70 percent at less than the present cost of generating electricity, according to analyses by efficiency guru Amory Lovins's Rocky Mountain Institute. Although the U.S. auto industry, forced by federal standards as much as by prices, made dramatic efficiency gains, the auto industry is still far from realizing the potential of diesel or gasoline engines, not to mention more advanced power sources.

Still, raising the price to some estimated real price would be a clumsy, slow, inequitable way of bringing about needed changes. First, there is nothing intrinsically good—and a lot bad—about high energy prices. What society needs is an inexpensive way to get necessary work done without the externalized costs. The question is: how do we get there in the most socially desirable way?

## WILL GOVERNMENT REGULATION WORK?

Direct government intervention is, despite market mania, often the best route. Japanese industries have become leaders in efficiency because "the government spurred their enthusiasm through a carefully coordinated, long-range program that continues even today," the *Wall Street Journal* recently reported. "One clear lesson to learn from Japan is that forcing core industries to become more energy-efficient is one thing that government *can* do well." Other industrialized countries are more energy efficient than the United States because of public investment in their public mass transit systems or because of explicit government strategies, such as Danish support of wind power.

Why hasn't the price of energy—even taking into account the decline in real oil prices in the mid-eighties —spurred more response? Consumers often are ill-informed about alternatives and find it difficult to make lifetime energy cost assessments (cheap initial cost of a regular incandescent bulb is more persuasive than the argument that lifetime costs of an expensive compact fluorescent are lower, for example). Even many industries simply don't understand how energy efficiency can benefit them. They insist that they recover the entire cost of efficiency investments in a year or two, although they might plan on recovering other investments in five years. Sometimes consumers don't directly make decisions: developers or landlords may make choices based on their costs, leaving tenants with higher bills.

* * *

There are large-scale institutional obstacles to change as well. Automobile manufacturers are to some extent captives of tastes they have created, but like the rest of the auto-oil-highway complex, they have a huge stake in keeping changes incremental—only anticipation of direct governmental edicts on alternatives to gasoline engines is leading manufacturers to gear up for electric vehicles. And private companies are largely incapable of making the kinds of massive investments needed for expanded rail or mass transit.

There are countless other ways in which businesses and consumers would not respond rationally or quickly even to prices that fully reflect environmental costs. Especially in making a major transition, the market is sticky, chaotic, and inefficient. For example, many farmers would like to shift from a less chemically intensive regime, especially as they become aware that it is not only economically viable but much healthier. But making the transition can be too costly —for example, suffering severe losses for several years until alternative controls of pests and weeds begin to work well.

Or take the case of photovoltaic cells, clearly a much-needed technology of the near future. Even though deep-pockets energy corporations bought up solar cell firms in the seventies, U.S. companies have been abandoning the field, in some cases selling off to European firms. This highlights another limit to the market model of efficiency: there are significant cultural differences, especially regarding long-term investment, and differences in levels of government support for alternative energy policies. Both affect market responses.

## REGULATION CAN HELP COMPETITION

Free-market enthusiasts insist that private businesses be allowed to innovate in response to market signals. But it is socially undesirable to treat the corporation as a black box, ignoring what goes on inside it and tinkering only with the price signals going in and then coping with what comes out. This is especially true in an era when large, multinational corporations dominate the global economy: their power, size, and internal governance distort idealized market responses to price signals.

Corporate policies vary significantly. At 3M Company, executives wisely instituted its "Pollution Prevention Pays" program and have saved $482 million since 1975, eliminated five hundred thousand tons of waste, and saved another $650 million through energy conservation. But what happens when a company compares polluting and nonpolluting alternatives and calculates that pollution does pay? Or take another example, representing a more familiar route in the eighties. Phillips Petroleum, under pressure of debt incurred in fighting off a hostile takeover, laid off experienced union workers and replaced them with ill-trained contract workers, took short-cuts on safety, and pushed production to the limit. The result was a major explosion in Pasadena, Texas, that killed twenty-six people and spread toxic materials throughout the environment.

Many businesses around the world have become more innovative and competitive as a result of strict environmental regulations. Both Germany and Japan have tougher standards than the United States and are growing faster. Some of the most strictly regulated U.S. industries, such as chemical, synthetics, and fabrics, have gained international competitiveness. Yet many businesses have chosen the path followed by a large segment of southern California's furniture industry: faced with tougher emissions standards, they fled to Mexico, where pollution laws are not enforced.

What makes one company prevent pollution while improving its ability to compete and another company endanger its employees and the surrounding community or flee abroad? Why does one business seize opportunities to become energy efficient and another respond to competitive pressures by shortchanging workers? How these distinct strategies emerge varies, but the general point is that when free marketeers talk about giving businesses flexibility and allowing the market to stimulate innovation, part of the flexibility and innovation will be socially good and part terrible. Why let private business make that momentous decision? Why should society wait until after the dirty deed is done to try to clean up the mess?...

## NIGHTMARE OF CONSUMPTION

Despite our own problems of inequality of consumption, which tear at the social fabric of the United States, an overemphasis on commodity consumption is the industrialized world's environmental nightmare. In mass-consumption societies self-fulfillment is defined in terms of buying more things, which leads to a disproportionate use of the world's resources and contributes to waste crises, from localized conflicts over municipal dumps to global destruction of the ozone layer. Of course, if raw materials were more accurately priced and if corporations were responsible for what happened to the waste they produced, there could be more reusable or at least recyclable packaging and less waste, all without a loss of meaningful consumption.

Environmentalists have contended that we must recognize limits to growth, a most unpopular prospect for both liberals and conservatives. Technically, the limit to a sustainable economy is the amount of solar energy falling on the earth that can reasonably be captured, even though there are much stricter limits on supplies of nonrenewable resources. The specter of global warming or holes in the ozone layer suggests that we could reach the limit of our use of nonrenewable fuels faster than we actually exhaust the earth's resources. Certainly there is no way that the earth can support the spread of wealthy, industrialized nations' current extravagant consumption to the world's poor. Environmentalists are divided over what are the limits to the earth's capacity, but markets have no way of even considering the question: unending growth is both their assumption and goal.

The alternative does not have to be for the richer nations to take vows of poverty. Some of our problems come from relying on the dynamics of commodity production rather than considering what needs we have and how those can be best served. We want homes and offices that are comfortable and well-lighted. But electric utilities want to sell electricity. It would be better for everyone if they devoted their resources to promoting energy efficiency, but they will only do so, in most cases, if they are compensated for part of sales forgone through efficiency-reduced demand. Increasingly, public utility commissions are enforcing such policies, and municipally owned utilities have aggressively pursued this service-oriented alternative because they are not profit oriented.

Environmental concerns should be added to many other motivations—political, philosophical, religious—to challenge the model of "economic man" that market society helps to create. The highly individualistic, cost-minimizing, profit-seeking mentality of market society is not a result of "human nature" but a cultural construction that denies a place for many values and feelings that have appeared in most human societies. True, there are flaky manifestations of new-age spiritualism associated with the environmental movement, but the desire for a sense of human community and harmony with the world is widespread and authentic.

The logic of free-market economics creates untenable abstractions, as Daly and Cobb, following economic historian Karl Polanyi, emphasize. In the laissez-faire market vision, nature becomes land. Then land itself is left out of the calculation, with the assumption that it is interchangeable with humanly created capital. Life becomes labor, or abstract labor-power, and patrimony becomes capital. All values are reduced to prices. Time is not concrete history, incorporating natural biological processes, but rather an infinite series of equivalent seconds. Places with distinctive features disappear into an interchangeable abstract space. By contrast, ecology reminds us that we live in a concrete world, and that we often end up committing real, not just intellectual, violence upon nature, humanity, and history.

## HOW DO WE DEAL WITH MARKETS?

So what do we do with markets? First, we must put them in their place, and that place is secondary to considerations of social values. The fundamental flaws in the market, from the environmental perspective alone, are enough to undo economists' claims for marketplace superiority. The market needs to be subordinated not only to nature but also to broader human values that form a limiting framework. That requires greater international cooperation. (This is already happening to a small extent with bans on whaling and the ivory trade and international agreements on reducing chlorofluorocarbons.) But ironically it also requires granting nations and communities power to enforce stronger standards to respond to their own local needs without having those undermined in the name of free trade.

Some environmentalists (including the Environmental Defense Fund and a group convened under senators Tim Wirth and the late John Heinz called Project 88) have argued that market-oriented regulations, such as tradable permits for discharges, will achieve environmental goals efficiently. The 1990 Clean Air Act revisions introduce such tradable permits, and the Chicago Board of Trade now plans a futures market in pollution permits. There are numerous objections: such trade *legitimates* pollution, it is likely to disadvantage the poor and powerless (especially if conducted on an international scale), regulatory regimes are already fairly flexible, and markets in such permits may be hard to establish and inefficient. The only evidence for efficiency so far comes from econometric studies already biased towards market solutions. Depending on the prices of permits or the level of taxes imposed, polluters could decide it was still cheaper to pollute.

Even more important, a focus on finding these market solutions diverts us from the main point. Nearly all these regulatory regimes represent attempts to control emissions, but as ecologist Barry Commoner argues in his book *Making Peace with the Planet,* regulatory efforts have at best slowed only slightly the rate of environmental deterioration. The real environmental successes have only come with outright bans of certain substances, such as lead in gasoline or paint. Instead of quibbling over how much toxic substance can be released, regulation should increasingly establish a standard of zero discharge. "The tax [on pollutants] can't work until you've done the wrong thing," Commoner says. "You can't have a market in pollutant rights until you have pollutants." The solution is prevention.

But prevention can't always be outright banning: for the foreseeable future, at least some hydrocarbons will be burned. In many cases, transitions to zero discharge may take time. During that period, using tradable permits or other market-oriented methods should be considered along with flexible regulation. But rather than a panacea, such devices represent an interesting gimmick of unproven value.

## WHAT FORCES WILL WORK BEST?

There is increased interest in energy or carbon taxes to discourage fossil-fuel use and give better signals on the true costs of burning hydrocarbons, especially non-renewable sources. Eliminating subsidies to dangerous or polluting sources, such as nuclear power, would also give more appropriate prices.

It's obvious that energy is mispriced and consequently misused, but relying on taxes to bring about a change through the market is likely to create great hardship for low-to-middle-income people and increase inequality. Ideally, a transition would not greatly increase energy bills but would increase energy prices steadily in tandem with changes to alternative, renewable energy sources, a different mix of technologies, and greater energy efficiency. If the government developed a strategy for transition to an essentially solar economy, then regular increases in energy taxes could be used for a variety of projects, including research. Federal, state, and local governments can have a tremendous impact: government purchases of solar cells or hydrogen- or electric-powered cars could speed the learning curve and cut prices quickly. Public investment would be needed to develop mass transit and railroads. A full-scale industrial extension service to promote energy efficiency and nonpolluting technologies could speed industrial transitions with less disruption. But

if energy taxes are going to work most effectively, it should not be simply through the indirect effect of higher prices but also through the investment of the new revenue in efficiency and alternatives.

\* \* \*

Green consumerism and protest already have had some impact. McDonald's, responding to a campaign against its styrofoam clamshell, has switched packaging and is considering composting of its food wastes. Other businesses sense a good market, although many are as duplicitous as Mobil Chemical, whose representative said its "biodegradable" plastic trash bags "are not an answer to landfill crowding or littering.... Degradability is just a marketing tool.... We're talking out of both sides of our mouths because we want to sell bags." Green consumerism is an important phenomenon but is likely to remain marginal without other reinforcing measures.

There must first be clear public policy. A mixture of direct government actions (purchases, subsidies, prohibitions, research, and technical assistance) can be combined with changed market incentives (for example, taxes and markets in efficiency) in ways that complement each other. Public policy, however, should determine the direction.

The disastrous effects of centralized government control in the communist countries should remain a reminder that government is no guarantee of virtue. Clearly government in the United States and elsewhere has often been the captive of corporate interests. Environmental values, like other values, must be cultivated among the electorate if public policy is going to change. In the long run, altering the "economic man" outlook of market society will make environmental goals easier to attain.

Much of the progress toward environmental sanity in the United States has come as a result of grass-roots protest, environmental impact fights, and legal action over local issues. Often dismissed as NIMBYism—not-in-my-backyard—these movements are often concerned about other backyards as well. Even now the grass-roots protesters among environmentalists exert pressure on the bigger, established environmental groups that are entrapped in the rulemaking squabbles of federal legislation and tempted to form alliances with big corporations (at times having an influence, yet also subtly losing their independence).

Besides guaranteeing a free and full role for citizen protest, which big corporations especially want to eliminate, it is important that workers have broad powers to influence the safety and health of their work environment. Like the proverbial canaries in coal mines of the past, they are the first victims of pollution and toxicity. Giving them powers to protect themselves, with mandated worker health and safety committees in every workplace, protects everyone else.

Environmental values lead to a model of society that subordinates the market to nature, but environmentalists cannot claim nature as their model any more than the free marketeers can call their model "natural." No model of society is natural; all are historical, cultural creations. And nature itself has forever been altered by human culture.

A new model of society can aspire to respect nature and to make culture and nature as compatible as possible. The implications of the environmental critique go beyond traditional ecological issues. Many similar critiques of the market can be made on behalf of other cultural values. The market, for example, does not take into account the externalities of human poverty and inequality, economic dislocation, stunted work lives, and destruction of community. It gives the wrong price signals, the wrong information. In taming the market to protect nature, we should not forget the well-being of those most curious natural creatures—ourselves.

# POSTSCRIPT

## Should Pollution Be Put to the Market Test?

For the past 25 years a massive effort has been put forth in the United States to advance environmental protection by using laws and regulation. Efforts can be traced back to the 1970 National Environmental Policy Act (NEPA), the first modern environmental statute that required environmental impact statements on federal projects. That same year, Congress also passed the Clean Air Act, which replaced a weak environmental statute with enforceable, federal clean-air standards and timetables for industry to meet. Seven years later, the Clean Water Act (1977) was passed. This act established standards and permits, and it attempted to limit discharges in navigable waters and protect wetlands from exploration.

At first, federal action was directed toward air- and water-pollution control; this was accomplished by issuing regulations and permits. The second set of initiatives focused on cleaning up hazardous waste dumps. This action was first authorized by the Resource Conservation and Recovery Act (RCRA) of 1976, which established a permit system for disposal sites and regulated underground storage tanks. Later initiatives in this area were authorized by the Comprehensive Environmental Response, Compensation, and Liability Act (CERCLA) of 1980. This act, known as the Superfund, created a fund to finance the clean-up of hazardous waste sites.

What is significant is that, until recently, efforts to control, contain, and eliminate pollution and its effects have been accomplished largely by government regulation. Economists such as Blinder have argued for policies that captured and utilized the strength of the market. However, as Moberg so effectively argues, the opposition has been successful in warning public policy away from a free-market perspective that would allow "the private owner to kill the goose that lays the golden egg" and in the process deny society "a perpetual stream of golden eggs."

For a review of the legislation in the air pollution area, see Richard H. Schulze, "The 20-Year History of the Evolution of Air Pollution Control Legislation in the U.S.A.," *Atmospheric Environment* (March 1993). For a discussion of some of the ethical issues surrounding the pollution permits, see Paul Steichmeier, "The Morality of Pollution Permits," *Environmental Ethics* (Summer 1993). And for other economic interpretations see Dwight R. Lee, "An Economist's Perspective on Air Pollution," *Environmental Science and Technology* (October 1993) and Joe Alper, "Protecting the Environment with the Power of the Market," *Science* (June 25, 1993).

# ISSUE 19

## Has the North American Free Trade Agreement Been a Success?

**YES: Paul Krugman,** from "How Is NAFTA Doing?" *The New Democrat* (May/June 1996)

**NO: Sarah Anderson, John Cavanagh, and David Ranney,** from "NAFTA: Trinational Fiasco," *The Nation* (July 15, 1996)

### ISSUE SUMMARY

**YES:** Paul Krugman, professor of economics at Stanford University, believes that assessment of the North American Free Trade Agreement (NAFTA) should be based on what things would have been like without it, and on this basis NAFTA has been a success.

**NO:** Sarah Anderson, fellow at the Institute for Policy Studies, John Cavanagh, codirector of the Institute for Policy Studies, and David Ranney, professor of urban planning at the University of Illinois, Chicago, argue that evidence is accumulating that NAFTA is not in the best interests of most of the people in Canada, Mexico, and the United States.

---

The North American Free Trade Agreement (NAFTA) was signed into law in fall 1993. The passage of NAFTA was no simple matter. Although the basic agreement was negotiated by the Republican Bush administration, the Democratic Clinton administration faced the challenge of convincing Congress and the American people that NAFTA would work to the benefit of the United States as well as Mexico. In meeting this challenge President Bill Clinton did not hesitate to use a bit of drama to press the case for NAFTA. He gathered together the former U.S. presidents (Bush, Reagan, Carter, Ford, and Nixon) and had them speak out in support of NAFTA. The public debate probably reached its zenith with a face-to-face confrontation between Ross Perot, perhaps the most visible and most outspoken opponent of NAFTA, and Vice President Al Gore on the *Larry King Live* television show. The vote on NAFTA in the House of Representatives reflected the sharpness of the debate; it passed by only a slim margin.

In pressing the case for NAFTA, proponents in the United States raised two major points. The first point was economic: NAFTA would produce real economic benefits, including increased employment in the United States and increased productivity. The second point was political: NAFTA would support the political and economic reforms being made in Mexico and promote further progress n these two domains. These reforms had made Mexico a "better" neighbor; that is, Mexico had taken steps to become more like the United States, and NAFTA would support further change. In fighting NAFTA, U.S. opponents countered both of these points. They argued that freer trade between the United States and Mexico would mean a loss of American jobs— Ross Perot's "giant sucking sound" was the transfer of work and jobs from the United States to Mexico. Opponents also argued that NAFTA did not do enough to protect the environment or to improve working conditions in Mexico. They felt that the notion of passing NAFTA as a reward to the Mexican government was premature; the government had not done enough to improve economic and political conditions in Mexico.

Implementation of NAFTA began in 1994. But events in Mexico during 1994 and 1995 took an interesting series of twists. By December 1994 the Mexican economy faced a balance of payments crisis, and the peso began to depreciate. In order to prevent a collapse of the Mexican economy, President Clinton organized a $50-billion multilateral assistance effort that included $20 billion of U.S. credit. The Mexican government also took action, including cuts in government spending and increases in interest rates. The net result of these events was a deep recession in the Mexican economy with a contraction of 7 percent during the first three quarters of 1995.

In assessing the impact of NAFTA, there are any number of different perspectives that can be employed. Should the focus be economic, political, or both? Should the evaluation concentrate on the benefits and costs to the United States, to Mexico, or both countries? How much of the history that follows NAFTA can be attributed to NAFTA and how much can be attributed to other factors? When is the appropriate time for an evaluation? In short, evaluation is no easy task.

Some of the difficulties of evaluation are captured in the following selections. Both were published at approximately the same time: three years after the passage of NAFTA and some two-and-one-half years after its implementation. In arguing that NAFTA should be considered a success, Paul Krugman is less concerned with the economic consequences of NAFTA. He believes that any realistic assessment of the economic benefits of NAFTA for the U.S. economy would have admitted that these benefits would be marginal at best. He believes that an assessment of NAFTA must concentrate, therefore, on its foreign policy implications. On these grounds, Krugman believes NAFTA is a success. Sarah Anderson, John Cavanagh, and David Ranney are more concerned with the economic implications of NAFTA and its impact on people. While not a total failure, they believe that NAFTA led to a series of economic problems, including Mexico's economic collapse and economic inequality in the United States, Mexico, and Canada.

# YES

**Paul Krugman**

# HOW IS NAFTA DOING?

More than two years ago, the United States, Canada, and Mexico entered into the North American Free Trade Agreement. Debate over the pact was marked both by extravagant promises about its benefits and by blood-curdling warnings about its costs. Now that some time has passed, it's fair to ask, "How is NAFTA doing?"

To many, the answer is obvious: Haven't events in Mexico—economic crisis, political unrest, the revelation of scandals—given the lie to NAFTA's supporters? But that visceral reaction misses the point. Whether we like what we see in Mexico or not, the place isn't going away. There are 100 million people right next door, with whom we must live one way or another. The right question to ask about NAFTA is not whether conditions in Mexico and our relations with it are all that we wish they were, but rather whether they are better under NAFTA than they would have been without it. And despite recent troubles, the clear answer is yes. Indeed, the real value of the new U.S.-Mexican relationship is best seen in adversity: Mexico is coping with its latest crises better than almost anyone would have imagined in the pre-NAFTA era.

NAFTA's defenders are saddled with a big public relations problem: The agreement was sold under false pretenses. Over the protests of most economists, the Clinton Administration chose to promote NAFTA as a job-creation program. Based on little more than guesswork, a few economists argued that NAFTA would boost our trade surplus with Mexico, and thus produce a net gain in jobs. With utterly spurious precision, the Administration settled on the figure of 200,000 jobs created—and this became the core of the pro-NAFTA sales pitch.

The overall number of U.S. jobs, however, was never going to be noticeably affected by swings in our trade balance with Mexico. Our economy employs more than 120 million workers; it has added more than 8 million jobs since 1992. Job growth has slowed since 1994, but not because those 200,000 export-related jobs failed to materialize (the real culprit is the Federal Reserve's interest rate policies).

From Paul Krugman, "How Is NAFTA Doing?" *The New Democrat* (May/June 1996), pp. 18–21.

If job creation isn't the point of NAFTA, what is? Another possible justification is the classic economic argument that free trade will raise U.S productivity and hence living standards. Few economists, however, thought the pact would yield large gains of this type. Mexico's economy is simply too small to provide America with the opportunity for major gains from trade. Typical estimates of the long-term benefits to the U.S. economy from NAFTA are for an increase in real income on the order of 0.1 percent to 0.2 percent.

So, where's the payoff from NAFTA for America? In foreign policy, not economics: NAFTA reinforces the process of economic and political reform in Mexico.

## MEXICAN REFORM: MYTHS AND REALITIES

As vast sums of money flowed into Mexico in the early 1990s, it became chic to talk about the "Mexican miracle." The country was lauded for its economic reforms; President Carlos Salinas became a business celebrity. But when enduring weaknesses in Mexico's political and economic systems manifested themselves in 1994—the peasant uprising in Chiapas, the assassination of presidential candidate Luis Donaldo Colosio—the same investors who had been euphoric about Mexico a few months earlier panicked. They were shocked—shocked!—to discover that Mexico, after all, isn't a combination of Switzerland and Singapore. And they began pulling their money out as fast as they had poured it in.

All of this could have been avoided if people had taken a realistic view of events in Mexico. By the early 1980s, the political and economic models that had ruled the nation for 50 years had reached a dead end. Mexico had tried to build political stability on the basis of one-party rule and economic development on the basis of a protected market and a powerful state sector. Eventually, it became clear that other developing countries' market-oriented, export-driven economies were leaving Mexico in the dust. It also became clear that serious economic reform could take place only along with a serious democratization.

The international debt crisis of the 1980s, which wreaked havoc with the Mexican economy, had the paradoxical effect of opening up the possibility for real change. During the crisis, the Mexican ruling party turned to technocrats—most of them U.S.-educated, and many of them possessing a strong sense of the virtues of U.S. institutions—to solve the country's predicament. Salinas turned out to have been less than a wholehearted reformer. Still, he brought into power a group that was astonishingly honest, pro-market, and pro-democracy by any previous Mexican standards.

And the technocrats produced real reform. Mexico's markets are far more open to U.S. exports than they have been since the early years of this century; many of the most wasteful and inefficient public enterprises have been privatized; a new economic base has emerged in the north, far from the inefficiency and corruption of Mexico City. Much has changed on the political front, too: Mexico's elections are freer and fairer than ever before.

Mexico may not be Canada, but it is a far better neighbor now than it has been in living memory. Even more important, a reformist Mexico led by pro-American technocrats is far preferable to the radical, anti-American nation we will surely face if the reformers fail. Clearly, it is in our interest to help the Mexican reformers succeed.

This is the context for judging the decision to go ahead with NAFTA. The agreement was a Mexican idea—proposed by Salinas to lock in the reforms he had begun and to build confidence about Mexico's future as a liberalized economy. How could we have refused? Rejecting Salinas's proposal would have been a devastating slap in the face for the reformers, who would have been taunted with the way that America rewards its friends.

Sensible NAFTA supporters had no illusions about Mexico. It is still a country with corrupt political bosses, tycoons whose fortunes are built on bribery, backward rural areas whose populations are virtually disenfranchised, and urban pockets of luxury ringed by slums. But it is less like that than before. Mexico's hope to become a better place and our hope to have a better neighbor depend on continued reform.

## CRISIS AND RESCUE

By early 1993, economists had begun to warn about the risks of a Mexican financial crisis. They were concerned about the dissonance between the wild optimism of investors, who were pouring money into Mexico at the rate of about $30 billion a year, and the still disappointing performance of the real Mexican economy, which was not yet delivering substantial improvements in living standards for ordinary families.

The failure of Mexican reforms to generate immediate rapid growth should not have been a big surprise. Economic reform is usually a painful process; the dislocations that are caused when old industries are no longer protected or subsidized tend to be more visible than the growth of new industries for at least several years. Chile did not begin to show a dramatic payoff to its market reforms until the mid-1980s, a decade after those reforms began; Eastern European nations like Poland and the Czech Republic, which escaped Soviet rule in 1989, are only now beginning to achieve solid growth. And the massive inflow of capital to Mexico between 1990 and 1994 in some ways actually delayed the economy's transformation. By leading to a severely overvalued peso, it slowed the emergence of new manufacturing exports—the engine of long-term economic growth.

Investors were too caught up in the investment boom to realize it was premature. Finally, their confidence began to falter in 1994 as Mexican politics and policies began to waver. The uprising in Chiapas posed no real threat to the government, but it was a reminder both of the vast, persistent inequities in Mexican society and of the limited progress made toward democracy. The assassination of Colosio, which remains something of a mystery, deprived the country of a much-needed leader and raised further doubts about stability. Also, during the run-up to the 1994 election, the Mexican government backslid on its record of responsible monetary and fiscal policies, printing and spending more money than it should have in an effort to buy votes.

The result was the crisis of December, in which a loss of confidence by investors forced a devaluation of the peso. By itself, the speculation against the peso need not have been a catastrophe. After all, currency crises are a common occurrence in the world of international finance. In fact, since 1990 major currency crises have forced devaluations not only in Mexico but in Britain, Finland, Ireland, Italy, Spain, and Sweden. The difficulties were increased when Mexico's devaluation was bungled, owing to missteps by a few officials (who were soon dismissed). They delayed the inevitable too long, carried out the devaluation half-heartedly, and managed in general to convey a sense of both arrogance and incompetence that further decreased confidence. Nonetheless, this too is fairly standard when there is a currency crisis, and Mexico's handling of the situation was no worse than that in many other countries.

The reason that Mexico's crisis soon ballooned to really dangerous proportions was that financial markets, which had been excessively euphoric about Mexico in the previous few years, overreacted in the opposite direction when the country hit a rough patch. This financial panic threatened to become a self-fulfilling crisis of confidence in the whole process of reform.

In simplified outline, this is what happened: As investors grew worried about Mexico during the second half of 1994, the country began running out of foreign exchange reserves. To maintain the peso's value, the government would have had to raise interest rates sharply, which would have pushed the faltering economy into a recession. Instead, the government let the peso fall. Investors, in turn, became so disillusioned that they withdrew all their money from Mexico, sending the peso into a freefall. To keep the currency from collapsing, which would have triggered explosive inflation, the Mexican government raised interest rates after all—indeed, to very high levels.

At this point, a vicious circle developed. For more than a year, interest rates in Mexico have been very high—so high

that investing there will be highly profitable unless there is a further huge fall in the peso. And there is no good economic reason to expect such a fall: Mexican exports are booming, the trade deficit has been eliminated, by any normal calculation the peso is undervalued. Investors, however, fear that the rule of the economic reformers in Mexico is in danger; that to put money into Mexico is to risk losing it when there is a nationalist backlash against the whole pro-market, pro-U.S. policy direction of the last decade. To induce them to keep their funds in Mexico despite such fears, the government has been forced to keep interest rates very high.

Why might there be a backlash? The biggest reason is the severe slump in the Mexican economy—a slump due mainly to high interest rates.

In short, investors are in effect saying, "I won't invest in Mexico unless I am offered a very high rate of return. I need that high rate of return to compensate me for the risks of a nationalist reaction, which may be sparked by the need to provide investors like me with such a high rate of return." It is a classic case of self-fulfilling pessimism.

What can be done? The best answer is to ride out the storm. In time, the vicious circle should become a virtuous circle. After all, at current interest rates, investing in Mexico is an extremely profitable proposition unless you fear either hyperinflation or expropriation. If time passes and these risks don't materialize, people will become more willing to invest in Mexico. This will allow interest rates to fall, which will produce an economic recovery, which will further reduce the perceived risks, and so on.

The great risk in 1995 was that the Mexican reformers would not be able to ride out the storm—that the financial markets' self-fulfilling pessimism would destroy their credibility before there was any chance to turn things around. It is in this light that one must understand the $50 billion rescue package put together by the United States and other advanced countries. We extended Mexico a large line of credit to buy the reformers some time.

The rescue attempt must be evaluated in terms of the alternatives. Should we have simply stood aside? This almost certainly would have doomed the Mexican reformers. If this had happened, it's a safe bet that Republican Sen. Al D'Amato, who held hearings to grill Administration officials over the decision to grant President Ernesto Zedillo's government a line of credit, would have instead held hearings demanding to know, "Who lost Mexico?"

Like the U.S. decision to go ahead with NAFTA in the first place, the rescue package was less an economic measure than a foreign policy move. Anyone who thinks it put too much taxpayer money at risk should try to make a realistic estimate of the cost of policing a 2,000-mile border with a hostile and angry neighbor. Even though the rescue plan was not guaranteed to succeed, it is hard to see how the United States could responsibly have done anything else.

## THE CURRENT PROSPECTS

The most important development in Mexico this past year is what has not happened. The ruling party has not abandoned its course of economic and political reform. Nor is there a serious challenge to the legitimacy of the government, either from armed peasants or populist politicians. The ruling party may well lose the next presidential election, but if it does, the likely victors will not be anti-market populists but pro-marketeers who will continue the process of reform. Mexico's political center is holding.

Meanwhile, it is beginning to look as if the virtuous circle Mexico's rescuers hoped for is materializing. Mexico's interest rates have dropped and its stocks have risen in recent months, and local economists are starting to talk about a fairly brisk short-term economic recovery. Furthermore, with private capital returning, Mexico has started to pay back its emergency loans. It now looks very likely that whatever else may happen, the American taxpayer will get his or her money back.

The recovery is still more a prospect than a reality, and things could still go very wrong. In particular, if U.S. politics turn protectionist and isolationist, it is hard to see how either Mexican recovery or Mexican reform can survive. But for now, at least, things are looking up.

Will this short-term stabilization prove to be the beginning of a new period of sustained growth? Has Mexico really turned a corner, or is this just the latest in a series of crises? Nobody knows. But this is the wrong question to ask. One cannot repeat it too often: *Mexico cannot be wished away.* We cannot wall it off behind an electrified fence and then forget about it. The important question for the United States is not whether we like everything we see south of the border. It is whether our interests would have been better served by the radicalized Mexico we would have faced if we had rejected NAFTA or denied it a financial lifeline last year—or by the struggling, troubled, but still reforming nation we actually have to deal with. By that test, NAFTA and the rescue that followed have been wise, successful policies.

# NO
## Sarah Anderson, John Cavanagh, and David Ranney

# NAFTA: TRINATIONAL FIASCO

One issue you can be sure that [1996 presidential candidates] Bob Dole and Bill Clinton will not disagree on is free trade. Both men were strong advocates of the North American Free Trade Agreement, which went into effect in January 1994. The peoples of North America have now lived with the agreement for [more than] 900 days and, contrary to the promises of Dole, Clinton and their advisers, NAFTA has turned out to be a losing proposition for all but the Fortune 500.

Rather than increasing by the hundreds of thousands, as promised, jobs have been disappearing in all three countries; those jobs that remain pay less with fewer benefits. The U.S.-Mexico border, already a development debacle when NAFTA was signed, is mired even deeper in health and environmental nightmares. Mexico's highly touted middle class has been slammed back into poverty. In Canada, one of the world's finest social welfare systems is under siege. Many more promises on funding, immigration, agriculture and other issues did not materialize. The leaders of the three NAFTA countries rarely mention the trade pact, fearing, perhaps, that they will remind voters of their exaggerated claims for it and how much needless misery it has produced.

Several dozen researchers and activists from all three countries have recently completed a series of comprehensive studies on NAFTA that debunk the prevailing myths. We focus here on five of the most prevalent ones. But first a caveat: We do not argue that NAFTA caused Mexico's latest economic collapse, nor did it create the growing inequality in all three nations, nor most of the other problems outlined below. NAFTA did, however, make them worse. In economic terms, NAFTA eased the movement of goods and investment among the three countries; it sped up the free-trade model that large corporations have been pushing for decades. NAFTA codifies an economic ideology that glorifies the market, that demonizes and defunds government and that regards human beings as little more than customers in a continental shopping mall.

## MYTH #1: NAFTA HAD NOTHING TO DO WITH THE RECENT MEXICAN CRISIS

The evidence of Mexico's economic failure, which burst into public view on the eve of Christmas in 1994, is so overwhelming that even the Clinton Administration doesn't deny it. What it says is that the fault lies with poor economic management by the Mexican government. Although NAFTA proponents claim that the crisis has postponed many of the benefits they predicted would emerge from the agreement, they argue that Mexico is continuing on the right free-trade track and that things would be much worse in the absence of NAFTA. In fact, NAFTA merely formalized and extended policies that were first imposed upon the country by the International Monetary Fund in 1982 in response to Mexico's massive foreign debt. These policies, popularly known as structural adjustment, represent an approach to economic development that requires slashing government expenditures and opening the country to foreign goods, services and capital without government regulation; in four words: Trade more, spend less.

In Mexico's case and for many other countries suffering structural adjustment, the effect of everyone exporting more drives prices down and makes servicing the debt even harder. Meanwhile, during the NAFTA negotiations, the International Monetary Fund and World Bank pressured the Mexican government to ease trade and investment barriers even further. As a result, foreign capital is increasingly coming in the form of speculative portfolio investment, or "hot money," which requires high interest rates that discourage productive investment.

In previous crises, Mexico saved scarce foreign exchange by using controls to exclude non-essential imports. But under NAFTA, this is no longer allowed, even during emergencies. The agreement also prohibits restrictions on foreign-exchange transactions without special permission. Finally, under NAFTA's "rules of origin" provisions, Mexico cannot impose requirements that could channel foreign investment into productive endeavors and away from speculation.

## MYTH #2: INCREASED EXPORTS WILL LEAD TO MORE JOBS

President Clinton boasted that NAFTA had created some 340,000 U.S. jobs. But the President's claim is based on an erroneous formula that asserts that every $1 billion in new exports creates another 15,000 to 20,000 jobs. The formula is flawed, in part because it considers only exports and doesn't subtract jobs lost when the United States imports goods that used to be produced here. Although U.S. exports to Mexico have grown some since NAFTA went into effect, the Administration's own numbers show that imports from Mexico have gone through the roof; a U.S. trade surplus of $1.7 billion in 1993 spiraled downward into a deficit of $15.4 billion by 1995. Hence, by the Administration's formula, many more U.S. jobs have been destroyed by NAFTA than have been created.

The Administration admits that 75,000 U.S. workers have been thrown out on the street as a result of the free-trade agreement. These figures are from the NAFTA Transitional Adjustment Assistance program, which provides retraining and other aid to U.S. workers who lose their jobs as a result of a shift in production to Mexico or Canada, or of increased imports from those nations.

The surge in Mexican exports to the United States should, in theory, have created many new jobs in Mexico. Indeed, Mexico's plummeting peso has drastically lowered labor costs for global companies operating there, and several hundred thousand new maquiladora jobs have been spawned on the border. However, this increase has been dwarfed by the 1.4 million to 2 million jobs that vanished during NAFTA's first two years, as record numbers of small and medium-sized businesses lost the battle with high interest rates and filed for bankruptcy. NAFTA proponents had claimed that the agreement would so improve the Mexican economy that pressures to migrate to the United States would greatly subside. In fact, displaced workers and peasants swelled the number of Mexicans apprehended in attempted border crossings by a dramatic 43 percent from 1994 to 1995.

And there is an even deeper flaw in the NAFTA jobs argument. Even if a country does have a trade surplus, it is faulty to assume that corporations always use profits generated by exports to create new jobs. Many successful exporting companies have instead chosen to use these profits to finance mergers or invest in labor-saving machinery, which can lead to job cuts. Firms like Zenith, Xerox, Caterpillar and Allied Signal are major exporters from the United States, yet all of them have eliminated thousands of U.S. jobs. A study of Illinois's top export industries showed they were laying off workers at a higher rate than other industries.

In Canada, an equally alarming job hemorrhage dates back to the Canada-U.S. Free Trade Agreement, which was signed in 1988. Between 1988 and 1994, Canada lost 17 percent of its manufacturing jobs, and unemployment rose from 7.5 percent in 1989 to just under 10 percent in 1995. A study by the Canadian Centre for Policy Alternatives shows that companies that lobbied hard for the free-trade pacts have been the biggest job slashers. Thirty-seven firms belonging to a pro-NAFTA business association have cut more than 215,000 jobs since 1988.

## MYTH #3: INCREASES IN PRODUCTIVITY WILL BE SPREAD TO WORKERS

In lobbying for the free-trade agreement, the corporate group USA*NAFTA claimed that "NAFTA itself will improve working conditions by generating economic growth, which will enable all three countries to provide more jobs with higher pay in a better working environment." To the contrary, NAFTA has given corporations increased power to drive down wages and working conditions.

The most direct method is through "whipsaw bargaining," or threatening to shift production to Mexico unless workers agree to concessions. Xerox used this technique effectively in Webster, New York, where workers agreed to reduce the base pay rate by 50 percent for new employees and cut workers' compensation in exchange for job guarantees through the year 2001. The Webster workers had reason to take the company's relocation threats seriously, since Xerox had recently moved jobs south of the border from plants in Illinois and Massachusetts.

Another common corporate tactic is to use the argument that increased international competition under NAFTA requires greater "flexibility" through hiring more workers on a part-time or temporary basis. Corporate-backed lawmakers are using the same argument to push antiworker legislation, such as the efforts to strip away the government's power to enforce health and safety regulations; outlaw union shops and unions' use of corporate campaigns; legalize company unions; and abolish overtime pay.

Thus, while corporations experience productivity growth, workers are not sharing in the benefits. In all three NAFTA countries, increases in real wages are lagging far behind increases in productivity. In Mexico, real wages as of May 1996 were 35 percent below their pre-1994-crisis levels. In Canada, as in the United States, real wages are stagnating and the proportion of full-time workers living in poverty continues to grow.

In response to NAFTA's critics, the Clinton Administration negotiated a labor side agreement, but it contains a narrow definition of worker rights and is weighted down with an enormously complex, time-consuming and bureaucratic dispute resolution mechanism. Not surprisingly, to date, complaints about violations of worker rights have been filed at only four plants (three in Mexico and one in the United States). Not a single worker involved in these complaints has benefited so far from the process. However, through tremendous persistence, unions and other groups have been able to use the agreement to draw more attention to the general problem of worker rights violations.

## MYTH #4: INCREASED INTERNATIONAL COMPETITIVENESS WILL BENEFIT ALL

"We must be internationally competitive." This is the mantra now parroted by heads of state throughout the world, including Clinton, Ernesto Zedillo in Mexico and Jean Chrétien in Canada. The benefits of such enhanced competitiveness, however, have turned out more often than not to be a mirage, as the evidence presented above indicates. But the tragedy of NAFTA and free trade runs deeper than lost jobs and falling wages. A key element of the drive for international competitiveness has been an assault on government.

*Nation* readers are familiar with the attack on social programs and federal regulations in the United States. In Canada, cuts in unemployment insurance reduced the number of unemployed Canadians who qualify for benefits from 87 percent in 1989 to 49 percent in 1994; this will fall to 33 percent when the latest round of cuts is fully implemented.

In Mexico, NAFTA has worsened conditions engendered by twelve previous years of austerity. These measures have been particularly devastating for rural Mexicans. A requirement for entry into the agreement was the removal of subsidies for family farmers, who also face drastic cuts in available credit and public services in areas such as veterinary medicine, agricultural extension and public health. In December 1995, Mexico's Institute of Social Security, which oversees health care and social security for salaried workers, was shifted from public to private administration and funding.

## MYTH #5: GROWTH FROM FREE TRADE WILL HELP CLEAN UP THE ENVIRONMENT

NAFTA supporters promised that the trade agreement would mean increased investment in environmental cleanup and a decline in the concentration of maquiladoras along the already heavily polluted U.S.-Mexico border. But as Public Citizen has documented, the increase in industrial activity in the border zone has not been met by any appreciable improvement in the disposal of industrial wastes or expansion of health care facilities. Many communities still lack access to both water and sewage systems. Today, only 10 percent of Mexico's yearly output of 7 million tons of hazardous waste receives adequate treatment, with the rest poured into clandestine waste dumps or municipal sewers.

Nor are NAFTA's environmental threats confined to the U.S.-Mexico border. Standards established through the struggles of environmental groups throughout each of the countries can now be challenged as "nontariff trade barriers." Groups trying to protect these standards will have to justify them according to the principles of "risk assessment"—the notion that health risks incurred because of lower standards must be great enough to justify the cost of restrictions on trade. Rather than the highest possible standards for a healthy environment, risk assessment leads to standards that pose the lowest restrictions on businesses.

As with labor, the Clinton Administration used the handy device of a side agreement to gain support of some environmental groups during the NAFTA fight. A number of them—dubbed "the shameful seven"—acquiesced. Yet the institutions set up under NAFTA have made little progress in addressing environmental concerns. The North American Development Bank has yet to fund a single cleanup project. Widely perceived as ineffectual, the North American Commission for Environmental Cooperation

was supposed to insure high levels of environmental protection and foster public discussion. Yet the C.E.C. has received only four petitions, three of which it has rejected. It has also been asked to investigate the mysterious mass death of birds in a reservoir in Guanajuato, Mexico.

* * *

NAFTA has not, however, been a total failure. Its most salutary effect was to catalyze new coalitions that crossed borders and political party lines, and embraced constituencies as diverse as workers, farmers, environmentalists, consumers and religious groups. Unfortunately, one would scarcely know this from press accounts. With its blinkered focus on officialdom, the press gave credence only to critics on the right. Hence, coverage of NAFTA opposition focused on Pat Buchanan, who, although correctly critiquing the agreement, presented a racist, "America First" solution that called for sealing U.S. borders to goods, capital and people from other countries.

The progressive opposition to NAFTA, on the other hand, has rejected the process, politics and policies of the pro-NAFTA forces. Opponents attacked the process because NAFTA was negotiated secretly, without a hearing from ordinary citizens; opponents advocated a transparent process that would bring all parties to the table. They condemned the politics because NAFTA's passage revealed how legislators' votes are often sold to the highest bidder in a system corrupted by corporate money. And on the policy level, they rejected the deregulatory framework of NAFTA and the new protections for corporations.

The main progressive citizen networks in the NAFTA countries proposed alternative policies that would protect worker rights, advance environmental standards and food security, and promote sustainable energy and agriculture. This approach was summed up in a document titled "A Just and Sustainable Trade and Development Initiative for the Western Hemisphere" by the key networks in all three countries that fought NAFTA.

These groups continue to fight for better economic alternatives. The Action Canada Network, which includes a broad array of social forces from the Canadian Labor Congress to cultural and indigenous movements, has helped forge an "Alternative Federal Budget" aimed at creating jobs through public investment and halting the dismantling of social programs.

In the United States, the Alliance for Responsible Trade, the Citizens Trade Campaign and many other groups from the economic and environmental justice movements continue to monitor NAFTA's impact and promote bi- and tri-national alternatives.

In Mexico, a similar array of citizen groups, represented by the Mexican Action Network on Free Trade, has worked with others to draft a twelve-point "Liberty Referendum," which outlines a national alternative to the government's neoliberal policies. At polling places around the country, half a million Mexicans signed their approval by November 1995.

NAFTA has unleashed a major war in all three countries over our economic future. While the pro-NAFTA forces won the opening battle, evidence continues to build that the agreement is not in the interest of the vast majority of people in any of the three countries. And in their silence over trade issues, candidates Clinton and Dole are acknowledging that they face even more difficult battles in new arenas: the trade deficit with China, NAFTA expansion to other countries and proposals to enhance the powers of the World Trade Organization.

# POSTSCRIPT

## Has the North American Free Trade Agreement Been a Success?

Krugman begins his assessment of NAFTA by identifying the perspective that he uses to evaluate it: are things better with NAFTA than they would have been without it? He states that the answer to this question should not involve a comparison of current reality with the exaggerated economic claims made on behalf of NAFTA by the Clinton administration when it sought support for the legislation. Rather, Krugman believes that the payoff to NAFTA involved foreign policy. In this regard, NAFTA should be considered a success because it reinforced the process of Mexican economic and political reform. According to Krugman, without NAFTA Mexico would have turned away from reform to radicalization.

Anderson, Cavanagh, and Ranney begin with an overview of their position on NAFTA: it did not create all the economic problems facing the United States, Mexico, and Canada, but it did exacerbate a number of them. To support their position, they concentrate on debunking five myths. They assert that NAFTA did contribute to the recent Mexican crisis; it has led to the loss of some 75,000 jobs in the United States; it has given business firms more control over wages and working conditions; it has facilitated attacks on social and economic programs designed to help workers; and it has not improved environmental conditions.

For a taste of the debate before the passage of NAFTA, both pro and con, see *NAFTA: An Assessment*, rev. ed., by Gary Clyde Hufbauer and Jeffery J. Schott (Institute for International Economics, 1993); "Grasping the Benefits of NAFTA," by Peter Morici, *Current History* (February 1993); "The North American Free Trade Agreement," *Economic Report of the President 1993*; "The High Cost of NAFTA," by Timothy Koechlin and Mehrene Larudee, *Challenge* (September/October 1992); and "The NAFTA Illusion" by Jeff Faux, *Challenge* (July/August 1993). On the issue of the relationship between NAFTA and the collapse of the Mexican peso, see "The Giant Sucking Sound: Did NAFTA Devour the Mexican Peso?" by Christopher J. Neely, *Review, Federal Reserve Bank of St. Louis* (July/August 1996). For the Clinton administration's views on the effects of NAFTA, see the 1996 and 1997 issues of *Economic Report of the President*. For a more complete assessment of the negative position presented by Anderson, Cavanagh, and Ranney, see their edited volume *NAFTA's First Two Years: The Myths and the Realities* (Institute for Policy Studies). Also see "NAFTA Shock," by James Cypher, *Dollars and Sense* (March/April 1995) and "Mexico," by Nora Lustig, *The Brookings Review* (Spring 1996).

# CONTRIBUTORS
# TO THIS VOLUME

## EDITORS

**THOMAS R. SWARTZ** was born in Philadelphia in 1937. He received a B.A. from LaSalle University in 1960, an M.A. from Ohio University in 1962, and a Ph.D. from Indiana University in 1965. He is currently a professor of economics at the University of Notre Dame in Indiana and the director of the Notre Dame Center for Economic Education. He writes in the areas of urban finance and economic education and has collaborated with Frank J. Bonello on a number of works, including *Urban Finance Under Siege* (M. E. Sharpe, 1993). In addition to *Taking Sides,* they have coedited *Alternative Decisions in Economic Policy* (Notre Dame Press, 1978) and *The Supply Side: Debating Current Economic Policies* (The Dushkin Publishing Group, 1983). Dr. Swartz is also the coeditor, with John E. Peck, of *The Changing Face of Fiscal Federalism* (M. E. Sharpe, 1990).

**FRANK J. BONELLO** was born in Detroit in 1939. He received a B.S. in 1961 and an M.A. in 1963 from the University of Detroit and a Ph.D. in 1968 from Michigan State University. He is currently an associate professor of economics and the Arts and Letters College Fellow at the University of Notre Dame in Indiana. He writes in the areas of monetary economics and economic education, and in addition to those publications he has coedited with Thomas R. Swartz, he is the author of *The Formulation of Expected Interest Rates* and the coauthor, with William I. Davisson, of *Computer-Assisted Instruction in Economic Education: A Case Study* (University of Notre Dame Press, 1976).

## STAFF

David Dean   List Manager
David Brackley   Developmental Editor
Ava Suntoke   Developmental Editor
Tammy Ward   Administrative Assistant
Brenda S. Filley   Production Manager
Juliana Arbo   Typesetting Supervisor
Diane Barker   Proofreader
Lara Johnson   Graphics
Richard Tietjen   Publishing Systems Manager

# AUTHORS

**ROBERT ALMEDER** is a professor of philosophy at Georgia State University and a member of the editorial board of the *Journal of Business Ethics*. He earned his Ph.D. in philosophy at the University of Pennsylvania and is the coeditor of *Business Ethics* (Prometheus Press, 1987).

**SARAH ANDERSON** is a fellow at the Institute for Policy Studies in Washington, D.C.

**RICHARD P. APPELBAUM** is a professor in and the chair of the Department of Sociology at the University of California, Santa Barbara. He is the author of *Karl Marx* (Sage Publications, 1988) and the coauthor, with John I. Gilderbloom, of *Rethinking Rental Housing* (Temple University Press, 1988).

**ROBERT A. BAADE** is in the Department of Economics and Business at Lake Forest College in Illinois.

**DEAN BAKER** is an economist at the Economic Policy Institute in Washington, D.C.

**ROBERT M. BALL** served as commissioner of Social Security between 1967 and 1973. He was a member of the 1994–1996 Advisory Council on Social Security.

**ALAN S. BLINDER** is the Gordon S. Rentschler Memorial Professor of Economics at Princeton University. He formerly served as vice chairman of the Federal Reserve Board and as a member of President Clinton's Council of Economic Advisers.

**MICHAEL J. BOSKIN** is the T. M. Friedman Professor of Economics at Stanford University in Stanford, California.

**GARY BURTLESS** is a senior fellow in the Brookings economic studies program. He is coauthor, with Martin N. Baily and Robert E. Litan, of *Growth With Equity: Economic Policymaking for the Next Century* (Brookings, 1993).

**JOHN CAVANAGH** is codirector of the Institute for Policy Studies in Washington D.C.

**THOMAS V. CHEMA** is an attorney practicing in Cleveland, Ohio. He was executive director of the Gateway Development Corporation of Greater Cleveland, a development agency.

**COUNCIL OF ECONOMIC ADVISERS** was established by the provisions of the Employment Act of 1946 and the Full Employment and Balanced Growth Act of 1978 to advise the president on the current economic status of the United States.

**CHARLES CRAYPO** is a professor of economics at Notre Dame University in Indiana.

**PAUL M. ELLWOOD JR.** is president of The Jackson Hole Group in Teton Village, Wyoming.

**MILTON FRIEDMAN** is a senior research fellow at the Stanford University Hoover Institution on War, Revolution, and Peace. He received the 1976 Nobel Prize in economic science for his work in consumption analysis and monetary history and theory and for demonstration of stabilization policy complexity. He and his wife, who also writes on economic topics, are coauthors of several publications, including *Tyranny of the Status Quo* (Harcourt Brace Jovanovich, 1984).

**JAMES K. GALBRAITH** is a professor of economics at the LBJ School of Public

Affairs at the University of Texas at Austin.

**DAVID F. GREENBERG** is a professor in the Department of Sociology at New York University in New York City.

**WILLIAM GREIDER** is the national affairs editor for *Rolling Stone*. He is the author of *Who Will Tell the People: The Betrayal of American Democracy* (Touchstone Books, 1993).

**ARTHUR L. KELLERMANN** is a professor in the Departments of Internal Medicine, Preventive Medicine, and Biostatistics and Epidemiology at the University of Tennessee in Memphis, Tennessee.

**MICHAEL KINSLEY** is a senior editor for the *New Republic* and the author of the weekly *New Republic* column "TRB from Washington," which also appears in the *Washington Post*, the *Los Angeles Times*, and the *Guardian of London*. He has been the managing editor of the *Washington Monthly* and a columnist for the *Wall Street Journal*. His publications include *Curse of the Giant Muffins and Other Washington Maladies* (Summit Books, 1987).

**PAUL KRUGMAN** is a professor of economics at Stanford University in Stanford, California. His publications include *The Age of Diminished Expectations: U.S. Economic Policy in the 1990s* (MIT Press, 1990) and *Pop Internationalism* (MIT Press, 1996).

**ROBERT KUTTNER** is a contributing editor for the *New Republic*, and he writes on social and political subjects. His publications include *The Economic Illusion: False Choices Between Prosperity and Social Justice* (University of Pennsylvania Press,

1987) and *The Life of the Party: Democratic Prospects in 1988* (Penguin, 1988).

**LESTER B. LAVE** is a James H. Higgins Professor of Economics at Carnegie Mellon University in Pittsburgh, Pennsylvania, with appointments in the Graduate School of Industrial Administration, the School of Urban and Public Affairs, and the Department of Engineering and Public Policy. He received a Ph.D. in economics from Harvard University and was a senior fellow at the Brookings Institution from 1978 to 1982.

**GEORGE D. LUNDBERG** is the editor of the *Journal of the American Medical Association*.

**JOHN H. McARTHUR** is a professor at Harvard Business School in Cambridge, Massachusetts.

**MATTHEW MILLER** is the economics editor at the *New Republic*.

**DAVID MOBERG** is the senior editor of *In These Times*.

**FRANCIS D. MOORE** is in the Department of Surgery at Brigham and Women's Hospital and at Harvard Medical School in Boston, Massachusetts.

**DANIEL D. POLSBY** is the Kirkland and Ellis Professor of Law at Northwestern University in Evanston, Illinois. He has also held academic positions at Cornell University, the University of Michigan, and the University of Southern California. He has published numerous articles on a number of subjects related to law, including employment law, voting rights, broadcast regulation, and weapons policy.

**DAVID RANNEY** is a professor of urban planning at the University of Illinois, Chicago.

**ROBERT RECTOR** is the senior policy analyst for welfare and family issues at the Heritage Foundation in Washington, D.C. This is a public policy research and education institute whose programs are intended to apply a conservative philosophy to current policy questions.

**MARTIN A. REGALIA** is vice president for economic policy at the U.S. Chamber of Commerce. Prior to that he was director of economics and research for the Savings and Community Bankers of America and a principal analyst in the Congressional Budget Office.

**FELIX G. ROHATYN** is the U.S. ambassador to France and a former partner in an investment firm in New York City.

**ROBERT RUBIN** is secretary of the U.S. Department of the Treasury. He previously served as assistant to the president for economic policy, directing the National Economic Council.

**THOMAS RUSTICI** was a graduate student in economics at the Center for the Study of Market Processes at George Mason University, Fairfax, Virginia, when he wrote this paper. An earlier version of it was awarded the 1984 Excellence in Liberty Prize by the Institute for Humane Studies.

**SYLVESTER J. SCHIEBER** is vice president and director with Watson Wyatt Worldwide, an economic consulting company. He was a member of the 1994–1996 Advisory Council on Social Security.

**CYNTHIA POLLOCK SHEA** is a senior researcher with the Worldwatch Institute, a research organization with an interdisciplinary approach to global environmental problem solving. She is a coauthor of the Worldwatch Institute's *State of the World* publication. Her principal interests include ozone depletion and energy and waste management technologies and policies.

**JOSEPH STIGLITZ** is senior vice president and chief economist at the World Bank in Washington, D.C. He is currently on leave from Stanford University, where he is the Joan Kennedy Professor of Economics. He previously taught economics at Princeton University.

**LESTER THUROW** is a professor in the Sloan School of Management at the Massachusetts Institute of Technology in Cambridge, Massachusetts. He received M.A. degrees from Balliol College and Harvard University in 1960 and 1964, respectively, and he received a Ph.D. from Harvard University in 1964. He is the author of *Poverty and Discrimination* (Brookings Institution, 1969), for which he won the David A. Wells Prize from Harvard University, and of *Generating Inequality: The Distributional Mechanisms of the Economy* (Basic Books, 1975).

**WILLIAM TUCKER,** a writer and social critic, is a staff writer for *Forbes* magazine. His publications include *The Excluded Americans: Homelessness and Housing Policies* (Regnery Gateway, 1989), which is the winner of the 1991 Mencken Award for best nonfiction, and *Zoning, Rent Control, and Affordable Housing* (Cato Institute, 1991).

**MICHAEL WISEMAN** is a professor of urban and regional planning at the University of Wisconsin–Madison and a visiting scholar at the Russell Sage Foundation.

**EDWIN W. ZEDLEWSKI** is a staff economist for the U.S. Department of Justice's National Institute of Justice.

# INDEX